Microsoft Press

GW00992235

Developing
User
Interfaces

for
Microsoft®
Windows®

Everett N. McKay

PUBLISHED BY
Microsoft Press
A Division of Microsoft Corporation
One Microsoft Way
Redmond, Washington 98052-6399

Library of Congress Cataloging-in-Publication Data
McKay, Everett N., 1961–
    Developing user interfaces for Microsoft Windows / Everett N.
  McKay.
        p.   cm.
    ISBN 0-7356-0586-6
    1. User interfaces (Computer systems) 2. Computer software-
-Development.   3. Microsoft Windows (Computer file)   I. Title
QA76.9.U83M44 1999
005.4'3769--dc21   99-13029
                                                        CIP

Printed and bound in the United States of America.

1 2 3 4 5 6 7 8 9 MLML 4 3 2 1 0 9

Distributed in Canada by Penguin Books Canada Limited.

A CIP catalogue record for this book is available from the British Library.

Microsoft Press books are available through booksellers and distributors worldwide. For
further information about international editions, contact your local Microsoft Corporation
office. Or contact Microsoft Press International directly at fax (425) 936-7329. Visit our Web
site at mspress.microsoft.com.

Acquisitions Editor: Ben Ryan
Project Editor: Devon Musgrave
Technical Editor: Jack Beaudry

*To my wife, Marie Séguin,
my children, Philippe Mathieu
and Michèle Audrey, and my
parents, George and Irma Jo.*

Contents

PART I

The Basics

Contents

PART II

Understanding Users

PART III

Design Concepts

Contents

Design Details

PART V

Testing and QA

Contents

Acknowledgments

There is no experience quite like writing a book. The closest thing to it I've ever done is run a marathon when I wasn't fully prepared. In both cases, although it's up to you to get the job done, you need the kindness of strangers to help you along the way.

I must first thank Ron Burk, editor of *Windows Developer's Journal,* who inspired me to write this book, although that inspiration was unbeknownst to him. I submitted to him a proposal for an article that would give a simple procedure for testing the user interfaces of Microsoft Windows programs. Let's just say that he lacked enthusiasm for my approach; he felt the presentation would be too abstract to be helpful. My first reaction was that it would take a long, boring book to cover the subject at the level of detail he suggested. My realization that I could present specific, practical Windows user interface development information in a fairly short and (hopefully) interesting book led to what you are holding in your hands. Ron was also helpful enough to give explicit instructions in "How to Write a Good Windows 95 UI Design Book" in the August 1997 issue of *WDJ.* I have tried to follow his advice as best I could.

I wish I could claim that every idea presented in this book is original. That would make me a pretty smart guy. Instead, the material in this book is a combination of my personal experience as a Windows programmer, the writings of many user interface experts, and the combined wisdom of all the talented user interface designers and programmers who have created the excellent programs I use every day. I would like to thank those experts whose insight into user interface design has helped me the most: Alan Cooper of Cooper Interaction Design, Tandy Trower of Microsoft Corporation, Donald Norman and Jakob Nielsen of Nielsen Norman Group, Bruce Tognazzini of Healtheon, and Virginia Howlett of Blue Sky Design, Inc. I'd also like to thank Hillel Cooperman, Chris Brown, Jan Miksovsky, Jordan Schwartz, and Kent Sullivan, all of Microsoft, whose presentations at the 1998 Microsoft Professional Developers Conference were inspirational, helpful, and timely. And thank you to Brian Hayes of Isys Information Architects, whose Interface Hall of Shame and Hall of Fame Web site served as an excellent reality check for many of my ideas.

I would especially like to thank all those people who gave me the opportunity do user interface development throughout my career, even when my skills weren't especially good. These people include Bob Headrick,

Greg Smith, Rick Fisher, Dennis Clark, Richard Speers, Flora Perski, Tom Weisz, Jacci Winchester, and Sean Cryan. Thanks also to Lawrence McMillin of the Webb School of California who taught me how to write at a time in my life when I didn't think writing skills were all that important. I also want to thank MIT's Nancy Lynch, my master's thesis advisor, for forcing me to remember those skills. Additional thanks to Meryle Sachs and Dave Myers for giving me insight on user interface development from the technical writer's point of view.

I am profoundly grateful to Microsoft Press for giving me this incredible opportunity. Thanks to Devon Musgrave, my project editor, and Jack Beaudry, my technical editor, for their help, guidance, and careful editing, and especially for not letting me get away with anything. I have a deep respect for the editing process now that I have experienced it. It is hard, tedious work, which, when done correctly, goes unnoticed by the reader. Special thanks also to Ben Ryan, my acquisitions editor, for seeing my potential and having faith that I could do the job and to Paula Gorelick, Alton Lawson, Karen Lenburg, Patricia Masserman, Joel Panchot, Julia Stasio, and Bill Teel for their fantastic editorial and production work.

Lastly, I give special thanks to my wife, Marie, and my children, Philippe and Michèle, who have had to endure my being attached to a computer for so many months. I could not have done this project without their support. I plan to spend the next few weeks trying to remember what we used to do when I had spare time on my hands.

Introduction

Good user interfaces matter. In fact, they matter a great deal to the success of a program. While a program's design and technology affects its overall capability and performance, as far as the user is concerned, the user interface *is* the program. If the user interface isn't good, the program isn't good. Don't expect users to look behind a bad user interface to see what lies beneath. They won't.

How many Microsoft Windows software products on the market that have bad user interfaces have been commercial successes? I am familiar with only one: a popular high-end image-processing program (which shall remain anonymous). Ask anyone who uses this program how they like it and you will get the same response: love the program, hate the interface. But this program is fairly unusual. It provides complex image manipulation that is unavailable in other programs, and its awkward interface allows for batch processing that its users love. As a good rule of thumb, if there are several programs competing in a particular market segment, the winner will be the one with the best user interface.

Since the ultimate goal of software development is to make successful software products that make lots of money (this is certainly my goal), it would stand to reason that most software developers would be obsessed with obtaining as much knowledge about user interface design as possible. Surprisingly, this is not happening. I have several explanations for this:

● The software development process and those who manage it are usually focused mostly on schedules and less on software quality. For every manager clamoring for better user interfaces, there are probably a hundred who are clamoring to get the product out the door. For programmers, this means that success lies in understanding the tools and technologies that help deliver software quickly. Focusing on quality user interfaces tends to have the opposite effect.

- Programmers are often encouraged not to do user interfaces. Programmers are often told that they aren't capable of being good interface designers. In large software companies, interface designs are often done by specialists, usually user interface designers or graphic designers. Consequently, programmers do not have much motivation for improving their user interface design skills. This is in spite of the fact that the user interface constitutes a significant portion of most modern programs.

- User interface design is not part of most computer science curricula, nor is it a prominent topic in most programmers' magazines. Some programmers' magazines have never run an article about user interface design.

- Many discussions about user interface design are deemed by programmers to be irrelevant or too academic to be useful. Often they are right. Many user interface books are focused on the theoretical, not the practical. They are often jam-packed with useless mumbo jumbo.

- Programmers might simply be unaware of how poor their user interfaces are. They might be aware of problems in other programs' user interfaces but not of problems in their own.

Since a significant portion of most modern software development is the user interface, a skilled programmer needs to have a solid understanding of user interface design. Very few programming jobs today require no user interface work at all. Even if a programmer works in an organization where specialists design the user interfaces, how can such a programmer do quality work without understanding what the interface is trying to accomplish? How can such a programmer identify problems, find bugs, or make appropriate changes? Understanding the fundamentals of Windows user interface design is essential for all programmers to create quality software.

The Audience

The target audience for this book is Windows programmers, specifically those programming Windows applications and utilities using MFC, the Windows API, or Microsoft Visual Basic. Many of the ideas I present also apply to other types of programming, such as programs designed for other operating systems, Web pages, and thin-client Windows DNA (Distributed interNet Applications architecture) programs, but I have not gone out of my way to address these specific subjects. Likewise, many of the ideas I present should be useful to software development team members other than programmers, such as managers, quality assurance testers, and technical writers, but again I haven't gone out of my way to address these specific audiences.

The Goals

To best present the subject of user interface design to Windows programmers, I have established several goals for myself:

● To focus on specific, practical, experience-based information. I've tried to focus on ways to avoid mistakes that I have seen myself and other programmers make.

● To present the information in short, self-contained chapters.

● To avoid vague generalities, user interface clichés, academic theories, and other forms of mumbo jumbo.

● To not try to explain everything about user interface design, but to focus on the key concepts that every programmer should know. You are referred to other sources for additional information when appropriate.

● To try to avoid "exercises" for the reader (at least the target reader). I try to provide specific examples in the text whenever practical.

This book is essentially a summary of what I believe a programmer needs to understand to create great user interfaces. These ideas and techniques have helped me tremendously in my work, and my ultimate goal is to share them in the hope that they will help you achieve great results.

What Is a User Interface?

So just what is a user interface? Interestingly, none of my favorite user interface books bother to define it. I use a fairly broad notion of user interface. To me, a user interface is much more than just the windows and dialog boxes – it is the entire user experience of using a program. In addition to the standard user interface elements, I believe the user interface also includes details like how the program installs, how the program integrates with Windows, how fast the program loads, how responsive the program is, how helpful the error messages and documentation are, and how well the program prints. Furthermore, developing a user interface is very much a team effort. I find it important to understand the roles of the other team members and how to help them help you make the best user interfaces you can.

All these factors play a role in how the user perceives a program. Consider how users react to a slow program. They don't say, "Oh, looks like this program has an inefficient internal algorithm." Rather, they say, "This program has a pokey user interface." Whether the slowness is caused directly by the user interface or not, the user interface gets the blame. Consequently, this book covers a number of subjects that relate to this total user experience that are not covered in most user interface books.

More of a Cliché than a Science

Alfred Hitchcock often said that one of his primary goals in filmmaking was to avoid the cliché. While I'm not exactly working at his level, I have made a sincere effort to avoid the standard user interface clichés and vague generalities. I have tried to avoid the common practice of describing user interface concepts in terms of analogies. There is no discussion of the KISS Principle. (And if you don't know what that is, I'm not going to tell you.) I'm not going to say that anything is more of an art than a science. Nor am I going to discuss being "user-friendly." I do include a "Keep It Simple" chapter, which is clearly titled after a vague generality, but the chapter mostly describes specific, practical techniques that a Windows programmer can use to simplify a user interface.

I've made an effort to focus on user interface techniques that are practical. The user interface techniques that I discuss are either standard techniques, techniques that I use, techniques that I used to use, or techniques that I could easily use when necessary. I don't suggest doing things that I would never do myself. I've also made an effort not to overstate the importance of things. Many things are important, but they are not all the most important. Many good user interface techniques can actually harm an interface when poorly done or overdone. I try to discuss both the right way and the wrong way and how to make sure you haven't overdone it.

Many of the user interface suggestions I make are easier to deal with early in the development process. Often this means that they are easy to implement in a new project but difficult to implement in an existing program. This is an unfortunate fact of life. If you're working on an existing program and you want to maintain a schedule, you simply cannot fix all user interface problems even if you want to. You have to choose your battles.

User interface development is a team effort, and it's important to have a realistic idea of when and how to involve the various members of the team in the process. I could say that you involve absolutely everybody in absolutely everything as early as possible, but this is clearly impractical. No one can work that way. So, for example, when I say you need to involve a technical writer early in the process, I try to give guidelines on just how early.

Finally, all rules have exceptions, so I try to explore exceptional cases whenever I can. To be practical, you can't just make blanket statements without exceptions.

User Interface Design Is No Longer a Mystery

I believe user interface design is no longer the mystery it once was. Today's typical Windows 98 user interface is far better than yesterday's typical Windows 3.1 interface. The behavior is much better and more powerful. The look is much cleaner and more professional. On the whole, Windows programs are more consistent because the Windows API and development tools like MFC have much higher-level user interface support built in. Today, you can create a good program framework in a matter of seconds by using the Microsoft Visual C++ AppWizard. An MFC program can provide advanced features like a print preview without any additional programming effort. These tools help make good user interfaces easier to implement, but they also raise the bar for the level of quality that users expect.

Most important, we now have a much better understanding of what a good Windows program looks like. The Windows 95 user interface really set the standard. We now understand the basic user interface components better: menus, toolbars, status bars, dialog boxes, property sheets, and message boxes. And we have a much better understanding of how user interface components fit together and their limitations. For example, we know that MDI isn't the right solution for all programs.

Since we are now creating user interfaces at a much higher level, your job should be easier. You can now create a good user interface by understanding the basic concepts of user interface design, understanding the Windows standards, understanding the basic user interface options, and making the right choices to help your users get their work done. There are many good Windows user interfaces that you can use as a model. What you don't have to do is design everything from scratch—there's little you have to invent. You don't need to have elaborate user testing facilities with two-way mirrors and videotaping. You don't need to perform elaborate user testing to determine the best way for a user to set the properties of an object. If you use the standard controls and follow the Windows standards for user interface design, most of this hard work has already been done for you. Many user interfaces have withstood the test of time. We already know they work.

One of my important goals in this book is to help you fully understand the Windows user interface components and how to make the right choices.

User Interfaces for Users

When you make user interface decisions, you need to remember that the ultimate goal is to help users get their work done. In fact, the best user interfaces go out of their way to help users get their work done. This is why they are called "user interfaces" and not "program interfaces."

While this observation might not seem especially profound, programmers often fail to make decisions based on what is best for the user. Rather, they often make user interface decisions based on what is best for themselves. Programmers choose to add inappropriate features because they are cool, because they are fun to program, or because they are easy to implement. Programmers rarely add inappropriate features because they are trying to help users get their work done.

To create good user interfaces, you have to become an advocate for users and put their goals ahead of your goals.

Programmers Can Create Good User Interfaces

In his otherwise excellent book *About Face: The Essentials of User Interface Design,* Alan Cooper flatly states that programmers are incapable of creating good user interfaces because they are too concerned about things like efficient algorithms. It is true that programmers have created some truly terrible user interfaces. However, I reject the notion that programmers are incapable of creating good interfaces because of some kind of innate inability. I'm just as concerned about efficient algorithms as the next guy, but it hasn't impaired my ability to create usable software.

Rather, I believe the problem is much more fundamental. Many programmers are simply not trained in the fundamentals of good user interface design. User interface design is not a standard part of the typical computer science curriculum (at least it wasn't for me), and it's not a popular topic in programmers' magazines. Programmers are fed a steady diet of "how-to" information that they need to get their work done, and interface design has not traditionally been presented in this manner. Without a solid understanding of the fundamentals, neither programmers nor anyone else can create good user interfaces. You cannot expect someone to have expertise in a skill they have never been trained in.

I believe it is important to understand that, like it or not, programmers are the ones doing most of the user interface work. Few organizations have specialized user interface designers. (For me, most of the projects I have worked on have been user interfaces with very little true core code. If you removed the user interface work from my projects, there wouldn't be much left.) Thus, there's a significant need for programmers to improve their user interface skills. And I believe programmers, with the right information, can create good user interfaces.

Controversial Ideas

Developing user interfaces is a highly personal subject. There is no one way to do it, nor is there one right way. That said, most of the advice I give in this book shouldn't be especially surprising since similar ideas have been described in other software development sources. However, in addition to believing that programmers can create good user interfaces, I have some other ideas that are not widely accepted, specifically:

- Users are not designers, so you cannot expect them to design your interfaces for you. Users can give you valuable information and they can test your program to tell you about its usability problems, but you will have to do the designing. Users can't turn a poorly designed program into a well-designed program. At best, they can turn a poorly designed program into a usable, poorly designed program. I believe the best way to design software is to work with users and other team members to create a program vision. You then use this vision as a decision-making framework.

- Prototyping can be very effective when done right, but it is easier to do wrong than most people think. Most prototyping efforts I've seen have been a waste of time. A couple of them were catastrophic disasters. To prototype effectively, you need to have a specific problem that needs to be solved; you need clear, realistic goals; and you need to know how to do proper user testing to get good feedback. Otherwise, don't waste your time. Finally, there are many types of design problems that prototyping cannot find.

- Programmers are primarily responsible for quality. Programmers can and should test their own user interfaces. The biggest hurdle is testing the program as a user by performing real tasks that users perform. Performing the same tests you used during debugging won't do the job. I've presented many practical techniques for testing user interfaces that any programmer should be able to use.

- User testing can be valuable, but you need to do programmer testing and QA testing first. User testing is more realistic than these other types of testing, but you can find many usability problems by using more cost-effective techniques.

Well, that's it. That is as controversial as I get. You might not agree with these ideas, but I'll do my best to talk you into them. These ideas reflect what I have experienced personally, and they have worked well for me. I have to call it as I see it.

A Word About Microsoft Software

I feel strongly about presenting practical, experience-based information in this book. Since it is important to understand why good programs are good and bad programs are bad, it is necessary to present real-world examples of both good and bad user interfaces. To make such examples practical and experience-based, I thought it would be a good idea to focus on products that I have extensive experience with and that most programmers are likely to have experience with as well. These would have to be programs I have used for years, not hours.

In my original proposal for this book, I chose several Microsoft products as examples of programs with good user interfaces and several non-Microsoft products as examples of programs with bad user interfaces. But when Microsoft Press agreed to publish this book, I immediately realized that I had a problem. It would be a little too cute for a book about user interface design from Microsoft Press to use Microsoft products for good examples and non-Microsoft products for bad examples. This would give my book a bias that I did not intentionally set out to give it.

My solution to this problem was to feature Microsoft products for all examples, both good and bad (with only a couple of exceptions). This approach has balance, and I'm happy to report that Microsoft Press made no effort to censor any of my criticism of Microsoft products. I realize that there are many other companies out there creating excellent user interfaces, but unfortunately these are not products I use on a daily basis.

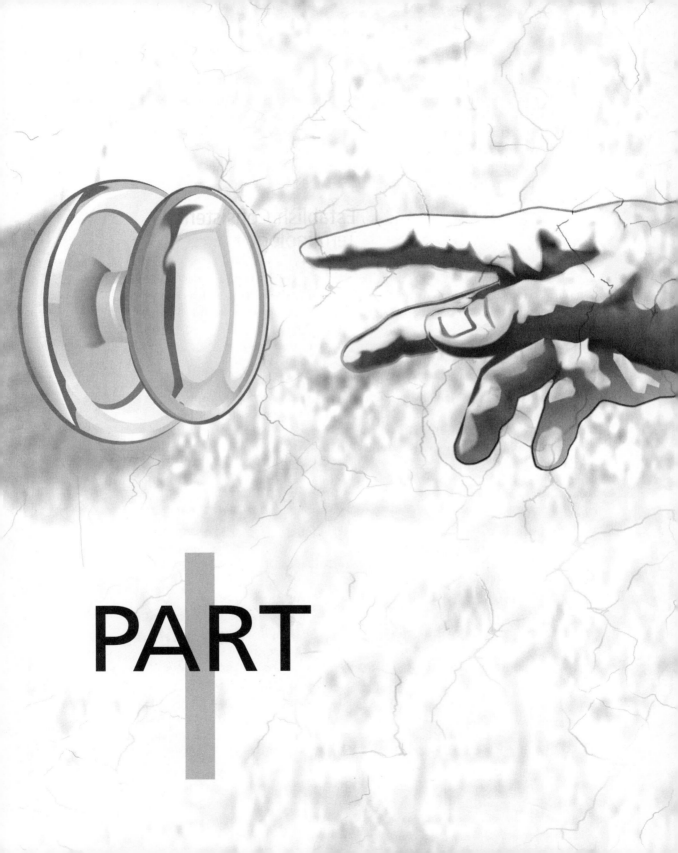

PART

The Basics

C
H
A
P
T
E
R

1

Know the Standards

Knowing, understanding, and applying the standards for Microsoft Windows user interface design allows you to create programs that the user already knows how to use. It also makes your programs more familiar and comfortable and ensures that they integrate well with the Windows environment. If you are doing user interface development, there is simply no excuse for not knowing the standards. Your knowledge of the standards is the absolute minimum requirement for programming user interfaces.

What Are the Standards?

I consider the following sources to be the standards for Windows user interface design.

Designing for the User Experience

These guidelines (formerly called *The Windows Interface Guidelines for Software Design*) cover user interface design principles, basic design concepts, visual design, the Windows environment, mouse and keyboard input, interaction techniques, windows, menus, toolbars, dialog boxes, controls, message boxes, online help, and Windows environment integration. This book is the single best source of Windows user interface information there is.

Microsoft Manual of Style for Technical Publications

This manual is a valuable reference that can help you make sure you're using the right terminology in your interfaces. While this manual is geared primarily for technical writers and not programmers, much of its information applies to the text in user interface elements such as dialog boxes, message boxes, menus, tooltips, status bars, and online help. Since text is a vital part of every user interface, using the right terms is critical to the clarity and consistency of the interface.

While I discuss this subject in detail in Chapter 3, note that the terminology used to describe many common Windows elements is different for programmers than for users. (Don't ask me how this happened.) For example, while programmer documentation refers to combo boxes, radio buttons, and subdirectories, user documentation refers to boxes ("combo" is never used), option buttons, and folders.

The Designed for Microsoft Windows Logo Requirements

The Designed for Microsoft Windows logo requirements are a set of requirements your program must satisfy to receive the Designed for Microsoft Windows logo. The specific requirements vary depending upon the type of program, but they are all geared toward making sure that your program integrates well with the Windows environment. They also help you provide optimum usability and ensure a consistent, accessible user interface.

Among the requirements are that your program must

- Use the Win32 application programming interface (API) and be in the Portable Executable (PE) format.
- Run in all current versions of Windows and Microsoft Windows NT.
- Use the registry and not the WIN.INI or SYSTEM.INI files.
- Register both large and small icons for each file type used.

PART

- Use system colors and metrics.

- Use the right mouse button for context menus and nothing else.

- Provide a setup program with complete uninstall capabilities, including automated setup and uninstallation.

- Reduce the chance of dynamic-link library (DLL) version conflicts by not installing globally shared DLLs in the Windows system directories.

- Support long filenames and universal naming convention (UNC) paths.

- Automatically add an extension when necessary before saving a file.

- Support hard drive volumes larger than 2 GB in size.

- Support users who upgrade from one version of Windows to another.

- Support accessibility by being compatible with the High Contrast option, providing keyboard access to all features, providing notifications of the keyboard focus location to support the Windows Magnifier, and providing customizable fonts and user interface timings.

While much of this information is covered in *Designing for the User Experience,* the Designed for Microsoft Windows logo requirements have much more detailed information specifically for programmers. The most important thing to understand about the logo requirements is that their goal is to make sure that your program integrates well with Windows and other applications. They are not arbitrary hoops you need to jump through.

I highly recommend that you review the logo requirements even if you could care less about using the Designed for Microsoft Windows logo. The new logo requirements form an amazing document that catalogs many guidelines to help make sure that your program integrates well with Windows. The information is useful, specific, and programmer-oriented. There is simply no better single source for this type of information.

TIP You should review the Designed for Microsoft Windows logo requirements, even if you could care less about obtaining the logo.

CHAPTER

Take the Quiz

While I clearly believe in the importance of knowing the standards, I want to convince you as well. But rather than trying to persuade you by begging and pleading, I want to give you a small quiz to test your user interface knowledge. These questions should be a snap if you have read *Designing for the User Experience* and the Designed for Microsoft Windows logo requirements.

Question 1—Ellipsis
The menu command to display a program's About box should have an ellipsis, as with "About My Program…"

a)   True
b)   False

Question 2—Static Text
Static text controls are the best way to display uneditable text in a dialog box.

a)   True
b)   False

Question 3—Message Boxes
When asking the user a question with a message box, the best approach is to ask the question, provide Yes and No buttons (and perhaps a Cancel or Help button, if appropriate), and the question mark symbol.

a)   True
b)   False

Question 4—Gray Backgrounds
A gray background indicates that a control is disabled.

a)   True
b)   False

Question 5—Determining Disk Space
The best way to report to the user the amount of free hard disk space is to use the GetDiskFreeSpace API function to determine the available disk space.

a)   True
b)   False

Question 6—Invisible Caret
There is never a need for a window to change the position of an invisible caret.

a)   True
b)   False

PART

8

The Quiz Answers

The answer to all of these questions is false. Here are the details:

Question 1—Ellipsis

Contrary to common belief, an ellipsis does not mean that a dialog box follows. Rather, it means that more information other than a simple confirmation is required to carry out the command. Since no additional information is needed from the user to display the About box, this command should not have an ellipsis. Interestingly, the Microsoft Foundation Classes (MFC) application AppWizard incorrectly provides an ellipsis with the About box menu command text. Even Charles Petzold himself incorrectly states: "The programmer indicates that a menu item invokes a dialog box by adding an ellipsis (...) to the menu item." Other common commands that should not have an ellipsis are Properties, Settings, Preferences, and Help Topics.

Question 2—Static Text

While static text is the best control for dialog box labels, read-only edit controls are much more useful for displaying other types of text. For example, the Windows Explorer Properties dialog box uses read-only edit controls for all the property text. Using read-only edit controls is more useful than static text since it allows the user to select the text, copy the text to the clipboard, and scroll the text if it is wider than the edit control.

Question 3—Message Boxes

The question mark symbol (MB_ICONQUESTION) is no longer recommended for message boxes because it is now used consistently within Windows 98 to signify context-sensitive help. In its place, the warning and critical message types are recommended. Note that using Yes and No buttons is much better than using the OK and Cancel buttons for questions since it is easier for the user to figure out what to do no matter how the question is phrased.

Question 4—Gray Backgrounds

Gray backgrounds are used to indicate that an object is read-only. Gray text is used to indicate that an object is disabled. By the way, this question was supposed to be the easy one.

Question 5—Determining Disk Space

The GetDiskFreeSpace API function is designed for hard disk volumes smaller than 2 GB, which is the limit with FAT16. With the new FAT32 file system, programs must use GetDiskFreeSpaceEx to handle hard disk volumes that are greater than 2 GB. (See the Designed for Microsoft Windows logo requirements, "Do Not Assume a Hard-Drive Size Limit of 2 GB.")

Question 6—Invisible Caret

To allow accessibility aids such as the Windows Magnifier to work properly, programs must provide Windows a notification of the current keyboard focus. While this notification is performed automatically with the standard Windows controls, custom controls that move the keyboard focus within themselves (such as a custom list control) need to notify Windows of the current keyboard focus. While there are several ways of doing this, often the easiest way is to create an invisible caret and move the position of the caret within the control. (See the Designed for Microsoft Windows logo requirements, "Provide Notifications of the Keyboard Focus Location.")

So What?

What's the big deal? After all, if everything else in your program is correct, having an ellipsis in the About box menu command isn't going to make your program difficult to use, is it? While that is certainly a valid conclusion, the premise is questionable. If you don't know the standards, what are the chances that everything else in your program is going to be correct? Bad user interfaces are usually not bad because they have one or two glaring problems. They're bad because they have dozens of small mistakes that can contribute to or directly result in the following problems:

- Inconsistency with other Windows programs and with the user's expectations
- Nonstandard mouse and keyboard input
- Nonstandard windows or dialog boxes that require nonstandard responses from the user
- Nonstandard controls or standard controls that behave in nonstandard ways
- Poor integration with the Windows environment
- Confusing and hard-to-understand error messages
- Inadequate accessibility
- Inadequate user assistance

Helping you make sure that your program conforms to what the user expects is exactly what the standards are for. Complying with the standards allows you to create programs that the user already knows how to use. For example, if you use a standard list box in a standard way, there's no need

PART

to document how to use it. And best of all, you don't have to do any of the really hard work—all of the design work and user testing has already been done for you. When you create programs that don't conform to the standards, you're pretty much on your own.

TIP Conforming to the standards makes your job easier, not harder.

I appreciate the fact that *Designing for the User Experience* is a fairly large book and can be difficult to read at times. However, it is effective as a reference and you really don't have to memorize it. Just have a copy within easy reach, know what's in it, know what you already know, know what you're less familiar with, and know when you need to refer to it. That's all!

When to Violate the Standards

While the guidelines specifically state that compliance is optional, I believe they say this just to be nice. You should conform to the standards unless you have an amazingly good reason to break them. Here are some good reasons for not conforming to the standards:

- You are trying to advance state-of-the-art user interface design, and you really know what you are doing. In this case, you should also have a significant budget for user testing.

- You are creating a radically new kind of program.

- Your program has extraordinary requirements.

- You are creating a game or multimedia program that is designed primarily to entertain, and you feel that conforming to the standard appearance is too boring.

- You have decided that achieving another goal is more important, and you are making a well-thought-out trade-off.

- You made an honest mistake and will fix the problem as soon as possible.

I consider the following to be really bad reasons for not conforming to the standards:

- You don't know what the standards are.

- You prefer to make up your own standards as you go.

- You find conforming to the standards too much trouble.

- You found a really cool ActiveX control on the Internet and want to use it in your program somehow, even though it doesn't conform to the standards.

People often note that Microsoft itself breaks the standards all the time. However, note that they do this to advance the state-of-the-art of Windows user interface design. Also note that they have a substantial budget to design and test new user interface designs. Microsoft typically unveils these new designs with their Office and Internet Explorer products and eventually incorporates them into the standards and other products. If you want to follow Microsoft's latest user interface designs and you have a good reason to, that is fine by me. Typically I plan to adopt them too, but I'm usually not in a big hurry to do so. I prefer to give myself, my users, and my tools (especially MFC) a chance to catch up.

TIP   Violate the standards to go forward, not backward.

Recommended Reading

- Cooper, Alan. *About Face: The Essentials of User Interface Design*. Foster City, CA: IDG Books Worldwide, Inc., 1995, pp. 499–501.

  Presents a good discussion of the importance of standards and when to break them.

- Microsoft Corporation. The Designed for Microsoft Windows logo requirements.

  You can find the logo requirements on the CD-ROM included with this book and in the MSDN Library.

- Microsoft Corporation. *Designing for the User Experience*. Redmond, WA: Microsoft Press, 1999.

  While you don't need to read this book from cover to cover, you should read the first two chapters and use the remainder as a reference. The first two chapters give a concise overview of the fundamental user interface design concepts. Definitely worthwhile.

- Microsoft Corporation. *Microsoft Manual of Style for Technical Publications, Second Edition*. Redmond, WA: Microsoft Press, 1998.

PART

CD-ROM Resources

The CD-ROM included with this book contains the following resources related to this chapter:

- An electronic version of the *Microsoft Manual of Style for Technical Publications, Second Edition*.
- The Designed for Microsoft Windows logo requirements.

CHAPTER

C
H
A
P
T
E
R

2

Read Other User Interface Design Books

I know it's a bit odd to start off a book about user interface development by saying that you should read other books about user interface design.

What I mean, of course, is that you should read other books because it is simply not possible for an author, including me, to present in a single book everything that one should know about user interface design. I clearly do not intend to try. In fact, I believe in this idea so strongly that I've included a Recommended Reading section at the end of each chapter. To further improve your interface designs, make sure you take a look at these other sources of relevant information.

In this book, I present user interface design from the Microsoft Windows programmer's point of view. Reading this book is an excellent start, but you should try to get other points of view as well. It's important to understand user interface design from the point of view of users, user interface designers, visual and graphic designers, and designers in other fields. I also find it useful to look at user interface design from the point of view of other platforms. Even though the fundamentals of good user interface design are largely platform-independent, looking at other platforms will give you a fresh perspective. Don't avoid a user interface book just because it isn't Windows-specific. Looking at other platforms can give you ideas that otherwise might never have occurred to you. In fact, I find books that discuss the Macintosh user interface to be far more relevant to my work than books that try to apply to all platforms.

In the remainder of this chapter, I will discuss some of my favorite books on user interface design. These are the books that I have found to be the most useful, and I will present them in order of their usefulness to me. I find these books to be practical, relevant, insightful, and worthwhile. Of course, your needs might be different than mine, so you might draw other conclusions. The Recommended Reading section in this chapter presents user interface–related books that I believe are worthy of honorable mention.

Alan Cooper's *About Face*

Cooper, Alan. *About Face: The Essentials of User Interface Design*. Foster City, CA: IDG Books Worldwide, Inc., 1995.

This book takes a comprehensive look at user interface design. It covers the goals of user interface design, how to deal with various implementation problems, the behavior of programs, interaction techniques, and the major user interface elements, such as windows, menus, dialog boxes, message boxes, toolbars, and controls. While the treatment of the subject matter ranges from practical to philosophical, Cooper discusses all of these subjects with incredible insight. His book includes more good ideas and observations about user interfaces and user interface design than any other book I have read. Best of all, the book is enjoyable to read and full of excellent examples.

A number of Cooper's chapters are masterpieces of user interface analysis. For example, Chapter 5, "Idioms and Affordance," gives an excellent analysis of metaphors vs. idioms. Chapter 11, "Orchestration and Flow," includes a great discussion on how to keep users focused on their work and not on the program. Chapter 12, "Posture and State," defines the different types of programs (postures) based on how they are used and how their type influences the appearance on the screen (state). Chapter 13, "Overhead and Idiocy," discusses how to recognize and eliminate unnecessary tasks. Chapter 21, "Dialog Boxes," discusses when and when not to use dialog boxes and compares the different types of dialog boxes. And Chapter 23, "Toolbars," compares menus to toolbars and makes it clear that menus are for teaching and toolbars are for convenience. Each of these chapters is a must-read.

PART

Cooper is not shy about taking controversial views on many user interface subjects. Happily, I agree with most of them. For example, he thinks that user interface metaphors are overrated: "There is an infinity of idioms waiting to be invented, but only a limited set of metaphors waiting to be discovered. Metaphors give first-timers a penny's worth of value but cost them many dollars' worth of problems as they continue to use the software." He believes that dialog boxes should be avoided: "Dialogs, for good or ill, interrupt the interaction and make the user react to the program instead of driving it." "A dialog box is another room. Have a reason to go there." "Dialogs break flow." And Cooper knows that usability testing is not a substitute for design: "The chief drawback of usability is that it sidesteps actual design. The process of testing is very different from the process of design. Design springs directly from the knowledge of goals. Usability derives from specific objects." Good stuff.

This is not to say that I agree with all his ideas. I find some of them downright loopy. For example, Cooper suggests that companies should establish a pronounced proprietary look for their programs: "As a software publisher, you can personalize your entire application. By putting identifying marks on all of the components of the program, you help in creating a branded product." He suggests that a good alternative to negative audible feedback (that is, beeping) is positive audible feedback: "Our programs would be much friendlier and easier to use if they issued barely audible but easily identifiable sounds when user actions were correct. The program could issue a soft 'coo' every time the user entered valid input to a field." Cooper also argues that it is better to allow users to enter questionable data into a database than to bother users with error messages when they enter questionable data: "Data integrity is a good concept on paper, but it dumps the burden of entering correct data in the user's lap rather than when—and if—the correct data is actually needed." He also proposes that programs should indicate that a drag operation has been cancelled by displaying a giant red "Drag Cancelled" stamp in the middle of the screen and by making a "thump" sound effect. Sorry, I don't think so.

I also think there are problems in the book's presentation. There is a bit too much attitude, too much ranting, and too much harsh language. I also believe there are too many unsupported opinions and too many analogies.

Despite its problems, however, what this book has is understanding and insight—and plenty of it. Even Cooper's worst ideas are worthwhile reading in that they are thought-provoking. The goal of reading this book shouldn't be to adopt Cooper's ideas without question but to let Cooper widen your thinking about user interface design and help you develop a better understanding of the fundamental user interface components. In my case, this book has helped me understand user interface design more than any other.

This is a must-have book.

Microsoft's
Designing for the User Experience

Microsoft Corporation. *Designing for the User Experience*. Redmond, WA: Microsoft Press, 1999.

I discussed this book in Chapter 1, so I'll keep my comments short here. I believe that this book is the single best source of Windows user interface information, and I refer to it often. Then why do I rank it second? While *Designing for the User Experience* does an excellent job of defining standard Windows appearance and behavior, it doesn't give you the understanding and insight that Cooper's book does. *Designing for the User Experience* explains what and how, and *About Face* explains why. I believe mastering why is ultimately more important.

This is a must-have book.

Virginia Howlett's
Visual Interface Design

Howlett, Virginia. *Visual Interface Design for Windows*. New York, NY: John Wiley & Sons, Inc., 1996.

This book presents user interface design from a visual designer's point of view. Virginia Howlett is a former director of visual interface design at Microsoft and was responsible for the team that designed the visual interfaces of Windows 3.1, Windows 95, and Microsoft Windows NT. Covering the fundamentals of graphic design and teaching you how to recognize common user interface mistakes, the book presents many important design principles, such as simplicity, balance, restraint, scale, contrast, focus, emphasis, grouping, and grid, as well as valuable information about using 3-D, fonts, color, and icons.

Howlett's book is especially important if you are creating highly visual, consumer-oriented programs, such as home, multimedia, or children's programs. While you most likely will be working with a graphic designer on such projects, it is still important to understand what this type of interface is trying to accomplish. Even if you are not working on multimedia-style programs, this book gives several excellent examples of common user interface mistakes that programmers are likely to make, such as poor use

PART

of color and contrast, poor use of 3-D, and screen design that lacks focus and balance.

The chapters on graphic design principles (Chapter 4, "Universal Design Principles," and Chapter 5, "Graphic Information Design Principles") as well as the chapters on visual design elements (Chapter 10, "Color"; Chapter 11, "Icons and Imagery"; and Chapter 12, "Fonts") are must-reads. The book also presents two user interface makeover examples that are outstanding (Chapter 13, "Interface Makeovers"). Short and to the point, they feature problems that programmers are likely to create. One of the examples is the makeover of Microsoft Encarta from the original version (apparently designed by programmers) to the current version, which is visually vastly superior. Finally, the last chapter (Chapter 15, "Common Pitfalls and How to Avoid Them") presents several useful tips on how to avoid common user interface problems.

One of the reasons this book is so effective is that it is a quick read. The ideas are well presented, and you're always given the essential information you need, typically with an excellent example screen shot to make the point. The subjects are not beaten to death, and there is only a tinge of mumbo-jumbo—you might be put off by the discussion of contextual inquiry, for example. This book would not be nearly as effective if it were larger. Page per page, it is possibly the best user interface book out there.

If you don't like the look of your programs, this is the first place to turn. In the author's own words: "Obviously, all of these topics could be treated in more depth, but my goal is to give you just enough information to inspire you to make better, more beautiful, Windows products." Enough said.

This is a must-have book.

Donald A. Norman's
The Design of Everyday Things

Norman, Donald A. *The Design of Everyday Things*. New York, NY: Currency/Doubleday, 1990.

This is an excellent user interface design book, but it does not directly discuss software user interfaces. By "everyday things," Norman means very common objects such as doors, telephones, refrigerators, cars, VCRs, and faucets. He only occasionally discusses computers. While at first this book might seem irrelevant to software user interface design, in fact it is nothing but relevant. Nearly every key idea applies directly to software user interface design with surprisingly little effort. One could argue that since the time this book was written, the computer has become an everyday thing. With today's sub-$1000 computers and with the Internet seemingly

19

everywhere, formerly "nontechnical" people are using computers in their
daily routine, and software user interface design needs to reflect this fact.
Even my two-year-old son Philippe is able to turn his computer on and off,
insert CD-ROMs (using caddies!), and start and use programs all on his own.

You need to read this book for two reasons: first, to understand basic
user interface design concepts, which are explained extraordinarily well in
this book; and second, to understand how to make complex software work
as simply as an "everyday thing" by eliminating unnecessary complexity.
Whereas Howlett's book helps you understand how a Windows program
should look, this book helps you understand how a Windows program can
be made easy to learn and use. This book has incredible insight.

Originally titled *The Psychology of Everyday Things*—the title was
changed to make the book more appealing to a broader audience—
Norman's book could be accurately titled *How Users Learn to Use Everyday
Things*. For software user interfaces, human psychology forms the vital link
between what the user sees on the screen and how the user decides what
to do (ultimately determining how the user learns to interact with the user
interface). It is therefore valuable to understand this psychology—how users
understand visual elements, explain them, remember them, form relationships between them, become confused, and make mistakes. Knowing this
information is fundamental to good user interface design. Since the book
focuses on simple, practical examples of everyday objects and avoids academic psychobabble, it is enjoyable reading for anyone.

Many design principles are examined throughout the book, the most
important being visibility, affordance, natural mapping, constraints, conceptual models, and feedback. User interfaces that implement these principles
well are easy for the user to learn, understand, and use. *Visibility* gives the
user the ability to figure out how to use something just by looking at it.
Affordance relates to the perceived and actual properties of an object that
suggest how the object is to be used. *Natural mapping* creates a clear relationship between what the user wants to do and the mechanism for doing
it. *Constraints* reduce the number of ways to perform a task and the amount
of knowledge necessary to perform a task, making it easier to figure out.
A good *conceptual model* is one in which the user's understanding of how
something works corresponds to the way it actually works. This way the
user can confidently predict the effect of his actions. Lastly, *feedback* indicates to the user that a task is being done and being done correctly.

Here's another interesting principle that Norman discusses: If a control needs a label, the design of the control has failed. While labels are
normally fine in software user interfaces, clearly a control that makes sense
without a label is better than a control that requires a label. Specifically,

edit boxes, which usually require labels to make sense, are not as effective as more constrained controls, such as combo boxes and slider bars, which are easier to understand without labels than edits boxes are. In terms of everyday things, a door handle is an excellent example. If a door looks like it should be pushed, people are going to push it. Only after a door fails to open after being pushed a couple of times do users bother to read the label that instructs them to pull.

I had many revelations while reading this book; I'll share just one. Many products are advertised as not requiring programming. What exactly does this mean? This distinction is somewhat arbitrary since you could argue that just about everything is "programmed" in some way. Doors are effectively programmed to open and close. Washing machines are effectively programmed to handle differing load sizes, colors, and fabrics. Certainly, using any sort of computer software is a form of programming. However, a task can be said to be performed without programming if there is a simple, visible, and direct mechanism that maps from what the user wants to do to how the object does it. Each control on the object has a single obvious function and provides some sort of feedback that the task is being accomplished correctly. On the other hand, a task requires programming when there is no direct relationship between what the user wants to do and how the object does it. For example, a digital watch requires programming and an analog watch does not. While it is possible to design a digital watch that doesn't require programming, its controls would support only a few functions. The reason digital watches require programming is to provide many features with a small number of controls. In the end, if given a choice, most users prefer to perform their work without programming.

This is a must-have book.

Bruce Tognazzini's *Tog on Interface*

Tognazzini, Bruce. *Tog on Interface.* Reading, MA: Addison-Wesley Publishing Company, Inc., 1992.

Bruce Tognazzini wrote this book while he was the human interface evangelist at Apple Computer. The book consists of many letters from developers and his responses (taken from *Apple Directions,* Apple's developer news magazine), techniques for the user interface design process, and basic design principles. The specific subjects covered include visibility, user-centered design, perceived stability, managing menus, managing dialog boxes, working with other team members, balloon help, agents, feedback, and dealing with user errors. Its coverage of user testing ("on the cheap") is the most concise treatment of the subject.

CHAPTER 2

While this information is mostly Macintosh-specific, much of it applies to Windows with little translation. But for a modern Windows programmer, the details are mostly irrelevant. A Windows programmer should not read this book for specific user interface techniques. Rather, the reason you should read this book is to gain insight on how to think about user interfaces, including the underlying principles of user interface design.

This book is especially dear to me because it was the first real user interface design book I ever read. It played a major role in rewiring my brain in just the right way so that I began to develop some understanding and insight about user interfaces. I would have ranked this book higher were it not for Cooper's book, which covers much of the same ground and is more relevant to modern Windows programmers.

Jakob Nielsen's *Usability Engineering*

Nielsen, Jakob. *Usability Engineering*. Chestnut Hill, MA: AP Professional, 1993.

User interface development is a difficult subject to write about. User interface books written by practitioners are typically the most relevant, since they discuss current technology and describe lessons learned from practical experience. However, such books are based largely on the opinion of the author and are rarely backed up by research. On the other hand, academic user interface books often have little practical information for programmers and are just plain boring. (How's that for an opinion!) Jakob Nielsen's *Usability Engineering* strikes a remarkable compromise. Nielsen's information is practical, interesting, well researched, well written, and very readable. And, because the subject of usability engineering is not based on any particular technology, the information is timely.

So, just what is usability engineering? The goal of usability engineering is to create software with the following attributes: learnability, efficiency, memorability, reduction of errors, and overall user satisfaction. Usability engineering is a collection of techniques that strive to obtain these attributes throughout the entire software development process. Since it is difficult for developers to predict what users want and how users will react to a program, the primary focus of usability engineering is working with users to establish program goals and evaluate results.

Usability engineering is similar in concept to user-centered design. One of the biggest problems I have with user-centered design is that it is based on the faulty assumption that developers have no clue how to design user interfaces and that the only way to develop a good user interface is through user testing. Nielsen knows better. Chapter 5, "Usability Heuristics" (which in any other book would be called "Basic Design Principles"), outlines many

PART

usability techniques that can be taken for granted in software design. Furthermore, Nielsen presents a realistic view of user-centered design and prototyping. He understands that user testing doesn't have all the answers, that users aren't designers, and that their feedback must be carefully interpreted. He states, "There are two major reasons for alternating between heuristic evaluation and user testing as suggested here. First, a heuristic evaluation pass can eliminate a number of usability problems without the need to 'waste users,' who sometimes can be difficult to find and schedule in large numbers. Second, these two categories of usability assessment methods have been shown to find fairly distinct sets of usability problems." This is great practical advice.

I have two minor complaints about this book. The first is that it expends a significant amount of effort describing formal usability measurement techniques. While such information is useful for researchers, it has little value for programmers. The second is that some of the research cited is fairly old. There's no particular reason to think any of the conclusions are wrong, but research based on character-mode user interfaces is clearly dated.

I find what Nielsen calls "discount usability engineering" to be the most useful and interesting information in this book. He understands that developers don't have unlimited budgets or time, so they need to use techniques that are quick and cost-effective. The inability to perform all of the processes described in this book should not be used as an excuse to avoid usability altogether. As Nielsen puts it, "Unfortunately, it seems that 'Le mieux est l'ennemi du bien' (the best is the enemy of the good) to the extent that insisting on using only the best methods may result in using no methods at all." Clearly, some usability engineering is better than none. Discount usability engineering consists primarily of user and task observation, scenarios (a minimal prototyping technique), user testing that employs thinking out loud, and heuristic evaluation. You shouldn't feel guilty about not using the ideal usability techniques. (I know I don't.) Instead, try to do the best you can.

This book is definitely a worthwhile read.

Laura Arlov's *GUI Design for Dummies*

Arlov, Laura. *GUI Design for Dummies*. Foster City, CA: IDG Books Worldwide, Inc., 1997.

I know—it's hard to believe. The saying that you can't judge a book by its cover definitely applies here. This is a solid book, definitely not for dummies. This book would probably sell much better if it had a different title.

Arlov's book has a balanced presentation, covering user interface design in both practical and theoretical terms. The issues are covered from

CHAPTER 2

many points of view, including programming, graphic design, and user psychology. Arlov also includes quite a lot of information about the design process and task analysis. This book would be an especially good choice if you are interested in creating a design process. While all the chapters are solid, I found that Chapter 6, "How Users Get Around: Navigation Models"; Chapter 11, "Making Your GUI Easy to Understand"; Chapter 13, "The ABCs of Visual Design"; Chapter 14, "Color Is Communication"; and Chapter 15, "Icons and Graphics," are especially good. My only complaint is that while this book covers most of the user interface subjects that I feel are important, the coverage isn't especially deep and the presentation is a bit too breezy for my taste.

If you have read Cooper's *About Face,* Howlett's *Visual Interface Design,* Norman's *The Design of Everyday Things,* and Horton's *The Icon Book,* much of Arlov's book will be review. On the other hand, if you haven't read these other books and don't plan to, this book would be a good choice for a summary of much important user interface design information.

Peter Bickford's *Interface Design*

Bickford, Peter. *Interface Design: The Art of Developing Easy-to-Use Software.* Chestnut Hill, MA: Academic Press, 1997.

This book is based on a user interface design column that Peter Bickford wrote for *Apple Directions.* (He took over the column after Bruce Tognazzini moved on.) It consists of 38 chapters, each covering a single subject. Among the subjects that I find the most interesting are transparency, error messages, preferences, icons, speed and feedback, usability testing, complexity, and providing intelligence. Though fairly short, each chapter typically has worthwhile insight that can be quite helpful. This book also has the advantage of being a relatively quick read.

Windows programmers should note that although Bickford made a token effort to expand the coverage to include Windows, this book is clearly written from the Macintosh point of view. While this in itself isn't a problem, the fact is that Bickford is a serious Mac-head with an agenda. You know what I mean: The Macintosh is ten years ahead of Windows. (He doesn't literally make this statement, but that's what comes across since every reference to Windows is negative.) All the user interface innovations developed in Windows are terrible. And so on. Try to ignore that stuff, and you'll find some really good ideas in this book.

Of course, these are my personal opinions. I can only guarantee that these books have helped me.

PART

Recommended Reading

I have presented the items in this list in order of their usefulness to me.

- Microsoft Corporation. Visual C++ Documentation, Using Visual C++, Visual C++ Programmer's Guide, Adding User Interface Features.

  While you could never learn how to design a user interface from this help information, it can be very helpful in addressing specific problems you may have when implementing your interface. I recommend reviewing this information just so you know what is out there. For some reason, this information is easy to overlook.

- Horton, William. *The Icon Book: Visual Symbols for Computer Systems and Documentation*. New York, NY: John Wiley & Sons, Inc., 1994.

  This book is the ultimate resource for icon design information. This is possibly the most narrowly focused book on a user interface subject ever written. However, while this information is intended to help you design icons, note that the same design principles apply to other visual symbols, such as toolbar buttons, cursors, and control indicators (such as the Windows close, minimize, maximize, and restore button graphics). Chapter 2, "How Icons Work"; Chapter 3, "Representing Ideas Graphically"; and Chapter 7, "Color in Icons," all contain valuable information general enough to be useful to those who never plan to create icons but who want to improve their visual design skills. This book will help you learn how to communicate visually. If you are having trouble expressing your ideas visually, this is the first place to turn.

- Kano, Nadine. *Developing International Software for Windows 95 and Windows NT*. Redmond, WA: Microsoft Press, 1995.

  Presents everything you need to know about internationalizing software. This isn't a user interface design book per se, but it's a fact that much of the effort in internationalizing a program involves the user interface. This book makes it clear that creating international software is much easier to do at the beginning of the development process than at the end, so this book is a must-read if you're planning to create international software. Don't be intimidated by the heft of this book—it's a quick read.

CHAPTER 2

- Microsoft Corporation. *Microsoft Manual of Style for Technical Publications, Second Edition*. Redmond, WA: Microsoft Press, 1998.

  Provides useful guidelines for all aspects of documentation. As I discuss in the next chapter, I believe it is important to establish consistent terminology in your interface, and this book is the best source I know of to help you accomplish this goal.

- Microsoft Corporation. *Microsoft Press Computer Dictionary, Third Edition*. Redmond, WA: Microsoft Press, 1997.

  This book is a good tool for making sure you are using the right term. Again, consistent terminology is crucial in interface design, and this book also helps accomplish that goal. Of course, this book is less helpful than the *Microsoft Manual of Style for Technical Publications* because the manual of style helps you understand which term to use and the dictionary just gives definitions.

- Microsoft Corporation. *Microsoft Windows 95 Help Authoring Kit*. Redmond, WA: Microsoft Press, 1995.

  This book is a good source of information on how to integrate context-sensitive help into a program. Third-party tools are available to help this process, but this book has useful information if you plan on doing it the hard way.

- Ezzell, Ben. *Developing Windows Error Messages*. Sebastopol, CA: O'Reilly & Associates, 1998.

  Discusses everything you ever wanted to know about error messages. While I think this book does an excellent job of identifying error message problems, I wouldn't use the proposed solutions presented here. Nevertheless, I find this book useful when considering error messages and error message problems.

- Thompson, Nigel. *Animation Techniques in Win32*. Redmond, WA: Microsoft Press, 1995.

  Despite its title, this book is an excellent resource for basic Windows graphics information, even if you never plan on doing any animation. The first three chapters provide a topnotch presentation on device-dependent bitmaps (DDBs), device-independent bitmaps (DIBs), video modes, colors, and palettes. It is essential reading if you need to do any bitmap or palette programming in your user interfaces.

PART

- Apple Computer. *Macintosh Human Interface Guidelines*. Reading, MA: Addison-Wesley Publishing Company, 1992.

   While many user interface books have bibliographies, the one presented in Appendix B of this book is possibly the best. It has excellent coverage, is well annotated, and is not Mac-specific. Unfortunately, it is getting a bit old. Check here first if you are doing advanced research.

CD-ROM Resources

The CD-ROM included with this book contains the following resources related to this chapter:

- An electronic version of the *Microsoft Manual of Style for Technical Publications, Second Edition*.

27

3
CHAPTER

Establish Consistent Terminology

Carmel, California, is world famous for its small-town charm and character. In addition to having Clint Eastwood as a former mayor, it has many other interesting characteristics, such as beautiful beaches, distinctive shops, fabulous art galleries, no franchise businesses, no mail boxes anywhere but at the post office, and most interestingly, no street numbers. Since I used to live two towns over in Monterey, I knew about these distinctions for years, but it wasn't until someone in Carmel gave me directions to their house that I fully appreciated the significance of not having street numbers. Without street numbers, residents can't just say they live at 123 Seventh Street. Rather, they must give directions such as "Our house is on Seventh Street, between San Carlos and Junipero. It is the light-gray house with white trim, on the north side next to the large oak tree...."

While not having street numbers might give Carmel character, not being able to easily find your way around does nothing for software. Yet programmers often seem reluctant to establish terminology to describe their

CHAPTER 3

programs. Often someone other than the programmers is responsible for deciding the names. But regardless of who is responsible, it is important to establish consistent terminology early in the software development process for all the significant elements of a program that will appear in the user interface. Because the terms you choose will often show up in the actual interface through menus, dialog boxes, status bar text, help systems, documentation, and so on, consistent terminology will both clarify the interface and make it more consistent. If you find yourself saying such things as "the second button on the window on the left-hand side of the screen—the Workspace window or whatever we end up calling it—needs to be larger…," you know you need to work on your terminology.

Why Terminology Is Important

Much of the reason is obvious. How do you discuss things without using names? How do you communicate if the names you use do not have consistent meanings? We use names to identify, to describe, and to seek out things. We use names to break down and get a grasp of something we are unfamiliar with. Using consistent terminology helps us understand issues better and communicate better—and simplifying and making our user interface terminology consistent helps our users understand and take advantage of the interfaces we design. Ask any technical writer what the biggest user interface problems are and you will find that inconsistent terminology is always at the top of their list.

Here's an example of how consistent terminology can affect how we think. I once worked on a document retrieval system that used at least six different equivalent terms to describe the documents it retrieved. The names were used consistently to describe different aspects of the same document retrieval process, yet there was absolutely no significant distinction between the terms from the user's point of view. (In case you are skeptical, the terms used were "document," "article," "topic," "subject," "heading," and "title." The terms "reference" and "citation" were also used, but those terms actually could be distinguished from the others.) It took me a fair amount of time to realize that all these terms described the same thing. Imagine how confused the program's users were.

Another good example is OLE. Or is that COM? No wait—it's ActiveX. To be honest, depending on the context, I'm not really sure—I have to look it up. Is it ActiveX automation? But isn't automation also part of COM? I think the official term is now just plain "automation."

Using different terminology to describe the same thing is one of the simplest things you can do to confuse everybody. And changing terminology after everyone is accustomed to it certainly doesn't help. Both situations make a program difficult to discuss, describe, and document. It even makes it difficult to program. For example, most of the MFC COM classes are still named OLE and are unlikely to change anytime soon because changing the names would break a lot of code.

TIP Use the same term to describe the same thing. Using different terms for items that have only subtle differences will confuse users.

Ultimately, a little work choosing consistent terminology early on will save everyone a whole lot of work later.

What to Name

Here are some typical interface-related objects that need to have names:

- The program itself
- The document types that the program uses
- The major activities the user performs with the program
- All windows, dialog boxes, and property sheets
- For primary program windows, all regions on the window
- Any nonstandard screen objects, commands, properties, interactions, or technologies

In short, anything that the user can see or interact with that shows up in the menus, toolbars, windows, dialog boxes, status bars, online help, or documentation needs to have a name. Of course, you should use preexisting names for any standard screen object. For example, you don't need to name the common dialog boxes since they already have names.

When to Name

Programmers often seem to be reluctant to name things. Considering names like PCMCIA, ISDN, and SCSI, perhaps this is a good thing. And some programmers believe that names really don't matter. They say things like "I don't care what you call it, just as long as it works." That's a bad approach. You should make a conscious effort to name an object as soon as you identify it as one requiring a name. Don't let the difficulty in naming be an excuse—pick the best name you can. Choosing a less than perfect name early in the process and using it consistently is far better than trying to choose the perfect name at the last minute. Naming early on at least indicates that the object needs a name and motivates people to think of better names. Avoiding choosing a name doesn't have the same effect.

TIP A good name now is usually better than a perfect name later.

Managers often "help" this situation by stepping in and assuming responsibility for choosing the names. When they do this, they sometimes don't assume the responsibility for choosing the name in a timely manner: "Have we chosen a name for Xanadu Project yet, Bob?" "Not yet, Joe. We've been having a lot of meetings lately. I won't be able to get on it for a while, I'm afraid." And sometimes managers seem to be under the impression that since the names they will eventually choose will be so fantastic, they can delay the decision until a week before the project ships. I once worked on a project where management chose the name after the product shipped. The user interface, documentation, and packaging all had to refer to the name of the data, never the product itself. Not good.

Whenever anyone takes responsibility for naming things, you should make sure they understand that choosing the names in a timely manner is a significant part of that responsibility.

TIP The responsibility for choosing names includes the responsibility for choosing the names in a timely manner.

How to Name

Many people have trouble naming because they want to choose the perfect name or a clever name. This is a flawed goal. The name doesn't have to be perfect, and it certainly doesn't have to be clever. Consider the names of the following Microsoft products: "Windows" for a windowed operating system, "Word" for a word processor, "Office" for a suite of business programs, "Money" for a personal finance program, and "Internet Explorer" for an Internet browser. These names are hardly clever, but they are excellent product names since they are easy to remember and clearly identify what the product does. Note that the more clever names "Xenix," "MultiPlan," and "Bob" did not help the products they were attached to become more successful.

This may seem obvious, but to come up with a good name, ask yourself what the object to be named really does and how it will be used. If you focus on its main behavior, a good name will usually be close at hand. Of course, you need to use a different approach for product names or feature names that you want to trademark. For trademarks, the more descriptive the name, the weaker the protection possible.

Naming Is Serious Business

It is important to understand that naming is serious business. You should avoid using joke names or any other kind of name that you wouldn't want the outside world to see, even temporarily. If your product is successful, those "temporary" names might be around for years and might be extremely difficult to change later on. For example, there are many "undocumented" Windows APIs that have unfortunate names, such as Death, Resurrection, TabTheTextOutForWimps, PrestoChangoSelector, BozoLivesHere, and various Bear and Bunny APIs. I'm sure these names have stuck around far longer than their originators expected. Avoid the temptation to use joke names, and use your creativity elsewhere.

TIP   Avoid choosing joke names.

Problematic Terms

Aside from terminology you create specifically for your program, there is already much established, standard terminology that you should use when appropriate. The *Microsoft Manual of Style for Technical Publications* contains a comprehensive list of standard software terminology. While the style manual is intended to be a reference, you can't know what's in it without reading it from cover to cover. Since reading the book from cover to cover is sheer torture—I have done it twice and hope never to do it again—I will spare you the misery and present a list of the terms that I find interesting or that I have made mistakes with in the past. Note that this list, beginning on the following page, applies to user documentation and that programmer documentation (such as this book) might use different conventions.

CHAPTER 3

A.M., P.M.	Not *am* or *pm*.
abort	Use *end* to refer to communications and network connections, *quit* for programs, and *stop* for hardware operations.
above	Use *preceding* or *earlier* instead.
accelerator	Use *shortcut* instead.
and/or	Use *or* instead.
application	Use *program* instead.
bars	*Taskbar* and *toolbar* are one word; all other bars (*scroll bar, split bar, status bar, title bar,* etc.) are two words.
below	Use *following* or *later* instead.
bitmap	Use *graphic* or *picture* instead.
boot	Use *start* instead.
box	Use *computer* instead.
boxes	*Toolbox* is one word; all other boxes are two words.
button	Use "click Cancel" instead of "click the Cancel button."
check	When referring to a check box, use *select* or *clear* instead.
choose	Use *click* or *double-click* instead.
close	Use for windows, documents, and dialog boxes. For programs and network connections, use *quit* and *end,* respectively.
combo box	Use *box* instead (for example, use "In the Font box…" instead of "In the Font combo box…").
context menu	Use *shortcut menu* instead.
context-sensitive	Always hyphenate.
corrupt	Use *corrupted* instead.
deselect	Use *cancel the selection* instead.
dialog	Use *dialog box* instead.
dialogue	Use *dialog box* instead.
directory	Use *folder* instead.
disabled	Use *unavailable* instead.
diskette	Use *disk* instead.
DOS	Use *MS-DOS* instead.
double-click	Always hyphenate.
edit	Use *change* or *modify* instead.
end user	Use *user* instead.
enter	Don't use as a synonym for *type*.

error message	Use *message* instead.
execute	Use *run* or *carry out* instead.
exit	Use as a command name only; use *quit* instead to refer to closing a program. For example, "use the Exit command to quit the program."
Explorer	Use *Windows Explorer* instead.
FAX	Use *fax* instead.
field	Use *box* or *option* instead.
file extension	Use *extension* or *file name extension* instead. For the actual extensions, use *.txt* instead of *.TXT* or *TXT*.
filename	Use *file name* instead.
fixed disk	Use *hard disk* instead.
floppy drive	Use *floppy disk* instead.
grayed	Use *unavailable* instead.
hard drive	Use *hard disk* instead.
his	Use *the* instead (for example, "the user can change the settings" instead of "the user can change his settings").
higher	Use *later* instead for product version numbers.
hyphens	Don't use in key combinations; use a plus sign instead (for example, "Alt+X").
illegal	Use *not allowed* instead, except when referring to matters of law.
install	Use *set up* instead when referring to software.
internet	Use *Internet* instead.
K	Use *KB* instead with a space following the number. For example, use *40 KB*, not *40KB* or *40K*.
legal	Use *allowed* instead, except when referring to matters of law.
list box	Refer to by its label and the word *list* (for example, use "In the Font list…" instead of "In the Font list box…").
log in/log out	Use *log on to* and *log off* instead.
lower	Use *earlier* instead for product version numbers.
machine	Use *computer* instead.
menu item	Use *command* instead.
message box	Use *message* instead.
mnemonic key	Use *access key* instead.
noncontiguous selection	Use *multiple selection* or *nonadjacent selection* instead.

NT	Use *Windows NT* instead.
open	Use for windows, files, documents, and folders—not for choosing a command, a menu, an icon, an option, or any other similar element that doesn't produce a working file in a window.
option button	Don't use in procedures. Use "click Landscape" instead of "click the Landscape option button."
output	Don't use as a verb. Use *write to, display to,* or *print to* instead.
pathname	Use *path* instead.
PC	Use *computer* instead.
pop-up menu	Use *shortcut menu* instead.
prompt	Do not use as a noun to mean "message."
property page	Use *tab* instead.
property sheet	Use *dialog box* instead.
pull-down menu	Use *menu* instead.
push button	Use *command button* instead.
press	Use *click* when an action can be performed with both the keyboard and the mouse.
radio button	Use *option button* instead.
Readme/Read Me	Use *readme* instead.
reboot	Use *restart* instead.
Registry	Use *registry* instead.
right-click	Always hyphenate.
(s)	Do not use to indicate that a noun can be singular or plural. Use the plural or *one or more* instead.
select	Use for data, not commands. For commands, use *click* or *double-click* instead.
subdirectory	Use *folder* instead.
terminate	Use *quit* or *close* instead.
Toolbar	Use *toolbar* instead.
tooltip	Use *ToolTip* instead.
will	Avoid; make present tense, if possible.
Wizard	Use *wizard* instead.

While it can be a chore to constantly look up terms in the *Microsoft Manual of Style for Technical Publications,* the second edition has a greatly improved electronic version that makes finding things a snap. I recommend installing the electronic version and its associated compiled HTML file so that you can look up things quickly without having to fool around with the CD-ROM.

PART

Speak the User's Language

The terminology recommended by the *Microsoft Manual of Style for Technical Publications* is specifically designed to be understood by a wide range of users. Any other terminology you use should be carefully chosen to be readily understood by your program's users. What terminology do your program's users understand? Of course, this depends on the target user. Unless your software is for programmers, you should avoid using computer jargon. Try to use common, everyday words instead. For example, the common term "separator" is much better than the technical term "delimiter" for most users. If technical terms are necessary, make sure they are terms that are likely to be in the user's vocabulary.

Terms to Avoid

There are also some terms that you should never employ in your user interfaces. While terms such as "execute," "kill," "terminate," "fatal," and "abort" are perfectly acceptable in programmer's documentation, they are extremely violent terms in all other contexts. When in doubt, check the term in the *Microsoft Manual of Style for Technical Publications* or the *Microsoft Press Computer Dictionary*.

Recommended Reading

- Microsoft Corporation. *Microsoft Manual of Style for Technical Publications, Second Edition.* Redmond, WA: Microsoft Press, 1998.

  Provides useful guidelines for all aspects of documentation. Be sure to check the Dialog Boxes and Property Sheets section to make sure you are using the right control names, the Menus and Commands section to describe commands correctly, and the Screen Terminology section to use the right terms for screen items. I find myself referring to these sections often.

- Microsoft Corporation. *Microsoft Press Computer Dictionary, Third Edition.* Redmond, WA: Microsoft Press, 1997.

  A good source for making sure you are using the right term.

- Nielsen, Jakob. *Usability Engineering.* Chestnut Hill, MA: AP Professional, 1993.

  Chapter 5, "Usability Heuristics," presents the results of research indicating that simpler terminology not only is easier to learn but also results in significantly fewer user errors.

CHAPTER 3

C
H
A
P
T
E
R
4

Establish a Consistent User Interface Style

While the standards for Microsoft Windows user interfaces described in Chapter 1 provide many specific rules and guidelines, there is still enough flexibility within the standards to create an endless variety of user interface designs. Of course, this flexibility is desirable because it gives you the ability to create user interfaces that satisfy practically any design objectives and that take advantage of any new user interface technology. Rigid standards that impede progress by requiring a user interface style that was popular at a specific moment in time wouldn't have much of a following.

While it might be desirable to take advantage of this flexibility by design, it isn't such a good idea to do so by accident. All the user interface elements in a program should have a certain consistency. At the very least, all the windows, dialog boxes, menus, and graphics in a program should look as if they were designed by the same person, even if they were designed by several people. For example, you shouldn't be able to look at a dialog box and figure out which programmer created it. Such consistency helps the user by making the user interface elements easier to recognize and understand. Furthermore, when all the programs developed by a company have a consistent appearance and behavior, the company's image is enhanced by the presentation of a uniform and recognizable appearance in the marketplace. And, when it comes to future development, it also makes it easier for the company to leverage user interface designs and code. Clearly, any organization needs to go beyond the standards and create companywide or projectwide user interface style guidelines to give its software a consistent appearance and behavior. This is especially true for companies developing software for multimedia programs, Web sites, games, and children's programs, which tend not to use the standard windows and controls. In such cases, the standards are somewhat less relevant.

Appearance vs. Behavior

The character of a program is determined primarily by its appearance—its "look"—and its behavior—its "feel." The focus of user interface style guidelines should be on the appearance of the program. While the guidelines can address the program's behavior, much of the standard Microsoft Windows behavior is already covered in *Designing for the User Experience*. But note that *Designing for the User Experience* doesn't specify all user interface behaviors. For example, should a command button respond to a double click? The book doesn't say, but such behavior would be a bad idea simply because users don't expect command buttons to respond to double clicks. (In fact, for the standard Windows buttons, only owner-draw and radio buttons receive a BN_DOUBLECLICKED notification code via the WM_COMMAND message. Radio buttons receive double clicks because they can be considered equivalent to a single-selection list, which also receives double clicks. However, a custom command button could respond to double clicks.) For another example, should a list box have a horizontal scroll bar? Again, the standards don't say, but it is generally accepted that horizontal scrolling should be avoided because it makes the list text difficult to read.

Guideline Goals

Don't create style guidelines just for the sake of having guidelines. Rather, make sure that you have specific goals for your guidelines and that satisfying these goals, not just following the specific guidelines, is your ultimate objective. I believe the following are reasonable goals for user interface style guidelines:

PART

- **Make appearance consistent** The guidelines should promote interfaces that have a consistent appearance to help make them easier to understand and use. The user interface elements should look like they belong together.

- **Make a company's image consistent** The guidelines should help ensure that different programs produced by the same organization promote the same image.

- **Simplify appearance and behavior** The guidelines should promote interfaces that avoid unnecessary visual complexity and nonstandard behavior.

- **Simplify development effort** The guidelines should make user interface development easier for programmers so that they don't have to figure out routine details or make as many decisions.

This last goal is especially important. Effective guidelines should make the programmer's job easier, not harder. They should help the programmer get his work done, not interfere with it.

TIP Effective user interface style guidelines make your job easier, not harder.

Rigid enforcement of style guidelines shouldn't be necessary, since programmers should be able to tell when the guidelines apply and when they don't. Furthermore, the existence of guidelines shouldn't be used as an excuse to stop thinking. Blindly following the style guidelines in circumstances in which they are inappropriate doesn't make sense.

TIP Having user interface style guidelines doesn't mean that you can stop thinking.

Guidelines for Guidelines

In addition to establishing goals, it's also a good idea to establish guidelines for the user interface style guidelines themselves. Here are some issues to consider:

- **Try to avoid repeating what is in the standards** The goal isn't to replace *Designing for the User Experience* but to supplement it. However, some redundancy is acceptable, especially when a guideline is easily overlooked or often violated. It's also acceptable to have some redundancy for completeness or convenience. For example, if you have five guidelines for menus but one of the guidelines is in *Designing for the User Experience,* you should probably include it anyway to make the guidelines easier to use. You should also cross-reference other documents as needed.

TIP User interface style guidelines supplement, not replace, the standards.

- **Try to avoid arbitrary guidelines** If a guideline appears arbitrary but has a good rationale, include the rationale in the guideline. For example, rather than saying something like "Don't use yellow," say "Avoid using bright yellow as a foreground color, since it is a distracting color and is often difficult to distinguish on white backgrounds." On the other hand, if a guideline really is arbitrary, don't include it. A weak rationale is a sure sign that a guideline is bad. To be effective, user interface guidelines need support from all developers, and developers will resist guidelines that don't make any sense.

TIP When appropriate, include the rationale in a guideline.

- **Try to make the guidelines easy to follow** Give plenty of screen shots and other examples to make the guidelines clear and more interesting. If you give both good and bad examples, make sure that the bad examples are clearly marked as bad. Also, clearly indicate what is considered a rule, which should be followed in most circumstances, and what is a guideline, which is a recommendation.
- **Try to keep the guidelines short** Long, tedious guidelines are ineffective, since they are less likely to be used.
- **Make sure the guidelines match the tools used** For example, dialog box guidelines for Microsoft Visual C++ programmers should use dialog units, and the same guidelines for Microsoft Visual Basic programmers should use twips.

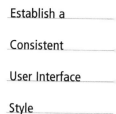

- **Try to avoid guidelines addressing Windows requirements**
  For example, don't include a guideline that says, "Child windows must be destroyed when the parent window is destroyed." In Windows, this always happens—there is no choice.

- **Try to focus on actual guidelines, not general user interface design principles**   If you want to establish baseline user interface design principles, use another document.

Create Resource Templates

One simple way to promote user interface consistency is to create resource templates. Although Visual C++ does not have direct support for user-defined resource templates—it does support predefined templates, such as dialog box templates for the large and small OLE property pages—you can make any resource into a template simply by copying and pasting an existing resource instead of creating a new one.

For dialog boxes, you can create the following templates:

- Wide, standard, and narrow dialog boxes with the main command buttons on the bottom.

- Wide, standard, and narrow dialog boxes with the main command buttons on the right.

- Wide, standard, and narrow property pages.

Note that the dialog box template size determines the width only. The height can be adjusted as needed. Also note that the template should contain preset guides and even placeholder group boxes and buttons. For example, you could use this dialog box template:

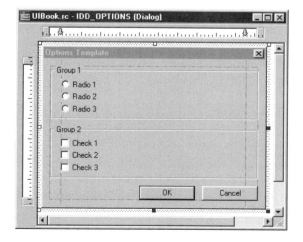

to create this dialog box:

While resource templates are most effective with dialog boxes, you can create templates for any other resource as well. The Visual C++ AppWizard makes what is in effect a template for the menu bar and toolbar, but you can go beyond that and create additional template menu commands and toolbar buttons that can be reused. You can also create template bitmaps and icons if you have graphics that can be used in several projects.

By using resource templates, different programmers can with little effort create resources with a consistent appearance.

TIP

Use resource templates to create consistent-looking resources.

Get "Le Look"

In Paris, fashion designers struggle with their haute couture to get "le look." I try to design user interfaces that have "le look" as well, but the particular look I'm after isn't trendy or attention-grabbing. Rather, I have the fairly modest goal of trying to create user interfaces that look normal. While it is difficult to precisely define what a "normal" user interface looks like, you can definitely tell when you are using one. As the fashion saying goes, if a person is poorly dressed you notice the clothes, but if a person is well dressed you notice the person. Similarly, if a user interface is poorly designed you notice the interface, but if a user interface is well done you notice

PART

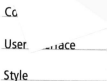

the program. This is the style I'm after. Normal-looking Windows programs have a familiar appearance that is immediately comfortable. They look like they are part of Windows. Programs that are not normal draw attention to themselves and clearly stand out but often in an undesirable way.

And now an interesting question: isn't my goal of getting "le look" in conflict with the previously mentioned goal of obtaining a consistent corporate image? The answer is that it can be but it doesn't have to be. If you want your programs to have a distinct image, you can do so with very subtle distinctions. The appearance of the bitmaps and icons; the way documents are displayed; the layout of the dialog boxes; the appropriate selection of controls; the use of advanced user interface features such as tooltips, previews, and direct manipulation; and the avoidance of annoying user interface problems all combine to make more of an impression than more obvious techniques like using custom controls just for the sake of being different.

In the following sample user interface style guidelines, I have tried to include guidelines that characterize this look.

Sample User Interface Guidelines

The following is a list of sample user interface guidelines that you might want to consider using. The items marked with an asterisk are considered rules and should be followed in most circumstances. The remaining items are guidelines. My personal criteria for rules is that either the rule must be followed to satisfy the standards, or the rule is objective (as opposed to subjective) and there is rarely a good justification for not complying. However, for me, there is no such thing as an absolute rule in user interface design. If I have an excellent justification for breaking a rule, it's broken. I rarely do.

Some of the guidelines give what might seem to be arbitrary sizes and spacing. However, the sizes and spacing given agree with the standards and are known to work well with the English language. If you have a good reason for using other sizes and spacing, you should do so. Just make sure to use whatever sizes and spacing you choose consistently throughout the program.

Lastly, note that in Visual C++ shortcuts are called "accelerators" and access keys are called "mnemonics." Normally, shortcuts are obtained with the Ctrl key, and access keys use the Alt key and are indicated by an underlined letter. The terms used here are consistent with *Designing for the User Experience* and the *Microsoft Manual of Style for Technical Publications, Second Edition*.

General appearance

- **Use consistency** A consistent appearance will make the user interface easier to understand and use. The user interface elements should look as if they belong together.

- **Use arrangement and flow** In Western cultures, people read from left to right and from top to bottom, so place the more important information on top and to the left. The upper left corner receives the most attention.

- **Use alignment** In general, use left alignment to make user interface elements easier to scan. Use decimal alignment or right alignment for numeric text. Avoid right alignment and center alignment for non-numeric text. You don't have to center everything or make everything symmetrical. Prefer having white space on the right side and bottom instead.

- **Use grouping** Group related user interface elements to show relationships. Display related information together. Place controls near the objects acted upon. Use white space, group boxes, lines and labels, or other separators to group related user interface elements.

- **Use emphasis** Try to draw attention to the user interface elements that need to be seen first, using focus, location, grouping, hierarchy, enabling/disabling, size, color, or font attributes. Try to visually indicate what the user should do next.

- **Use visual clues** Try to use like sizing and spacing to indicate that user interface elements are similar and different sizing and spacing to indicate that user interface elements are different.

- **Use white space** Use white space to create "breathing room" that makes window layout easier to understand and more comfortable to view. The spacing should appear more or less balanced and even, with no awkward gaps. However, avoid having too much white space. If possible, try to make the window smaller instead.

- **Watch for vanity** Don't plaster company or product names and logos all over the place. While large company or product names and logos are perfectly acceptable in splash screens or about boxes, the available space in other windows should be used for something else. If there is nothing else, try to make the window smaller instead.

PART

- **Watch sizing**   Make user interface elements resolution independent. Use either system metrics (using the GetSystemMetrics API function) or text metrics (using the GetTextMetrics or GetTextExtentPoint32 API functions) to determine the size of user interface elements. Any object that displays text, such as dialog boxes or printed text documents, should use text metrics. Avoid using pixels for sizing.

- **Consider using resource templates or predefined layout grids**   Resource templates or predefined layout grids will help you obtain consistency between different windows.

Note how the second dialog box below, unlike the first, has a compact, left-to-right, top-to-bottom flow; left-aligned labels that are easy to scan; and edit boxes aligned and sized to give them an organized, balanced look.

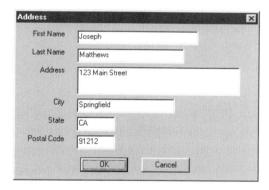

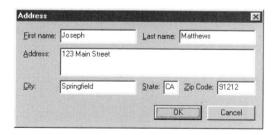

Windows visual affordance

Affordance relates to the ability of a user to determine how to use an object just by looking at its visual clues. Maintain the following visual affordances used in Windows:

- Raised items can be clicked.

- Items that become highlighted when the mouse cursor passes over them can be clicked.

- Recessed items cannot be clicked.

- Items with a white background and a flashing vertical bar can be edited.

- Items with a gray background cannot be edited.

- Gray items are disabled.

- Raised lines can be dragged.

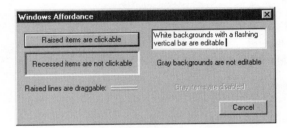

Interaction

- **Try to provide keyboard access to all features**   Ideally, all functions, except graphical functions like drawing, should be accessible with the keyboard alone.

- **Try to provide mouse access to all features**   Ideally, all functions, except text entry, should be accessible with the mouse alone.

- *** Make sure that activities that have significant consequences require explicit selection from the user**   The user needs to be fully aware that he is about to do something dangerous or destructive.

- *** Give feedback for all time-consuming operations**   Make sure there is a wait cursor, progress meter, or some other visual feedback during lengthy operations. The user should be able to cancel lengthy operations. Label the button Cancel if canceling undoes the operation, otherwise label the button Stop.

- *** Visually indicate modes**   Give the user visual feedback to indicate when he has entered a mode, typically by changing the cursor or the title bar text.

PART

- *** Make sure single-clicking and double-clicking are consistent** Use single-clicking for selection for nonbuttons. Use double-clicking for selection plus performing the default action. In other words, double-clicking (in a list box, combo box, or any other control that takes a double click) should have the same effect as selecting an item in the control and pressing the Enter key.

- *** Use the right mouse button only for context menus** Make sure the right mouse button is used for context menus and not for any other purpose.

- *** Do not use the middle mouse button** If the user has a mouse with a middle mouse button, let the user assign the behavior using the Mouse utility in the Control Panel.

- **Assign shortcut keys consistently** Use function keys and Ctrl key combinations for shortcuts. Don't use Alt key combinations except by convention, since they are used for access keys. Never combine Alt and Ctrl keys, since such combinations make shortcuts cumbersome and less accessible.

- *** Always make shortcut keys redundant** Never make a shortcut key the only way to access a command. Give the user a more visible alternative.

- **Avoid horizontal scroll bars** Unlike vertical scrolling, horizontal scrolling is undesirable because it makes it difficult to read an item. As an alternative, try to use a vertical scroll bar, make the window wider, shorten the text, or wrap the text instead. Of course, use horizontal scroll bars if you really must.

Programs

- *** Only main program windows have title bar icons, menu bars, toolbars, and status bars** Secondary windows must not appear on the taskbar, since clicking on a primary window taskbar button also activates any secondary windows. Secondary windows should not have the complexity to warrant a menu bar, toolbar, or status bar. Title bar icons are used as a visual distinction between primary windows and secondary windows. Also, never use the default Windows icon (the flying window icon) as a window icon.

- **Make the default configuration very simple** Let users grow into a program at their own pace.

CHAPTER 4

- **Applications should use either a multiple-document interface (MDI) or a single-document interface (SDI)** These program interfaces match the usage pattern of applications.

- **Applications should be maximized by default** The user is usually more productive when the full screen is dedicated to an application.

- **Utilities should use either an SDI or a dialog box interface** These program interfaces match the usage pattern of utilities. Using an MDI interface is not recommended for utilities because it requires too much effort to manage all the windows.

- **Utilities should work in a small screen space** Utilities are often used in conjunction with another program, so they need to run in a small screen space. Utilities should have a flexible window layout so that they can accommodate a wide variety of sizes. Utilities rarely run maximized.

- *** SDI programs that use actual documents must support running multiple instances** Running multiple instances will allow the user to work with several documents at a time.

- **Use an Exit command to quit a program** Use Exit to quit a program, Close to remove primary windows and modeless dialog boxes, and Cancel to remove modal dialog boxes. Use Close instead of Exit for primary windows when closing the primary window doesn't imply terminating the process. For example, closing a printer status window doesn't cancel the outstanding print jobs.

Terminology

- **Use the same term to describe the same thing** Using different terms for items that have only subtle differences will confuse the user.

Defaults

- **Save and restore user selections** A program should restore itself to the state it was in when last quit. MDI programs should restore the size and location of document windows. Dialog boxes should generally use the last input values for defaults.

- **Provide appropriate defaults** Help users get their work done by eliminating unnecessary effort through appropriate defaults. Give the default value that is most likely to be right, given how the setting is actually used. Often the best default is the last setting that the user input.

PART

- *** Consider safety when selecting default values**   Irreversible or destructive actions should never be the default. Never use a default value that would surprise the user.

Dialog boxes

- **Dialog boxes should display correctly in all video modes**   When displayed in VGA mode (640 x 480), a dialog box should be no larger than 640 x 460 (saving 20 pixels for the taskbar). This will guarantee that the dialog box can be displayed in all video modes.

- *** Make modal dialog boxes modal**   Make sure that all modal dialog boxes that have parent windows supply the correct parent window handle instead of a NULL handle. (Note that the correct parent handle is automatically supplied when using MFC.) If the parent window handle isn't supplied, the parent window is still active, so the dialog box really isn't modal.

- *** Never use scrollable dialog boxes**   That is, never use dialog boxes that require the use of a scroll bar to be viewed completely. Such dialog boxes are difficult to use and completely unnecessary. Redesign the dialog box instead.

- *** Never use menu bars in dialog boxes used as secondary windows**   Such dialog boxes require too much effort to use. Note that menu bars are acceptable in dialog boxes used as primary windows (such as the Find utility). Also note that context menus and menu buttons are acceptable in all dialog boxes:

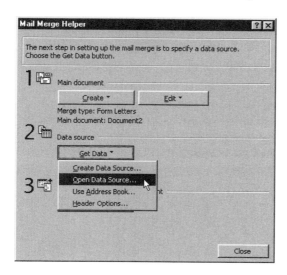

51

- *** Never use title bar icons in dialog boxes used as secondary windows** Title bar icons are used as a visual distinction between primary windows and secondary windows.

- *** Never display dialog boxes used as secondary windows on the taskbar** Note that clicking on a primary window taskbar button also activates any secondary windows.

- **Use the following layout and spacing within a dialog box:**

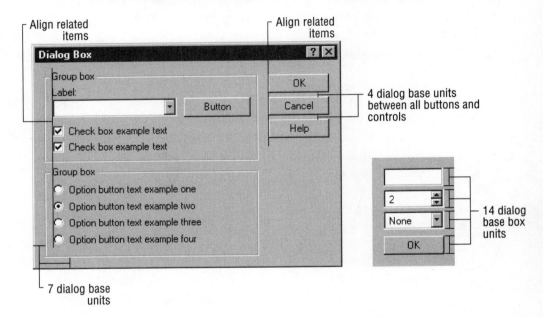

- **Between similar dialog boxes, use control locations to emphasize similarity** If the same control with the same meaning appears in several similar dialog boxes, it should appear in the same location. On the other hand, avoid placing different controls that could be confused in the same location.

- **Prefer dockable toolbars to modeless dialog boxes** Dockable toolbars are functionally equivalent to modeless dialog boxes but allow for more flexible placement.

- **Set input focus strategically** Set the initial input focus on the control that is most likely to be used first.

- **Don't put ellipses in dialog box title text** For example, a dialog box that is displayed as the result of choosing the Print Options... command should have the title *Print Options*. An exception is to indicate that a command is in progress, such as with "Connecting To The Internet…"

- *** Assign access keys to all controls that can handle access keys** Access keys help users keep their hands on the keyboard and make a program more accessible. You can assign access keys to controls such as command buttons, radio buttons, and check boxes directly in their captions. You can assign access keys to controls such as edit boxes, list boxes, and combo boxes by supplying a static text label or group box with an access key that precedes the control in tab order. Don't assign an access key to a group box in other circumstances—this is confusing. An OK button doesn't have an access key, since it is selected with the Enter key when it is the default button. A Cancel button doesn't have an access key, since the Esc key is used to dismiss a modal dialog box. If possible, avoid assigning an access key to a lowercase *g*, *j*, *p*, *q*, or *y*, or to a character immediately preceding or following one of these characters. The underline doesn't look right against the character's descender. Of course, the access keys must be unique.

- **Avoid using bold text** Use bold text sparingly. Bold text was used in Windows 3.1 dialog boxes to draw disabled text on old video hardware (that is, dithered gray). Since modern video hardware can draw gray text without dithering, Windows now uses normal text in dialog boxes for a much cleaner look. Use bold text only for emphasis. Most dialog boxes should not use any bold text.

- **Provide context-sensitive help** For more complicated dialog boxes, supply context-sensitive help for the entire dialog box (accessed with a help button or the F1 key), control-specific help for individual controls (accessed with the What's This? button or the Shift+F1 key), or both.

Dialog box main command buttons

- *** Separate main command buttons from the main body of a dialog box** Main command buttons are command buttons such as OK, Cancel, Close, Help, Stop, Hide, and other related buttons. This separation makes the main command buttons easier to find and identify.

- **Choose the dialog box orientation carefully**   In Western cultures, people read from left to right and from top to bottom, so main command buttons are easier to find if they are across the bottom or on the right. You should chose the orientation that makes the aspect ratio of the dialog box more similar to the aspect ratio of the screen, which is typically 3 units high to 4 units wide. This makes the dialog box appearance more comfortable and easier to position on the screen. Put the buttons across the bottom if they have different sizes. When in doubt, put the buttons across the bottom, since this orientation is more common and easier to read.

- **Right-align main command buttons placed across the bottom**   Right-aligned main command buttons follow the left-to-right flow. You might want to make an exception by centering the main command button when there is only one.

- **Avoid multiple rows or columns of main command buttons**   Multiple rows or columns of main command buttons will overwhelm the user. If you have many main command buttons, note that you can usually place more buttons in a single column on the right than in a single row across the bottom. Alternatively, consider using a command menu instead. If you must have many buttons, note that multiple rows are preferred to multiple columns.

- *** For modal dialog boxes, always provide OK and Cancel buttons**   To use a dialog box, the user needs to be able to easily identify how to move forward (with the OK button) and backward (with the Cancel button). You can replace OK with a more specific command, but never replace Cancel in a modal dialog box, except with Stop to indicate that the effect of an operation in progress cannot be cancelled.

- *** For modeless dialog boxes or dialog boxes used as primary windows, provide a Close button but do not provide OK and Cancel buttons**   Using OK and Cancel for a modeless dialog box or primary window makes the dialog box appear to be a modal dialog box. Furthermore, OK and Cancel are not meaningful when used in a modeless context. Use Close instead to eliminate any confusion.

- *** Always put the OK button first, Cancel second, Help last**   OK or its equivalent should always be the first main command button. Cancel should be to the right of or below OK. Place the OK and Cancel buttons next to each other. The Help button

should be the last button. If there is no OK button, place the Cancel button just before the Help button. This makes the main command buttons easier to find and identify.

● *** Label the OK and Cancel buttons correctly** The OK button should be labeled *OK*, not *Ok* or _OK_. The Cancel button should be labeled *Cancel*, not _Cancel_ or *CANCEL*.

● *** Make sure the Cancel button really cancels** When cancelled, the program state should be exactly the same as it was before the modal dialog box was displayed. If not, the Cancel button should be replaced with a Stop button. The Cancel button in the body of a modal dialog box should have the same effect as the Close button on the title bar. Property sheets are an exception, since the Cancel button doesn't cancel or undo changes that have already been applied.

Property sheets and property pages

● **Have property pages work independently** Avoid having the behavior or operation of one property page depend upon another. Users are unlikely to discover such dependencies between property pages. There should be no restriction on the order in which property pages are used. The user should be able to view any property page at any time.

● **Lay out property pages independently** The contents of several property pages aren't always going to take exactly the same amount of space. The layouts of the property pages that take less space than the largest property page should not be formatted differently because there is extra space available.

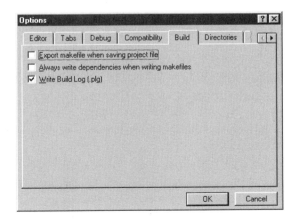

Avoid centering.

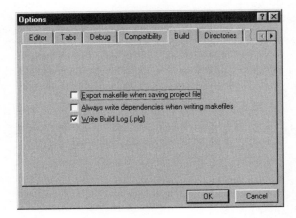

- **Prefer property sheets to dialog boxes with tab controls**
  There is no significant usability advantage to using property
  sheets rather than tabbed dialog boxes except for additional consistency. Alternatively, use property sheets for dialog boxes that
  actually display an object's properties and tabbed dialog boxes
  for other uses.

- *** Always use property sheets for properties, even if there
  is only a single page**   Always use a property sheet to make it
  clear that the user is viewing properties and not a regular dialog box. A property sheet has an Apply button to help the user
  experiment with settings.

- *** Never use more than two rows of tabs**   A single row of tabs
  is preferred, but two rows are acceptable. Having more than two
  rows of tabs is too many. Use hierarchical property sets or multiple dialog boxes instead.

- *** Always implement the Apply button for properties**   Again,
  providing an Apply button helps the user experiment with settings.

- *** Always put the word *Properties* and the name of the object in the title of a property sheet that displays properties**   Again, note that not all property sheets are used to display
  properties.

- *** Always place command buttons in the right location**   Command buttons that apply to all pages must be outside
  the tabbed page area. Command buttons that apply to individual
  pages must be inside the tabbed page area.

Wizards

- **Use wizards for advanced, complex, or infrequent tasks**
  Wizards are helpful for tasks that are sufficiently advanced or
  complex that the extra effort required to use them is worth the
  trouble. Wizards are most effective when used for tasks that are
  rarely performed. Using wizards for common tasks makes those
  tasks cumbersome.

Controls

- **Prefer the standard controls**   Use the standard controls (the
  six original basic controls and the new Win32 common controls)
  whenever possible. Programs that use nonstandard controls don't
  look or behave like most other Windows programs. Use custom
  controls only when you have a good justification.

- **Customize standard controls with caution**   Be careful when
  changing the standard appearance or behavior of the standard
  controls. It is often a mistake.

- *** Disable invalid controls**   Disable controls that don't apply
  in the current program state.

- **Eliminate unnecessary scroll bars**   If possible, make controls
  long enough or wide enough to eliminate the need for scroll bars.

Command buttons

- **Use a minimum width and a standard height**   Command
  buttons with text captions should have a minimum width of 50
  dialog units (1095 twips in Visual Basic) and a standard height
  of 14 dialog units (375 twips in Visual Basic). Try to limit the number of different sizes for command buttons with text to no more
  than two. Owner-draw buttons or command buttons without a
  text caption (such as "…") may be any size. This guideline gives
  command buttons a consistent, simple appearance. Command
  buttons that have a height greater than 14 dialog units tend to
  look amateurish. While there is no maximum width for command
  buttons, a command button wider than 200 dialog units (4380
  twips in Visual Basic) is questionable. See the screen shot on the
  following page for examples of command buttons.

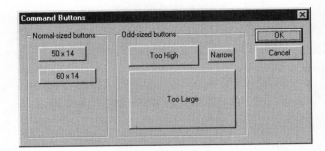

- **Consider widening buttons for internationalization**   While a width of 50 dialog units is a good minimum width for English text, it might be too small for programs that are to be localized for other languages. For programs that need to be translated to other languages, a minimum command button width of 60 dialog units (1335 twips in Visual Basic) might be easier to work with.

- *** Disable invalid command buttons instead of giving error messages**   Never have enabled commands that will result only in an error message.

- *** Always use ellipses to indicate more information is required**   An ellipsis in a command indicates that more information other than a simple confirmation is required to carry out the command. An ellipsis does not mean that a dialog box follows.

- *** Never assign a behavior to a double click**   Users do not expect command buttons to respond to double clicks, so they are unlikely to discover this behavior.

Check boxes

- *** Use check boxes to turn options on and off, radio buttons to change modes**   Check boxes are effective in turning options on and off but confusing when used to change modes to a state other than on or off. For example, you can use a check box to indicate that a toolbar is displayed or not, but using a check box to toggle a printer between landscape mode and portrait mode would be very confusing. Use a group of radio buttons with landscape and portrait modes instead.

- **Avoid groups of check boxes with more than eight (or so) items**   Consider using a check box list instead, since it takes up less space, but remember that a check box list will require more effort to use if scrolling is required. While check boxes are preferable if there is plenty of space or to be consistent with the use of other check boxes in the same window, more than eight or so check boxes is just too many.

- **Consider putting related groups of check boxes in a group box**   Such grouping will make the relationship between the check boxes more apparent.

- **Prefer vertical alignment**   A group of check boxes is easier to scan if aligned vertically, although horizontal and rectangular alignments are acceptable if they result in a better layout.

Radio buttons

- **Avoid groups of radio buttons with more than eight (or so) items**   Consider using a list or combo box instead, since they take up less space. Remember, however, that these elements require more effort to use. While radio buttons are preferable if there is plenty of space or to be consistent with the use of other radio buttons in the same window, more than eight or so radio buttons is just too many.

- **Avoid radio buttons for on/off or yes/no choices**   Use check boxes instead.

- *** Always put radio buttons in a group box**   Since radio buttons form a set of mutually exclusive choices, a group box makes it clear what the choices are.

- **Prefer vertical alignment**   A group of radio buttons is easier to scan if aligned vertically, although horizontal and rectangular alignments are acceptable if they result in a better layout.

Combo boxes

- *** Always give combo boxes a label**   Labels are necessary to identify what the combo box is for.

- **Make combo box drop-down lists at least five lines long**   Lists with fewer than five lines don't have a usable scroll bar thumb, making scrolling difficult. Note that if a combo box doesn't have enough items to fill the list, the list length is automatically shortened.

- **Avoid combo box lists with fewer than four (or so) items**   Consider using radio buttons instead, since they are easier to use, although they do take up more space. Combo boxes with only a few items are preferable if space is at a premium or for consistency with other combo boxes in the same window.

59

Edit boxes

- *** Always give edit boxes a label**   Labels are necessary to identify what the edit box is for. If the label is on the left, vertically align the label text with the edit box text.

- **Avoid edit boxes for constrained input**   Use edit boxes for input where the user can enter any text or numbers for numeric edit boxes. For constrained input, use other controls, such as combo boxes, lists, sliders, and spin boxes. Use the date and time picker control for dates and times.

- **Make edit boxes visible with spin boxes and browse buttons**   Spin boxes and browse buttons are simple, visible mechanisms that help the user give valid input in an edit box. Avoid forcing the user to type input. Use an edit box with a spin box only for numeric input, and be sure to use the AutoBuddy style for the spin box. For text, use a combo box instead.

- **Set the width of edit boxes to suggest the size of the expected input**   The width of an edit box is a visual clue of the expected input. For example, if the user is entering an address, a State field that is about two characters wide clearly suggests entering a two-character state abbreviation. If the expected input has no particular size, choose a width that is consistent with other edit boxes or controls.

- *** Always use numeric edit boxes for numeric input**   The user should never have to receive an error message for entering non-numeric text into a numeric field.

Sliders

- *** Always give sliders a label**   Labels are necessary to identify what the slider is for. Typically, sliders also need labels to indicate the meaning of the high and low values as well as of the current selection—all without colons, of course.

Static text

- **Left-justify static text labels**   Left-justification gives the labels an organized look and makes them easy to scan.

- **Prefer to place static text labels on the left, not on top of their associated control**   This alignment makes the labels easier to find and the combined label and control easier to scan. Obvious exceptions are tall controls, such as lists, trees, and multiline edit boxes.

- *** Always use colons at the end of static text labels used to identify a control**   Using a colon clearly indicates that the text is a control label. Labels used to give supplemental information about a control should not have a colon, such as labels used to interpret a slider control. Colons are also used as a clue by screen readers.

- *** Always use read-only edit boxes for nonlabel text**   Read-only edit boxes allow the user to copy the text to the clipboard and scroll the text if it is longer than the control.

- *** Never put static text on a raised border**   Static text on a raised border looks like a button, and users will try to click it. (The static text Modal frame extended style in Visual C++ will raise the border.)

List boxes

- *** Always give list boxes a label**   Labels are necessary to identify what the list box is for.

- **Make list boxes at least five lines long**   Lists with less than five lines don't have a usable scroll bar thumb, making scrolling difficult. Using a shorter list box is acceptable if the list box will not have a scroll bar.

- **Consider using check box lists for multiple selection**   Check box lists make the ability to select multiple items more obvious. If a check box list isn't acceptable, use a multiple-selection list with static text indicating the number of items selected to clearly show that multiple selection is possible.

- **Consider providing Select All and Deselect All commands for multiple-selection lists**   These commands make it easier for the user to make multiple selections, since it is common to want to select or deselect everything.

List views

- *** Always give list views a label**   Labels are necessary to identify what the list view is for.

- **Make list views at least five lines long**   Lists with fewer than five lines don't have a usable scroll bar thumb, making scrolling difficult. Using a shorter list box is acceptable if the list box will not have a scroll bar.

CHAPTER 4

- *** Use a clickable header only if the list is sortable**   Clickable headers should not be used for anything other than sorting. The first click should sort the list in normal order; the second click should sort the list in the reverse of normal order.

- *** Always make a list view sortable if it can contain more than about 30 items**   Giving the user the ability to sort long lists makes it easier to find information.

Scroll bars

- *** Use scroll bars only for scrolling**   Use sliders or spin boxes to set values.

- **Make scroll bars long enough to have a usable scroll bar thumb**   Scroll bars without a usable scroll bar thumb make scrolling difficult.

Group boxes

- **Use group boxes to group related controls**   While group boxes are traditionally used to group radio buttons, they can be used to group any type of control. Avoid group boxes with only a single control except to maintain consistency with other group boxes in the same dialog box.

- **Consider using static lines and text labels instead of group boxes**   A problem with group boxes is that they can take up a lot of space if there are many of them. A good alternative if space is at a premium is to group controls using a combination of a static text label and a static line (actually a static etched frame with a height of one dialog box unit).

- *** Don't use colons at the end of group box labels**   The box or line associated with a group makes the colon unnecessary and confusing.

Menus

- *** Always use single words for menu titles**   A multiple-word menu title on the menu bar looks like multiple menu titles.

- *** Never put gaps between the text on menu bars**   Nonuniform menu bar text looks awkward and serves no purpose.

- *** Avoid multiple-line menu bars**   While any menu bar can take multiple lines if you make the parent window narrow enough, avoid having so many menu bar items that multiple lines are likely in ordinary usage.

- *** Keep menus stable**   Disable, don't remove, invalid menu items. However, if a menu item is never valid during the instance of the program, remove it.

- **Order menu items strategically**   Group related items. More important commands should appear at the top of the menu, less important commands at the bottom.

- *** Disable invalid commands instead of giving error messages**   Menus should never have enabled commands that will only result in an error message.

- *** Assign access keys**   Access keys help users keep their hands on the keyboard and make a program more accessible. If possible, avoid assigning an access key to a lowercase g, j, p, q, or y, or to a character immediately preceding or following one of these characters. The underline doesn't look right against the character's descender. Of course, the access keys must be unique within a menu.

- *** Always use ellipses to indicate more information is required**   An ellipsis in a command indicates that more information other than a simple confirmation is required to carry out the command. An ellipsis does not mean that a dialog box follows.

- **Use the standard menus**   Avoid not supplying File, Edit, and Help menus. Since these menus are standard, users expect them. For example, users expect to find commands like Print and Exit in the File menu, even though these commands have nothing to do with files. Similarly, users expect to find Cut, Copy, and Paste in the Edit menu, and at least the About command in the Help menu.

- **Place the Find and Options commands consistently**   Always put the Find command in the Edit menu, and always put the Options command in the Tools menu if there is one or the View menu if not.

- *** Use check marks to turn options on and off, radio groups to change modes**   Check marks are effective in turning options on and off, but confusing when used to change modes to a state other than on or off. For example, you can use a check mark to indicate that a toolbar is displayed or not, but using a check mark to toggle a printer between landscape mode and portrait mode would be very confusing. Use a radio group of landscape and portrait modes instead.

- *** Never use multicolumn drop-down menus**   Multiple columns add unnecessary complexity to a menu.

- *** Never use "Bang" menus**   Bang menus are items on the menu bar that look like drop-down menus but are actually commands that execute immediately upon selection, such as Exit! Obviously, users expect menu titles to act as menus and not commands.

- *** Never right-justify menu titles**   This menu style is obsolete and only makes the menu hard to use. (You can right-justify menu titles using the Help property in Visual C++.)

Context menus

- **Consider using context menus, but make them redundant**   Context menus shouldn't be the only way to access a command. Typically, commands in a context menu should also be available from the menu bar. Use context menus to make command access more efficient.

- **Avoid including shortcut keys in context menus**   Rather, put the shortcut key assignments in the menu bar. Context menus are for quick access and are accessed with the mouse, not the keyboard.

Toolbars

- *** Keep toolbars stable**   Disable, don't remove, invalid toolbar buttons. However, consider removing entire toolbars that do not apply when the user enters a mode.

- *** Disable invalid commands instead of giving error messages**   Toolbars should never have enabled commands that will only result in an error message.

- **Use large toolbar buttons for utilities** A good utility toolbar is usually quite different from an application toolbar. It is far simpler and has much larger buttons. A utility toolbar should include only a few obvious commands with descriptive text and graphics.

- **Use movable, customizable toolbars for applications, fixed toolbars for utilities** Applications need flexible toolbars to support their typical usage pattern. Users typically do not use utilities long enough to need to customize their toolbars.

- **Provide an option to show or hide the toolbar** If there are multiple toolbars, provide options to show or hide them individually.

- *** Always use tooltips** Tooltips help the user understand what the toolbar buttons do.

Tooltips

- **Make your toolbar tooltip text informative, yet brief** Avoid stating the obvious. Consider using an ellipsis to indicate that more information is required to carry out the command. If the command has a shortcut key assigned, display the shortcut as well.

- **Aim toolbar tooltip text at intermediate to advanced users** Use tooltips to briefly identify or remind, not to teach.

- **Use tooltips to display useful information** Use tooltips in places other than toolbars. Tooltips are a great way to provide useful information to the user with very little effort. But use tooltips with restraint—they lose their value if there are too many of them. Don't use tooltips for controls like command buttons or static text.

- **Don't automatically remove tooltips that contain a lot of text** Tooltips automatically remove themselves after about 10 seconds by default. If the tooltip contains a lot of text, this will not be enough time for the user to read the text.

Text

- **Avoid unnecessary abbreviations** Try to either give the text more room or rewrite the text to take up less space. Abbreviations make text harder to understand.

- **Avoid unnecessary uppercase text** Never use words with all uppercase letters unless the word is an acronym. This makes it look as if you are shouting at the user.

CHAPTER 4

- **Avoid complex punctuation**   Prefer simple punctuation such as periods, commas, question marks, and dashes. Avoid semicolons, exclamation points, parentheses, brackets, and so on.

- *** Use consistent capitalization**   Use book title capitalization for text in window titles, menus, command buttons, column headers, property page tabs, and toolbar tooltip text. Use sentence capitalization for text used in labels, radio buttons, check boxes, group boxes, and menu item help. (Book title capitalization is the capitalization of the first letter of every word except articles or prepositions not occurring at the beginning or end of the title. Sentence capitalization is the capitalization of the first letter of the initial word and any words that are normally capitalized— such as proper nouns.)

- **Avoid distracting backgrounds**   Place text on solid, neutral-colored backgrounds. Make sure to create a good contrast between the text and the background.

- **Avoid offensive language**   Avoid violent terms such as *fatal, execute, kill, terminate,* and *abort.*

Message boxes

- **Carefully select the right message box type**   Use the Information message box with an OK button to provide the user with information about the results of a command. Use the Warning message box with Yes, No, and possibly a Cancel button to ask a question or alert the user to a condition or situation that requires the user's input before proceeding. Use the Critical message box to inform the user of a problem that requires correction before work can continue.

- *** Do not use the Question message box type**   The question mark symbol (MB_ICONQUESTION) is no longer recommended for message boxes because it is now used consistently within Windows 98 to signify context-sensitive help.

- **Avoid unnecessary message boxes**   Don't use error messages to report normal behavior. Instead, use them to report unusual or unexpected results. Don't use confirmations for actions that can be easily undone.

- **Ask questions with yes or no answers**   When asking the user a question, use the Yes and No buttons instead of the OK and Cancel buttons. Using these buttons makes the question easier to understand. Unlike in dialog boxes, the OK and Cancel buttons are rarely used together in message boxes.

- **Make sure the message box option buttons match the text** For example, never give Yes and No as responses to non-questions. Also, don't give multiple option buttons that have the same effect. For example, don't give both No and Cancel button options unless they have different results. The No button should perform the operation, whereas Cancel should cancel the operation.

- **Carefully select the default button** Make the safest or most frequent option the default button.

- **Avoid unhelpful help** Don't provide a Help button unless you can provide additional information that really is helpful. Don't supplement a meaningless message box with meaningless help.

- **Consider using system-modal message boxes for critical errors** Use system-modal message boxes to notify the user of serious, potentially damaging errors that require immediate attention. A system-modal message box is the same as an application modal message box except that the message box has the WS_EX_TOPMOST style. Unlike in 16-bit Windows, being system modal has no effect on the user's ability to interact with other programs.

Error messages

- **Avoid error numbers** Never give error numbers unless the user can actually do something useful with the number.

- **Avoid blaming the user** Avoid using the words *you* or *your* in the error message text. If necessary, use the passive voice when referring to user actions. It's better to say the equivalent of "mistakes were made" than the equivalent of "you screwed up."

- **Avoid hostile language** Avoid using the terms *bad, caution, error, fatal, illegal, invalid,* and *warning* in the error message text. Try to use more specific, descriptive terms instead. Try to explain what exactly is wrong.

- **Use plain English in the error message text** Be brief, clear, consistent, and specific. Never use words with all uppercase letters unless the word is an acronym. This makes it look like you are shouting at the user. Use full sentences and the simple present or past tense. Avoid abbreviating words.

- **Avoid trying to be funny or clever in the error message text**
Users do not find error messages funny, and any attempt at humor will not be well received.

- **Allow the user to suppress noncritical error messages** For noncritical errors that occur often, give the user an option to suppress the error message in the future.

Fonts

- ***Respect the user's font selections** Windows allows the user to select fonts for title bars, menus, message boxes, and tooltips. Handle the WM_SETTINGCHANGE message so that font changes happen immediately and completely.

- **Avoid distracting fonts** Generally, typefaces other than Arial, Tahoma, and MS Sans Serif should be avoided. Verdana, Trebuchet MS, and Century Gothic are also good choices for a slightly different look. Any serif fonts in an interface should be considered distracting, although serif fonts are fine in a document. Don't use monospaced fonts except to indicate user input or mimic a typewriter.

- **Avoid using bold or italic fonts** Use bold fonts to attract attention and italic fonts for emphasis, but do so rarely.

- **Avoid mixing typefaces** Any window that does not contain a document should have at most two different typefaces.

Color

- ***Use the system colors** Respect the user's color selections. Avoid using fixed colors. Don't force the user to use your color selections. Avoid distracting text colors, generally anything other than black. Use the system colors COLOR_BTNTEXT or COLOR_WINDOWTEXT for text. There is absolutely nothing wrong with black text (COLOR_WINDOWTEXT) on a white background (COLOR_WINDOW). Handle the WM_SYSCOLORCHANGE message so that color changes happen immediately and completely.

- ***Select the system colors based on their description, not their appearance** Do not mix and match system colors that are part of a set. For example, don't mix COLOR_BTNTEXT with COLOR_WINDOW.

- **Consider using the system halftone palette for graphics**
Using the halftone palette avoids a palette flash in 256-color mode.

PART

- *** Never use color as the sole means of conveying information** Not depending upon the ability to distinguish colors makes a program more accessible to color-blind users and usable on a monochrome monitor.

3-D

- **Avoid unnecessary 3-D effects** Avoid 3-D static lines and rectangles, except when grouping controls. Prefer using white space to separate controls. Never surround 3-D rectangles with other 3-D rectangles. Avoid 3-D text.

- **Use subdued 3-D effects** Note how the more subtle 3-D effects used in Windows 98 are much more effective and pleasing to look at than the 3-D effects used in Windows 3.1. While most real-world objects have highlights, very few real-world objects have solid black borders. Windows 98 creates 3-D effects by using black borders only on the right and bottom for raised objects and on the top and left for sunken objects.

CHAPTER 4

- *** Use a consistent 3-D effect**   Make sure the light source for 3-D effects is the upper left corner of the screen.

Miscellaneous details

- *** Never beep or blink**   Nothing is more annoying than a beeping, blinking program. A good exception is flashing a program's taskbar window button to notify the user of a pending message.

- **Avoid unnecessary audio effects**   At the very least, make them optional. Ideally, they should be turned off by default and the user should have to explicitly request them.

- **Improve the accessibility of documents with a zoom feature**   A program that displays documents can improve accessibility as well as overall usability by providing a document zoom feature.

- *** Handle the WM_DISPLAYCHANGE message**   A program should be able to appear and function correctly after a display resolution change.

- **CD-ROM–based programs should support AutoPlay**   AutoPlay should display a list of options, including setup, when the CD-ROM is inserted into the drive. AutoPlay should not run if the program is already installed.

- **Support the user's locale**   Use the date and time picker control for date input, the GetDateFormat and GetTimeFormat API functions for date formatting, the GetCurrencyFormat and GetNumberFormat API functions for currency and number formatting, and the LCMapString API function for sorting. Consider using the RichEdit control for text input and output. Lastly, use the WM_INPUTLANGCHANGE message to handle changes to the input language.

Related Chapters

- Chapter 1—Know the Standards.

  Presents the Windows user interface standards, consisting of *Designing for the User Experience,* the Designed for Microsoft Windows logo requirements, and the *Microsoft Manual of Style for Technical Publications, Second Edition.*

- Chapter 10—Good User Interfaces Are Visible.

  Offers several suggestions on how to make user interface functionality self-evident.

- Chapter 11—Good User Interfaces Are Invisible.

  Offers several suggestions on how to prevent user interfaces from drawing attention to themselves—the ultimate goal of "le look."

- Chapter 15—Keep It Simple.

  Presents a Windows user interface roadmap that compares the various Windows user interfaces and shows how to decide which one to choose, primarily with the goal of obtaining simplicity.

- Chapter 16—Prefer the Standard Controls.

  Describes the advantages of the standard controls, both good and bad reasons to use custom controls, and how to select a custom control.

- Chapter 29—Check Your Dialog Boxes.

  Gives a list of useful items to check to make sure your dialog boxes are done correctly.

- Chapter 30—Check Your Error Messages.

  Gives a list of items to check to make sure your error messages are necessary, helpful, informative, and easy to understand.

Recommended Reading

- Arlov, Laura. *GUI Design for Dummies.* Foster City, CA: IDG Books Worldwide, Inc., 1997.

  Chapter 7, "The GUI Standard," and Chapter 22, "Ten Things a Project Leader Can Do," give useful tips for creating guidelines, and Chapter 13, "The ABCs of Visual Design," and Chapter 16,

"The Right Widget for the Job," give useful ideas for the content of your guidelines. The book's CD-ROM includes a draft project GUI standard.

- Capucciati, Maria R. "Putting Your Best Face Forward: Designing an Effective User Interface." *Microsoft Systems Journal,* February 1993.

  Gives many excellent ideas for guidelines and has several screen shots of user interfaces that definitely do not have "le look." While this article was written for Windows 3.1, almost everything discussed still applies to Windows 98.

- Cooper, Alan. *About Face: The Essentials of User Interface Design.* Foster City, CA: IDG Books Worldwide, Inc., 1995.

  Chapter 22, "Dialog Box Etiquette"; Chapter 25, "Imperative and Selection Gizmos"; and Chapter 26, "Entry and Display Gizmos," give useful ideas for guidelines, but don't be surprised if you disagree with some of the ideas presented in these chapters.

- Howlett, Virginia. *Visual Interface Design for Windows.* New York, NY: John Wiley & Sons, Inc., 1996.

  Chapter 10, "Color"; Chapter 11, "Icons and Imagery"; Chapter 12, "Fonts"; and Chapter 15, "Common Pitfalls and How to Avoid Them," give useful ideas for guidelines for more subjective, visual interface design issues.

- Microsoft Corporation. *Designing for the User Experience.* Redmond, WA: Microsoft Press, 1999.

  The baseline Windows user interface standards. Your user interface style guidelines should supplement these standards. This is the first place to look when you have a question about guidelines. The chapters on windows, secondary windows, menus, controls, toolbars, and visual design should be of particular interest when creating guidelines.

- Nielsen, Jakob. *Usability Engineering.* Chestnut Hill, MA: AP Professional, 1993.

  Chapter 8, "Interface Standards," gives research-based information about interface guidelines, including the benefits of guidelines for both users and developers, the dangers of poor or misused standards, and suggestions on how to create and evaluate standards.

- Weinschenk, Susan; Jamar, Pamela; and Yeo, Sarah C. *GUI Design Essentials*. New York, NY: John Wiley & Sons, Inc., 1997.

  This book consists of two parts; the second part is dedicated to design guidelines. These guidelines are intended to be used as companywide standards. Some of the guidelines given are a bit too obvious to be interesting. The book's CD-ROM includes a design guidelines document.

CD-ROM Resources

The CD-ROM included with this book contains the following resources related to this chapter:

- A copy of the sample user interface guidelines presented in this chapter in Microsoft Word format that you can customize.

- Sample resource templates.

CHAPTER 5

Pay Attention to Other Programs

I find it highly educational to pay careful attention to other programs' user interfaces while I am using them. Looking at other programs is an interesting exercise for a programmer because it turns the tables on you by turning you into a user. This helps you focus on the program's usability rather than its implementation or technology.

Everyone has their favorite programs, and everyone has programs they can't stand. You should try to understand why you feel the way you do about a program. What is it about the user interface that makes the program good, and what is it that makes it bad? This understanding will help you improve your own programs. Of course, if you like all programs, you probably need to be a bit more critical—there are plenty of bad ones out there.

TIP Think like a user instead of a programmer. Trying to understand why you feel the way you do about a program will help you improve your own programs.

I find that the programs I like best have many of the same characteristics, which are described below.

General Characteristics

- The interface is attractive yet has a standard look and familiar feel. It feels comfortable the first time I use it.

- The interface is consistent with the standards and with itself. The interface looks as if it were designed by one person.

- The dialog boxes have an organized layout and don't try to present too much information at a time.

Easy to Learn

- The interface is easy to learn without your having to read any documentation.

- The menus are simple and well organized and provide a road map to the program's functionality.

- The toolbar icons have obvious meanings. They are not distracting and use subdued colors.

- When I have a question, the context-sensitive help answers it with a click or two of the mouse.

Configurability

- The interface is easily configurable and is automatically initialized to my preferred configuration.

- The interface readily adapts to any screen resolution or number of colors.

- My input or selections are remembered and used as defaults the next time input is required.

PART

Operation

- The tasks are accomplished by directly manipulating objects on the screen instead of filling in dialog boxes.

- The interface is responsive. Most commands are performed quickly, and those that are not show accurate processing progress.

- My input results in visual feedback.

- My mistakes can be easily undone.

- The information I need is readily accessible. Tooltips are used to provide information when appropriate.

Details

- The program integrates well with Microsoft Windows and with other programs.

- The data can be exported in a variety of formats to files or the clipboard.

- The status bar actually has useful status information, rather than useless information such as "Ready."

- Setup and uninstallation are easy to perform.

When I am creating user interfaces, I try to take the above ideas and apply them whenever I can. When it comes to attributes like these, you simply can't have too much of a good thing.

Interestingly, none of the above characteristics is directly related to any specific technology, which is generally the aspect many programmers like to focus on. As a user, I don't care if a program was created using the Windows API, MFC, Active Template Library (ATL), or Microsoft Visual Basic, or if it uses standard controls, custom controls, or Microsoft ActiveX controls. I don't care if its graphics use device-independent bitmaps (DIBs), device-dependent bitmaps (DDBs), or Microsoft DirectX. The specific technology matters to me only as much as it contributes to these characteristics and helps me accomplish my goals, which are what led me to use the program in the first place.

Case Study: Visual C++

For a specific example, let's consider Microsoft Visual C++ version 5.0, an application many Windows programmers know and love. On the whole, I believe it's an excellent application. Following are lists of what I like and dislike about it. Making such lists in response to various programs will help you set goals for your own user interfaces.

Likes

- Visual C++ has successfully integrated what used to be several individual programs, including a compiler, an editor, a debugger, a resource editor, online help, Microsoft Developer Network (MSDN), and source-code control. Having all these tools available in one application is a great convenience. I also like the ability to seamlessly integrate third-party tools, such as other source-code control systems and debugging tools.

- The AppWizard and Class wizards are extremely useful and help eliminate having to write and maintain boilerplate code.

- The Visual C++ environment makes routine tasks simple, often by providing direct manipulation. I especially like the ability to view variable values using tooltips, the ability to drag and drop text from an editor window to the Watch window, and the ability to lay out the toolbars by directly moving, dragging, and sizing the toolbar controls.

- The environment is highly configurable. I can configure the size and location of the Workspace and Output windows. I can also configure just about every detail of the toolbars, which I use all the time.

- Visual C++ can display a variety of document formats. Although I normally use it to edit C++ text and Windows resources, I especially appreciate the ability to edit and view HTML files. The syntax-coloring feature works well with HTML files because it clearly indicates syntax errors. The hex dump window is also convenient.

- The compiler performance is excellent. I also like the incremental linking and intelligent rebuilding that doesn't recompile files unless it is necessary.

- Visual C++ has a powerful debugging environment that gives you the ability to trace into DLLs, the MFC source, and even inline functions. I also like the just-in-time debugging ability.

PART

- There are many more features that I have not even used, such as a configurable keyboard map, custom AppWizards, and macros. The product has amazing depth.

- The basic online help included with Visual C++ is awesome. If you need more information, the MSDN help files are available.

- Given all this functionality, the Visual C++ menus and dialog boxes are relatively easy to figure out.

Dislikes

- Visual C++ routinely rearranges my toolbars whenever I minimize the application while debugging, and the result is never what I would like. Believe it or not, this rather small item bothers me more than anything else about the program, since it seems to happen to me all the time.

- The paste function has a tendency to paste the two last items cut, instead of just the last one.

- Unlike normal text files, you can edit a resource file even if it or any of its dependent files are read-only. Read-only file attributes are a common occurrence when using source-code control. This can mean that either you lose your work or—as in the case where the resource file is writable but the header file isn't—your resource can become corrupted.

- Project settings, options, and customizations are spread across three dialog boxes and two menus. I always seem to choose the wrong menu the first time and have a lot of difficulty finding the setting I want to change.

- You cannot save project or program settings to a file. (OK, you can save the project settings to a makefile, but this isn't what I want to do.) If I could save the settings, I could compare different projects to determine whether they have consistent settings and, after finding any problems, restore the settings that were changed accidentally. There are other ways to accomplish this goal, but it would be handy to have some convenient way to manage settings, especially across projects.

- Although I can easily install MSDN into Visual C++, I can't easily uninstall it. No matter what I do to remove MSDN, the Visual C++ help system insists on accessing the MSDN CD-ROMs. The only way I can completely remove MSDN is to uninstall and reinstall Visual C++ and reset all my settings. Not good.

CHAPTER 5

- Visual C++ often remembers my previous input but often forgets it as well. For example, when I create a dialog box with the ClassWizard, I usually save it to files named "dialog.cpp" and "dialog.h," yet the wizard always attempts to save them to files named after the class name, thereby forcing me to change the filenames. This can be very irritating after a few hundred times— a good user interface should adapt to the user. A history list of previous input would be useful in such situations.

- The text windows have the full pathnames in the window captions. While this is normally useful, it is a problem when the windows are minimized and the default directory is different from the file's path. In this case, instead of captions like "Myfile.txt," all the captions become something like "C:\...\Folder...," which is next to useless. I can view the full file path using tooltips, but that feature doesn't seem to work well. I think it would be more useful if the caption included only the filename when a window is minimized.

- If you change a file and then give the Go command, Visual C++ asks whether you want to rebuild before running. If you select Yes but the rebuild fails, the old version of the program is run without any notification. This results in debugging the wrong code, which is a huge waste of time. It would be better if the program didn't run when the build failed.

- For some reason, you can't toggle between decimal and hexadecimal displays from the Quick Watch window, but you can from the Watch window. I find this inconvenient.

- I find it too difficult to change the name of a file and even more difficult to change the name of a project.

- Although the resource editor is nice enough to automatically assign resource IDs, it would be an improvement if there were a way to keep the IDs contiguous as the resources are maintained. For example, the MFC message map macros ON_COMMAND_ RANGE and ON_UPDATE_COMMAND_UI_RANGE are easier to use with contiguous IDs.

What I find most interesting about the lists above is that the bad items are rather trivial when compared to the good items. This is typical of a good program. Of course, the fact that the bad items are minor makes them no less irritating. Details matter! A program could have the most awesome features in the world, but if it has many minor user interface problems, users are going to find the program aggravating. You could take any good program and come up with lists similar to mine—what is important is the overall trend. In most cases, the trend will be for a good program's positive attributes to largely match the characteristics I outlined at the beginning of the chapter.

TIP Details matter! The fact that a program's problems are minor makes them no less irritating.

On the whole, the best programs don't just allow me to get my work done—they go out of their way to help me get my work done. Visual C++ accomplishes this through its wizards, debugger, configurability, and remarkable integration. As you use other programs, paying attention to how the programs fail at or achieve this goal will go a long way toward helping you understand the different ways of creating great user interfaces.

TIP Good programs go out of their way to help users get their work done.

Recommended Reading

- Howlett, Virginia. *Visual Interface Design for Windows.* New York, NY: John Wiley & Sons, Inc., 1996.

  Chapter 13, "Interface Makeovers," presents a couple of case studies of interface makeovers, including a makeover of Microsoft Encarta. These interface makeovers illustrate how to achieve some of the user interface characteristics presented in this chapter.

PART II

Understanding Users

C
H
A
P
T
E
R
6

Beginning vs. Advanced Users

Because a user's skill level is a primary factor determining how the user will interact with your program, understanding your users' skill level plays a significant role in your user interface design. This chapter explores the different types of users, how their different skill levels result in different interface designs, and some methods for creating a program that can accommodate all types of users.

Types of Users

As I describe the three fundamental types of users—beginner, intermediate, and advanced—in detail, note that each skill level is really a combination of two different factors: Microsoft Windows experience level and application experience level. The more important factor is the user's overall level of experience with Windows. Since Windows programs are usually created from the same user interface building blocks, the skills a user acquires from

85

using one Windows program usually apply to other programs. An experienced Windows user should be able to figure out how to use many other Windows programs (that is, if those programs have good interfaces) with very little help. The less significant factor is the user's overall level of experience in using the program in question and in performing the program's tasks. For example, I have been using Windows for years, but I am pretty much a beginner when it comes to three-dimensional animation programs or computer-aided design (CAD) programs. Understanding Windows doesn't help me much with such programs.

Beginning Users

Beginning users are determined largely by how much they know about Windows alone. And beginning users don't know much. Of course, this doesn't mean that beginning users aren't smart, but it does mean that certain user interface features are probably inappropriate for them. For example, if your program uses only context menus to accomplish a task, chances are that a beginning user won't be able to figure out how to do that task. The beginning user's experience just doesn't encompass advanced user interfaces such as context menus. Luckily for user interface designers, while all users start out as beginning users, few users stay beginners for long—with more and more experience with Windows, beginning users quickly become intermediate users. So, while it makes sense to make your program beginner-friendly, your real emphasis should be on accommodating intermediate and advanced users.

Intermediate Users

Intermediate users understand how to use the standard features of Windows fairly well. They are comfortable with context menus and dragging and dropping. They understand more subtle details, such as the difference between single-clicking and double-clicking. They have also used your program enough to know roughly how it works, but they don't understand all of its features, especially its advanced features. Intermediate users use your program only occasionally. If they used your program more often, they could become advanced users.

Advanced Users

Like intermediate users, advanced users understand almost all of the standard Windows user interface features. What separates advanced users from intermediate users is that advanced users understand most of the functionality of your program and they want to get their work done as quickly as possible. (Intermediate users are more willing to trade some efficiency for simplicity and ease of use.) Advanced users want to use toolbars and context

86

menus instead of the menu bar. They want to keep their hands on the keyboard and use keyboard shortcuts whenever they can. They prefer to manipulate objects directly and want to see as few dialog boxes as possible. Advanced users typically use your program for several hours a day.

Since the difference between intermediate and advanced users has less to do with their Windows skills and more to do with how much they use a program, the majority of a program's users are intermediate users. As we will see in the next chapter, users typically spend most of their time with a few applications, eventually becoming advanced users of those programs. This leaves them too little time to master all the other programs they use. For example, users rarely become advanced users of utilities, simply because they don't use them long enough. I used the Find utility in Windows literally hundreds of times before I bothered to check its menu bar, and even then the reason I checked the menu bar was out of curiosity, not out of necessity. I can't imagine not checking the menu bar of an application. The difference between applications and utilities is discussed in detail in Chapter 7.

Choosing Appropriate Interface Features

Now that I've established the different types of users, you might be asking, "Does this really make a difference in user interface design? Should I really design an interface differently for beginning users than for advanced users?" The answer to both questions is yes, and in this section as I further compare the types of users and the user interface features suitable for each, I think you'll see why this is true. You'll find that users with different skill levels have different needs, and that many Windows user interface features are appropriate for some skill levels and not others.

Beginning Users

Because a beginning user is unfamiliar with the more sophisticated interface elements, the key to success in designing for beginning users is to make the user interface visible. A user interface is visible when a user can figure out how to use it just by looking at it. With a typical visible user interface, a user is able to perform tasks by making selections in menus and dialog boxes. Visible tasks don't require knowledge of special keyboard sequences or mouse selections or any other mechanism that isn't apparent on the screen.

The point is that obvious visual clues indicating how to perform a task give the beginning user a good chance at getting his work done. If there are no obvious visual clues, it's highly unlikely the beginning user will figure out how to do his job. Note that interface mechanisms such as context menus, dragging and dropping, and keyboard commands are clearly not visible. For example, there is no way to determine that a window has a context menu simply by looking at it. In Chapter 10, "Good User Interfaces Are Visible," I discuss in detail making user interfaces visible.

Let's look at some specific user interface elements that are good for beginning users.

Menu bars

Menu bars are the best way of showing beginning users how to use your program. Menu bars make an excellent teaching tool. A program's menu bar is effectively a hierarchically organized catalog of all the program's features. If you want to get a quick overview of what a program does, scanning its menu bar gives you a concise summary. A menu item's state (enabled vs. disabled) indicates when the user can perform a task. The menu item text itself indicates the shortcut key and access key (for example, the Ctrl+S shortcut and the underlined letter "S" access key in the Save command).

Menu bars are an excellent teaching tool.

It is important to keep the menu bar stable. You should indicate that a command is available only by changing the menu item's state. You should not indicate that a command is unavailable by dynamically removing it from the menu. Changing the menu structure can be confusing for all users but especially for beginning users. For example, note that Microsoft Word 95 removed all menus except the File and Help menu when all the documents were closed. Word 97 fixed this mistake.

Keep menus stable. Disable, don't remove, invalid menu choices.

Dialog boxes

While simple tasks are best performed directly from the menu bar, dialog boxes are the best way of showing beginning users how to perform more complex tasks that require additional input. Dialog boxes are also an excellent teaching tool. A good dialog box conveys what the task is, what the options are, and what input is needed to perform the task.

Wizards

Wizards are a good mechanism for performing highly complex tasks, regardless of the user's ability. However, an interesting difference between wizards and dialog boxes is that wizards make poor teaching tools. In fact, wizards don't teach anything. They effectively say "give me all the information and I will do all the work." This approach is effective for rarely performed tasks that the user probably doesn't really need to understand, such as connecting to a network. However, wizards are a poor choice as a sole mechanism for performing important tasks that are central to a program, since they do not help users understand how to accomplish such tasks on their own.

Redundant menus

While context menus are excellent for advanced users, using only context menus to perform certain tasks virtually guarantees that beginning users won't be able to perform them. To satisfy all types of users, make sure that all commands in context menus are also available in the menu bar. For example, Windows Explorer allows the user to perform many useful file commands from the file context menu, but all these commands are duplicated in the menu bar and the toolbar.

Now let's look at some specific user interfaces that are inappropriate for beginning users.

Cascading dialog boxes

While presenting a single modal dialog box to a beginning user isn't a problem, presenting a complex cascade of dialog boxes can be very confusing. The problem is that beginning users don't really understand the modality of modal dialog boxes, especially when they are in a big pile. There is no strong visual clue—aside from the disabled caption bar, which is rather weak—that the dialog boxes underneath are really disabled when they appear enabled. Disabling the controls of a disabled dialog box would provide a stronger visual clue, but this technique is currently not standard in Windows programs.

Double-clicking

Beginning users have trouble understanding when double-clicking is necessary. While advanced users understand that single-clicking means selection and double-clicking means selection plus performing the default action, beginning users do not. Consequently, they either don't double-click at all or they double-click everything until they eventually figure out the difference. Note that the general Web page user interface, which does not use double-clicking at all, is very popular with beginning users because they find it easy to understand.

Status bars

While knowing the status is certainly a good thing and status bars are visible, beginning users are not yet in the habit of checking the status bar for information. If you use the status bar as the sole method of providing important information, chances are beginning users will not see it.

Edit boxes

Edit boxes are good for beginning users when just about any input is acceptable. However, when specific input is required, it is better to give beginning users controls that are constrained to valid choices. When possible, use radio buttons, lists, or combo boxes instead.

Nonstandard controls

Nonstandard controls are easier to understand when you already have a frame of reference. For example, it is easier to conclude "Oh, that's just a funky combo box" when you already know what a combo box is. While beginning users probably don't know what controls are standard and what controls are not, they have probably seen and used all of the standard controls and therefore have some basis for understanding how to use nonstandard controls.

Intermediate/Advanced Users

The key to success in designing for advanced users is to make the user interface convenient and efficient. Advanced users want to get their work done as quickly as possible. They don't want to fool around. Intermediate users aren't quite at the same level as advanced users, but they have essentially the same goals—to work quickly and efficiently. While all users benefit from having a visible user interface, more advanced users want the option of employing more efficient user interface mechanisms, which are commonly not visible. If you do not provide these mechanisms in your interface, you run the risk of frustrating these users or, worse, preventing them from working at the speed that will let them meet their goals.

Let's look at some specific user interface elements that are good for intermediate and advanced users and consider why they are not good for beginning users.

Toolbars

Toolbars are something of a cross between menus and modeless dialog boxes. Either way, advanced users prefer using toolbars to using the menu bar because the interaction is so much easier—just move the mouse over the toolbar button and click. While toolbars can also benefit beginning users, they are not quite as effective as the menu bar because the menu bar is more comfortable if you are inexperienced.

Why? Because the menu bar provides context. When you browse the menu bar, you know the menu category. Is the command in the Edit menu? If so, it is for editing. Is the command in Tools menu? If so, the command is a tool. When you drop down a menu, you also see all the other possible selections. If you are not sure you've selected the right command, you can review all the other commands in the same menu until you are sure. Typically, some help text appears on the status bar that explains what the menu item does. Lastly, by using an ellipsis, a menu item gives you a clue as to what is going to happen when you select it. If there is no ellipsis, no further input is required, so there is no chance to bail out if you change your mind. While more convenient because they require less effort to use, toolbar buttons provide the user with none of this information and, as a result, are less comfortable to the beginning user.

Keyboard shortcuts

If you have your hands on the keyboard and you want to work quickly, you want to continue to keep your hands on the keyboard. Constantly moving your hand from the keyboard to the mouse and back again requires additional effort and time. Keyboard shortcuts allow you to perform commands directly from the keyboard, and they are by far the most efficient technique for giving commands if you already know the shortcut.

The problem with keyboard shortcuts for the beginner is that they are not visible. The easiest way to learn about a keyboard shortcut is from the menu bar itself, since keyboard shortcuts are shown on the right-hand side of menu items that support them. You can also learn about keyboard shortcuts in a program's documentation and by knowing the standard Windows keyboard shortcuts. However, all these techniques require time, experience, and memorization (usually achieved through repetition), and to place such expectations on a beginner is not realistic.

Context menus

Advanced users enjoy using context menus because they are extremely convenient. You don't have to move the mouse much to call them up, and all the commands relevant to an object are consolidated in a single location rather than spread across several menus as they are in the menu bar.

As noted earlier for keyboard shortcuts, the problem with context menus for beginners is that they are not visible. You have to know that you can click an object with the right mouse button to see its context menu. You also have to get in the habit of doing this to see whether objects have context menus.

Direct manipulation

Advanced users like direct manipulation because it allows them to interact with an object directly with the mouse instead of having to use dialog boxes. For example, to change the name of a file using Windows Explorer, you just have to select the filename, click it to put it in edit mode, and type in the new name. Compare this process to having to use a dialog box—a dialog box is not nearly as convenient.

As with all the other advanced user interface techniques, direct manipulation isn't visible, although some types of direct manipulation are suggested by cursor hinting. For example, you can tell whether a dialog box is resizeable because the cursor changes to a shape that suggests resizing when you move it to the edge of the dialog box.

Handling All Types of Users

What do you do if your program needs to support all user skill levels? After all, it is a reasonable goal for most programs to support a wide range of users. Happily, while the needs of beginning and advanced users are not the same, they are not exclusive either. You can accommodate a wide range of user skills by making your user interface visible; allowing the user to perform all tasks using the menu bar and dialog boxes; providing optional toolbars, context menus, and keyboard shortcuts; and providing advanced interface features such as direct manipulation and drag-and-drop functionality. Windows Explorer, Microsoft Internet Explorer, and Microsoft Word are examples of programs that support a wide range of user skills.

Here are some additional ideas you should consider:

- Make sure the program, however complex, at least appears simple to beginning users. Consider Windows Explorer as an example. While Windows Explorer has a significant amount of depth, its menu bar structure is fairly simple.

PART

- Make sure that the advanced interface features are never the only means of accomplishing important tasks.

- Make the user interface highly configurable. Configurability always helps satisfy a variety of user levels, since one size rarely fits all.

- Unless your program is only for beginning users, focus the design effort on intermediate and advanced users. Going out of your way to accommodate beginning users will likely frustrate all other users. Remember that beginners don't stay beginners for long.

Avoid User Modes

When trying to accommodate a wide range of user skill levels, you might be tempted to solve the problem by having user modes: one mode for beginning users, another mode for advanced users. User modes can also be configured for different roles—one mode for a manager, one for a worker, one for an executive, and so on.

I believe user modes are always a mistake, simply because they aren't necessary, and adding the complexity to support user modes makes the interface more difficult to use and understand for all users. I find that if you improve the usability for all users and make the program flexible and configurable, user modes aren't needed.

Consider Microsoft Word. This is an application that is used by a wide variety of users, all with different skill levels, all performing different tasks. People use Word to write letters, create reports, create brochures, write articles, write books, write poetry, prepare résumés, do homework, write term papers, and so forth. Each of these activities has different goals and requires different levels of skill. You might be able to make a convincing argument that the needs of different types of writers are so varied that different modes are necessary. Yet Word doesn't have user modes and it doesn't need them. It accommodates a wide range of users by providing easy-to-use functionality that is flexible and highly configurable. It helps users perform a wide variety of tasks through templates and wizards. In effect, this flexibility allows users to create their own modes. Having fixed user modes would only get in the way.

Don't use fixed user modes. Provide enough flexibility and configurability so that users can create their own modes.

Choose the Default Configuration Carefully

As users gain experience with your program, they will make the transition from beginner to intermediate to advanced. Your program can accommodate this transition by providing enough depth in functionality to satisfy the more advanced users. Your program might provide things like multirow toolbars, several types of docking windows, and floating palette windows. Whatever you do, don't display all these windows on the screen by default. If your program has a lot of functionality, let users grow into it at their own pace. You don't need to show every feature in the beginning—let the user choose to display these other windows when they are ready. If you initially present your program with a clutter of windows, the reaction isn't going to be "Cool, look at all these neat features!" Rather, more likely the reaction is going to be "Whoa, what is all this junk?" Users unfamiliar with a program are rarely impressed by a clutter of windows.

 TIP

Make your program's default configuration very simple. Let users grow into the program at their own pace.

Making your program highly configurable also helps accommodate a wide range of users. But make sure that the default program configuration is usable for beginners without modification. Users typically don't start to configure a program until they become familiar with it.

Understanding your users' skill level plays an important role in a program's user interface design. Users with different skill levels have different needs and different goals. Consequently, you need to make sure to select those user interface elements that are appropriate for your target users. Ideally, your program should have enough depth to accommodate a wide range of users and to allow a user to grow into it.

Once you understand the type of user you are dealing with, are you ready to start designing the user interface? Well, no—there is one more step. You also need to understand the type of program you are designing and the implications of the different program types. These are the subjects of the next chapter.

PART

Related Chapters

- Chapter 7—Using Applications vs. Utilities.

  Explores the different types of programs and how they result in different interface designs.

- Chapter 10—Good User Interfaces Are Visible.

  Presents a discussion on why visibility is important, and gives several specific techniques for making Windows programs more visible. Visible user interfaces are essential for beginning users.

- Chapter 15—Keep It Simple.

  Presents several techniques for simplifying Windows programs. Keeping your program simple helps all users, regardless of skill level.

Recommended Reading

- Cooper, Alan. *About Face: The Essentials of User Interface Design.* Foster City, CA: IDG Books Worldwide, Inc., 1995.

  Chapter 19, "The Meaning of Menus," presents an insightful discussion of the different menu types and how users naturally use menus to learn how to use new programs. You should take full advantage of this natural ability. Chapter 31, "Good at What You Do," presents an interesting discussion of different user levels and the needs of the users at each level.

C
H
A
P
T
E
R
7

Using Applications vs. Utilities

In the last chapter, I discussed how the user's skill level should affect your user interface design. Clearly, understanding how the user actually makes use of your program should affect the design even more. While there are many different types of programs and ways of using a program, most programs can be described as either an application or a utility, and this simple categorization can help you make significant decisions about your user interface design. In this chapter, I'll explore these types of programs and how each type influences user interface design. One interesting conclusion is that program type strongly impacts the user's skill level with the program. This chapter, then, can be regarded as the flip side of the previous chapter—the user's skill level affects the program's design, but the program's design also affects the user's skill level.

CHAPTER 7

Types of Programs

While it might seem as if there are an unlimited number of different program types, from the point of view of user interface design most programs fall neatly into one of two types: application or utility. Each program type is defined below in terms of how a program of that type is used.

Applications

An application is a program designed to perform a specific task, such as word processing, creating spreadsheets, creating presentations, or database management. However, the specific activity being performed isn't what makes a program an application. The determining factors are both the level of the tasks being performed and how long the tasks are performed. Users tend to use applications for long periods of time, possibly all day long, and applications provide a high level of functionality to support this amount of usage. By contrast, any program used for a few minutes at a time is a utility, no matter how sophisticated it is. Although Microsoft Word and WordPad both perform word processing, Word is an application because it is typically used for hours at a time and it has the functionality required for this level of usage, while WordPad falls into the utility category because it is typically used to quickly view or edit a document and has relatively basic functionality.

Running an application for many hours at a time has several implications. The first is that an application is usually run maximized, since the user is more productive when the full screen is dedicated to the task. Another implication is that a key to success in designing an application is to make its user interface convenient and efficient. Application users want to get their work done as quickly as possible. Lastly, since users spend so much time using applications, they quickly become intermediate to advanced users. Users grow into applications and make an effort to learn more advanced techniques to become more productive. Consequently, applications should be designed primarily for advanced users. While, ideally, beginning users should be accommodated, this accommodation should not be at the expense of advanced users.

TIP Applications are usually run maximized. Design applications primarily for advanced users.

Utilities

A utility is a program designed to perform a narrowly focused task (for example, a function related to system management). Utility tasks are often simple, and users tend to use a utility for only brief periods of time to accomplish a task quickly. Once done performing the task, the user usually minimizes or closes the utility to get it out of the way and then resumes using an application.

The fact that utilities are run for short periods of time has several implications. For example, it's safe to assume that a utility will be used in conjunction with another program. As a result, to work effectively with another program, a utility must run in a small screen space. Utilities are almost never run maximized. In fact, it's desirable for the utility to have a flexible window layout so that it can accommodate a wide variety of sizes well. Another implication of a short running time is that the utility's user interface should be visible so that a user can immediately figure out how to use the utility. Utility features should be simple and obvious—in other words, they should not stall the user. Lastly, since users spend so little time using utilities, they don't advance much beyond the beginner-to-intermediate level. Utility users are best described as perpetual intermediates with little motivation to become advanced users. They probably won't discover advanced or subtle user interface features. Consequently, utilities should be designed primarily for beginning users.

Utilities need to work in a small screen space. Utilities are almost never run maximized. Design utilities primarily for beginning users.

Of course, certain programs don't fit into either the application or the utility category. Consider system programs, such as device drivers, that run in the background—these programs are rarely seen by the user except for an occasional dialog box. System software and hardware drivers that appear on the taskbar System Tray are another example. Their user interfaces also consist of simple dialog boxes. None of these examples, however, are particularly interesting when it comes to user interface design. Such programs should have the same user interface characteristics as utilities.

CHAPTER 7

Choosing Appropriate Interface Features

Given the differences between how applications and utilities are used, it should be clear that not all user interface features work equally well in both program types. The user interface features suitable for each program type are discussed below.

Applications

The following list describes user interface strategies and characteristics appropriate for an application:

- An application can use either a multiple-document interface (MDI) or a single-document interface (SDI).

- For an SDI application that manipulates actual documents, the program must support running multiple instances in order to handle multiple documents simultaneously.

TIP SDI programs that manipulate actual documents must support running multiple instances.

- An application's main window should be maximized by default. For MDI applications, the MDI child document windows should most likely be maximized by default as well. Of course, the application should allow users to override these defaults.

- Since applications are used for an extended period of time, an application's appearance should not be distracting or fatiguing. Consequently, its overall appearance should be low-key and its colors subdued.

- An application should include an optional, configurable toolbar to support advanced users.

- An application should support advanced user interfaces—such as keyboard shortcuts, context menus, and direct manipulation— to support advanced users.

PART

Utilities

The following characteristics and strategies are appropriate for utilities:

- A utility can use either an SDI or a dialog box interface. Using an MDI is definitely not recommended, since it requires too much effort to manage all the windows.

- For an SDI utility that manipulates actual documents, the program must support running multiple instances in order to handle multiple documents simultaneously.

- A utility's main window should have a flexible layout so that it can be used in a variety of sizes. The utility's main window should never be maximized by default.

- Since utilities are not used for an extended period of time, a utility can use more and brighter colors than an application does to help the user quickly distinguish its features.

- A utility can use animation, such as with the Find utility and ScanDisk.

- A utility either does not include a toolbar or offers a simple toolbar using large buttons and text to describe the buttons. If the utility includes a toolbar, the toolbar shouldn't depend upon tooltips to explain its buttons.

- If a utility supports advanced user interface features (such as keyboard shortcuts, context menus, and direct manipulation), those features should not be the only way to accomplish the task. Utility users are more likely to employ the more visible means of using the program.

Multiple-document interfaces are not suitable for utilities because they are just too complex for the simple, quick tasks performed by utilities. An MDI utility would force the user to manage too many windows; SDI and dialog box interfaces don't require this additional effort. This is at least one reason why Windows Explorer is a much better program than the old File Manager.

As explained in the last chapter, menus are more suitable for beginners than toolbars are because a menu is an excellent teaching tool, providing the user with context missing from toolbars. Note that few of the utilities that come with Microsoft Windows have toolbars. (I know, many of the Microsoft Windows NT Administrative utilities use toolbars, but these are clearly aimed at more advanced users.) If a utility does use a toolbar, the toolbar is usually quite different from an application toolbar. Far simpler and much larger, a utility toolbar includes only a few obvious commands with descriptive text and graphics.

Lastly, note that utilities can get away with nonstandard interfaces more easily than applications can. Since a utility is generally used in small doses, nonstandard buttons, graphic backgrounds, and bright colors are acceptable because these features won't be used long enough to grow tiresome.

Exceptions to the Rule

While most programs fall neatly under the application or utility category, exceptions that are harder to categorize do exist. For example, what kind of program is Windows Explorer? In many ways, it's like an application. It has fairly extensive functionality, much more than most utilities. With the exception of the bright yellow folder icons, it has a low-key appearance, using subdued colors. It supports many advanced user interfaces, such as drag-and-drop operation, direct manipulation, and context menus. Interestingly, it doesn't support any keyboard shortcuts beyond the standard Cut, Copy, Paste, Undo, and Select All.

However, given the way Windows Explorer is used, it is clearly a utility. Using Windows Explorer isn't an end in itself. Users don't run it to create files as they do with applications; rather, they run it to find and maintain files. Also, users employ Windows Explorer for brief periods of time to accomplish small tasks quickly; because they use it so often, users keep it running instead of closing it when done. Since it is often used in conjunction with other programs, it's usually not maximized but is run instead in a somewhat-less-than-full screen window as a drag-and-drop source or target.

Windows Explorer differs from other utilities simply in that it is used so much that its users quickly become advanced users. Features that are suitable for advanced users work effectively in Windows Explorer. In fact, its target user is intermediate-to-advanced, although one could argue that Windows Explorer targets beginning users with the View As Web Page mode. Interestingly, this significant time-of-use difference makes Windows Explorer a bad design model for most utilities.

PART

Are there other exceptions? I believe that the other major programs that are part of Windows, such as Microsoft Internet Explorer, Microsoft Outlook Express, or any other system program used several times a day, straddle the definition of utility and application the same way that Windows Explorer does.

Program Categories

Now that I have defined what an application and a utility are and defined a program as software that can be either an application or a utility, I'll use these terms consistently throughout the rest of this book. Usually I'll use the term *program,* since most of the material applies to both applications and utilities.

While I'm at it, I'll define one more term, *program category.* I'll use program category to describe a group of programs considered together based upon their similar purpose, type, or audience. There are many program categories, such as:

- Business and professional programs
- Multimedia programs and programs designed for home users
- Internet sites and applets
- Games
- Children's programs

I've focused this book on the business and professional category. Some of the ideas I present don't apply to the other program categories. However, to make a daring generalization, I think you can usually treat programs in the other categories as utilities, with the exception that they are often run maximized and not in conjunction with other programs. The need for visible user interfaces targeted to beginning users is the primary reason they should be treated as utilities. Users run programs in these other program categories primarily for entertainment, and they aren't willing to make a significant effort to learn how to use them. Users use them because they want to, not because they have to.

I find it interesting that each of these program categories has a fundamentally different user interface style. Users expect a Web site to look like a Web site, a game to look like a game, and so on. A single user can move easily from one program category to another, easily adjusting his expectations to match the category. For example, a user would not expect a game or multimedia program to look like a business application. This difference in program category style results partly from the designers in each program category understanding that their users have alternatives. For example, the

CHAPTER 7

user of an online encyclopedia could easily perform the same activities using a printed encyclopedia, so the online encyclopedia's designers make sure that it has a visual appeal on a par with a printed encyclopedia.

Related Chapters

- Chapter 6—Beginning vs. Advanced Users.

  Explores the different types of users, how their different skill levels result in different interface designs, and methods for accommodating all types of users in a single program.

- Chapter 10—Good User Interfaces Are Visible.

  Presents a discussion on why visibility is important and gives several specific techniques for making Windows programs more visible. Visible user interfaces are essential for utilities.

Recommended Reading

- Cooper, Alan. *About Face: The Essentials of User Interface Design*. Foster City, CA: IDG Books Worldwide, Inc., 1995.

  Chapter 12, "Posture and State," presents an insightful discussion of the different types of programs based on how they are used. Cooper refers to this as posture and defines the four most common postures: sovereign (applications), transient (utilities), daemonic (system programs), and parasitic (programs that monitor ongoing processes). He then discusses the three window states (normal, maximized, and minimized) and their significance. Lastly, he discusses when it is appropriate to use MDI.

- Howlett, Virginia. *Visual Interface Design for Windows*. New York, NY: John Wiley & Sons, Inc., 1996.

  Presents useful information for designing multimedia programs.

CHAPTER 8

Users Aren't Designers

As you make user interface design decisions, you need to understand that the ultimate goal of most software is to help users get their work done. The connection between a program and a user is called a *user interface* and not a *program interface* for a reason. Users are what user interfaces are all about. Given the importance of users, it only makes sense to have users involved in the user interface design process in some way. After all, if you incorporate users directly into the design process, you are certain to satisfy the user's goals and have a successful product, right? Well, maybe. While user satisfaction is the ultimate measure of a good user interface, the fact is that users are not designers, so they don't necessarily have the knowledge or ability to give you all the information required to create a good user interface design. So, although users can play an important role in the design process, I believe that it's up to you in your role as a software designer to design the user interface.

Directly involving users in the user interface design process is referred to as user-centered design. A typical user-centered design process involves talking to users, creating a prototype interface, having users test the prototype, and iterating through the process until everyone is satisfied with the results. While I agree that the goals of any user interface design should be user centered, it is less clear that the design process itself needs to be user centered. This chapter will describe user-centered design and its various alternatives. It will also describe the alternative that I prefer to use, which I call vision-centered design.

One alternative to user-centered design that I won't be discussing is programmer-centered design. Naturally, this is the approach typically preferred by programmers, but it has a poor track record. The problem is that programmers are not users. Programmers and users typically have different needs and goals, as well as different knowledge and preferences. I'll discuss the specific differences between programmers and users in detail in the next chapter.

TIP   Users are not you. You need to be an advocate for the user by putting the user's goals ahead of your goals.

Determine the Target User

A good user interface is specifically designed for the people who are going to use it. Clearly, the first task is to determine the target user. You need to answer the following questions:

- Who are the program's users?
- Are they a member of a specific group of users or the mass market?
- What is their background or profession?
- What is their software skill level?
- What are their specific needs and goals?
- Why will they buy the program?
- Why will they like it?

Of course, at this point the answers to many of these questions are theoretical. You'll get much more realistic answers from your target users in the next step.

PART

TIP Establish the target user to help you make design decisions.

Suppose that as you identify the target user, you determine that your program is a mainstream, mass-market product to be used by everyone. Programs such as Microsoft Internet Explorer or even Microsoft Windows itself are good examples of such products. Appealing to a broad market doesn't mean that you can't define a target user. While it is possible for a single program to accommodate a wide variety of users, not all users can be accommodated equally well. As I discussed in Chapter 6, "Beginning vs. Advanced Users," users with different skill levels have different needs. Such a mainstream program should be targeted squarely at intermediate users. Going out of your way to accommodate beginning users will likely frustrate all other users. Furthermore, beginners don't stay beginners for long. Targeting advanced users will clearly frustrate beginners.

Identifying and understanding the target user is valuable even if your program is used by a wide variety of people. The target user sets the direction in which you want to aim your program. Identifying and understanding the target user will help you make better design decisions.

TIP Always identify a target user, even if your program will be used by a wide range of users.

Talk to Target Users

Now that you have identified target users, the next step is to actually talk to them. You need to understand them and their goals in more detail. You need to ask target users the following questions:

- What is their work environment?

- What tasks do they do? How can software improve those tasks? Can the tasks be made more productive and more enjoyable? What are the biggest problems?

- What is their skill level for the task that the program will perform? What is their software skill level?

- What hardware do they feel comfortable using? What hardware do they have?

- What Windows features do they understand?

- What terminology do they understand? What languages do they speak? (Obviously, not everyone speaks English.)

- How often will they use the program? For how long?

- How much training will they receive?

If you are able to, you should watch users perform their work. (This is referred to as a *site visit*.) See what they do. Ask them why they do it. Try to understand what tasks are really necessary and what tasks are unnecessary overhead. See what mistakes they make. Not only will this allow you to understand the tasks better, but it will also allow you to identify problems the user isn't even aware of. Also, try to determine the accuracy of your target user profile. Is the typical user similar to the target user or is the target user only the center of a broad spectrum of users?

The goal behind this research is to really understand your program's users and their needs and goals. What you want to do is to create a framework that you can use to make good design decisions. You definitely want to avoid speculating on what tasks users might want to do or how they might want to do them—work from the direct knowledge of your users that your research gives you.

TIP

Avoid designing user interfaces based on speculation of the user's needs and goals. Work from direct knowledge whenever possible.

As I discussed in Chapter 6, "Beginning vs. Advanced Users," and Chapter 7, "Using Applications vs. Utilities," the answers to these questions really do make a difference in the design of a program. These chapters describe how knowing that a program is a utility targeted specifically for beginning users leads to an understanding that certain design possibilities are appropriate and others are not. Specifically, a program aimed at beginners should have visible features so that the user can figure out the program just by looking at it. The program shouldn't rely upon interface elements that are not visible—such as context menus, direct manipulation, or keyboard shortcuts—and should avoid elements like edit boxes and interactions like double-clicking. A program that is a utility should be simple to use and have a flexible layout that works well in a small space. It should not use MDI, be initially maximized, or have a complex toolbar.

While understanding the type of user and type of program will help you choose which user interface elements to use, understanding your users' needs and goals will help you decide everything else. This knowledge will help you determine factors critical to the success of the program, such as what features to provide, what data is required, how the tasks should be performed, how all the program activities should fit together and how they should be implemented. This information will also help you make decisions about design details, such as the importance of the mouse vs. the keyboard, the performance of the target hardware, and whether it is appropriate to use audio. For example, using audio is inappropriate in an office environment but can be appropriate in other settings.

 TIP Use specific target user information to make decisions about design details.

User-Centered Design

The goal of talking to the target users is to determine their needs. But nobody knows users' needs better than the users themselves. Instead of asking them high-level task-related questions, as outlined earlier, why not go one step further and ask them low-level detailed questions? Why not involve them directly in the user interface design process itself? Why not have them evaluate the entire user interface design?

Designing user interfaces with the direct assistance of user feedback is the core of user-centered design. A user-centered design process typically includes the following steps:

1. Talk to users (as discussed earlier).
2. Quickly design a user interface based on user information.
3. Create a prototype of the design.
4. Have users test the prototype.
5. Repeat the process until satisfied.

In this user-centered process, the user is the key player. The user, not the programmer, is setting the program's goals and requirements based on his needs. The user, not the programmer, is determining what the product should look like and how it should behave. Furthermore, the user has ample opportunity to evaluate the user interface by testing the prototype so that he can identify problems early in the design process. In short, the user is getting exactly what he wants. The programmer is simply implementing what the user asks for in the intermediate prototypes and the final product.

What could be better for satisfying the user's goals? If you do every-thing the user asks for, how could this process not result in a successful product? How could such a process possibly go wrong? Well, there is one small problem: users typically don't have the knowledge or ability to play this role, even if they want to.

Users Aren't Designers

For users to play such a critical role in the user interface design process, they need the following abilities:

- Users need to know what they want and be able to articulate it.
- Users need to understand the solutions possible using current technology.
- Users need to understand basic user interface design principles.
- Users need to determine if the prototype is acceptable.

Unfortunately, users typically do not have these skills. The fact that users often lack these skills doesn't mean that they aren't smart—it simply means that users aren't software designers or software engineers and there-fore have no experience designing software. However, note that while users can't tell you if a design is good, they can certainly tell you if a design is bad. They can tell you whether they understand it and can perform tasks with it. They can tell you if they are confused or don't know what to do next. User testing is the best way to obtain this information during the develop-ment process and it is discussed in detail in Chapter 27, "User Testing."

Let's look at these problems in a bit more detail. While users are cer-tainly experts on the tasks they perform, the goal behind creating new software is to help users perform the tasks more efficiently and effectively—in other words, differently than the way the tasks are done now. If the tasks are currently performed without software, most likely users will want to perform them roughly the same way with software. Users are unlikely to use radically different thinking or employ new software technology. While users might know how to improve their current process, they probably don't have the ability to translate this directly into a software solution. In other words, they might know what they want in general terms (for example, "I want to access the Internet more efficiently"), but probably won't have a clue how to do that in more specific terms. Likewise, they might not be fully aware of the ways in which software can improve their tasks. Also, it's possible that some users won't have the ability to communicate their ideas effectively. Besides being able to say that they don't like something ("My current Web browser is a pain to use"), they might not understand or be able to communicate specifically why they feel that way.

The fundamental concept behind user-centered design is something like, "We software developers don't know how to design software that satisfies user's goals, so we are going to have users tell us what they want." While a group of users can lead you to a user interface design that they really like, there is no guarantee that other users will feel the same way. If the first group of users don't understand fundamental user interface design principles, this outcome is virtually guaranteed. After all, users aren't designers.

Problems with Prototyping

User interface prototyping holds many promises. Prototyping can help you get user feedback quickly. Prototypes allow you to try new ideas easily, without much commitment. And they allow you to make sure that users are satisfied with the user interface design early in the process before the real development begins—at least in theory.

As noted earlier, for the user-centered design process to work, the user needs to determine whether the design is acceptable by evaluating a prototype. This task is much more difficult than it appears. For a user to identify design problems in a prototype, the user must:

- Use the prototype long enough to realize that there is a problem
- Be able to recognize the problem
- Be able to recognize that the problem lies in the design of the prototype and not in the user's actions
- Be able to clearly articulate any problems or concerns with the prototype

Having users evaluate a design through a prototype is much harder than it appears.

Let's consider why these tasks are difficult. The first question to ask is: what exactly is a prototype? A user interface prototype is a mock-up of a user interface. What exactly is a mock-up? Many forms exist, ranging from a paper mock-up to a nearly fully functional user interface, but all user interface prototypes or mock-ups have one thing in common: they are not the real user interface. For a prototype to have any sort of cost or time advantage over the real user interface, it must have some significant functionality missing. While the basic user interface elements will probably be present, many of the details will not. If data is involved, the prototype data might not be real. There might not be detailed features that help the user eliminate unnecessary effort. The prototype might lack error messages and advanced features. For these and other reasons, the prototype won't give a realistic indication of the eventual program's actual performance. However, these details can be extremely valuable in evaluating the usability of the interface. Such details often make the difference between a collection of windows and dialog boxes and a usable program.

Now let's look at some of these problems in more detail. If a user is testing a mock-up user interface with mock-up data, how long can you expect the user to evaluate the prototype? For a half-hour, maybe an hour if you're lucky. Unfortunately, it takes users a fair amount of time before they can identify many types of problems. For example, if a task is unnecessarily repetitive, it might not be obvious from performing it once or twice. But it will certainly be obvious after performing the task a few dozen times when the program is in the real world. Some user interface problems take a while to become annoying.

It can be difficult to recognize even routine problems with a prototype. How so? Suppose you introduce a prototype by saying, "This prototype is a rough idea of what we have in mind. Clearly, the finished product will be different." This seems reasonable to say, but what you are basically saying to the user is, "Don't criticize the details because they haven't been addressed yet. In fact, don't criticize the prototype at all unless it is way off the mark." This is what is often understood, anyway. Even if you explicitly ask users to report every detail they don't like, it is hard to be critical of a prototype that you know isn't the finished product. A user can easily explain away all minor shortcomings by thinking, "Well, this is just the prototype. All these minor problems will be fixed in the real interface."

TIP It is hard for a user to be as critical of a prototype user interface as of a real user interface.

Users that are unfamiliar with a prototype clearly know that they are unfamiliar with it. Suppose a user evaluating a prototype repeatedly makes a mistake. There is a strong possibility that the user will blame himself for the problem, not the prototype. Such a user is likely to think, "Gosh! I did it again," rather than conclude that the user interface design is at fault.

Lastly, the user needs to be able to communicate any problems or concerns that he has with the prototype. But if an interface is bad, don't expect the user to understand why or how to fix it. Suppose a user says: "I find this task too difficult to do, but I don't know why." How do you interpret this? Is the problem with the user interface design? Is the problem with the incompleteness of the prototype? Is the problem with the user's lack of experience? The only safe conclusion is that it is a problem with the user interface design. Now how do you fix it?

I clearly have a problem with the overreliance placed on *functional prototyping* (prototyping with operational software) in the typical user-centered design process. The effectiveness of prototyping cannot be taken for granted. To find many types of problems, you need to test real software with real data using real tasks. While I believe users should play an important role in the user interface design process, there is a limit to what they can do. They can't turn a poorly designed program into a well-designed program. At best, they can turn a poorly designed program into a usable poorly designed program. On the other hand, I do believe that prototyping can be a very effective technique for solving specific user interface problems. Moreover, I prefer nonfunctional prototyping techniques—such as prototyping by example, paper prototypes, scenarios, and resource prototypes—to functional software prototypes. I'll discuss these issues in detail in Chapter 14, "Prototype with Caution."

Many of these functional prototyping problems can be addressed by evaluating the prototype with a proper user testing procedure, as described in detail in Chapter 27. You can obtain valuable information by combining prototypes with user testing. The problems I describe here can occur when functional prototypes are not combined with user testing, which I have seen happen quite often. To solve many of these problems, you need to actually watch users test the prototype and you need to ask them to think out loud while they use it. This way, you directly experience the problems instead of relying on the users to communicate and interpret them. You can't just hand users a functional prototype and expect them to give you useful feedback.

Marketing-Centered Design

A reasonable alternative to user-centered design is marketing-centered design. After all, the primary goal of marketing is to identify needs and wants in the marketplace and target a company's products and services to satisfy those needs and wants. In effect, it is a marketer's job to talk to users, understand what users want, and make sure that the resulting product satisfies those wants. This sounds much like the goal of user-centered design. However, since marketers have a better understanding of the big picture and of the capabilities of current technology than users typically do, they are able to identify solutions that users are unable to see. And unlike some users, marketers have no trouble expressing their ideas. They are not known for being shy.

While marketing plays an important role in creating successful software, marketing-centered design isn't a guaranteed road to success. While marketers understand users and, in a sense, represent users, the fact is that marketers aren't users. In terms of user interface design, they are no more representative of users than engineering or management. Furthermore, marketers aren't designers either. Like everyone else, marketers have their point of view about user interfaces, but their opinion about user interface design has no overly special significance compared to anyone else's.

 TIP   Marketers aren't users.

One common mistake that marketers make is asking users what they want and believing what the users tell them. They forget that users can't always be taken at their word. Many users say something like "I don't want a whole bunch of fancy features. I just want to get my work done." But, while I'm sure that users honestly believe this, I wouldn't recommend using this statement to identify what users actually want to buy. For example, Microsoft makes two office productivity products: Microsoft Office and Microsoft Works. Office is the full-blown product, whereas Works is the simplified product, but each allows the user to perform roughly the same tasks. Guess which one sells more. I personally prefer Office. Why? Works might do everything I need, but I would prefer not to find out the hard way. I prefer the safer bet.

One of the world's largest and most successful consumer product manufacturers set out to create a new product that would overwhelm its competition. The company employed its vast marketing and research resources to create a product that a majority of consumers said they preferred over the competition during the direct testing of over 200,000 people. They launched the product with a $100 million advertising campaign and received what is estimated to be over $1 billion in free publicity. Yet ironically, instead of being one of the greatest marketing successes of all time, it was one of the worst marketing disasters in history. When the product was released in 1985, it was an embarrassing failure. Of course, I am referring to Coca-Cola's New Coke product. While there are many explanations for this disaster (the company didn't listen to its loyal customers, who preferred the old Coke, but instead listened to its competitors' customers; what customers say they like isn't necessarily what they will buy; and so forth), you need to understand that decisions based on extensive market research and user testing are not guaranteed to be successful.

 PART

While you should always listen to your users, you should not incorporate their suggestions uncritically. There is a difference between what users say they want and what users actually want. A wise software developer learns to recognize the difference.

TIP While you should always listen to your users, you should not incorporate their suggestions without question. There is a difference between what users say they want and what users actually want.

Vision-Centered Design

Users, programmers, designers, marketers, and management are all important players in the software design process. Yet, as I have shown, none of these players has everything it takes to create an excellent user interface on their own. Clearly, all the players need to work together. But work together to do what? To directly design the software? Probably not, since all the players don't have design skills. Rather, I believe all the players need to work together to establish a vision of the program and of its user interface.

Establish a Product Vision

A vision is the ultimate objective of a program to help it satisfy the user's needs and goals. It is the strategic goal that transcends any specific design details or immediate problems. It is the objective for the current release as well as future releases. It is the compass your design team uses to make product direction and design decisions. Furthermore, a vision needs to be shared. It needs to be understood and agreed upon by everyone involved with the project.

TIP Establish a shared product vision to make product direction and design decisions.

Where does a product vision come from? It doesn't really matter. It could come from the users, from marketing, from management, or even from the programmers. The origin of the vision isn't significant. What is significant, however, is that the vision is based on satisfying the users' needs and that it works as a decision-making framework.

Case Study: Information at Your Fingertips

Let's look at an example of a successful product vision. In the early 1990s, Microsoft announced that their vision for Windows was to provide *Information at Your Fingertips*. Microsoft realized that users don't really use computers to run programs. Rather, users use computers to gather, retrieve, process, manage, and manipulate information. Windows at that time supported an applicationcentric model, where future versions of Windows would support a datacentric model. This simple vision helped Microsoft fundamentally change how it viewed Windows. This datacentric vision of Windows required a more object-oriented way of doing tasks. Users needed the ability to create, identify, access, view, combine, share, distribute, store, and link objects. Applications were no longer viewed as ends in themselves but as collections of components that provide services to manipulate certain types of objects. This vision led to the development of COM and OLE, and object-oriented, component-based software is now a fundamental Windows technology.

You might argue that a vision like this affects the system architecture more than the user interface design itself. Perhaps, but the user interface is what the user sees of the underlying system functionality. The two are related although the linkage doesn't have to be direct. You cannot create a user interface that fulfills the user's needs without an underlying system design that also supports that fulfillment. If you believe that the ultimate goal of software is to help users get their work done, you have to understand that this means more than designing a particular set of windows and dialog boxes. Those user interface elements have to be there for a reason.

How does a vision like this affect the user interface? It affects it in many subtle ways, but the biggest difference is that Windows now has a datacentric model. As the result of this model, Windows handles file extensions, icons, drag-and-drop functionality, context menus, and object properties differently. The Windows shell is extensible to accommodate new types of data and data commands. MDI applications are now less desirable because they tend to be applicationcentric instead of datacentric. Even the layout of a program's title bar text format has been changed (from "App – Doc" to "Doc – App") as a result of this vision.

The *Information at Your Fingertips* vision has resulted in a significant change in how we regard Windows programs. The COM programming model is revolutionary all by itself. Note that while it is possible that such a vision could have been established directly from users or from prototyping, it is extremely unlikely.

PART

Vision-Centered vs. User-Centered Design

To put everything together, let's compare a typical vision-centered design process to a typical user-centered design process. A typical user-centered design process looks something like the following:

- Ask users what they want.
- Throw together a prototype based on user input.
- Have users test the prototype.
- Evaluate results with users and with the design team.
- Determine what changes need to be made.
- Repeat until done (possibly many times).

One could argue that the phrase "throw together" should be replaced with "carefully design." Admittedly, I used the phrase "throw together" to make the process sound hasty, but it isn't too far off the mark. Again, the basic concept behind user-centered design is that software developers don't know how to design software that satisfies user's goals, so such a process views careful design as a waste of time. In fact, the above process is often referred to as *rapid prototyping,* since more emphasis is placed on obtaining feedback quickly than on design. This is a highly iterative, feedback-driven process—made possible through rapid prototyping—that tries to discover what users really want.

TIP

Rapid prototyping and careful design are mutually exclusive design techniques.

User interfaces developed this way potentially have many desirable attributes. The user is very much in the center of the process. The user interface is subjected to plenty of user testing and user evaluation. But there are serious problems as well. The software isn't really designed by anyone. If the results are poor, users might be able to help identify the problems. But if the results are passable, but mediocre, user testing probably won't help much. Users often have trouble articulating problems and blame themselves for making mistakes or being confused. The success of this process depends upon users having skills and knowledge that they probably don't have.

I consider the following vision-centered design process to be a much better alternative:

- Talk to users and understand their needs and goals.

- Identify the critical user needs and goals.

- Identify critical features to accomplish the critical user needs and goals.

- Establish product goals and a product vision.

- Incorporate the information into a design.

- Review the design to make sure it achieves the goals and vision.

- Present the design to users for feedback and carefully interpret the feedback. Use prototyping combined with user testing as necessary to solve specific problems.

- Repeat until satisfied.

At their core, these two processes are similar in that satisfying the user is the primary objective of both. But while the ultimate goal is the same, the emphasis is completely different. In this process, the role of the user is significantly reduced. User input is used to determine the high-level requirements and to evaluate the results. All user feedback is carefully interpreted. The design team, not the user, is responsible for the actual design of the software. The design itself is focused on high-level issues, such as the product vision and critical features. The process doesn't depend upon creating prototypes and bothering users to make every design decision. Not every dialog box and not every icon is designed with direct feedback from the user. While obtaining good user feedback is desirable, the results of the process aren't completely dependent upon it.

TIP User-centered design shouldn't result in user-designed software.

While user interfaces are for users and user satisfaction is the ultimate measure of a good user interface, the fact is that users are not designers. You can't expect to go to your users with a blank sheet of paper and say, "Tell me what you want," and expect to come up with a well-designed system. Rather, it is your responsibility to design the user interface, not the user's. To properly design the user interface, you need to identify the program's target users and then talk to them to understand their needs and goals. You need to work with users, designers, marketers, and managers to establish a product vision. This vision will help you make good decisions about the product and its user interface. Lastly, you need to have the target users test your user interface, but you need to carefully interpret their feedback. Mindlessly implementing everything your users tell you isn't a recipe for success.

Related Chapters

- Chapter 9—Users Aren't You.

  Compares users to programmers and describes how programmers and users usually have different needs and goals, as well as different knowledge and preferences.

- Chapter 14—Prototype with Caution.

  Describes the problems with functional prototyping, some alternatives to functional prototyping, how to establish realistic goals for prototyping, and how to select a prototyping method to accomplish those goals.

- Chapter 27—User Testing.

  Describes how to perform user testing and gives a specific procedure to make sure you get good feedback.

- Chapter 28—Talk to Your Other Team Members.

  Describes how to involve nonprogrammer team members in the software development process. These other team members include management, marketing, graphic designers, technical writers, technical support staff, and quality assurance testers.

- Chapter 36—Learn How to Play QA Gefahren.

  Describes how to handle feedback, specifically bad feedback, from the QA (quality assurance) process. This information is also useful in interpreting feedback obtained during the design process and from prototyping.

CHAPTER 8

Recommended Reading

- Capucciati, Maria R. "Putting Your Best Face Forward: Designing an Effective User Interface." *Microsoft Systems Journal*, February 1993.

  This article states, "User feedback should be analyzed for trends and common threads rather than taken at face value. Sometimes the best feedback comes not from users, but from looking at other products and talking with people who have a similar vision for the application."

- Cooper, Alan. *About Face: The Essentials of User Interface Design*. Foster City, CA: IDG Books Worldwide, Inc., 1995.

  Chapter 34, "Where Do We Go from Here?", states "One of the central tenets of usability engineering is that design should be 'user-centered.' This certainly sounds good, but it has serious problems. The biggest problem is that it is widely interpreted to mean that your users can tell you how to design software. Saying 'user-centered software design' is like saying 'fish-centered aquarium design.' You wouldn't ask the fish, would you?"

- Cooper, Alan. "Goal-Directed Software Design." *Dr. Dobb's Journal*, September 1996.

  In this article, Alan Cooper presents his method of user-centered design called "Goal-Directed Design™." The approach is "goal-directed" as opposed to "task-directed," since achieving the user's goals is ultimately more important than performing a set of tasks. He makes a very convincing case using a goal-directed group-calendar program as an example. In this case, he notes that one of the tasks of the program is to set meetings but the user's goal is to avoid meetings.

- Microsoft Corporation. *Designing for the User Experience*. Redmond, WA: Microsoft Press, 1999.

  See the chapter on design principles and methodology for a brief introduction to user-centered design, from the point of view of both user interface design principles and the design process itself.

- Nielsen, Jakob. *Usability Engineering*. Chestnut Hill, MA: AP Professional, 1993.

  This book contains valuable information about user-centered design, user testing, prototyping, how to interpret user feedback, and usability in general. If you want more information about developing a process for usability, this is the place to turn.

- Norman, Donald A. *The Design of Everyday Things*. New York, NY: Currency/Doubleday, 1990.

Chapter 2, "The Psychology of Everyday Actions," gives a good account of how users don't always report problems when they blame themselves for mistakes. User mistakes are often attributed to user error instead of a bad user interface.

CHAPTER 9

Users Aren't You

Users aren't you. More specifically, users aren't programmers. As a programmer, you have goals, knowledge, and preferences that are definitely not the same as those of a typical user. For example, no user ever liked using software because it was fun to program or because it was developed using an interesting programming tool or technology. This chapter explores the ways in which users are different from programmers, why understanding this difference is important, and how to deal with it.

Users Have Different Goals

Your goals are often in conflict with the user's goals. The following lists describe typical programmer goals and typical user goals.

Typical Programmer Goals

- Programmers want their software to be fun to program, often by using new tools and technologies.

125

- Programmers want to write their software quickly, often by using third-party solutions, so that it can be delivered on schedule.

- Programmers want their software to be easy to implement, often by avoiding user interface details, documentation, and gory debugging.

- Programmers want to advance their career by working with technologies that are in demand.

- Programmers enjoy technical challenges and want to know how software works.

- Programmers don't care much about installation, documentation, and technical support—these are perceived as somebody else's job.

Typical User Goals

- Users don't generally use software because they enjoy using software. (Games are an obvious exception.) Rather, they use software to get their work done.

- Despite the fact that users generally don't use software because they enjoy using it, users want to get their work done enjoyably.

- Users want to get their work done quickly.

- Users want to get their work done without having to read documentation or ask for help. They don't want to know how the software works.

- When they have to read documentation, users want it to answer their questions with a minimum amount of effort.

- Users want software to install and uninstall easily.

No big surprises here, but notice that programmers and users have fundamentally different goals.

Users Have Different Knowledge

Your knowledge about your software (and software in general) and the user's knowledge about such matters are also often in conflict. The following lists contrast typical programmer software knowledge and typical user software knowledge.

Typical Programmer Knowledge

- Programmers are expert computer users.

- Programmers are expert Microsoft Windows users.

PART

- Programmers understand their software better than anyone else does. They know all the features that aren't visible directly on the screen or on the menus. All program behavior is understood and expected, even if confusing or nonstandard.

- Programmers know exactly why their software doesn't work and how to fix the problem.

Typical User Knowledge

- Users typically are not expert computer users. They might not even like using computers.

- Users typically are not expert Windows users. They generally have some ability to change settings from Control Panel and Properties dialog boxes. They generally know nothing about the Windows registry. They might have only a vague understanding of what a dynamic-link library (DLL) or ActiveX component is.

- Users often understand only the features that are visible on the screen or from scanning the menu bar. They do not know any nonstandard mouse actions or keyboard sequences. They will not click on screen items that don't look as if they can be clicked. Any nonstandard program behavior is unexpected and confusing.

- Users typically do not understand why the software doesn't work, even if you carefully document the problem.

- Users typically don't read documentation.

Again, no big surprises. You can eliminate these conflicts by designing an interface that can be used by a wide range of users and by making the user interface features visible and easy to configure.

Users Have Different
Personal Preferences

Of course, everyone has different personal preferences. Different users prefer different screen layouts, screen colors, fonts, and other options. Some users prefer to use the mouse, and others prefer the keyboard. Some prefer to use toolbars and context menus, and others prefer the menu bar. And some users are more cautious and constantly save their work, while others never save their work. If you provide users the ability to set, save, and restore their preferences, they will find using your program much more enjoyable.

Key Questions to Ask

When you realize that you are about to make a user interface decision—say, to add a feature—that is based on your goals, knowledge, and preferences rather than on the user's, ask yourself the following questions:

- Does this feature help the user get his work done?
- Is the program better with or without this feature?
- Will the user understand how to use this feature?
- Will the user want to use this feature the same way I do?
- Can I satisfy more users by making this feature optional?

If adding the feature really does help the user, go for it. If not, why do it? If not all users will want to use it, make it optional. If not all users will use it the same way, make it configurable. It seems obvious, doesn't it? Yet you don't have to look hard to find programs that have unnecessary or inflexible features.

What Does All This Mean?

A programmer's goals, background, and preferences necessarily form the basis upon which he makes decisions about how to implement software. Unfortunately, many poor user interface decisions have resulted from programmers putting their goals ahead of the users'.

The next time you see a programmer create an awful user interface, ask him what his motivation was. You probably won't get an answer like "I was trying to help the user accomplish this task more efficiently." You are more likely to hear something like "I found this neat ActiveX control on the Internet and wanted to use it in the program somehow. Isn't it cool?" Sorry, it's not cool. It's really lame. You cannot possibly create a good user interface with this type of thinking.

TIP Be an advocate for the user. Put the user's goals ahead of your goals.

Some people believe that programmers can't create good user interfaces because they are incapable of looking at software from the user's point of view. I don't buy this idea at all. Programmers can create good user interfaces, but they need to understand how to do it right, just like anyone else. Universally declaring that programmers can't create good user interfaces doesn't help anyone. And hearing that they are incapable certainly doesn't encourage programmers to improve their user interface skills.

Understanding that there really is a conflict between your goals as a programmer and the user's goals is half the battle. If you look at the user interface from the user's point of view and become an advocate for helping the user get his work done, you are well on your way to creating great user interfaces.

TIP Looking at the user interface from the user's point of view is the first step in creating great user interfaces.

Related Chapters

- Chapter 10—Good User Interfaces Are Visible.

  Suggests ways to make your program's functionality visible to the user.

- Chapter 19—Configurability Is Cool.

  Suggests ways to make your programs configurable.

Recommended Reading

- Cooper, Alan. *About Face: The Essentials of User Interface Design*. Foster City, CA: IDG Books Worldwide, Inc., 1995.

  Chapter 1,"Goal-Directed Design," and Chapter 2, "Software Design," present an excellent discussion of why software often doesn't satisfy user's goals. Chapter 34, "Where Do We Go from Here?", presents an interesting but not so excellent theory that programmers can't design user interfaces.

- Norman, Donald A. *The Design of Everyday Things*. New York, NY: Currency/Doubleday, 1990.

  Chapter 6, "The Design Challenge," discusses why designers have different goals than users and how designers are not typical users, giving several good examples.

PART III

Design Concepts

CHAPTER 10

Good User Interfaces Are Visible

A user interface is visible when a user is able to figure out how to accomplish tasks just by looking at it. With a typical visible user interface, a user is able to perform tasks by making selections in the menu bar and dialog boxes and by manipulating objects on the screen with the mouse. Visible features don't require knowledge of special keyboard sequences or mouse interactions or any other mechanism that isn't visible on the screen.

So what specifically does it mean for a user interface to be visible? When a user interface feature is visible, its existence and functionality are obvious by simple inspection. A feature's existence is obvious by simple inspection when one of the following phenomena is true:

- The feature appears directly on the screen, such as a command button or a hyperlink.

- The feature appears on the screen when the user clicks on a standard drop-down interface, such as a menu bar or a combo box.

CHAPTER 10

- The feature is suggested when the mouse cursor passes over it, such as a sizeable window frame or a dynamic window splitter.

A feature's functionality is obvious by simple inspection when it meets one or more of the following requirements:

- The functionality is clearly suggested by its visual attributes, such as a command button or a sizeable window frame.

- The functionality is obvious with simple experimentation, such as the tools in a paint program.

- The functionality is understood with the help of a tooltip, such as a toolbar button.

- The functionality is visible and understood because of standards or convention, such as the behavior of check boxes and radio buttons, the double-clicking of a desktop icon, or the single-clicking of a hyperlink.

- The functionality is visible and readily understood by common sense or real-life experience, such as a calendar control or the buttons in the Calculator utility.

- The functionality is not visible on the screen at all but is standard enough that it is understood by users, such as moving a window by dragging its caption bar. In this case, while the caption bar appears on the screen, there is no visual indication that the user can move the window by dragging the caption bar.

While a modern graphical user interface such as the one provided by Microsoft Windows is highly visual, not all the user interface elements of a typical program can be figured out by inspection alone. You must have some basic knowledge about how graphical user interfaces work to perform even the simplest tasks. Consider a program's menu bar. While the menu bar is visible on the screen, to use it you have to understand why you need to use a menu, how to recognize a menu bar, how to pull down a menu, and how to make a selection. Without this basic knowledge, you can't do anything with a menu bar. In fact, menu bars would not be appropriate in environments where the user cannot be assumed to be a computer user, such as in a walk-up kiosk. But for normal Windows programs, using the menu bar is so basic that even the most beginning user (with, say, more than an hour's experience) can be assumed to know how to use a menu. This basic knowledge makes the menu bar a highly visible, hierarchically organized catalog of a program's features.

Clearly, there is more to making a feature visible than simply displaying it visually on the screen. The user not only has to be able to see it but also has to be able to understand it. No matter how artistic a feature's visual appearance is, if the user doesn't understand it, it really isn't visible. The understanding can come from the user's knowledge of the real world, the user's common sense, the user's basic knowledge of graphical user interfaces, or completely from the feature's visual properties. One way or another, a feature is visible if a user with basic graphical user interface skills can easily figure out how to use it just by looking at it.

> There is more to making a feature visible than displaying it visually on the screen. The user has to be able to understand it.

Visible user interfaces often result in what is called a noun-then-verb form of interaction. You see something (the "noun" in the construction above) that you want to manipulate on the screen, you select it, and then you perform some action (the "verb"). Visible user interfaces can also be viewed as being object-oriented in that you select an object and then change its properties or perform commands.

A visible user interface is similar to an intuitive user interface (which, by the way, should really be called an "intuitable" user interface to reflect that fact that the user, not the interface itself, is doing the intuiting). A user interface feature is intuitive when it meets all the criteria below:

- The feature is visible as defined above, not counting the case in which a feature is understood only because it is standard.

- The feature has visual or functional attributes that are consistent within the program and with other programs.

- The feature has visual or functional attributes that are consistent with real-life experience.

In other words, a feature is intuitive if its existence and functionality are obvious by simple inspection, if it is consistent with the user's real-world experience and other software experience so that the user can infer its meaning, and if it doesn't require the user to have any knowledge of the standards.

> Intuitive = Visible + Consistent − Standards

CHAPTER 10

When describing a user interface, I prefer the terms "visible" and "consistent" over "intuitive" for two reasons. First, the "intuitive user interface" has become such a cliché that it hardly means anything anymore. Too many horrible, difficult-to-use user interfaces have been described as intuitive. Second, the terms "visible" and "consistent" are more specific and are both significant user interface attributes in their own right. Burying these two important design concepts in a single design cliché is a far less effective way of characterizing user interfaces.

Windows Visual Affordances

Although I don't care for the term "intuitive," the properties I have just outlined are significant in user interface design, since even a first-time computer user is able to instantly figure out a feature that has these properties. Such a feature has the highest level of visibility.

A better way to describe such a feature is to say it has *affordance*. Affordance relates to the ability of a user to determine how to use an object just by looking at its visual clues. For example, people understand how to use everyday items such as doorknobs, hand tools, and kitchen utensils just by interpreting the appearance of these items. Of course, our understanding of each object's use is gained through real-world experience (for example, through the opening of doors), but once gained that understanding is permanently associated with the object. A doorknob's affordance, then, is the set of properties related to its use that comes to mind when we see a doorknob: the doorknob is "grabbable," "turnable," "related to the opening of a door," and so on. I'll discuss both affordance and its interpretation in more detail in Chapter 12, "Learn from *The Design of Everyday Things*."

Windows uses several visual affordances, specifically:

- Raised items can be clicked.
- Items that become highlighted when the mouse cursor passes over them can be clicked.
- Recessed items cannot be clicked.
- Items with a white background and a flashing vertical bar can be edited.
- Items with a gray background cannot be edited.
- Gray items are disabled.
- Raised lines can be dragged.

You should take advantage of these affordances whenever possible and maintain them, unless you have an extraordinarily good reason not to. For example, note that a command button has affordance because it is drawn with a raised 3-D rectangle that looks like it can be pushed. If something looks like a button, users had better be able to push it because they are certainly going to try. On the other hand, users aren't going to click something that is recessed, since the visual clue indicates that it isn't clickable. Note how the modern two-dimensional menu bars and toolbars maintain their affordance by becoming raised when you pass the cursor over them. This is known as hot-tracking. This is a simple yet effective mechanism for making it clear when an item can be clicked that has the benefit of reducing the visual complexity on the screen. However, note that this technique works well for menu bars and toolbars because users can easily identify them and know that they can click them. Using the cursor to reveal affordance in other circumstances is most likely a bad idea, since the user would have to pass the cursor over all of the program's graphic elements to distinguish the interactive graphics from decorations.

Visible Interfaces

Now for some specifics. A summary of the common visible interfaces used by Windows programs follows.

Commands

- **Menu bars**   Menu bars are a highly visible, hierarchically organized catalog of a program's features.

- **Toolbars with tooltips**   Toolbars are less visible than menu bars because they lack the context that menus provide. Menus have a clearly indicated hierarchy with submenus, cascading menus, and separators to show relationships. Toolbars do not have descriptive categories, and the placement of buttons on a toolbar is far less significant than the ordering of commands in a menu. Also, a menu command can include an ellipsis to indicate that giving the command will require more input, but toolbar buttons do not use ellipses.

- **Coordinated menu bars and toolbars**   Using the same icons on both menu commands and toolbar buttons adds extra visibility by giving a visual indication that the commands are the same. (See the screen shot on the following page.)

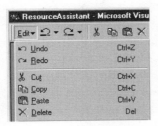

● **Hyperlinks**   The popularity of the World Wide Web has made hyperlinks an especially popular user interface. Just point and click. However, the best way to make sure that hyperlinks are visible is to use the standard hyperlink colors to clearly indicate that the text is a hyperlink and not just underlined text. Unfortunately, hyperlink colors are not yet in the system colors—I think they should be—but you can get the hyperlink colors used by Microsoft Internet Explorer by reading the registry values *Anchor Color* and *Anchor Color Visited* under the *HKEY_CURRENT_ USER\Software\Microsoft\Internet Explorer\Settings* key.

Windows

● **Dialog boxes**   A well-designed dialog box with instructive labels and with controls organized to clearly show their relationships is a very visible mechanism for performing tasks.

● **Wizards**   A well-designed wizard that doesn't require any external information to be used is a very visible way to help the user perform complex tasks.

Controls

● **Command buttons**   A command button with clear, descriptive text is one of the most basic visible user interfaces. Note how the animation performed when a command button is clicked reinforces its correspondence to real-world buttons and clearly separates it from other nonclickable user interface elements.

● **All other controls except edit boxes**   All controls except for edit boxes have a high degree of visibility. Edit controls are visible only when the user is free to enter any text or numeric input, since only then is its functionality obvious by inspection. When the input is constrained, other more specific controls are much more visible, as in these examples:

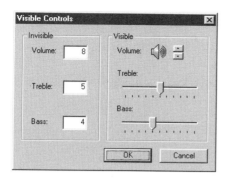

- **Edit boxes with spin boxes and browse buttons**   Providing spin boxes for numeric input and browse buttons for file paths is a simple, visible mechanism to help the user give valid input in an edit box. In this case, the edit box still really isn't visible but the associated control is.

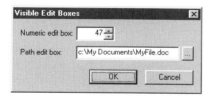

Visual Feedback

- **Plain old text**   Just because Windows is a graphical user interface doesn't mean you can't use text. In fact, sometimes the most visible way to communicate with the user is to just say something. For example, Microsoft Outlook and the Find utility indicate when no information is available by showing "There are no items to show in this view." This text also eliminates the need to display a notification message reading "No matches found." You can't get more visible than that.

- **Previews**   Previews are an effective way to give the user feedback on the results of a command without the user having to perform the command. They make features self-explanatory and easy to understand, reducing the need for documentation.

CHAPTER 10

- **Tooltips**   Tooltips make the functionality of toolbar buttons and other user interface elements visible by displaying a little popup window with brief context-sensitive information. However, you should never use tooltips as an excuse not to make the meaning of your icons and other screen elements obvious.

- **Cursor hinting**   Cursor hinting allows the cursor to change shape when it passes over an object; the cursor's new shape suggests what the user can do with that object. Cursor hinting is commonly used to visually indicate text that is editable, a window or other object that can be moved or resized, or a dragged object that can be dropped.

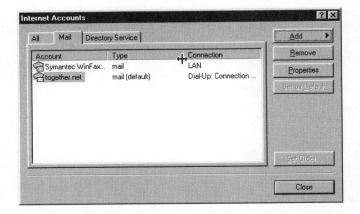

- **Status bars**   Status bars work well to make status information and feedback for background tasks visible. Status bars can be used to make selections more visible. For example, the visibility of a multiple-selection list can be significantly improved by indicating how many items are selected, as done with the Windows Explorer status bar. This technique not only helps the user know what has been selected but also makes it obvious that multiple selection is possible in the first place.

- **Animation**   Animation is a visible way to indicate that a command is being performed or that an object is being manipulated. Animations such as zoom rectangles can also show cause-and-effect relationships. For example, when you access the Find dialog box in Microsoft Word, zoom rectangles go from the Select Browse Object button below the vertical scroll bar to the Find dialog box. When you close the Find dialog box, the zoom rectangles go from the dialog box back to the button. This action makes the relationship between the Find dialog box and the Select Browse Object button (as well as the Previous Find and Next Find buttons) very visible.

Other

● **Grabbers** Grabbers are raised lines on a window that indicate that the item can be dragged. For example, the new 2-D menu bars have grabbers on their left-hand side to indicate how they can be moved. For another example, the Open and Save As common dialog boxes in Windows 98 clearly indicate that they can be resized through a combination of grabbers in the lower right corner and cursor hinting.

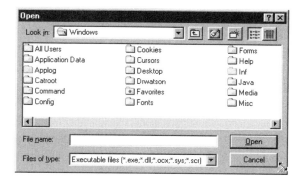

Edit boxes are especially challenging to make visible. While an edit box that allows any kind of input in any format is visible, an edit box that requires the user to enter text according to some constraint is not visible. For example, requiring the user to enter −1 into an edit box to indicate a special state makes the edit box's functionality invisible. On the other hand, a check box used to indicate such a state is visible, even if the −1 value is stored internally. Another example is an edit box that requires a date to be entered in a special format, such as "07FEB1961." In this case, using the new date and time picker control is much more visible. If you want to make a constrained edit box visible, the best alternatives are to

● Use spin boxes for numeric input and browse buttons for file paths

● Supply an appropriate default value in the required format

● Put the required format in the label or other nearby static text

Visual Feedback

So far the discussion has been focused on making features visible. For complete visibility, a program needs to provide visual feedback to indicate to the user that a task is being done either correctly or incorrectly. Visual feedback is very important for direct manipulation to indicate that an object has been changed. Any task that a program does automatically should have some visual indication. For example, when Word saves a file automatically, a floppy disk icon appears on the taskbar. All time-consuming operations also need feedback. Make sure there is a wait cursor, progress meter, or some other visual feedback for all operations that take more than a second to complete. It is important to give the user a clue that the program will be unresponsive while a command is being performed. The previous list of visual interfaces gave several examples of visual feedback. Feedback is discussed in more detail in Chapter 12.

Invisible Interfaces

According to our definition of a visible user interface, a feature should be considered invisible if its existence and functionality are not obvious by simple inspection. There are many ways to fail these visibility requirements. Any user interface feature can be invisible if poorly done. Many invisible user interfaces include various kinds of inexplicable buttons, bitmaps, and icons that do not pass the visibility test even though they are in plain sight. While their existence is obvious, their functionality clearly isn't. Another example is a standard user interface element that is programmed to have a nonstandard behavior. Because the user will assume the standard behavior for the element, the element's functionality isn't visible.

As I discussed previously, the user's experience is also a factor. Most of this chapter assumes that the user is familiar with Windows. Any program designed for all users, such as a kiosk, a point-of-sale display, or a museum exhibit, cannot assume that the user knows anything about graphical user interfaces. For this type of user, interface elements such as menus, toolbars, status bars, splitter windows, and cursor hinting should not be considered visible. In fact, for this type of user, pretty much everything should be considered invisible except for text, graphics, command buttons, simple list boxes, edit boxes for which all input is either valid or well understood (such as a password), and possibly check boxes and radio buttons. For this type of user, all the controls used should be simple and have affordance.

For users with at least some graphical user interface experience, the following features are invisible and therefore should never be the sole means of performing a task.

Invisible Existence

- Keyboard shortcuts, especially Alt and Ctrl key sequences and function keys
- Double-clicking
- Nonstandard mouse interactions, such as triple-clicking or chord-clicking
- Context menus

Invisible Functionality

- Buttons with incomprehensible text.
- Incomprehensible icons and bitmaps. The old saying that a picture is worth a thousand words doesn't apply to such graphics.
- Toolbars without tooltips.
- Edit boxes that require a specific format or special values.

Perhaps the ultimate in invisible user interfaces is the MS-DOS prompt box. All that is visible is the command line with the default drive and path and a blinking cursor. If you don't know what to do with it, you will never figure it out just by looking at it.

Examples of Visible Interfaces

The following are some simple examples of visible interface elements compared to their invisible counterparts.

Taskbar vs. Alt+Tab

The Alt+Tab keyboard shortcut was added to Windows 3.1 to help users switch between programs. While this shortcut is convenient, there is no visible clue anywhere in the Windows 3.1 interface that this command exists. Consequently, since beginning users are unaware of the command, this technique for switching programs is used primarily by advanced users. In fact, many advanced users and laptop users still prefer the Alt+Tab technique because it is almost effortless—once you get used to it—since you don't have to move the mouse. On the following page is an example of an Alt+Tab window.

CHAPTER 10

By contrast, the taskbar introduced in Windows 95 visibly shows the running programs with buttons that have both the program icon and title. The active program is displayed with a depressed button, and all other running programs are displayed with buttons in their normal state. Using the taskbar, you can switch between running programs simply by clicking the button representing the program you want. The taskbar mechanism is so simple and obvious that its functionality is clear to even the most beginning user.

Check Box List vs. Multiple Selection List

The standard Windows list box control has three different selection modes: single selection, multiple selection (that is, the LBS_MULTIPLESEL style), and extended selection (that is, the LBS_EXTENDEDSEL style). In single selection mode, you can select only a single item at a time and selecting an item removes any other selections. In the multiple selection mode, clicking any item toggles its selection state regardless of the Shift and Ctrl keys. Lastly, in extended selection mode, clicking a single item produces the same result as in single selection mode and the selection can be extended by dragging or with the Shift and Ctrl keys.

Multiple selection list boxes have been part of Windows since the very beginning. However, multiple selection lists suffer from the fact that they are visually indistinguishable from a single selection list. Also, although a multiple selection mode list is fairly obvious once you start clicking on it, an extended selection mode list (which is used far more often) has a behavior that is indistinguishable from a single selection mode list unless you do a drag select (which most users don't normally do) or you click with the Shift or Ctrl keys (which a user isn't likely to do unless he already knows the list is an extended selection mode list). So, while you can provide the user the ability to make multiple selections with an extended selection mode list, the user has no obvious clue that the list isn't a single selection list and is therefore unlikely to make multiple selections.

By contrast, check box lists indicate selections with a check box instead of a highlight, making it essentially a scrollable list of check boxes. A check box list, then, is a clear visual indication of multiple selection. Note that a check box list does not use a standard list format. You need to use either an owner-draw list box control (in multiple selection mode, not extended selection mode), the MFC CCheckListBox class, or the new Internet Explorer 4.0 ListView control with the LVS_EX_CHECKBOXES style.

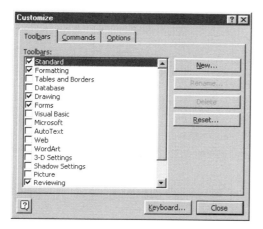

What's This? Button vs. Shift+F1 Key

Context-sensitive help has been part of Windows since Windows 3.0. When you are in context-sensitive help mode, a question mark is added to the cursor and you receive help related to the next item you click. While experienced users know about accessing regular help with the F1 key, few users are aware that you can get context-sensitive help with the Shift+F1 key. Why? Partly because there is no visual indication that such help is available in this way and partly because in the past few programs actually bothered to implement this type of help (primarily because few users knew about it).

The solution, of course, is to make context-sensitive help more visible. One approach is to put a context-sensitive help command in the Help menu and on the toolbar. While this approach is good, an even better approach is to use the What's This? button, which was introduced with Windows 95. This simple and obvious solution makes it clear when context-sensitive help is available and how to obtain it.

Properties Button vs.
Properties Context Menu Command

The standard technique for accessing the properties of an object in Windows 98 is to right-click the object to view its context menu and then to select the Properties command, which is usually the last item in the menu. Unfortunately, context menus are not visible, and beginning users often don't know about them. As a result, many Control Panel applets, for which setting properties is an essential activity, use Properties command buttons instead of context menus. This technique ensures that the way to set properties is obvious to all users.

TIP Make an extra effort to ensure that essential features are visible.

While these examples are simple, they all demonstrate the importance of visibility. If a feature is visible, the user will know that the feature exists and will be able to figure out how to use it simply by looking at it. Visibility is the ultimate goal of a graphical user interface.

TIP Visibility is the ultimate goal of a graphical user interface.

Related Chapters

● Chapter 11—Good User Interfaces Are Invisible.

Presents several suggestions on how to prevent user interfaces from drawing unwanted attention to themselves. User interfaces can be too visible and, when they are, they can be annoying.

● Chapter 12—Learn from *The Design of Everyday Things*.

Discusses the attributes of visible navigation and techniques to make navigation visible. Discusses affordance, including how users interpret visual clues. Also describes the attributes of good feedback and compares the different forms of feedback.

● Chapter 13—Learn from the Web.

Discusses the techniques used by the Web to make features more visible by embedding commands and help in the context where they are needed. The Web also makes navigation more visible by showing the current context and by using home pages, navigation bars, and the Web Browser Navigation Model.

PART
III

- Chapter 20—Previews Are Cool.

  Presents the types of previews and examples of each type. Previews are an excellent way to provide visible feedback.

Recommended Reading

- Arlov, Laura. *GUI Design for Dummies*. Foster City, CA: IDG Books Worldwide, 1997.

  Chapter 11, "Making Your GUI Easy to Understand," discusses how to make interfaces easy to use by providing feedback and affordance.

- Armstrong, Strohm, "Previewing the Common Controls DLL for Microsoft Internet Explorer 4.0, Part II." *Microsoft Systems Journal*, November 1996.

  Discusses the new ListView control, including the LVS_EX_ CHECKBOXES style.

- Cooper, Alan. *About Face: The Essentials of User Interface Design*. Foster City, CA: IDG Books Worldwide, Inc., 1995.

  Chapter 5, "Idioms and Affordances," discusses affordance, particularly with respect to our instinctive understanding of how to use things with our hands. It also discusses what it means for an interface to be intuitive. Chapter 12, "Posture and State," has a good comparison of the taskbar and the Alt+Tab command. Chapter 15, "Elephants, Mice, and Minnies," has a good discussion about cursor hinting.

- Horton, William. *The Icon Book: Visual Symbols for Computer Systems and Documentation*. New York, NY: John Wiley & Sons, Inc., 1994.

  The ultimate resource for icon design information. Confusing icons are definitely not visible.

- Howlett, Virginia. *Visual Interface Design for Windows*. New York, NY: John Wiley & Sons, Inc., 1996.

  Chapter 8, "Affordance, Realism, and Dimension," discusses affordance, realism vs. abstraction, and the use of 3-D as an affordance. It also discusses the effectiveness of icons at conveying their meaning. Unfortunately, that effectiveness isn't great, so graphics and text together (for example, tooltips or text captions) are often the best solution.

CHAPTER 10

- Microsoft Corporation. *Designing for the User Experience*. Redmond, WA: Microsoft Press, 1999.

  See the chapter on general interaction techniques for guidelines on how to give feedback for selection, editing, and direct manipulation. See the chapter on special design considerations for the advantages and disadvantages of using sound for feedback.

- Norman, Donald A. *The Design of Everyday Things*. New York, NY: Currency/Doubleday, 1990.

  Discusses how users learn to use everyday things through their design attributes of visibility, affordance, natural mappings, constraints, conceptual models, and feedback. Norman helped popularize the concept of affordance and defined it as "the perceived and actual properties of the thing, primarily those fundamental properties that determine just how the thing could possibly be used."

- Tognazzini, Bruce. *Tog on Interface*. Reading, MA: Addison-Wesley Publishing Company, 1992.

  The first words in the Introduction are "The Visible Interface." The introduction makes the distinction between a visible user interface and a graphical user interface. Appendix B, "Index of Principles and Guidelines," presents guidelines that make an interface visible. An interesting list, but not the most practical advice for Windows programmers.

CD-ROM Resources

The CD-ROM included with this book contains the following resources related to this chapter:

- The DevUI MFC Extension Library, which contains a McShow-ZoomRect function to help show the relationship between a user action and its effect.

CHAPTER 11

Good User Interfaces Are Invisible

During the ultimate user interface experience, the user is totally focused, in a groove, on a roll, and very productive. He is so focused on his work that he is in a kind of dreamlike state—completely absorbed by the task at hand but oblivious to the program being used to accomplish the task. As we know, however, this state is a fragile one, and it can be easily broken by a silly dialog box like this:

This chapter summarizes the most common ways this state of focus is broken.

CHAPTER 11

While its title makes this chapter seem to contradict the previous chapter, there is actually no contradiction because the two chapters address entirely different subjects. Although I could have named the last chapter "Good User Interfaces Are Easy to Learn" and this chapter "Good User Interfaces Don't Draw Attention to Themselves," I think the apparent contradiction in the titles I've chosen helps these concepts counterbalance each other in an interesting way. A user interface that is *too* visible draws attention to itself and by doing so breaks the user's flow.

TIP A user interface that is too visible draws attention to itself and breaks the user's focus.

Death Comes to Bob the Waiter

The experience of an invisible user interface is a subject that begs for analogies. Alan Cooper compares the user's state of easy concentration and productivity to the exhilarating experience of planing in a racing dinghy—that is, of skimming across the surface of the water at a very high speed. (Apparently he is unaware of sailboards, which plane far more often than dinghies.) He describes this as "flow" and introduces flow this way: "Tom DeMarco and Timothy Lister in their book *Peopleware, Productive Projects and Teams* define flow as a 'condition of deep, nearly meditative involvement.' Flow often induces a 'gentle sense of euphoria' and can make you unaware of the passage of time. More significantly, a person in a state of flow can be extremely productive, especially when engaged in process-oriented tasks such as 'engineering, design, development, and writing.'"

But my favorite analogy for this subject comes from Peter Bickford's chapter (first an article) "Transparency, or Death Comes to Bob the Waiter," in which he compares an invisible user interface (or, as he calls it, a transparent interface) to a good waiter: "This is the concept that computer interfaces should attempt to serve the user as unobtrusively as possible (like a good waiter). It lets users concentrate on their work—not on the interface itself." He further states, "Great waiters serve your food, refill your glass, and clear your dishes without ever interrupting the flow of conversation." By contrast, bad waiters "shatter any sense of romance by stopping by every five minutes to ask 'How's everything going?' and 'How's everyone's warm duck salad tonight?'" This is why we hate bad waiters.

Now let's look at the ways in which a user interface can act like Bickford's bad waiter.

How a Program Draws Unwanted Attention

So just how does a program draw unwanted attention to itself? Any user interface problem effectively draws unwanted attention; however, some problems are much worse than others. Let's round up the usual suspects, in order of their heinousness.

Capital Crimes

Of all the ways to draw unwanted attention, these are by far the worst:

Beeping or blinking

Whatever you do, don't make your program beep or blink. Nothing is more annoying than a beeping, blinking program. Enough said. (A good exception is flashing a program's taskbar window button to notify the user of a pending message.)

Using unnecessary customization

Some programmers try to customize everything—custom windows, custom title bars, custom menus, custom toolbars and tooltips, and so on. These custom features typically do not have the standard Microsoft Windows appearance. Often they do not have the standard Windows behavior either. The interesting thing about such customizations is that they usually make the program worse, since they are confusing and do absolutely nothing to help users get their work done. I am constantly amazed at the extraordinary effort some developers put into creating truly awful user interfaces. (If you must create a highly customized user interface, try to change only the appearance and not the behavior.)

Using unnecessary audio effects

Avoid unnecessary audio effects. At the very least, make them optional. Ideally, they should be turned off by default and the user should have to ask for them explicitly. The user and his neighbors can close their eyes, but they can't close their ears.

Using distracting text

Avoid distracting text colors, generally anything other than black. Use the system colors COLOR_BTNTEXT or COLOR_WINDOWTEXT for most text. Avoid distracting fonts, generally typefaces other than Arial, Tahoma, or MS Sans Serif. Verdana, Trebuchet MS, and Century Gothic are also good choices for a slightly different look. Any serif fonts in an interface should be considered distracting, although serif fonts are fine in a document. Don't use monospaced fonts except to indicate user input or to mimic a typewriter. Avoid unnecessary uppercase text. It's OK to label a button OK, but never label a button CANCEL.

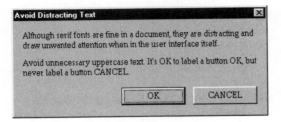

Using distracting backgrounds

Avoid distracting backgrounds, especially backgrounds with poor contrast. Few interface problems are sillier than making text illegible by displaying it on a distracting background. Users are never impressed by this, so what's the point? Remember that there is absolutely nothing wrong with black text (that is, COLOR_WINDOWTEXT) on a white background (COLOR_WINDOW).

Using harsh colors

Avoid harsh colors (that is, highly saturated colors), especially in windows that the user sees often. Harsh colors demand the user's attention. Don't make your program look like a cartoon, unless it is supposed to look like a cartoon. A limited number of muted, coordinated colors works well.

Using distracting graphics and animations

Avoid distracting bitmaps, icons, and animations. When used properly, graphics and animation can add a great amount of style to your program. When misused, they can make your program look ugly and amateurish. Make sure that prominent graphics are necessary and well designed. Don't think eye candy, and definitely don't think eye Velcro.

Of course, distraction is a subjective experience. I thought for sure that I would find the Microsoft Office Office Assistants to be way over the top. I forced myself to use the Clippit Office Assistant in Microsoft Word just so that I could understand exactly why I would find these animations to be irritating. I am fairly surprised to say that after using the Clippit assistant for an extended period of time, I don't mind it at all. (Still, I don't care for the Office Logo assistant since its colors are much too distracting, especially when they are flashing. The Clippit assistant uses a very limited and muted palette, which is almost certainly why I don't mind it much. It would be even better if it didn't wiggle around as often.) While I don't use the Office Assistant by default anymore, I no longer rush to get rid of it either.

Being unforgiving

Users make mistakes, but some programs really make the user pay for making a mistake. This is especially frustrating when the mistake is easy to make. Try to design your programs to prevent the user from making mistakes, and provide some degree of forgiveness, ideally by providing an undo/redo feature. Forgiveness is especially important for programs designed for beginners.

Using cumbersome metaphors

Good metaphors help users get their work done by modeling program tasks after real-world tasks. Bad metaphors do not help the user; they just get in the way and draw unwanted attention to the program. A good metaphor makes perfect sense and is so natural the user might not even be aware of it. A bad metaphor just seems dorky.

Metaphors are most successful when they have the following attributes:

- They are simple.

- They make sense. Choose a metaphor that uses real-world properties to help the user grasp the task at hand.

- They are not driven into the ground. Don't try to force similarities that don't really exist.

- They don't constrain the user to real-world limitations. The whole point of using computers is to make things easier, not to do things exactly as they are done without computers.

For example, suppose you are creating a program that lets users buy products. There is nothing wrong with using a shopping cart as a metaphor when referring to the collection of items the user selects for purchase. Using a shopping cart metaphor is much better than using technical terms such as a selection database or purchase subset. But don't drive it into

155

the ground by extending the metaphor to shopping aisles, checkout lines, and squeaky wheels that wobble around. The world really doesn't need a wobbly wheel metaphor.

TIP Use a metaphor only if it is simple and helps the user accomplish the task without constraining the user to the real-world limitations of the metaphor.

Note that the world's most successful software metaphor—the desktop—is very simple and barely reflects the real-world properties of an actual desktop. The desktop in Windows is just a place to put things you need while you are working. People don't really put recycling bins or wallpaper on their real-world desktops, but this doesn't harm the metaphor. Folders are another example of a good, simple metaphor. It is far easier for a beginning user to understand what a folder is than a subdirectory. Windows uses many other simple metaphors, such as files, menus, the Clipboard, the Recycle Bin, the Briefcase, mail, forms, lists, and push buttons. Of course, Windows itself is a metaphor for a way to view information on the screen.

The irony of most bad metaphors is that in their quest to leverage the user's assumed relevant knowledge of real-world tasks, designers are all too willing to abandon the standard controls that users in fact already know how to use. Does this really make sense?

Felonies

These problems draw unwanted attention but are not quite as serious (at least in small quantities):

Using unnecessary dialog boxes and message boxes

Unnecessary dialog boxes and message boxes are one of the worst ways that a program can draw attention to itself. While one or two unnecessary dialog boxes or message boxes aren't that big of a deal, the problem is that this is a fairly easy mistake to make, so it is quite common. For every distracting background or cumbersome metaphor, there are probably hundreds of unnecessary dialog boxes and message boxes out there.

Unnecessary dialog boxes and message boxes break the user's flow because the user is no longer in control of the program. Rather, the program is now controlling the user. Furthermore, even the most beginning user is fully aware of which dialog boxes and message boxes are really necessary and which ones aren't, so you shouldn't think that this problem will escape the user's notice. It's important to realize just how much these boxes break the user's train of thought: users often greet such boxes with a groan. I'll discuss unnecessary dialog boxes and message boxes in detail in Chapters 22 and 23.

TIP Unnecessary dialog boxes and message boxes break the user's flow because the user is no longer in control of the program. Rather, the program is controlling the user.

Using commands that are hard to find or difficult to access

Make sure that it is easy for the user to find commands. The user shouldn't have to hunt for commands as if on some sort of bizarre command safari, because this will certainly break the user's concentration. Make sure all commands are easy to find in the menu bar and easy to access through context menus and keyboard shortcuts.

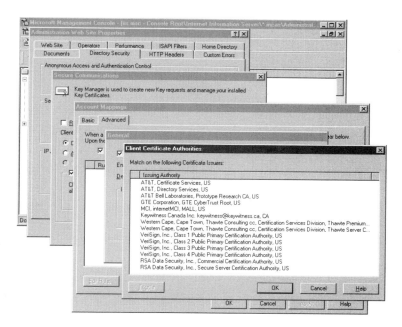

Not conforming to standards and not integrating well with Windows

A program that doesn't conform to standards definitely attracts unwanted attention, since this usually means that the program doesn't behave the way the user expects. The same is true if the program doesn't integrate well with Windows.

Being just plain stupid

Sometimes a program is just plain stupid, such as when it:

- Prevents the user from doing something that he clearly should be able to do.

- Asks the user for input and then promptly forgets it. Your program should save input and use it for future default values to eliminate unnecessary repetitive tasks.

- Asks the user a question when the program already knows the answer.

- Presents poorly worded, unhelpful error messages.

- Blames the user for problems.

- Uses offensive language, such as "execute," "kill," "terminate," and "abort."

- Doesn't present a wait cursor or progress dialog box to indicate a time-consuming operation, thus giving the appearance of being hung.

Misdemeanors

These problems also draw unwanted attention to a program, but they are much less serious than the others:

Using three-dimensional effects unnecessarily

A restrained use of 3-D effects can give your program style. Too much use of 3-D effects draws attention to the interface, but not in a flattering way, and makes your program look amateurish.

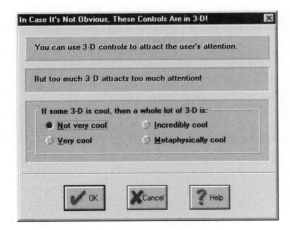

PART
III

158

Using unnecessary nonstandard controls

Using unnecessary custom controls draws unwanted attention by making your program look strange. Programs that use nonstandard controls don't look or behave like most other Windows programs, and nonstandard controls often draw attention to interface elements that shouldn't really be receiving attention.

Using inconsistent terminology

Inconsistent terminology draws unwanted attention simply by confusing the user. For more on this subject, see Chapter 3, "Establish Consistent Terminology."

An interesting observation about these problems is that the worse the offense, the more likely the problem was caused by the developer trying to impress the user. Animation, sound effects, and wild backgrounds might seem cool while you are developing a program, but to the user they grow tiresome quickly. Also, none of these problems are necessary. They often reveal a lack of good judgment and restraint. While many of these problems are minor, each acts as an irritant, like a pebble in your shoe. And no matter how good the shoes are, all you want to do is get rid of that pebble.

When in doubt, ask yourself whether the user benefits from the feature you are considering. For example, animation that shows the progress of a lengthy task benefits the user by showing the user how much work needs to be done, how much work has already been done, and that progress is being made. The animation also helps the user pass the time. Such animations are used throughout Windows and are very easy to justify. However, if a feature doesn't help the user get his work done (or, as in the animation example just mentioned, doesn't help the user when he is not able to do any work) and is merely to show off, you shouldn't use it. If you look at the user interface from the user's point of view and become an advocate for helping the user get his work done, you'll understand that you are not doing the user a favor by creating a user interface that draws attention to itself.

TIP Be an advocate for the user. Put the user's goals ahead of your goals.

CHAPTER 11

Related Chapters

- Chapter 12—Learn from *The Design of Everyday Things*.

  Describes the use of metaphors in affordance and conceptual models. Notes the potential problem with using metaphors: a metaphor can give the user a wrong impression of what an object can do.

Recommended Reading

- Cooper, Alan. *About Face: The Essentials of User Interface Design.* Foster City, CA: IDG Books Worldwide, Inc., 1995.

  Chapter 5, "Idioms and Affordances," presents an insightful discussion comparing idiom paradigm interfaces to metaphor paradigm interfaces. Unlike metaphors, idioms are not based on the real world and require the user to learn the idiom's attributes. In general, he prefers idiomatic learning: "Searching for that magic metaphor is one of the biggest mistakes you can make in user interface design." Metaphors "have a host of other problems as well, including the simple fact that there aren't enough metaphors to go around, they don't scale well, and the ability of users to recognize them is questionable." Also, "There is an infinity of idioms waiting to be invented, but only a limited set of metaphors waiting to be discovered. Metaphors give first-timers a penny's worth of value but cost them many dollars' worth of problems as they continue to use the software." This is good stuff. He also blasts the General Magic MagiCap user interface, which in my opinion is one of the worst user interfaces ever invented. Why? Because the designers of this interface placed their needs as designers ahead of helping the user get his work done. This interface takes metaphors to a ridiculous extreme. Chapter 11, "Orchestration and Flow," discusses flow and how invisible user interfaces help users maintain their flow. Chapter 30, "Undo," presents useful information on why undo is important and tips on how to implement it.

PART

- Bickford, Peter. *Interface Design: The Art of Developing Easy-to-Use Software.* Chestnut Hill, MA: Academic Press, 1997.

  Chapter 5, "Transparency, or Death Comes to Bob the Waiter," makes an interesting comparison of an invisible user interface (in his words, a transparent interface) to a good waiter. I find this simple analogy very helpful. The same information can be found in *Apple Directions*, November/December 1992.

- Howlett, Virginia. *Visual Interface Design for Windows.* New York, NY: John Wiley & Sons, Inc., 1996.

  Chapter 1, "An Introduction to Visual Interface Design," discusses some of the properties of an invisible user interface; Chapter 6, "Graphic Information Design Principles," discusses basic design principles, including the use of color and fonts; and Chapter 8, "Affordances, Realism, and Dimension," presents useful information about the use of 3-D effects, especially mistakes to avoid.

CHAPTER 11

CHAPTER 12

Learn from
The Design of
Everyday Things

Donald A. Norman's *The Design of Everyday Things* presents several fundamental user interface design principles that he derived by looking at the design of everyday things, such as doors, telephones, refrigerators, cars, VCRs, faucets, and such. While it can be fun and educational to consider the design of some everyday things and try to gain insight that can be applied to software, the goal of this chapter is to examine the design principles Norman presents and apply them directly to user interface design for Microsoft Windows.

How Users Learn to Use Everyday Things

As I mentioned in Chapter 2, Norman's book was originally entitled *The Psychology of Everyday Things,* but I think it could be accurately entitled *How Users Learn to Use Everyday Things.* For software user interfaces, human psychology forms the vital link between what the user sees on the screen and how the user decides what to do and, ultimately, how the user learns to interact with the user interface. It is therefore valuable to understand this psychology—how users understand visual elements, explain them, remember them, form relationships between them, become confused, and make mistakes. Knowing this information is fundamental to good user interface design.

The specific user interface design principles from *The Design of Everyday Things* that I want to focus on in this chapter are

- **Visibility** Gives the user the ability to figure out how to use something just by looking at it.

- **Affordance** Involves the perceived and actual properties of an object that suggest how the object is to be used.

- **Natural mapping** Creates a clear relationship between what the user wants to do and the mechanism for doing it.

- **Constraints** Reduces the number of ways to perform a task and the amount of knowledge necessary to perform a task, making it easier to figure out.

- **Conceptual models** A good conceptual model is one in which the user's understanding of how something works corresponds to the way it actually works. This way the user can confidently predict the effects of his actions.

- **Feedback** Indicates to the user that a task is being done and that the task is being done correctly.

These are not six random design principles; they all fit together to help a user learn how to perform and understand a task. Let's look at how these principles work together when a user is learning how to perform a task using software:

- The user decides he needs to perform a task. *Now I need to perform this task...*

- The user needs to identify the features that he can use to perform the task. This step is facilitated by visibility. *Hmm, I think this feature might do it...*

- The user needs to determine how those features are used. This step is facilitated by affordance. *Now how does this object work? Oh, I get it...*

- The user needs to understand how the features perform the task. This step is facilitated by natural mapping. *To perform my task, I need to select this option, enter that information, and then press this button...*

- The user needs to know what to select or enter. This step is facilitated by constraints. *Oh no, what do I have to enter here? OK, I just have these choices...*

- The user needs to understand how the feature works to correctly predict what the program will do. A correct prediction leads to understanding and confidence, whereas an incorrect prediction leads to confusion and insecurity. This step is facilitated by a good conceptual model. *To perform the task, I provided the necessary information and gave this command...and it seems to work as I expected it to.*

- Lastly, the user needs to see the results, whether indicating success or failure. These results must be easy to interpret. This step is facilitated by feedback. *Great—it worked!* or *Oops! I made a mistake and here is how I correct it. Now I understand, and I'll try again.*

In other words, to perform a task, the user needs to identify the right program features, determine how to use those features, determine how to perform the task using those features, correctly predict the outcome of all the actions, and see the results. These fundamental design principles help users learn how to use your program. User interfaces that implement these principles well are easy for the user to learn, understand, and use. They make the difference between software that is easy to use and a bunch of windows on the screen.

Users Perform Tasks, Not Features

Users perform tasks. Programs provide features. That's a problem. Since users perform tasks but programs provide features, users often cannot do what they want to do directly. Rather, they have to understand the program's user interface enough to translate the task into a sequence of steps to take using the features provided by the program. This translation can be difficult, or it can be easy. The easier this translation, the easier the program is to understand and use. The harder the translation, the more the user has to learn. Your job as a user interface designer is to make this translation easy.

CHAPTER 12

TIP Your job as a user interface designer is to make the translation from tasks to program features easy.

Levels of Learnability

There are several levels of learnability, from the case in which the user interface provides no clue at all about a feature to that in which the user interface provides everything the user needs to perform a task. These levels of learnability, starting with the most difficult case for the user, include the following:

- **A feature**   A feature exists. The user needs to learn about the feature's existence and functionality from a source external to the program, such as online help, printed documentation, or a coworker. A typical example is any MS-DOS command.

- **A visual feature**   A feature exists and is displayed visually on the screen, but its meaning and functionality are unclear. The user needs to learn about the feature's functionality from a source external to the program. A typical example is an indecipherable toolbar icon that doesn't have a helpful tooltip.

- **A visible feature**   A feature's existence and functionality are obvious by simple inspection. However, its functionality might not be obvious as a result of the visual properties of the object but because of standards or convention instead. For example, a feature implemented with a hyperlink is visible because its existence and functionality are obvious by inspection but only if you already understand hyperlinks.

- **A feature with affordance**   A feature's existence and functionality are obvious by simple inspection. Its visual properties suggest how it is to be used, so the user can figure it out without knowing any standards or conventions. For example, a command button has a raised 3-D border that makes it look like it can be pushed. As with this example, the interpretation of affordance is often dependent upon real-world experience. Such a feature could also be described as an intuitive feature.

- **A visible task**   The steps required to perform a task are obvious by simple inspection. The user interface makes it clear how to combine all the features required to perform a task. This ultimate level of learnability can be achieved by using a good conceptual model and natural mapping to combine visible features.

PART

Visible user interfaces are the fundamental building blocks of good user interface design, and I have stressed this point in several chapters, including Chapter 10, "Good User Interfaces Are Visible." But although good user interfaces have visible features, the best user interfaces have visible tasks.

TIP The ultimate user interface design goal is to create visible tasks.

The Evolution of Everyday Things

Before we look at Norman's user interface design principles, let's consider the design of everyday things for a moment. Specifically, I find it interesting how the design of a product evolves. There is a fairly common design lifecycle that most products seem to follow, whether the product is a remote control unit or software. Let's look at this evolution process from the point of view of an everyday item like a VCR remote control.

Phase 1   The design goal is to make the object easy to implement with existing technology. Such designs are simple, but they have poor affordance. For example, first-generation remote controls were created using the various cases, buttons, and switches that were available at the time. All the buttons on the remote looked and behaved exactly the same.

Phase 2   The designers learn from their mistakes in Phase 1, so the design goal is to make minor improvements while still using existing technology. Such designs still have poor affordance, but they have better mappings. For example, second-generation remote controls were likely to use the same basic controls but might use two different-shaped buttons instead of one shape. They also had better button layouts, more descriptive labels, and perhaps different color buttons.

Phase 3   The designers realize that they are not restrained to existing technology, so they come up with a better design that uses custom technology. Such designs have greatly improved affordance, since the controls have properties that suggest what they do. However, since this new technology is still unproven, the designers use it sparingly. For example, third-generation remote controls might have used completely different button styles for the Channel and Volume controls as well as for the Play and Stop buttons. These buttons have a different feel so that you get feedback just from their touch. These remote controls might have also used special buttons with totally different behaviors, like a special Record button designed to prevent accidental pressing.

Phase 4   Brimming with confidence from their success in Phase 3, the designers use new technology for everything they can think of. Unfortunately, they overdo it, and the designs are a disaster. Despite the designers' best intentions, such designs have poor affordance and mapping, so users no longer have a clue how to use them. Such designs seem like a good idea at the time but are considered silly in retrospect. For example, fourth-generation remote controls might have looked like a spacecraft control panel, complete with several different-shaped buttons, all with different behaviors and colors. Because these designs had a lot of buttons, some designs hid infrequently used buttons to not overwhelm the user. Interestingly, one successful innovation from this era was VCR Plus, which presented a much better conceptual model for programming VCRs.

Phase 5   Now humbled, the designers focus on designs that employ the best ideas using the best technology. They focus on designs that help users do their tasks and not on showing everyone how clever they are. Focused on the user's goals, they use restraint to reduce complexity. For example, fifth-generation remote controls have a minimum number of buttons with only a few different shapes and colors. The buttons are now easier to find, understand, and use.

   Does this evolutionary life cycle sound familiar? It should. I wanted to come up with an example of this process that used Windows user interface technology. I didn't have to think too hard. Consider this highly simplified version of the evolution of the Windows user interface design:

Windows 1.0 (Phase 1)   Designed to get to market as quickly as possible, using a visual appearance similar to popular graphical user interfaces at the time, primarily Apple Lisa, Apple Macintosh, and Xerox Star.

Windows 2.0 (Phase 2)   Fixes the mistakes in the first version. Also adds a few minor improvements, primarily overlapping windows.

Windows 3.0 (Phase 3)   Designed with a significantly new user interface look to take advantage of VGA display technology. Screen windows and dialog boxes are still 2-D with white backgrounds, but the design includes a limited use of 3-D effects for buttons.

Windows 3.1 (Phase 4)   Completely out of control—no restraint at all. Everything is 3-D on a gray background, whether it needs to be or not. The look is inconsistent, ugly, and overused. Since the basic Windows controls are still primitive, Windows programs use many custom controls that are inconsistent in both appearance and behavior. It seemed like a good idea at the time.

PART

Windows 95 (Phase 5) Sanity is restored. Windows now provides more powerful common controls to give programs a more consistent look and behavior. The use of 3-D effects is minimized, and the 3-D effects used are much less severe.

While it can be argued that this evolution is a natural progression and unavoidable, we could save a whole lot of time and money if we were able to go directly from Phase 1 to Phase 5. But that never seems to happen. There seems to be quite a lot of momentum in the design process, and the evolutionary life cycle requires a substantial amount of learning. You have to wait for technology to catch up with you, and then you have to catch up with technology.

Visible Navigation

Making the translation from a task to a set of features can be simple, especially if there is a direct mapping from the task to a single window and the path to that window is obvious. The translation is most difficult when the user is required to navigate through a series of windows, especially when the path between the windows isn't obvious. In this section, I will focus on the problems of navigation and show how to make navigation visible. Visible navigation is an essential requirement for creating visible tasks.

Wilderness Training

How do you make a task easy to navigate? Well, what do you need to navigate easily in the real world? To navigate in the real world, you need an easily identifiable starting point, a clearly understood destination, and a clearly marked path from the starting point to the destination. At any point in time, you need to have an idea of where you are, how to go forward, and how to go backward.

In wilderness training, you are taught how to identify landmarks and find your way using a map and compass. Interestingly, the ability to go backward is given almost as much attention as going forward. You are taught to periodically turn around so that you can recognize where you came from and how to get back to where you started. You would clearly prefer to get to your destination instead of your starting point, but if you can always get back to your starting point you can then determine what you did wrong and either try again or give up. The inability to move forward to your destination or return back to your starting point is known as being lost.

CHAPTER 12

Navigation Essentials

Since the typical user hasn't had wilderness training, your user interface needs to guide the user through the task. Here are the essentials to visible navigation:

- **A starting point**   Provide a clearly marked starting point so that the user can readily determine how to begin the task. A menu command is often the best starting point because the menu text combined with the command's context within the menu help the user understand the command. Toolbar buttons and keyboard shortcuts work well as alternative shortcuts to the starting point. Make sure the starting point is in the program itself and not within some other program. If the task is performed by another program, use the menu command to make the link; otherwise, the user will never find it.

- **A destination**   Make it easy for the user to predict which starting point will lead to the desired destination. This is accomplished by using natural mapping, which I will describe in detail later in this chapter.

- **An escape route**   Provide a clearly marked exit command in case the user changes his mind or wants to start over. This is usually accomplished with a Cancel button or through direct access to the starting point, as with a Home button.

- **The current step**   Provide a clear indication of where in the process of the task the user is, especially when multiple windows or multiple steps appear within a window. This is usually accomplished with a descriptive window caption. In a multistep process, adding text like *(Step 1 of 7)* also helps.

- **The next step**   Make it clear to the user how to get to the next step. This is usually accomplished by providing the user appropriate options and commands. Make sure that the command buttons are descriptively labeled so that the user can accurately predict what clicking a button will do. Also make sure that the labels clearly differentiate the available choices so that the user can select the right option. Often, adding an extra word or two makes a big difference.

- **The previous step**   Make it easy for the user to get back to the previous step. This is usually accomplished with a Cancel button in modal dialog boxes or a Back button in wizards.

PART
III

In short, at any time the user should know where he is, where he has been, and where he is going.

What to Do

You need to help the user navigate within a window and between windows. Let's now look at some specific ways to make navigation visible.

Identify the steps within a window

You need to make navigation clear within a single window. This is typically accomplished by arranging the controls in logical groups and displaying the groups in a logical order, usually from top to bottom. One effective technique to make the steps in a task clear is simply to number them and describe them within the window. Don't rely on Help to sort things out. This example from Microsoft FrontPage makes it clear that creating a new FrontPage Web requires two steps and what those steps are:

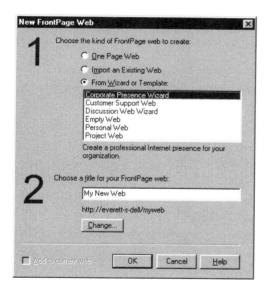

The numbers used in this example are quite large, and it's possible that they might distract the user from the instructions. Smaller numbers will do just fine.

Use a single window whenever possible

When possible, the easiest solution is to let the user perform a task using a single window. You can combine related windows into a property sheet or a dynamic dialog box, such as with this Page Setup common dialog box in Windows:

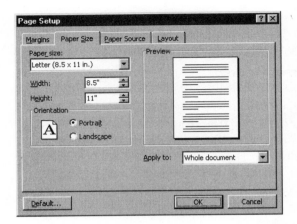

Putting everything the user needs to perform the task in a single window is a technique commonly used in Web pages. Web browsers also have a highly visible navigation model. I'll discuss this subject in more detail in Chapter 13, "Learn from the Web."

Use wizards

Wizards are ideal for complex tasks because they guide the user through the task and allow the user to focus on one step at a time. Wizards have all the elements required for visible navigation: they clearly identify the starting point, ending point (with the Finish button), escape route (with the Cancel button), next step (with the Next button), and the previous step (with the Back button). Some problems with wizards are that they require too much effort for commonly used tasks and they are modal so the user can do only one task at a time.

Use modal dialog boxes

Cascading dialog boxes, while inelegant, can provide visible navigation. Although you want to avoid performing a task with a big pile of modal dialog boxes, they can be effective when there are only a few of them. Again, a problem with using modal dialog boxes is that the user can do only one task at a time.

What to Avoid

Now let's look at some examples of what to avoid.

Don't use unrelated windows

The most invisible form of navigation is when the user has to access several unrelated windows to perform a task. These windows might be accessed from different menu commands or, worse yet, from different programs. In this case, the user simply has no clue what the steps are or even where to start. For example, suppose you want to use the Find utility to look for a system file, such as Commctrl.dll. If you can't find the file, you might be tempted to change an option by using the Options menu.

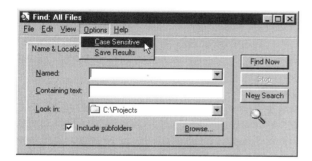

Unfortunately, the only option you have is for a case-sensitive search. To search for system or hidden files, you have to use the View tab of Windows Explorer's Folder Options property sheet.

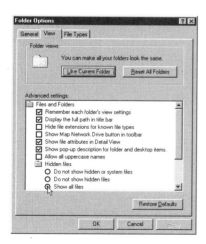

In this case, the starting point isn't obvious. Navigation doesn't get any more invisible than this. Note, however, that there is some logic behind this technique. The Folder Options property sheet sets the folder options for

CHAPTER 12

the entire Windows system, and the Find utility is regarded as part of the system. But how many users know this? Clearly, the Find utility would be easier to use if you could change its options directly from its Options menu.

TIP

The most invisible form of navigation is when the user has to access several unrelated windows to perform a task. Try to make the connection between such windows visible.

Don't cross paths

Another common navigation problem: two tasks that have similar steps cross paths, making it difficult for the user to figure out what the next step is and how to get the paths uncrossed. For example, suppose you have two different tasks that share their first three steps. You could combine the starting point for both tasks and have the user determine which task to pursue at the fourth step. Although this technique requires you to write less code, it's very confusing. There isn't a clear relationship between what the user wants to do and the mechanism for doing it. Furthermore, the user is unable to predict what is going to happen in the initial steps. How is the user supposed to know that he will be able to choose what he really wants to do in the fourth step? A far more visible navigation technique is to offer two independent paths right from the start.

My favorite example of a crossed path is the Add/Remove Programs Control Panel applet:

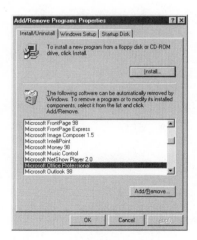

Can you predict what clicking the Add/Remove command button will do? If you didn't read the instructions carefully, you might predict that clicking the button will uninstall the selected program. But that is only partially true since clicking this button also allows you to add or remove components to an installed program. Consider the navigational hurdles a user has to leap over to add a component to a program. First the user has to know that the way to add a component isn't through the program or the setup program but from the Add/Remove Programs Control Panel applet. The user then has to understand that even though he doesn't want to either add or remove a program, the way to install a component is by clicking the Add/Remove button. Even expert Windows users have trouble with navigation like this.

There's nothing wrong with using the Add/Remove Programs Control Panel applet to add components. What's missing is visible navigation. There needs to be a link to this applet from the Help menu of a component-based program as well as a link from the setup program. There then needs to be two separate, well-labeled buttons: one that says *Add or Remove Program Components...* and another that says *Add or Remove Program....*

Affordance

Norman defines affordance as "the perceived and actual properties of the thing, primarily those fundamental properties that determine just how the thing could possibly be used." In other words, affordance relates to the ability of a user to determine how to use an object just by looking at its visual clues.

As noted earlier, an object having affordance is similar but different from an object being visible. An object is visible when a user is able to determine how it is used just by looking at it. What is the difference? The difference is that a user can determine how to use an object with affordance solely by interpreting its visible characteristics. A user can determine how to use a visible object by interpreting its visible characteristics or by knowing the standards and conventions. A command button and a hyperlink are both visible user interface elements, but only the command button offers affordance, because it has a raised 3-D border that makes it look like it can be pushed. Consequently, a first-time computer user is able to figure out instantly how to use a command button, whereas the same user would have to experiment with a hyperlink to understand its function. We can say an object has affordance when all of the following are true:

- The object is visible on the screen, but using the object doesn't require knowledge of the standards or conventions.
- The object has constraints that suggest how it is used. For example, parts of the object move in a certain way and other parts are stationary.

- The object has visible characteristics and usage that are consistent with real-life experience.

- The object has visible characteristics and usage that are consistent within the program and with other programs.

Consistency is also required for affordance, since inconsistent behavior of objects of similar visible characteristics undermines the user's ability to figure out how to use an object just by looking at it.

Human Anatomy vs. Metaphor

For affordance to work, the user needs to be able to interpret an object's visual clues. How does the user do this? The user combines the object's visual clues with real-world knowledge and perhaps some common sense. Often this real-world knowledge depends upon basic human anatomy, especially the properties of the human hand. The hand can point, grab, lift, pull, push, and rotate. Raised 3-D rectangles, such as command buttons, look as if they can be pushed, whereas raised 3-D lines, such as gripper bars, look as if they can be grabbed. And, if something looks like it can be pushed, pulled, grabbed, rotated, and so on, users are going to try to do it. By changing the cursor pointer to the appropriate shape that matches an object's visible features, the mouse in effect becomes an extension of the user's hand.

Another common technique for interpreting an object's visual clues is through metaphor. An object on the screen looks like a common, everyday object that the user already understands and knows how to use. For example, the drawing tools in a typical paint program use metaphors. Instead of calling a free-form line-drawing tool a "free-form line-drawing tool," paint programs call it a "pencil." Selecting the pencil tool changes the cursor to a pencil shape, completing the metaphor. Now the user knows what to do.

However, as I will discuss in the section "Conceptual Models," using metaphors can potentially be a problem because a metaphor can give the user a wrong impression of what an object can do. For example, since real-world pencils don't work in a similar fashion, the user might not realize that a pencil tool can be constrained to draw straight lines. Likewise, the affordance of a push button is strong: because we push real buttons all the time in the real world, we know exactly how they work. And have you ever had to double-push a real push button? To conform to this real-world experience, you should never assign double-click behavior to a command button. It would simply never occur to anyone to try it.

> **TIP**
>
> Users understand affordance through real-world knowledge, including knowledge of human anatomy, metaphors, and experience with everyday objects.

Windows Visual Affordance

Windows maintains the following visual affordances:

- Raised items can be clicked.
- Items that become highlighted when the mouse cursor passes over them can be clicked.
- Recessed items cannot be clicked.
- Items with a white background and a flashing vertical bar can be edited.
- Items with a gray background cannot be edited.
- Gray items are disabled.
- Raised lines can be dragged.

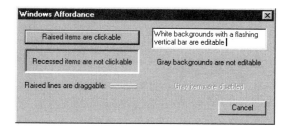

The following cursor pointers reinforce the affordance of the objects they manipulate:

Natural Mapping

A natural mapping creates a clear relationship between what the user wants to do and the mechanism for doing it. It creates an obvious and predictable relationship between actions and their effects. Good mappings work without descriptive labels. In fact, the need for a descriptive label is an indication that a mapping isn't natural.

TIP The need for a label indicates that a mapping isn't natural.

So, how can a mapping be natural? A natural mapping must correspond to the user's preexisting knowledge of the real world. Such real-world knowledge could be from the following sources:

● **Physical** The mapping corresponds to the laws of physics. Alternatively, a control has a physical resemblance to a real-world and familiar object. For example, a car seat control has a natural physical mapping if its shape models the car seat.

● **Spatial** The mapping corresponds to our perception of space. The spatial mapping might apply to a single control or to the relationship between several controls. For example, we perceive *up* to mean on, more, or forward, whereas we perceive *down* to mean off, less, or backward. For a natural mapping, an up arrow must be above a down arrow and a left arrow must be to the left of a right arrow. Any other relationship would be unnatural, as shown here:

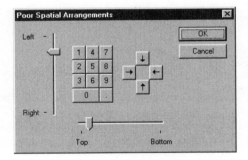

● **Cultural** The mapping corresponds to cultural customs. For example, the symbol for a male is usually shown wearing pants, and the symbol for a female is usually shown wearing a dress. This distinction is cultural and is understood even though the symbol isn't always accurate. (What I mean, of course, is that females often wear pants as well.)

● **Biological** The mapping corresponds to biological attributes or distinctions, especially the attributes of human anatomy. The shape of a mouse and the layout of its buttons correspond to the shape of an adult's right hand. The left button is often larger than the right button because of the anatomical preference to point with the index finger.

- **Standard**   The mapping corresponds to well-known standards. For example, the QWERTY keyboard is a natural mapping simply because it is standard, whereas other keyboard layouts do not have what would be considered a natural mapping.

Natural Mapping Attributes

A natural mapping tends to have several of the following attributes.

A one-to-one correspondence between action and result

A single control performs a single function, so controls are not overloaded to perform multiple functions. A good example of an overloaded control is the Add/Remove button from the Add/Remove Programs Control Panel applet discussed earlier.

No translation required

No translation is required, so the user doesn't have to know anything to use a function. This is often accomplished by selecting the appropriate type of control. For example, you should use check boxes to turn options on and off and radio buttons to change modes. You could use a check box to change modes, but doing so would require the user to translate the off state into the opposite mode of the label. In the following dialog box, the user would have to know that the opposite of portrait mode is landscape mode.

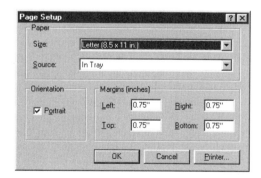

For another example, note that Shift+A doesn't require translation, since it is obviously a capital A, and Ctrl+Alt+A needs translation because its meaning isn't obvious.

Speaking the user's language

Closely related to the concept of not requiring translation is that of speaking the user's language. This could mean the user's spoken language, such as English, or any other type of expression understood by the user, such as numeric formats, currency formats, dates, times, and such. This attribute applies to other forms of perception as well, such as color. Note that color selection is always performed in terms of hue, saturation, and luminosity because that's how the eye perceives color. It's easy to understand what changing the saturation of a color does, whereas changing a specific RGB value is much harder to understand since its perceived effect on the color depends upon the other values. For example, adding more red to a shade of red makes the color more brilliant, but adding more red to a shade of cyan makes it less brilliant.

An appropriate metaphor

Metaphors are often used to map between a user interface and the user's knowledge of the real world. Although an appropriate metaphor isn't required for natural mapping, an inappropriate metaphor destroys a natural mapping because it causes the user to draw an incorrect conclusion about what will happen. I'll give an example of this problem in the next section.

Consistency

Consistent behavior reinforces a mapping; having a control or interaction do different things in different circumstances weakens a mapping. Using different terminology for the same task or feature also weakens a mapping. For example, how many clicks does it take to launch a program in Windows? It depends, since it takes a single click to launch a program from the Start menu but a double click to launch from the desktop. Consistency makes a mapping easier to understand and remember.

When to Use Unnatural Mapping

Sometimes a natural mapping simply isn't practical or possible. After all, there's a limit to the number of controls you can use. A good example is the keyboard: every key can be overloaded by using the Shift, Ctrl, or Alt keys. If you have to overload a control, try to do so in a way that doesn't seem arbitrary.

Constraints

Constraints reduce the number of ways to perform a task and the amount of knowledge necessary to perform a task, making it easier to figure out. Norman describes this as knowledge in the world, as opposed to knowledge

PART

in your head. If there is enough knowledge contained within an object itself, the user doesn't have to remember anything to use it. For example, you don't have to remember the exact layout of the buttons on a telephone since the telephone itself contains that information. Which key do you press for the letter *A*? The correct answer is *2*, not *1* as you might guess. But you never have to guess because that information is always available. As Norman puts it: "Why the apparent discrepancy between the precision of behavior and the imprecision of knowledge? Because not all of the knowledge required for precise behavior has to be in the head. It can be distributed—partly in the head, partly in the world, and partly in the constraints of the world."

There are several ways to use constraints in a user interface, but they all involve removing or disabling invalid choices. When you do this, the user doesn't need knowledge about which choices are valid and which are invalid because they are all valid. Note that good constraints do not inhibit the user since they remove only invalid choices. Constraints also eliminate the need for error messages because they make it impossible for the user to make a mistake.

Good constraints eliminate invalid choices while making the remaining valid choices easier to use.

Types of Constraints

The following constraints are commonly used in user interfaces.

Remove invalid choices

You can constrain the user's choices by disabling or removing choices that don't apply. The user should never be able to select a choice that will only result in an error message. Remove choices in menus or controls that are never valid during an instance of a program; otherwise, disable choices whenever they don't apply. Whenever you give a list of choices, filter out the ones that don't apply to the current context or that the user doesn't care about. For example, you should filter out printer fonts from a list of fonts for the display.

You can also constrain the user's choices by enforcing consistency between controls. Making a selection in one control can enable or disable another control, as well as change its value. A good example is the Settings tab of the Display Control Panel applet, shown on the following page. In this case, selecting more screen area can reduce the number of colors, whereas selecting more colors can reduce the screen area. Note that all selectable combinations are valid.

CHAPTER 12

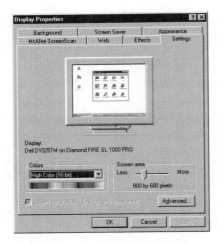

Constrained controls

Use constrained controls whenever possible. In other words, avoid using edit boxes for anything other than unconstrained text and numeric input. For constrained input, use other controls such as combo boxes, lists, sliders, and spin boxes. Use the date and time picker control for dates and times.

Constrained modes

You can constrain the user by using modes. Modal dialog boxes and wizards are obvious examples. In this case, the user must respond to the modal dialog box or wizard before he can do anything else, which is good if that is the behavior you want.

Another example of constrained modes is the modal tools used by paint programs such as Microsoft Paint. When you select a modal tool, the other tools and their attributes are effectively disabled. While the user can't make an error by setting text attributes when using the pencil, disabling attributes that don't apply serves to make the program less confusing.

Constrained manipulation

While direct manipulation is easy to learn as well as quick and convenient to use, it can make it difficult to manipulate objects precisely. Programs that support direct manipulation often allow you to use the keyboard to obtain precise manipulation. For example, in paint programs it is difficult to get a perfect circle or square. Microsoft Paint uses the Shift key to constraint an object's shape. An oval drawn with the Shift key depressed is a circle, a rectangle is a square, and lines are constrained to be at angles that are multiples of 45 degrees. Tools like dialog box editors allow you to set grids and guides to help obtain consistent control sizing and alignment.

PART
III

Standards

You can constrain the user's choices by following conventions. In this case, there might be several ways to perform an action, but only one of them is an accepted standard. If all the user's programs follow the standards, the user might not even be aware that alternatives exist. For example, what happens when you press the Page Up key in a document? In all Windows programs (hopefully), the document remains fixed and the window is moved up relative to the document to see what is above the current view. I once used a workstation where pressing the Page Up key kept the window fixed and moved up the document relative to the window, allowing you to see what was below the current view. Were some Windows programs to use the fixed-document approach and others to use the fixed-window approach, users would have to know which technique was used to be able to scroll a document. For another example, the Microsoft Photo Editor doesn't follow the standards since it uses the mouse wheel for zooming instead of scrolling.

Conceptual Models

A good conceptual model is one in which the user's understanding of how something works corresponds to the way it actually works. This allows the user to confidently predict the effect of his actions. As Norman states, "This requires that the principles of operation be observable, that all actions be consistent with the conceptual model, and that the visible parts of the device reflect the current state of the device in a way consistent with that model."

There are three different conceptual models involved in this process in a program's user interface:

- **The design model**   The conceptual model created by the user interface designer. This model is how the user interface designer intends the user to see a program.

- **The user's model**   The conceptual model of the user interface as understood by the user.

- **The system image**   The visible user interface that the user observes to form the user's model. This image can be different from how the software is actually implemented, which I will call the implementation model.

Ideally, the design model, the user's model, and the system image are all in agreement. When this happens, the user understands how the program works and has well-founded confidence in his ability to use it. The user can accurately predict what the program will do as the result of his actions. When this doesn't happen, the user is confused and unsure of what to do.

Notice that the user's model isn't fixed but that as the user interface designer you have no direct control over it. All you can do is create a design model that makes sense and a system image that matches the design model. You also need to do plenty of user testing on the program to make sure that users understand it. Aside from user testing, users and designers do not communicate directly except through the user interface; that is, through the program's system image.

Interestingly, these conceptual models happen whether or not you intentionally design them. The more normal your program is—the more it follows the standards and has a familiar appearance that is immediately comfortable—the less likely the design model and user's model will diverge. You'll have to worry more about this issue when you create new, nonstandard interfaces; use nonstandard controls; or include complex features.

TIP Conceptual models happen whether or not you intentionally design them.

Conceptual Model Problems

To help them understand how a program works, users naturally make conceptual models based on whatever knowledge they have. Of course, that knowledge might be completely wrong. When this happens, the user becomes confused, finds the program hard to use and learn, and makes many mistakes.

I recently encountered a simple example of a conceptual model problem with my two-year-old son Philippe. I upgraded his computer to Windows 98, which had the side effect of turning on the energy saver feature. Soon I discovered that he was turning the computer on and off quite often. In the design model for Windows, the monitor is blank when

● The computer is turned off.

● The energy saver has turned on.

In my son's user model, the monitor is blank when

● The computer is turned off.

● The computer has crashed.

He has no idea what energy is or why anyone would want to save it. When he sees a blank screen, he thinks the computer needs to be reset. Although in this case he could turn the monitor on by simply pressing a key or moving the mouse, he knows there is no reason to try this if the computer is off or has crashed. By turning off the energy saver feature, I was able to make the design model agree with his user's model and the problem was solved. While this is clearly an example of a conceptual model problem, the conceptual model in question isn't necessarily bad. After all, young children are not the target user for most hardware. But this is clearly an example of how an incorrect user's model leads to confusion.

How to Choose a Design Model

Bad things happen when the design model doesn't match the user's model. An obvious question to ask is: Why bother with a design model at all? Why not make the implementation model (as I said, how the software is actually implemented) the design model? Won't this eliminate any opportunity for confusion? Perhaps—this approach could eliminate some confusion and would certainly be easier to program. But the design model is intended to hide the gory details of the raw implementation model that users don't want to see. For example, MS-DOS is a much more accurate reflection of the way computers work than Windows. Tag-based word processors are a more accurate reflection of a word-processing file than WYSIWYG editors. The problem with implementation models is that they expose too much, much more than users need to deal with to get their work done. For example, the user doesn't care which tag is used to make text bold; he just wants the text to be bold. By working at a higher level, design models make user interfaces easier to understand and use, and they help make the user more productive.

A good design model focuses on what the user needs to do and wants to understand. A good design model for a user interface

- Is focused on the user's needs.

- Is simple.

- Is easy to understand and remember.

- Hides implementation details that the user doesn't need to know.

- Makes it easy for the user to predict what the user interface will do.

It is possible that the best design model is in certain cases the implementation model. For example, system utilities typically hide little from the user. But whatever model you use, the key to success is to do plenty of user testing to make sure that users understand the model.

An Example Conceptual Model

An interesting example of a conceptual model is Windows Explorer. Windows Explorer largely matches the raw hierarchical file system, in which files are contained in folders, each of which can contain other folders and files. On the other hand, the Windows Shell Namespace makes system objects not directly related to the file system appear to be part of it. Specifically, Windows Explorer makes network drives, the Control Panel, the Recycle Bin, the Briefcase, and printers look like files and folders. Even the Microsoft Internet Explorer home page and current page are integrated into the Windows Shell Namespace. This technique gives the user common access to all these features from a single program.

Metaphors as Conceptual Models

A popular technique for conceptual models is to pattern the model after a common real-world object. This way the user can readily identify what the object is and understand how to use it. While using a metaphor can help the user grasp the conceptual model quickly, it runs the risk of having the user's model differ from the design model. The problem is that user interface metaphors rarely match the exact behavior and properties of their real-world counterparts, and in that case they can mislead the user as to what an object will do. In other words, the real-world properties of a metaphor can be counterproductive if the interface behaves differently.

A classic example of this problem is the Trash icon on the Apple Macintosh desktop. You can delete a file by dragging it to the Trash. You can also eject (but not erase) a floppy disk or CD-ROM by dragging it to the Trash. This disk-ejection technique bothers everybody, especially beginners. The real-world properties of a trashcan suggest that placing a disk in the Trash should be akin to throwing away its contents. While Apple has several reasons for this design decision, it ruins the metaphor and, conversely, the real-world properties of the metaphor ruin the program feature by making you not want to eject disks this way. Had a metaphor not been used—had the Trash been given a meaningless name like Storage Munger— there wouldn't be a problem. Of course, the real problem here isn't using a metaphor but assigning it a behavior that is counter to our common real-world experience.

Feedback

Feedback indicates to the user that a task is being done and that it is being done either correctly or incorrectly. Your program needs to inform the user what it is doing. Without feedback, the user is giving commands without any knowledge of their results. Feedback completes the loop by letting the user know that the commands worked. Since the user needs to know when an action cannot be done or is being done incorrectly, error messages are an important form of feedback.

PART
III

Good feedback is both immediate and obvious. Feedback delivered after the user needs it or that the user doesn't understand is worthless. For example, some programs are slow to display a wait cursor or progress indicator when they start a time-consuming operation, causing the user to think that nothing is happening. Feedback can be made obvious by placing the feedback mechanism in close physical proximity to the causal action. While a taskbar can be used effectively for status-related feedback, taskbars are too far away from the causal action to be effective in general. Feedback to a time-consuming operation can be made obvious by indicating how much work has been done and the total amount of work to do.

Feedback Interfaces

The following interfaces are commonly used to provide feedback. Interestingly, all but the first four of these forms of feedback have something in common: they are annoying when misused. You should choose the least obtrusive interface that does the job, so I have ordered the interfaces by their obtrusiveness, the least obtrusive first.

TIP   Choose the least obtrusive feedback interface that does the job.

Show the results

Often the best feedback technique is to simply show the results. You can show that an operation is complete by showing the results of the operation. For example, you can show that an object has been manipulated by showing the resulting selection, deletion, moving, copying, sizing, and so on. Such results are indicated by either changing the physical properties of the object or how the object is drawn. For example, selection is shown by changing an object's background color.

Show a preview of the results

Previews are an effective way to give the user feedback on the results of a selection without the user having to make the particular selection. They make features self-explanatory and easy to understand, reducing the need for documentation. They also make the user more productive by reducing the chance of making bad choices.

Use tooltips

Tooltips are a simple and effective way to give dynamic feedback in a way that requires almost no effort from the user. They truly implement the "information at your fingertips" concept.

CHAPTER 12

Cursor hinting

Changing the cursor is a simple way to give feedback. The wait cursor is a good choice to show that an operation is going to take a few seconds. Other cursor shapes are good for indicating direct manipulation, such as when resizing, moving, or using a specialized tool (as found in a paint program).

Control enabling

You can give effective, unobtrusive feedback simply by enabling or disabling controls to show that an operation is running or to show an object's status. For example, the Microsoft Visual C++ Compile, Build, and Rebuild All toolbar buttons are disabled while code is compiled and are enabled when the operation has finished.

Color

Color can be used for feedback, but it has several problems. The first is that color is difficult to interpret by itself. You can use red to indicate danger and yellow to indicate caution, but even these color interpretations are culturally dependent. Another problem is that many users either are color-blind or use monochrome displays. Consequently, color is best used to reinforce another form of feedback.

Status bars

Status bars work well for status information and for feedback about background tasks such as printing or formatting. As noted earlier, status bars suffer from not being obvious, so they are a poor choice for critical information. However, they work well with progress indicators since progress indicators use both motion and color, making them easy to notice on a status bar.

Progress indicators

Progress indicators are useful for operations that take more than about five seconds to perform. They provide more information than a wait cursor by indicating how long the operation will take, how much work has already been done, and that progress is being made. If you display a progress indicator in a modal dialog box, you can also give the user the ability to stop the operation.

Taskbar

Flashing a program's taskbar window button is a good way to notify the user of a pending message.

Taskbar System Tray

The taskbar System Tray is a good way to provide feedback for a system task or a utility. The problem is that the System Tray is overused; many programs display System Tray icons that do little more than take up space.

188

The best way to use a System Tray icon is to display it only when you need to provide feedback to the user. The sudden appearance of an icon in the user's peripheral vision draws far more attention than changing a permanent icon's appearance.

Animation

You can use an animation control as an alternative to a progress indicator to show that an operation is in process. You can also use animation to show that an object has been manipulated, such as when a button is pushed. Lastly, you can use animation to show the relationship between cause and effect, such as with the zoom rectangles shown whenever you display the Find dialog box in Microsoft Word. The best animations are kept small and simple to avoid distracting the user.

Sound

Sound can also create effective feedback, but it too has several problems. The first is that it can be just plain annoying, especially in an office environment. While people can close their eyes, they can't close their ears. Sound is a poor feedback mechanism for those who have hearing disabilities, those who are in a noisy environment, or those who don't have their sound turned on (which is true in my case). If you decide to use sound for feedback, make it optional and redundant.

Message boxes

Message boxes with a brief, clear, consistent, and specific message are an effective way to give feedback. The message box text must provide enough information so that the user can understand the issue and know what to do about it. The problem with message boxes is that they force the user to stop working to respond to them. Consequently, message boxes should be used for feedback only when necessary. A message box confirmation is appropriate to give feedback that the user is about to perform a dangerous or destructive operation. By contrast, you should never use a message box to report that a command has completed successfully. Such good news can be taken for granted.

The Need for Design

Creating user interfaces with these important design principles doesn't happen by chance—it happens only by design. As Norman observes: "The next time you pick up an unfamiliar object and use it smoothly and effortlessly on the first try, stop and examine it: the ease of use did not come about by accident. Someone designed the object carefully and well."

CHAPTER 12

Related Chapters

- Chapter 10—Good User Interfaces Are Visible.

  Describes visibility in general by discussing what makes a feature visible, what makes a feature invisible, and examples of visible features and feedback.

- Chapter 11—Good User Interfaces Are Invisible.

  Discusses some of the more undesirable forms of feedback, such as beeping, blinking, sound effects, and unnecessary dialog boxes. Also discusses avoiding cumbersome metaphors and the characteristics of a good metaphor.

- Chapter 13—Learn from the Web.

  Discusses the techniques used by the Web to make navigation more visible, such as showing the current context, using home pages, using navigation bars, and using the Web browser navigation model.

- Chapter 17—Direct Manipulation Is Cool.

  Presents the techniques to make direct manipulation visible through feedback.

- Chapter 20—Previews Are Cool.

  Presents the types of previews and gives examples of each type. Previews are an excellent way to provide visible feedback.

- Chapter 23—Unnecessary Message Boxes Are Pure Evil.

  Unnecessary message boxes are the worst forms of feedback. This chapter discusses the various types of message boxes and gives tips on how to eliminate the unnecessary ones.

- Chapter 27—User Testing.

  Discusses how to perform user testing and gives a specific procedure to make sure you get good feedback. You need to do user testing to make sure that users understand your conceptual models.

- Chapter 30—Check Your Error Messages.

  Gives several suggestions on how to make sure your error messages provide helpful, easy-to-understand feedback.

Recommended Reading

- Arlov, Laura. *GUI Design for Dummies*. Foster City, CA: IDG Books Worldwide, Inc., 1997.

  Chapter 5, "Pin Up Those Super Models," discusses conceptual models, primarily with a case study. Chapter 6, "How Users Get Around: Navigation Models," covers how to improve navigation models, especially in database programs. Chapter 11, "Making Your GUI Easy to Understand," describes how to make interfaces easy to use by providing feedback, affordance, mapping, and metaphors.

- Bickford, Peter. *Interface Design: The Art of Developing Easy-to-Use Software*. Chestnut Hill, MA: Academic Press, 1997.

  Chapter 1, "Constraints," discusses how constraints reduce complexity by using an example of how constraints are used to eliminate user errors by Japanese vending machines. Chapter 11, "Speed and Feedback," describes the importance of providing feedback to improve the perceived speed of software. Chapter 38, "Apocrypha and Secret Lore: Interface Oddities and Ephemera," attempts to justify the Macintosh design of having users drag disks to the trash to eject them.

- Cooper, Alan. *About Face: The Essentials of User Interface Design*. Foster City, CA: IDG Books Worldwide, Inc., 1995.

  Chapter 3, "The Three Models," discusses conceptual models and the problems with basing user interfaces on the implementation model. Chapter 5, "Idioms and Affordances," discusses affordance, particularly with respect to our instinctive understanding of how to use things with our hands, and problems with using metaphors in user-interface design. Chapter 8, "Lord of the Files," discusses the problems with the conceptual model of the file system, which Cooper believes is based too closely on the implementation model.

- Howlett, Virginia. *Visual Interface Design for Windows*. New York, NY: John Wiley & Sons, Inc., 1996.

  Chapter 7, "An Introduction to the Psychology of Perception," discusses how users perceive, focusing on vision, mental models, and cultural differences. Chapter 8, "Affordance, Realism, and Dimension," considers affordance, realism vs. abstraction, and the use of 3-D as an affordance.

CHAPTER 12

- Nielsen, Jakob. *Usability Engineering*. Chestnut Hill, MA: AP Professional, 1993.

  Chapter 5, "Usability Heuristics," discusses mappings, conceptual models, and metaphors and shows how metaphors can mislead users by giving them false expectations. This chapter also discusses feedback, especially as it relates to response time.

- Norman, Donald A. *The Design of Everyday Things*. New York, NY: Currency/Doubleday, 1990.

  Discusses how users learn to use everyday things through their design attributes of visibility, affordance, natural mappings, constraints, conceptual models, and feedback. Discusses other design attributes as well, such as simplicity, consistency, forgiveness, and conformance to standards. Chapter 2, "The Psychology of Everyday Actions," presents the seven states of action that ties all these design attributes together.

- Tognazzini, Bruce. *Tog on Interface*. Reading, MA: Addison-Wesley Publishing Company, Inc., 1992.

  Chapter 17, "Conceptual Models," gives guidelines on how to create conceptual models. He stresses the importance of simplicity, memorability, familiarity, and focusing on the user's needs.

PART
III

1 CHAPTER 3

Learn from the Web

The World Wide Web has profoundly changed how we view computing; we can now use computers as a global information appliance. It shouldn't be surprising to discover that the Web has also changed how we view user interface design. What's remarkable about the Web is that users are able to visit a Web site they haven't seen before and quickly figure out how to use it with little effort—even without a help system or documentation. While Web sites tend to have rich, highly visual content, the user interface mechanisms provided by HTML are fairly primitive compared to those available through the Microsoft Windows API. This simple document-based approach to user interface design has many benefits that we can incorporate into our standard Windows programs.

The goal behind learning from the Web isn't to be trendy. I'm not suggesting that you redesign all your user interfaces to use this technology because it is a cool thing to do. In fact, I'm not necessarily suggesting that you redesign anything. You don't have to make your program look like a Web site. Rather, I suggest that you see whether you can improve the way you create programs by looking at user interface design from a different, simpler perspective. The goal is to make software easier to use. And you can do a good bit of this by making small changes to your existing user interfaces.

TIP The goal behind learning from the Web isn't to be trendy but to make software easier to use.

If you have spent much time on the Internet, you know that there are many things that you should not learn from the Web. You can find many astoundingly bad Web sites out there that are the result of poor design decisions, such as presenting text on distracting backgrounds, overusing graphics, prominently displaying useless distracting animations, and making poor use of color. These Web sites have a tendency to draw unwanted attention to themselves. The lesson to learn from this aspect of the Web is how to use restraint.

In Chapter 5, "Pay Attention to Other Programs," I suggested that you analyze other programs' user interfaces while you use them. The same applies to the Web. Ask yourself why you like the Web sites you do. Try to understand why you like them or dislike them. If you find them easy to use, try to understand why. If you find them difficult to use, try to figure that out as well. Then try to see whether you can apply the methods and principles you find effective to your user interfaces.

The Limitations of HTML

Let's start by trying to understand why the Web is easy to use. The most fundamental element of a Web site is an HTML page. If you are a hammer, every problem is a nail; if you are a browser, every problem is an HTML page. Interestingly, HTML is essentially a document format, not a user interface format, and it has the ability to display the following:

- Text
- Hyperlinks
- Graphics
- Tables
- Frames

- Forms
- Controls
- Tooltips (that is, ALT text for graphics)

That's pretty much it. You can go well beyond these basic capabilities, such as with cascading style sheets, scripts, ActiveX controls, and browser plug-ins like Macromedia ShockWave, but the fundamental building block of the Web is the standard HTML page. By contrast, standard Windows programs have many more user interface features, such as:

- Multiple windows
- Multiple-document interfaces (MDI)
- Dialog boxes and property sheets
- Message boxes
- Menus
- Toolbars
- Cursors
- Help systems
- Status bars

In terms of interaction, Web pages support single-clicking and mouse hovering, whereas Windows programs support single-clicking, double-clicking, dragging and dropping, and sometimes even triple-clicking as well as hovering. Windows programs also support keyboard shortcuts and access keys.

Interestingly, I believe the most useful user interface innovations for the Web were developed to work around the lack of all these user interface elements. Let's look at the list of Windows interface features again and see how typical Web pages compensate for lacking each feature:

- **No multiple windows or MDI** Web pages compensate for not having multiple windows by putting all the elements required to perform a task in a single window. The contents of a Web page can be created dynamically, so it is easy to tailor the contents of a window to the specific task at hand. Web pages can have complex layouts through the use of tables and frames. Hyperlinks make it easy to access other pages as needed. The browse buttons (such as Back, Forward, Stop, Refresh, and Home) and the History and Favorites commands further simplify navigation between pages.

CHAPTER 13

- **Dialog boxes**   Web pages compensate for not having dialog boxes by either putting what would be a dialog box on a separate page or by integrating the dialog box into the page. For example, most sites that have search capabilities have the search dialog box incorporated into the appropriate pages.

- **Message boxes**   Web pages compensate for not having error messages by clearly marking any input fields that have invalid information and providing instructions on how to fix the problem. This makes problems easy to identify and correct.

- **Menus and toolbars**   Web pages compensate for not having menus by embedding commands directly in the context of the page where they are needed. This technique establishes a clear relationship between what is on the screen and what you can do with it.

- **Help systems and status bars**   Web pages compensate for not having help systems by providing help information directly in the page itself. If the user needs additional information, there is often a link to help information pages. Status-related information is also embedded directly into the page.

- **Single-clicking**   Web pages avoid the need for interactions other than single-clicking. You can select text and graphics in a Web page for copying to the clipboard by clicking and dragging, but otherwise there is no other mode of selection. You cannot select a standard HTML object to perform a command on it. Consequently, there's no need to distinguish between single-clicking and double-clicking, so all actions are performed with a single click.

- **Keyboard shortcuts and access keys**   Web pages have relatively primitive keyboard support. You can navigate within a Web page by using the Tab and Shift+Tab keys, and you can jump from a link or push a button with the Enter key.

You can apply these Web user interface innovations in standard Windows programs by using the following techniques:

- Using HTML documents

- Considering hyperlinks

- Simplifying navigation

- Simplifying interaction

- Using in-place help

- Simplifying windows
- Eliminating dialog boxes

In the remainder of this chapter, I'll explore each of these techniques in detail.

Using HTML Documents

You should consider using HTML documents instead of other formats for read-only text in your program. For example, the new help system used by Windows 98 is all HTML-based, as is the new Microsoft Developer Network (MSDN) Library. Using HTML allows you to provide rich text with graphics and tables easily.

Consider using HTML to display textual information in your program, such as text, tables, and reports. This is true even if the information is fairly simple and looks nothing like a typical Web page. For example, consider text as ordinary as that in the Build tab of the Output window in Microsoft Visual C++.

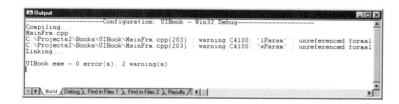

How could you implement this window in MFC? The first possible approach is to create a window derived from CScrollView. While the scroll view allows you to display and scroll text with little effort, you have to implement any additional functionality yourself. For example, you would need to write code to be able to select text, copy text to the clipboard, or print text. You would also have to write code to allow the user to double-click on an error message to see the corresponding source code. Alternatively, you could derive from CEditView, but this approach also has drawbacks. In an edit view, you can use only a single font and the view can contain a limited amount of text. (There is a 64 KB limit in Windows 98.) You would also have to handle double-click messages and convert the clicked window locations to error message line offsets to show the source code. Furthermore, the text is editable by default, so you have to make it read-only, which has the side effect of making the background gray. You then have to change the background color.

Assuming you know how to tag text in HTML (which is very easy), the simplest way to implement this window in MFC is with CHTMLView. Not only will an HTML window display and scroll the text without any size limitations, but this approach gives the user the ability to select, copy, and print text. You can embed hyperlinks to allow the user to jump from error messages to source code. HTML makes this connection visible, whereas the original does not, so the user doesn't have to know to double-click the error messages to see the source code. Furthermore, if your requirements change and you want to make the text look better by using different fonts or perhaps tables, all you have to do is add a few HTML tags and you are finished. Of course, you could also add the ability to export HTML files with almost no effort, allowing the user to view rich text on practically any platform. HTML documents are easy to create and very flexible.

The key points I want to make are that HTML documents allow you to create better text user interfaces even if the document looks nothing like a Web page and often requires less effort than the alternatives. Of course, if you want rich content, HTML documents are the best way to go.

 TIP

Consider using HTML documents even if the document looks nothing like a Web page. They are flexible, powerful, and easy to program.

Considering Hyperlinks

Hyperlinks are vital to the Web—links make the difference between having a World Wide Web and a bunch of random, unconnected HTML pages. It's helpful to understand the difference between a hyperlink and a command button and when to use hyperlinks in a standard Windows program. It's also helpful to understand how to create a good hyperlink and how to apply the same technique to creating good button labels.

PART

III

On a Web page, a hyperlink is used to directly change the contents of the window, whereas a button is used to perform a command, which might indirectly change the contents of a window. For example, a Search button submits a search command that in turn changes the window contents. While this type of activity occurs often in a browser, it rarely happens in a standard Windows program. I think hyperlinks make sense in a standard Windows program for three purposes:

- To change the contents of a window, as in HTML help or a program's home page. (I'll discuss home pages in the next section.)

- To launch a browser to display a Web page, such as for technical support information.

- To launch a Mailto email message window. You could use a hyperlink to send questions to technical support, for example.

Admittedly, that isn't much. However, I find the real benefit in considering hyperlinks isn't in their physical attributes—after all, command buttons have an advantage because of their affordance (that is, they look like they can be pushed) and because they provide positive visual feedback when you push them—but in understanding how to label them correctly. Jared Spool, in *Web Site Usability: A Designer's Guide,* points out that the success of a hyperlink depends upon:

- How well the user can predict where the link will lead
- How well the user can differentiate one link from another

These requirements make perfect sense because a typical Web page has several links and the user needs to have enough information to choose the right one. Interestingly, Spool discovered that users usually expect links to take them to another page and they are confused when links are used to move within a page or to change the contents of the same page. Web pages accomplish these predictability requirements by using verbose links, with just enough descriptive text to make it clear what the link will do.

 TIP

Users need to be able to predict where links will lead and differentiate one link from another.

CHAPTER 13

With these ideas in mind, consider the Add/Remove Programs Control Panel applet:

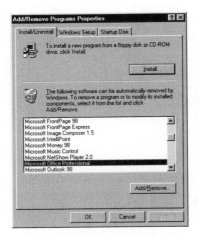

Can you predict what clicking the Add/Remove command button will do? If you didn't read the instructions carefully, you might predict that clicking the button will uninstall the selected program. But that is only partially true since clicking this button also allows you to add or remove components to an installed program. In the case of Microsoft Office, clicking this button allows you to add or remove installed components, restore missing files or settings, uninstall the program, or perform online registration. Would it surprise you to find out that most users don't know this? From the point of view of hyperlinks, a far better approach would be to use the following slightly more verbose descriptions:

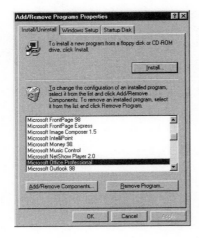

The possibility that these different command buttons might lead to the same place is not significant, although ideally they should go to different places. After all, Web pages frequently have redundant hyperlinks without causing confusion. What is important is that if you add an extra command button and a few more words, the user can now predict what is going to happen before clicking the button. I like this example because thinking about the Web clearly shows a flaw in this dialog box's user interface that uses no Web technology at all. Finding problems like this just requires a small change in perspective: pretend that your command buttons are hyperlinks, and then try to predict where they will take you.

TIP

Pretend that your command buttons are hyperlinks, and try to predict where they will take you.

Simplifying Navigation

Hyperlinks are hardly a trouble-free technology. The problem is that since navigation is no longer linear, it becomes difficult for users to understand where they are. I like to refer to this state as being hyperlost. Although Web designers struggle to organize their sites in an understandable hierarchy, Jared Spool has discovered through user testing that often users have no clue what that organization is. This problem is a least partially solved by having both browsers and Web sites make navigation more visible using the following techniques:

- Showing the context
- Using home pages
- Using navigation bars
- Using the Web browser navigation mode

Let's look at each of these techniques in more detail.

Showing the Context

Hierarchically arranged Web sites often indicate directly in the page where the user is, such as in the following Yahoo! example.

CHAPTER

13

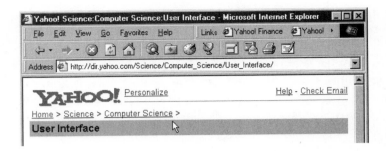

This technique makes it clear where the user is and where he has been. Windows Explorer in effect does the same with the Address bar:

For one more example, notice how Microsoft Encarta dedicates the left-hand side of its window to display an outline of the currently displayed subject to give the user the context.

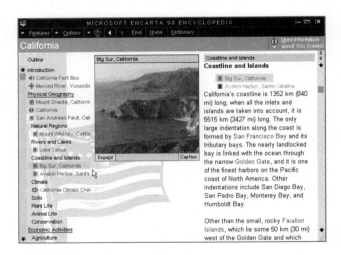

In all three cases, the interface helps make it clear to users where they are, where they have been, and how to get back to where they came from. Showing the context helps prevent users from getting lost.

Using Home Pages

The typical Web site uses a home page as a launch pad to the other pages in the site. The home page is a simple, visible, and convenient mechanism to display the features that are available. A good home page contains all the features a user would commonly want to use. For example, Microsoft Outlook Express displays its home page when nothing specific is selected. The home page shows the features that are available and provides a simple means to access them. This is what the user sees the first time he runs the program.

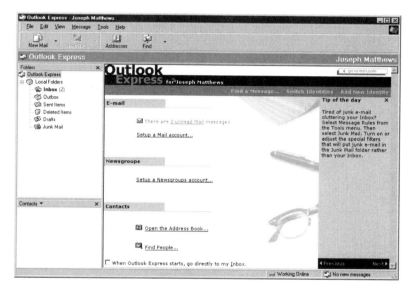

Note that if the home page weren't displayed in this case, the alternative would be to display an empty window or a meaningless graphic. The home page takes full advantage of the available screen space.

The Microsoft Money home page, shown on the following page, packs even more functionality, providing quick access to charts, accounts, and overdue bills.

CHAPTER 13

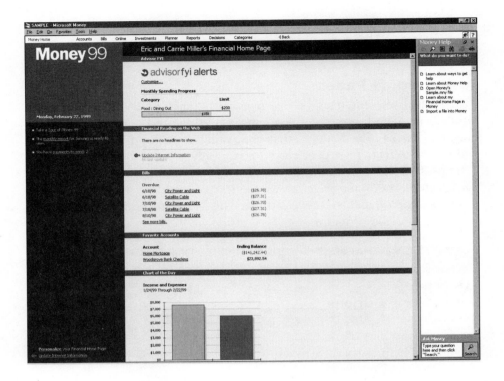

Using Navigation Bars

Another Web technique used to make navigation visible is a navigation bar. A navigation bar is similar to a toolbar, except that it is used to quickly access Web pages instead of to issue commands. The previous screen shots from Money and Encarta show typical navigation bars at the top of each window. Microsoft Outlook has a more standard-looking navigation bar, called an Outlook bar, on the left-hand side of the window. These navigation bars list the important places where a user is likely to want to go. Ideally, the user should be able to get where he wants to go with just a couple of mouse clicks.

Using the Web Browser Navigation Model

In the standard Windows navigation model, the user selects a command that results in a new window being displayed. The user interacts with the new window and either gives another command resulting in another window or closes the window by clicking the OK, Cancel, or Close button and returns to the original window. This procedure can create a stack of windows. As long as only a couple of windows are displayed at a time, this model works fairly well, but it breaks down when it results in a big pile of windows on the screen. The windows used in such cases are usually modal dialog boxes, which is preferable. Having a modal dialog box display a modeless dialog box that in turn displays another modal dialog box would be confusing. Perhaps the most significant problem with the Windows navigation model is that beginning users don't understand modal dialog boxes. They become frustrated when they click something they want to use on the screen and receive a beep instead of the expected results.

TIP   Beginning users don't understand modal windows.

The Web browser navigation model eliminates these problems. A browser displays only a single page at a time, so windows never pile up on the screen. With only one window displayed at a time, all interactions are modeless. As a result, you can never click an element on a Web page and receive a beep as an error. Instead of displaying multiple windows, a Web browser displays multiple pages one at a time in a single window and relies on the ability to navigate between these pages. Browsers simplify this navigation by providing the Back, Forward, and Home buttons in addition to the Favorites menu (providing favorite pages selected by the user) and the History list (providing pages recently accessed by the user). If the user gets lost, all he has to do is click the Back or Home button to return to a familiar place. The single modeless window with easy access to the most useful pages makes the Web Browser Navigation Model much more simple and uniform than the standard Windows navigation model.

Windows Explorer makes an interesting use of the Web Browser Navigation Model. By providing Back and Forward buttons, it makes it easy to toggle between two folders anywhere on the network. Also, the Up button lets you easily navigate up the folder hierarchy, and the Favorites menu lets you easily access often-used folders. My only complaint is that Windows Explorer favorites are jumbled together with the Microsoft Internet Explorer favorites. When I'm using Windows Explorer, I just want to see my favorite folders, not Web pages.

For one last example, consider how Outlook and Outlook Express handle navigation from the home page. Whenever you navigate from the home page to another Web-style page, that page always has a Back link displayed at the top of the window to visibly maintain the navigation model, as shown in the screen shot on the following page.

CHAPTER 13

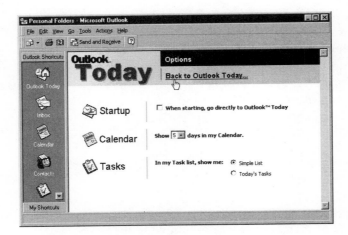

Simplifying Interaction

Web pages simplify interaction through two techniques: single-clicking and eliminating menus. Let's look at each in more detail.

Single-Clicking

The most basic form of interaction in Windows is the mouse click. But what does a single mouse click do? The problem is that it depends on what is being clicked. For example, single-clicking a command button gives the command, but single-clicking an icon on the desktop doesn't open the shortcut but selects the icon instead. In this case, you have to double-click to open the shortcut. So, the clicking rules are:

● Buttons perform their action with a single click.

● Nonbuttons are selected with a single click, whereas double-clicking selects the object and performs the default action.

For a user to understand how an object is going to behave when clicked, the user needs to understand these rules and the visual distinction between a button and a nonbutton, which isn't easy to do. To help make this visual distinction, program icons should not look like buttons—they should not have raised rectangular 3-D borders. Not surprisingly, many users don't understand these distinctions. Some users single-click everything, some double-click everything, and others (like my two-year-old son Philippe) just keep blasting at it until they get what they want. These users are confused by the most basic form of Windows interaction. Such confusion cannot be good.

Web pages eliminate this problem by using single-clicking for every-thing. (This is true for HTML at least—Microsoft ActiveX controls can do what-ever they want.) They can do this because there is no notion of selection in a Web page, so there is no need to distinguish between single clicks and double clicks. Selection is usually accomplished through check boxes, as with this example from Amazon.com:

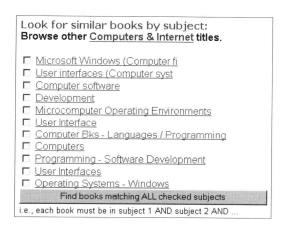

Note that in this example you can immediately view a subject by clicking its hyperlink or you can select several subjects and click the Find button. An-other selection technique used by Windows Explorer in the Web-style mode is hovering: an item is selected when you hover the cursor over the item for about a second. I don't know about you, but using this selection tech-nique for any length of time drives me nuts, since I am constantly select-ing objects accidentally. Clearly, selection in Web pages is fairly primitive.

So what should you do? I recommend the following:

● Consider single-clicking when selection isn't necessary. You can visually indicate that an object uses single-clicking by giving it a raised rectangular 3-D border, as done with command buttons, or by underlining its caption and using the visited or unvisited links color, as done with hyperlinks.

● When selection is necessary, make sure that selectable objects are visually distinct from objects that are not selectable. In other words, selectable objects should never have raised rectangular 3-D borders or underlined captions.

TIP   Consider single-clicking when selection isn't necessary, but make sure that there is a clear visual distinction between single-clickable objects and double-clickable objects.

Eliminating Menus

Menus are fundamental to basic interaction in modern user interfaces, yet Web pages don't have menus. (OK, Web pages can have menus, but Web page menus are supported by scripting, not through HTML.) Web pages compensate for not having menus by embedding the commands directly in the context of the page where they are needed. This technique establishes a clear relationship between what is on the screen and what you can do with it.

In Chapter 6, "Beginning vs. Advanced Users," and Chapter 10, "Good User Interfaces Are Visible," I explained that menu bars are the best way of showing beginning users how to use your program because the menu bar is effectively a hierarchically organized catalog of all the program's features. (This makes menu bars an excellent teaching tool.) But there are exceptions to this rule. For example, dialog boxes don't use menu bars because all the controls needed to use the dialog box already appear in the immediate context where they are needed. The command technique used by Web pages is simply an extension of this approach. If done well, placing commands right where they are needed eliminates the need for the user to go through a learning process to use the program.

If you do decide to put commands in context, you should review the commands you leave in the menu bar. You don't want to constantly change the contents of the menu bar, because this can be disorienting. You want the menus to appear stable. Consequently, you should use the menu bar for universal commands that apply in most contexts.

TIP   Consider embedding commands directly in the context where they are needed. If you do, use the menu bar for universal commands that apply in most contexts.

Using In-Place Help

Web sites don't have help systems or other forms of documentation. Suppose standard Windows programs didn't have Help or documentation. You could compensate by putting detailed instructions in the user interface

PART
III

itself, as in the case of displaying the Printers folder using Windows Explorer in the View As Web Page mode.

Of course, you don't need to use an HTML page to give in-place help. Wizards routinely provide in-place help, although this is much less common in dialog boxes. A good example of a dialog box that does give in-place help is the Windows Explorer Organize Favorites dialog box.

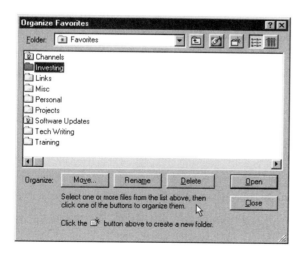

Notice that the in-place help doesn't have to be long or complicated. In this case, two short sentences do the job.

Simplifying Windows

Users typically perform one task at a time. Why not put everything the user normally needs to perform the task in a single window? Web pages cannot have multiple windows, so there is no choice, but standard Windows programs can benefit from using a single window.

Of course, sometimes the user needs the power and flexibility provided by multiple windows. MDI programs such as Microsoft Word, Microsoft Excel, and Visual C++ need to provide this capability to users to help them accomplish their tasks since users often need to access multiple documents simultaneously. But the problem with MDI programs is that the power and flexibility provided by multiple windows has a cost—that cost is the added complexity of managing and viewing all those windows. MDI programs often have a significant amount of screen clutter. By contrast, single window programs require very little window management, as you only occasionally need to size the program window or move a window splitter. Your objective should be to give the single window the most useful layout by default so that the user doesn't have to change the layout just to perform a task.

Web pages use tables and frames to divide a single window into multiple regions. Frames are equivalent to splitter windows, and they are a good substitute for MDI in many situations. The home page used in Microsoft Money, shown previously, is a good example of a frame used in a standard Windows program. Programs such as Windows Explorer, Outlook, Microsoft FrontPage, and Encarta also use frames, and they work fine in a single window. Admittedly, frames have a bad reputation in Web design, but this is related more to the fact that some browsers don't handle frames well rather than to usability problems.

TIP

Don't use multiple windows when a single window will do. Try to have users perform a single task in a single window.

A small but visually significant difference between Web pages and standard Windows programs is that a Web page is a document. Normally, this means that all windows, by default, would have a white background. Standard windows programs tend to use a light gray background for each

PART

window that isn't a document window, such as dialog boxes, message boxes, and menus. Gray backgrounds help you create 3-D effects, but the trend is to use less 3-D because it has been terribly overused in the past. By using white backgrounds and fewer 3-D effects, you can give your windows a cleaner appearance, one that is easier to read and that has better contrast and focus. For example, this checking account window from Microsoft Money uses a light-colored background with the account information to make it easy to read and to focus the user's attention on the main task. Peripheral activities are given a dark background so that they will receive less attention.

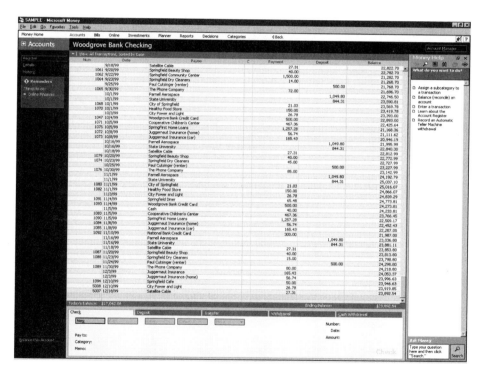

TIP Try to use more white backgrounds and fewer 3-D effects to give your windows a cleaner appearance.

Eliminating Dialog Boxes

Web pages compensate for not having dialog boxes by either putting what would be a dialog box on a separate page or by integrating the dialog box with the page. I'll discuss eliminating dialog boxes in detail in Chapter 22, "Unnecessary Dialog Boxes Are Evil," but let's look at one example now. If you want to search for text in a message using Microsoft Outlook, the search dialog box is incorporated directly into the window, as shown here:

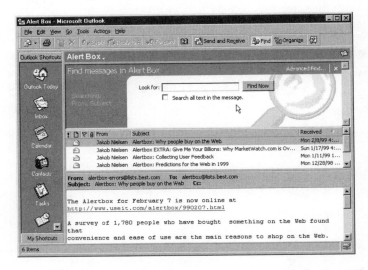

This technique eliminates the need to use a modeless dialog box and allows the user to access both the Find window and the Messages window at the same time.

If you want to make your program look like a Web site, that's fine by me, but that's not what this chapter has been about. Instead, I've emphasized that you can learn from the Web to make programs that are simpler and easier to use and features that are easier to find. While Money is clearly intended to look like a Web site, Windows Explorer, Outlook, and Outlook Express are notable in that they look like ordinary Windows programs, aside from a few details. In other words, you don't have to radically change your user interface design to learn from the Web. Instead, I've described several ways to take advantage of Web innovations while maintaining a normal Windows program appearance. More than anything else, learning from the Web requires that you change the way you think about user interfaces.

Related Chapters

- Chapter 15—Keep It Simple.

  The goal of learning from the Web is to make software simpler and easier to use. This chapter presents a Windows user interface road map that compares the various Windows user interfaces and helps you decide which one to choose, primarily with the goal of obtaining simplicity.

- Chapter 22—Unnecessary Dialog Boxes Are Evil.

  This chapter explains why unnecessary dialog boxes are undesirable, how to identify unnecessary dialog boxes, and how to eliminate them.

Recommended Reading

- Spool, Jared M.; Scanlon, Tara; Schroeder, Will; Snyder, Carolyn; and DeAngelo, Terri. *Web Site Usability: A Designer's Guide.* San Francisco, CA: Morgan Kaufmann Publishers, Inc., 1999.

  While I think learning from the Web is a good idea, you might want to make sure that you are learning the right things. In this book, Jared Spool and his associates describe performing extensive usability testing on nine different Web sites and asking users to perform four tasks at each site (although each user didn't test every site). The results contradict some widely held beliefs about Web site usability. For example, this group found that there needs to be a link between content and navigation and that shell pages that are independent of the site's contents are ineffective. The user needs a clear indication of what he is going to get before clicking a hyperlink. It also found that graphics are a neutral factor in the user's ability to perform tasks (except that users find animations to be annoying) and that users are often basically clueless about the overall structure of a site. Also, interestingly, it found that certain users don't use the Back button at all and always try to get where they want to go by going forward or returning to the home page. Finally, Web pages with little white space seem to do well. This book will help you learn from the Web because it provides research data rather than opinions and assumptions.

CHAPTER 13

C
H
A
P
T
E
R

14

Prototype
with Caution

A user interface prototype is a mock-up interface that has selected functionality designed to demonstrate how a program is going to look and behave. Its purpose is to solve specific problems and to obtain early feedback from users and other team members. Prototyping allows you to get feedback more quickly and cost effectively than normal production software.

Software prototyping is at least in part a reaction to the classic "waterfall" software development lifecycle model, which goes from requirements to specification, to design, to implementation, to testing, and then to maintenance. The problem with this lifecycle model is that it is heavily weighted to the earlier phases in the development process. There is often no visible output until late in the implementation phase. If the output of this process is found to be unacceptable, the consequences are often disastrous.

Prototyping is used to shorten this feedback loop so that users, customers, and other interested parties can determine early in the process whether the results are acceptable.

User interface prototypes exist in many forms, ranging from paper mock-ups to nearly fully functional user interfaces. But in all cases a prototype cannot be a real user interface. For a prototype to have any sort of cost or time advantage over the real user interface, it must have some significant functionality missing. While the basic user interface elements might be present, many of the details are not. If data is involved, the prototype data might not be real. Also, there might not be detailed features that help the user eliminate unnecessary effort, error messages, or advanced features. Furthermore, the prototype might not give a realistic indication of the actual performance.

I have to admit that I'm not a big fan of what is normally considered prototyping—that is, *functional prototyping,* or the creation of prototypes consisting of functional, working code. I've worked for two small start-up companies that went down the tubes, and I believe that improper functional prototyping was a major factor in the demise of each company. In both cases, what was supposed to be a prototype became the actual product. Both projects were disasters. Easily foreseeable disasters, in fact. In one case, management did realize that the prototype-based product was a serious problem, so they hit the reset button and started over. This would have been a good move, but by that time their capital (financial and otherwise) was pretty much gone. It was all spent on developing the prototype.

You can see that it's very important to have a realistic understanding of what prototyping can and cannot do. It's important to understand the potential hazards of prototyping and how to avoid them by setting proper, realistic objectives. Lastly, you need to understand that there are effective prototyping techniques that do not involve creating functional software. You should prefer these nonfunctional techniques whenever possible. Misguided prototyping can be dangerous, so be sure to prototype with caution.

The Promise of Prototyping

User interface prototyping holds many promises. User interface prototypes can help you get user feedback quickly. Prototypes allow you to try new ideas easily, without much commitment. There is little risk in creating prototypes since you can always throw them away. Most importantly, they allow you to make sure that users are satisfied with the user interface design early in the process before the real development begins. At least in theory.

The Myths of Prototyping

Unfortunately, the reality of prototyping is a bit more complicated. There are several traps with functional prototypes that a hapless software developer can easily fall into. The problem is that effective prototyping isn't as easy as it appears. Some of the myths about functional prototyping that help explain why include:

- Prototypes are easy to create and change.
- Prototypes are thrown away.
- Prototypes are designs.
- Prototypes provide good user feedback.
- Prototypes make good specifications.

Let's look at each of these problems in detail. Note that in this discussion I'm referring primarily to functional prototypes (again, prototypes consisting of functional, working code). Later in this chapter, I'll discuss other forms of prototypes, which do not involve functional code. The following problems do not necessarily apply to nonfunctional prototypes.

Prototypes Are Easy to Create and Change

Functional user interface prototypes are often justified because they are easy to create and change. Easier to create and change than what? Than fully functional production code? Perhaps, but they are not easier to create or change than paper designs. You can sketch out a window design on paper in seconds. To create the equivalent functional window design with your favorite prototyping tool will take minutes, if not hours. Of course, the more detail in the prototype, the longer it takes. I have seen people spend several months to create a prototype.

Try the following experiment: Draw a complete dialog box design on a sheet of paper. Now throw it away and do a completely different design. How do you feel? Not too bad, I assume. Now create the same dialog box using your favorite programming tool. Write whatever code it takes to make it functional. Now throw that away and implement a completely different design. Be sure to make that design functional as well. How do you feel now? Undoubtedly, you feel like you have wasted a great deal of time and effort. The extra time and effort required to program creates a sense of commitment to the design and a resistance to change. Try asking someone to completely redo a prototype that they have spent a couple weeks on and see how they react. It won't be with enthusiasm—unless they are paid by the hour.

14

C
H
A
P
T
E
R

TIP The more time and effort you spend creating a prototype, the harder it is to change—defeating the very purpose of the prototype.

Prototypes Are Thrown Away

Functional prototyping promises to be a low-risk activity because the prototype code is going to be thrown away. Its disposability allows you to cut many corners and adapt the shortest of short-term thinking. You can easily justify skipping most of the normal design process and developing horrible code for a prototype, safe in the knowledge that all that rubbish is going to be thrown away. Why spend valuable time doing things right when the prototype is headed for the trash heap anyway?

After you have made all the changes and everyone is satisfied with the results, you throw away the prototype and completely redesign and implement real production code. Well, that's the theory, but the reality is usually different. If the prototype is successful and everyone is happy, everything changes. Instead of throwing it away, why not "evolve" it into commercial code? You don't really have to start completely over, do you? After all, the project is behind schedule, and the code "almost" works. Why not fix what is wrong and move on? Whatever problems the prototype has can be fixed with a few tweaks here and there, and everything will be fine.

In marketing, the tactic of advertising one thing and selling another is known as *bait and switch,* an illegal practice that leads to criminal penalties and fines. In software development, this tactic is often known as *rapid development,* because it gives the illusion of quick progress. At least initially. When a project is under schedule pressure (and what project isn't?), the temptation to "evolve" the prototype into the end product becomes irresistible. As a result, functional prototypes are rarely thrown away.

Once this fateful decision is made, the situation don't seem so bad at first. After all, the project seems to be progressing nicely. There is plenty of software to show. But over time, you begin to discover why careful design is important. You discover that adding minor features that should be simple are in fact quite difficult. In fact, any change becomes very difficult and the initial rapid progress comes to a screeching halt. A single word describes code that was evolved from a rapidly developed prototype. That word is *dreck.* In programming, few tasks are more tedious and time-consuming than maintaining poorly designed, poorly implemented code. Ironically, this situation often happens as the result of misguided effort to achieve "rapid development."

TIP If you don't throw it away, it isn't a prototype.

Prototypes Are Designs

Some programmers like to design, but others are uncomfortable with it. They feel more comfortable holding a keyboard and mouse than a blank sheet of paper and a pencil. But all programmers like to program—that's why they are programmers. If they really liked to design, perhaps they would be designers instead. If you give a programmer a programming tool and ask him to design a user interface, the programmer is totally happy. While you might call this process designing, in reality it's programming.

Why? Because the focus is on writing code. When you are implementing code, the decisions you make are implementation decisions, not design decisions. The issues considered don't include whether the dialog box is necessary or whether the navigation to and from the dialog box works well. Rather, the issues considered are more along the lines of how to use the programming tool and how to implement the dialog box functions. The issues considered aren't what the behavior of the dialog box should be, but how to implement it. This leads us to a general conclusion: the more programlike a design is, the less effective it is as a design.

When someone presents a functional prototype to me, I too look primarily at such implementation issues. Although I should know better, the fact is that when you're looking at a functional prototype, it's difficult to consider anything other than implementation. For example, when someone asks me to check out a dialog box they've designed, I look at things like command button placement or the labels on the controls. While I would like to examine the larger design issues, often I can't. What are the user's goals in using the program? What are the goals of the program's design? What task is this dialog box for? How does the user get to the dialog box? Is using this dialog box the best way to perform that task? Who knows? I can't tell just by looking at the dialog box—I need to understand the task at hand and the program's design. If a programmer asks your opinion about a dialog box and instead you ask him all these questions, don't expect him to ask for your advice in the future. His goal is to get help implementing that dialog box, not to get a lecture about user interface design principles.

Focus on design-related issues during the design process. Design, and then implement. Don't implement, and then implement again.

CHAPTER 14

TIP

Programming is programming, not matter what you call it.

Prototypes Provide Good User Feedback

While one of the most important objectives in prototyping is to get good user feedback, the fact is that getting user feedback can be difficult to do and the results are often difficult to evaluate. There are several reasons for this. The first is that prototypes are mock-ups that must have significant functionality missing. As a result, users adjust their expectations and react to prototypes differently than to real programs. It's hard to use a mock-up exactly the same way as a real program. It's also hard to be critical of a user interface that you know is a mock-up. A user can easily explain away all minor shortcomings by thinking, "Well, this is just the prototype. All these minor problems will be fixed in the real interface." Furthermore, users don't use prototypes for long, and, because of their lack of experience, users often blame themselves for errors, instead of the prototype.

TIP

Users know that a prototype user interface isn't a real user interface, so they use it and evaluate it differently. It is harder for a user to be critical of a prototype user interface than of a real user interface.

The user needs to be able to communicate any problems or concerns that he has with the prototype. But if an interface is bad, don't expect the user to understand why or how to fix it. In fact, the user might feel embarrassed to say anything at all. I have seen prototypes that were just horrible, yet they received what could be interpreted as positive feedback. (Part of the reason this occurred was that the entire program was prototyped and evaluated as a whole. Had the prototype focused on individual tasks, its failure would have been much more obvious.) The effectiveness of prototype evaluation cannot be taken for granted. To find many types of problems, you need to test real software with real data on real tasks with real problems. I discussed these prototyping problems in detail in Chapter 8, "Users Aren't Designers."

Prototypes Make Good Specifications

Suppose up to now that you have done everything right. You have created a real functional prototype that you are actually going to throw away. During the process, you focused on design issues, not implementation issues. You developed it quickly, and you were able to get excellent user feedback and make appropriate changes to satisfy everyone. Now what? You now have to turn the prototype into a software design. But you can't just hand a prototype to a team of programmers (often referred to as *throwing it over the wall*) and say, "Here, implement this, only do it the right way—with plenty of design and all that." You need to provide much more information than just the prototype.

Again, the problem is that prototypes are mock-up user interfaces with significant functionality missing. You need to interpret the prototype. You need to indicate which parts of the prototype are intentional and which parts are arbitrary. You need to specify which parts need to be changed and which parts are missing. In fact, what you really need to do is create a complete design document. The prototype itself is not a good specification.

TIP You need to interpret a prototype by creating a design document.

Avoid Vaporware—
The Prototype of Doom

As I've said, a prototype is a prototype only if it is thrown away. When a functional prototype starts to have a life of its own, you know you're in trouble. Always be aware of the motivation behind a functional prototype. If the motivation really is to resolve a user interface design issue that cannot be resolved any other way, then sure, make a functional prototype. But if the motivation is something else, such as making the project look further along than it is or giving marketing demos, you are in trouble. You are going down a dangerous path.

Suppose management or marketing comes to you and says something like "A customer is coming in next Tuesday. Can we add this one feature to the prototype to show them what the product is going to look like? We'd also like to show the prototype at the trade show next month. We just need to show a little progress." When this happens, a light should start flashing and an alarm should sound, saying "Warning! Dangerous vaporware! Leave the area immediately!" The problem is that once you begin on this path it's difficult to stop. There are always more customers. There is always another trade show. The next thing you know, the prototype is the product. You have been sucked into the vaporware tar pit up to your neck, there is no way out. The product is doomed.

CHAPTER 14

> **TIP** Avoid dangerous vaporware. Never prototype to give someone the impression that a program is further along than it actually is. Never prototype to make marketing demos. Prototypes are for design, not for marketing.

The Goals of Prototyping

Most problems with prototyping stem from having the wrong goals or motivations. The odds of successful prototyping improve significantly if you have practical, realistic goals and use a prototyping technique that can accomplish these goals. Let's look at some good and bad reasons to prototype.

Good Reasons to Prototype

I consider the following to be good reasons to prototype:

- **To resolve problems** You need to understand and resolve a specific user interface problem.
- **To visualize a design** You need to visualize a specific user interface design.
- **To help communicate a design** You need help to communicate a complex or unusual user interface design.
- **To obtain immediate feedback** You need to obtain immediate feedback from users and other team members about a specific design problem.
- **To design task flow** You need to analyze the flow between the different user interface windows in a task and understand how the user will navigate between the windows in a task and between tasks. You might also need to determine whether the user is able to discover if a feature exists.
- **To create a radically new design** You need to create a completely different user interface design that uses new, nonstandard controls or new forms of user interaction. The more leading-edge your interface is, the more you need to prototype.

These goals have several attributes in common. The first is that there needs to be a specific objective—usually a specific design problem to be solved, a lesson to be learned, or a solution to be discovered. You shouldn't prototype for the sake of prototyping but instead to accomplish something specific. The second is that these goals do not necessarily require a functional prototype. You can use a nonfunctional prototype to solve problems, to visualize interfaces, or to communicate. Lastly, there is usually no need to prototype the entire user interface. You should prototype just enough to accomplish the goal at hand.

Sure, sometimes a full-blown, functional prototype that covers the entire user interface is warranted. If I were responsible for designing the next generation of the Microsoft Windows user interface, I would have no trouble justifying extensive prototyping of all the new user interface elements and the major system components. Without hesitation—no questions asked. After all, everything is new, the stakes are high, and the budget is there. But situations like this are relatively rare. Most programs simply don't have the type of problems that warrant such extensive prototyping. Rather, they have specific problems that justify specific prototyping.

Bad Reasons to Prototype

I consider the following to be poor reasons to prototype:

- **To simulate progress**   The worst reason to prototype is to give someone the impression that that the program is further along than it actually is. Functional prototypes are an excellent way to fake progress.

- **To create marketing demos**   If your marketing team asks you to create a prototype so that they can give a dog and pony show, recommend that they give a Microsoft PowerPoint presentation instead.

- **To adhere to a rigid design process**   You have a design process where prototyping is always required, regardless of the need for it.

Prototyping Success Factors

For a prototype to be effective, the following must be true:

- The prototype must have significant functionality missing. If the prototype is fully functional, it isn't really a prototype.

- The prototype must be easily disposable. If you are reluctant to throw it away, it's not a good prototype.

- The value of a prototype must exceed its cost.

- The prototype must have clear, realistic goals.

CHAPTER 14

If you write a program that is fully functional and you don't throw it away, it isn't a prototype—by definition. Regardless of what you call it or what you think it is, it is in reality production code. Furthermore, prototyping is essentially an economic activity. The only reason to prototype is to save time and money. Consequently, an effective prototype must save more time and money than it costs to create. This is where ineffective prototyping efforts usually fail. Lastly, the prototype must have clear, realistic goals, such as any of the goals I mentioned earlier. Specific task-oriented prototypes are much more likely to produce useful information than unbounded prototypes. For a prototype to be effective, make sure you have a good reason for doing it.

My Favorite Prototyping Techniques

A wide spectrum of activities can be called prototyping. Not all of them involve writing functional code. In fact, none of my favorite prototyping techniques require writing any significant code at all. This makes the prototypes easy to create and change, easy to throw away, easy to focus on specific design problems, and cost-effective. They are also 100 percent vaporware-proof.

Here they are, in my order of preference.

Prototyping by Example

What I call *prototyping by example* (or *by pattern,* if you prefer) involves designing a user interface by modeling program features after characteristics of existing programs. This technique is also called *competitive analysis.* The characteristics of the existing programs allow you to evaluate and test their appearance, behavior, and overall usability in an efficient, cost-effective manner because the working code already exists. Furthermore, testing an existing, fully functional program is more realistic and enlightening than testing a partially functional prototype.

Of course, it is important that any models you choose are appropriate for your program. A user interface from a game is likely to be a poor model for a business application. And an interface from a utility designed for beginners will most likely be a poor model for an application intended for advanced users. In Chapter 7, I point out that Windows Explorer is likely to be a bad design model for utilities since its usage pattern is different from most other utilities.

Suppose you want to design a user interface for an audio CD player utility. There are dozens of such utilities in existence. Instead of designing everything from scratch, you could review as many of these programs as you can and analyze what you like and don't like about them. You might decide you like the convenience of one program, the look of another, and the functionality of another still.

While competitive programs often have the most similar interface ideas to what you need, you can employ user interface ideas from practically any program, even programs from other platforms. Look at other successful programs for guidance. You might choose to model a program's preview functionality after features found in Microsoft Word. You might want to consider using some of the direct manipulation techniques found in Microsoft Outlook. You can even cobble together bits and pieces of existing user interfaces to create a totally new concept.

An example of a user interface model that has been reused in many user interfaces is the classic Macintosh Font/DA Mover utility interface:

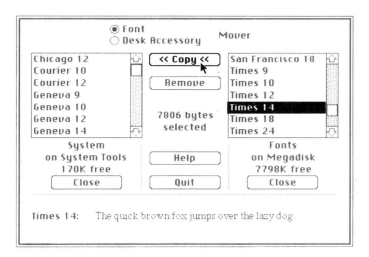

Does this look familiar? This is a user interface design pattern that has launched a thousand clones. It allows users to select which fonts and desk accessories they want to use from a list of available choices. Today countless user interfaces are patterned after this utility, such as the Customize Toolbar dialog box (shown on the following page) that is built into Windows.

CHAPTER 14

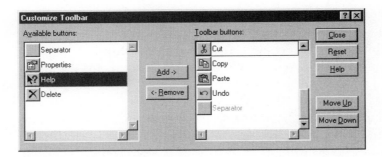

This prototyping technique allows you to design a user interface based on existing user interfaces that are known to be effective. You don't have to write any code to visualize them, to communicate them, to get feedback about them, or to determine their usability. You just have to say something like "Let's pattern the script editor after the Font/DA Mover, but let's also support drag and drop editing." If everyone agrees, your work is done and you can move on to the next design problem. (Of course, you might also have to give a demo if nobody knows what the Font/DA Mover is.)

This is not a suggestion to steal anyone's copyrighted software. Rather, the goal is to collect, evaluate, analyze, and compare ideas and gather inspiration from the user interface elements of existing programs. The user interface you create should be a result of your own interpretation of these patterns, with your own innovations and improvements. There are plenty of good user interface design models out there. Why reinvent the wheel?

Use prototyping by example to design new user interfaces by modeling them after appropriate user interface elements of existing programs.

Paper Prototypes

If you need to create a new design, usually the best way to do it is on paper. After all, paper and pencil are the most powerful, efficient design tools available. Paper prototypes are easy to create, easy to modify, and easy to throw away. Paper prototypes are effective in designing window layouts, menus, dialog boxes, and other user interface elements, as well as the navigation between windows. Anyone can create a paper prototype since it doesn't require any special skills. Best of all, paper prototypes force you to focus on high-level design. When using another design tool, you are often focused on using the features of the tool—for example, getting the control sizes exactly right and making sure the buttons are aligned. Design details like precise control sizes and alignment clearly aren't relevant to a paper prototype and receive no unwanted attention.

TIP Paper and pencil are the most powerful, efficient design tools available. Use paper prototypes to create new designs.

Interestingly, software development is the only engineering field where sketching out design ideas on paper is referred to as prototyping. In all other fields, this activity is just a normal part of design. For example, in architecture, a blueprint design is not considered a prototype. The distinction between a paper design and a paper prototype is that a paper prototype is intended for user testing whereas a regular paper design is not. In fact, paper prototypes intended for user testing try to simulate a working program by having each screen (that is, window, dialog box, menus, combo box, and so on) on a separate piece of paper so that a user can actually perform tasks with the prototype. You have to act as the computer to display the appropriate screen based on user actions.

It is harder to misinterpret a paper prototype than a functional prototype. Nobody expects the controls to line up perfectly or even the text to be spelled correctly. Fonts and colors aren't issues. Nobody can be confused in determining what is intentional and what is arbitrary. Only the core ideas in a paper prototype are intentional—all the concrete details are arbitrary. In fact, the sloppiness of a typical paper prototype is one of its strengths, since it forces you to judge it by its design merits and not by its visual appearance. On the other hand, a poor design created with a good design tool might have an excellent visual appearance, making its usability flaws harder to see.

As I discussed earlier, people are reluctant to change a functional prototype. Just the opposite is true with paper. Even if you come up with something on paper that appears to be a very good design, few people will resist putting it aside, at least momentarily, and looking for alternative designs. After all, you are just dealing with paper. You can try a more spacious layout and then try a more compact one. You can completely rearrange the flow of the window. You can try to eliminate controls that might be unnecessary. You can even try to find ways to eliminate the window altogether. Best of all, you can do all of this in a matter of minutes. Paper prototyping allows you to do whatever you want without fooling around.

14 CHAPTER

The ability to easily change paper prototypes makes user testing more effective as well. You can incorporate user suggestions and make other changes on the spot. Users are more willing to make suggestions because they understand that paper designs, unlike functional prototypes, are preliminary and easy to change. Their feedback is likely to be more honest and direct. And they are more willing to say that they don't like the user interface at all if it is on paper, which is something they might feel reluctant to say about working code.

Scenarios

Another effective technique is to prototype tasks using scenarios. The idea is to describe a specific task and walk through how the user is to perform that task. Depending upon the situation, either you do the walk-through (for a design meeting or a customer presentation) or the user can do the walk-through (for user testing). In either case, the person doing the walking needs to verbalize his thoughts (which is called *thinking out loud*) so that everyone knows what is going on. You can use whatever means you have at your disposal for walking through the task, including paper prototypes, resource prototypes (as discussed below), functional prototypes, or even whiteboard drawings. The specific media don't matter as long as the prototype is easy to create, change, view, and save. The objective is simply to walk through the important program tasks and make sure that the proposed user interface supports them in an acceptable manner. Such task analysis does not require functional code.

TIP   Use scenarios to prototype specific tasks.

Resource Prototypes

I also really like to create what I call *resource prototypes*. Using only program resources, you can design windows, menus, toolbars, bitmaps, icons, and dialog boxes. If you want, you can also use a small amount of code to glue everything together to show how the user navigates from window to window. The ability to go back and forth between windows is the prototype's only functionality.

Using resource prototypes has many advantages. They are easy to create and change, since the resource-editing tools in Microsoft Visual C++ and Microsoft Visual Basic are quite productive. They are easy to throw away because nothing of value needs to be thrown away. You can keep the resources, since an acceptable resource is an acceptable resource. Any glue

PART

code you create is so simple that it isn't worth keeping. Since you aren't creating a functional prototype, all the focus is on design. And lastly, since the results are nonfunctional, there is no danger of vaporware exposure.

Every screen shot in this book of a dialog box that isn't from an existing program is a resource prototype with absolutely no code behind it. Not one line of code. All the dialog box screen shots were captured while in Test mode in the Visual C++ resource editor. I did have to program the menu screen shots, but only because there isn't a test mode for menus in the Visual C++ resource editor. Although I didn't create any property sheet screen shots, I would have had to write some code for them as well.

TIP Use resource prototypes to create nonfunctional prototype programs without writing any code.

Are there disadvantages to using resource prototypes? A couple. They are clearly inappropriate if you want to test actual functionality, since they don't have any. To evaluate a resource prototype with users, you pretty much have to talk users through the program, since they can't do anything with the prototype on their own. Because of this, I find that resource prototypes work especially well with scenarios. Lastly, there is a risk of misusing resource prototypes. If you find yourself focusing on minor details such as control sizes and locations and not on more critical design issues like usability, you should probably use paper prototypes instead.

These four prototyping techniques allow you to accomplish the goals of prototyping in a way that steers clear of the hazards of prototyping. They are all nonfunctional and do not require you to write any code, and they are effective in achieving the goals of prototyping in that they are easy to create and change, easy to throw away, focused on specific design problems, and cost-effective. I find them so natural that I don't really consider them to be prototyping at all. I consider them to be part of the normal design process.

Make sure you have the right prototyping goals and are using the right prototyping technique. Time spent building the wrong prototype is still time wasted.

TIP Prefer nonfunctional prototypes. Avoid writing prototype code.

CHAPTER 14

Functional Prototyping

If your prototyping goals are such that only a functional prototype will do, you are going to have to write some code. Again, you need to have proper, realistic, specific goals for creating your prototype. For a functional prototype, you should try to accomplish your goals by writing as little code as possible. Restraint is essential. Consider establishing a strict time limit for the creation of a functional prototype, such as a week at most. Unbounded functional prototypes rarely have benefits that justify their costs. The best way to get useful information from functional prototyping is through user testing, as described in Chapter 27.

There are two basic types of functional prototypes. A horizontal prototype implements most of the major functionality but with very little depth. Such a prototype gives a good feel for what the appearance of the program as a whole will look like, but the individual features might lack significant functionality if they work at all. By contrast, a vertical prototype implements enough features to perform a single task or a small set of tasks but doesn't attempt to implement the remainder of the program. Such a prototype gives an accurate model of the ability to perform those tasks but little else. Of course, it is possible to combine these techniques and create a horizontal prototype with enough features implemented to perform a few tasks.

TIP If you must create a functional prototype, try to implement as little functionality as you can. Create either a horizontal or vertical prototype and establish a strict time limit.

Visual Basic vs. Visual C++

What tool should you use for making functional prototypes or resource prototypes? As a Windows programmer, you are most likely using either Visual C++ or Visual Basic for your main programming tool, so I would recommend using these tools for prototyping as well. Many people immediately think of Visual Basic when they think of prototyping, since it has a reputation of being an effective prototyping tool. After all, Visual Basic programs are developed by creating the user interfaces first and then writing the code, so programming in Visual Basic forces you to put the user interface ahead of the underlying code. Visual Basic also frees you wasting time compiling and linking and will not let code be changed while the program is running.

PART

However, I wouldn't automatically recommend using Visual Basic as a prototyping tool. Instead, I would recommend using the tool you are most familiar with. Using the most familiar tool has two advantages:

● One of the keys to success in prototyping is to save time and effort. If you feel more comfortable using a certain tool, you will be more productive using that tool for prototyping.

● Prototypes created with a tool tend to look like they were created using that tool. If you program using Visual C++, there is no point in jumping through hoops just to make the results look like a Visual Basic program. For this reason, I consider using HTML inappropriate for designing anything other than Web pages.

For my personal use, I believe using Visual C++ for prototyping has additional advantages over using Visual Basic. I usually make resource prototypes, so the ability to write code quickly isn't an advantage. In fact, I think it is a disadvantage, since it might give me the temptation to write code. If I do decide to write prototype code, it is usually only enough to glue the various resources together to show the program navigation—the Visual C++ AppWizard and ClassWizard tools help do this quickly.

Note that if you do create a resource prototype using Visual Basic and want to implement the program using Visual C++, you don't have to start completely over. Rather, you can import Visual Basic forms and icons into Visual C++ by using the Resource command from the Insert menu. In the Insert Resource dialog box, select the Import command, and then select a Visual Basic form or icon. Using this command to import Visual Basic resources can save a lot of time.

Related Chapters

● Chapter 8—Users Aren't Designers.
Describes user-centered design and some of the problems of using prototypes in the design process.

● Chapter 27—User Testing.
Describes how to perform user testing and gives a specific procedure to make sure you get good feedback.

CHAPTER 14

Recommended Reading

- Arlov, Laura. *GUI Design for Dummies*. Foster City, CA: IDG Books Worldwide, Inc., 1997.

  Chapter 6, "How Users Get Around: Navigation Models," describes using prototyping to design navigation models and the benefits of using paper prototypes.

- Cooper, Alan. "The Perils of Prototyping." *Visual Basic Programmer's Journal*, August/September 1994.

  In this article, Alan Cooper, "the father of Visual Basic," concludes that Visual Basic should not be the mother of all prototypes. He believes that paper and pencil are a superior design tool. As he states, "Everyone knows that Visual Basic is a great tool for prototyping, so many VB programmers design user interfaces by prototyping them. They are misinterpreting programming for design, and make no mistake about it: prototyping is programming and it is harder than concrete to change." I agree.

- Dent, Andy. "Paper Prototypes." *Windows Tech Journal*, June 1997.

  Discusses the advantages of paper prototyping and describes a design process that uses paper prototypes.

- Nielsen, Jakob. *Usability Engineering*. Chestnut Hill, MA: AP Professional, 1993.

  Chapter 4, "The Usability Engineering Lifecycle," presents several different prototyping techniques and ways to evaluate them. The prototyping techniques discussed include horizontal and vertical functional prototypes, scenarios, and competitive analysis. The chapter also describes the problem of using a prototype as a specification. Chapter 6, "Usability Testing," describes the difficulty of evaluating prototype test results and the difficulty of getting suitable test users.

- Weinschenk, Susan; Jamar, Pamela; and Yeo, Sarah C. *GUI Design Essentials*. New York, NY: John Wiley & Sons, Inc., 1997.

  Chapter 3, "Design," presents a detailed design process that uses prototyping. I especially like the fact that the authors recommend using a paper prototype (or a "lo-fi" prototype, as they call it) in the design phase.

15

Keep It Simple

Keep it simple. Now there's an original idea! While "keep it simple" is a well-established design cliché, I believe that simplicity is the most important quality of good user interface design. While saying that it's important to keep your user interfaces simple might seem a bit, well, simplistic, much of the user interface development process involves simplifying and refining the interface in some way. Refinement has been defined as the process of obtaining simplicity. Typical user interface refinements include eliminating unnecessary screen clutter; eliminating unnecessary features; eliminating unnecessary windows, dialog boxes, or message boxes; and simplifying how the user interacts with the program. Remember—no bad user interface has ever been made into a good interface by adding stuff.

TIP Simplicity is the most important quality of good user interface design. Much of the user interface development process involves simplifying the interface in some way.

A Windows Interface Road Map

One interesting characteristic of Microsoft Windows is that it provides such rich user interface functionality that often you can implement a user interface feature in several different ways. It's a useful exercise to lay out the various options and to understand the relationships between them. This knowledge will help you understand your options and help you make the right choices when simplifying your user interfaces. Very often the difference between a simple user interface and a complex one lies in making the right choices among these options.

 TIP Windows typically allows you to implement a user interface feature in several different ways. Often the difference between a simple user interface and a complex one lies in making the right choices among these options.

Primary Windows

Several types of primary windows are commonly found in Windows programs, including the following.

Single-document interface (SDI) window

An SDI window is a single primary window, with possibly a menu bar, toolbar, and status bar. This approach is simple and is suitable for both applications and utilities. Since there's a one-to-one relationship between a document and its window, an SDI program is easy to understand and manage. A good example is the Microsoft WordPad program.

Split single-document interface (split SDI) window

A split SDI window includes a single primary window and a window splitter, with possibly a menu bar, toolbar, and status bar. This approach is also simple and is suitable for both applications and utilities. The splitter gives you additional flexibility to add a second view of a document or a tree view or a list view to control the contents of the document window. The one-to-one relationship between a document and its window makes a split SDI program easy to understand and manage. Good examples are Windows Explorer and Microsoft Internet Explorer. In fact, this style window is sometimes referred to as an Explorer-style interface.

 PART
III

238

Multiple-document interface (MDI) window

An MDI window includes a collection of any number of document windows within a single frame, almost always with a menu bar, toolbar, and status bar. MDI applications often also have docking windows. This approach is fairly complex and is suitable only for applications. The biggest problem with an MDI application is simply the fact that the user has to manage all of these windows. Also, there's no clear relationship between documents and windows, especially if the user can display multiple windows containing the same document. Good MDI examples are Microsoft Word and Microsoft Visual C++. While it's fashionable to suggest that there are better (that is, more document-centric) alternatives to MDI, such as workspaces, workbooks, and projects, I don't buy it. The fact is that for complex applications like Microsoft Excel and Visual C++, MDI works well.

Dialog box window

A dialog box window is a dialog box used as the primary window, possibly with a menu bar and status bar. A dialog box program is typically used to view or change some values—no document is involved in the usual sense. This approach is simple and is suitable for utilities. Good examples are the Windows Find utility and the Calculator utility.

Secondary Windows

Secondary windows are used to provide information or supplemental interaction to the primary window. Of course, your interface will be simpler with fewer secondary windows, and your first choice should be to eliminate the need for secondary windows when possible. For example, Chapters 22 and 23 present many suggestions on how to eliminate unnecessary dialog boxes and message boxes. The most common forms of secondary windows follow.

Modal dialog boxes

A modal dialog box is a modal secondary window used to collect additional information from the user. Because the dialog box is modal, the user cannot use the primary window until the dialog box has been dismissed.

Modeless dialog boxes

A modeless dialog box is a modeless secondary window typically used to help the user interact with the primary window. Modeless dialog boxes are fairly awkward, since it is difficult to position them without having them in the way. Consequently, modeless dialog boxes are rarely used today and toolbars, docking windows, and palette windows are used in their place.

CHAPTER 15

Convertible dialog boxes

A convertible dialog box is a secondary window that the user can make either modal or modeless, often by clicking on a "push-pin" button. For example, the Visual C++ resource properties dialog boxes are convertible. This type of dialog box is a good choice when either mode makes sense. It lets the user decide.

TIP A convertible dialog box is a good choice when either the modal or modeless state makes sense. It lets the user decide.

Toolbars

A toolbar is a modeless dockable frame that contains a set of controls, often buttons and combo boxes, that are typically used to issue commands and set options. Toolbars are functionally equivalent to modeless dialog boxes but are far more convenient since they don't obscure the document window. For example, Visual C++ supports text searching through both a modal dialog box and a set of toolbar controls. There is nothing you can do with a modeless text search dialog box that you can't do with a search toolbar.

Docking windows

A docking window is a modeless dockable frame that contains any type of controls or information. Docking windows are similar to toolbars except that they are larger and they are not used primarily to issue commands.

Palette windows

A palette window is a modeless floating secondary window typically used to help the user interact with the primary window. While palette windows are similar to modeless dialog boxes, they have a smaller caption bar and typically contain only a small set of nonstatic controls. Palette windows are often obtained by undocking toolbars.

Commands and Options

Giving commands and selecting options are two frequent user activities. The most common techniques for presenting commands and options follow.

Menu bars

Menu bars are used to present most of the commands and high-level options available in a program. Users can quickly determine what a program does simply by scanning through the menus. This technique makes menus an excellent teaching tool for beginning users.

Buttons

Note that there is a strong relationship between buttons and menus. For example, this menu:

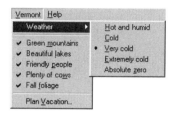

is functionally equivalent to this dialog box:

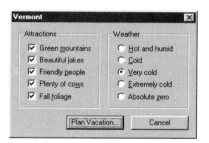

In fact, both approaches result in the same WM_COMMAND messages being sent to the appropriate window.

Programmers often try to simplify their interfaces by using buttons instead of menus. If there are only a few commands, this approach is effective because all the options are displayed right in front of the user, so the user doesn't have to hunt for the right menu item. However, this technique works with only about eight or fewer buttons.* (You can, however, get away with many more buttons if there is an obvious relationship between them—the Calculator utility is a good example.) With too many buttons, this becomes a poor trade-off since the user is overwhelmed with screen clutter and will have trouble finding anything. In this case, a better approach is to place the most common commands on the screen using buttons and place all the infrequently used commands in the menu bar. The Find Utility on the following page is a good example of this technique.

---

* Miller, George A. "The magical number seven, plus or minus two: Some limits on our capacity for processing information." *The Psychological Review* (1956), 63, 81–97.

CHAPTER 15

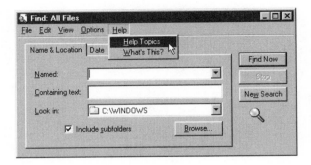

Context menus

Context menus are displayed when you right-click an item that has a context menu. Context menus are an excellent way of simplifying the presentation of commands and options. Since you can gather all the commands and options relevant to an object in a context menu, you can sometimes simplify the structure of the menu bar. Windows Explorer is an excellent example of this technique. Note how simple Windows Explorer's menu bar is, given the amount of functionality this program provides.

The problem with context menus is that they're not visible. You can't tell if an object has a context menu just by looking at it. You have to know to right-click the item to see whether there is a menu. This problem makes context menus a poor choice for programs that are targeted at beginning users. While a program aimed at beginners can use context menus, such programs should always provide alternative methods visible on the screen. As a result, Windows Explorer presents the most commonly used commands on the toolbar in addition to the context menu.

Context menus aren't visible, making them a poor choice for programs that are targeted at beginning users.

Toolbars

Toolbars are an excellent technique to simplify the user interaction required to give a command or select an option. They offer the simplicity and visibility of buttons but eliminate the screen clutter. However, toolbars are most effective once the user has experience with a program. Typically, a user learns how to use a program first by using the menu bar and then graduates to the toolbar once he feels more comfortable. Given the amount of time users spend with applications compared to utilities, toolbars are most effective with applications, since this graduation process is less likely to happen with utilities. Note that few of the utilities that come with Windows 98 use toolbars.

PART

Keyboard commands

The keyboard is still a good way to give commands and select options. This is by far the most efficient technique if the user knows the keyboard shortcut and already has his hands on the keyboard. All programs should support the standard key assignments discussed in *Designing for the User Experience*. Programs should also have shortcut keys assigned for the most common commands and options. Using the keyboard greatly simplifies the effort required by intermediate and advanced users.

Control Grouping in Dialog Boxes

Organizing related controls into clearly related groups is one of the best ways to simplify an interface. It's important to understand that you don't have to display everything in a single dialog box. The technique of presenting information only as it is needed is called *progressive disclosure*. The most common techniques for grouping controls in dialog boxes follow.

Property sheets

Property sheets have done wonders in simplifying complex dialog boxes. Instead of cramming dozens of controls into a single dialog box or having complex and confusing multiple dialog box sequences, property sheets allow you to consolidate a significant number of controls into a single dialog box in a way that is still quite usable. The only potential problem with property sheets is using too many tabs. Two rows of tabs, as shown here in the Options dialog box in Microsoft Word, is about the limit for tabs.

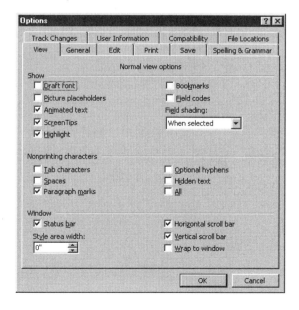

CHAPTER 15

Another approach is to use scroll bars to allow the user to scroll the tabs. While this approach eliminates screen clutter, it makes it difficult to find a tab. Perhaps the best solution to this problem is to consolidate several categories of settings on a single tab, as in this example from Visual C++.

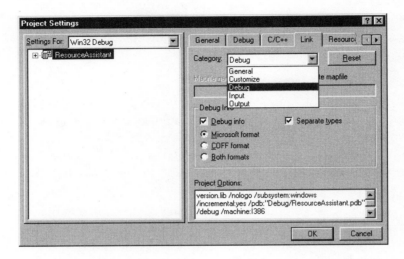

Using hierarchical property sets is a good way to reduce the number of tabs while still making it easy to find settings without much effort. Note how awkward it would be to have multiple link tabs, such as "Link—General," "Link—Custom," and so on.

Should you ever use a property sheet with a single tab? If you are using a property sheet to display an object's properties and not using it as a dialog box with tabs, then yes. Always use property sheets for properties, even if there is only a single property page. Using a property sheet makes it clear that the user is viewing properties and not a regular dialog box. A property sheet (like the one on the following page) has an Apply button to help the user experiment with property settings.

Group boxes

Group boxes are used to group related controls within a dialog box or a property page. While group boxes are traditionally used to group radio buttons, they can be used to group any type of control, such as the Debug Info in the Visual C++ Project Settings dialog box shown earlier.

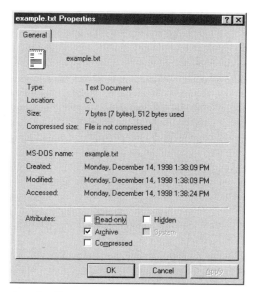

Static lines and text

One problem with group boxes is that they can add too much complexity to a dialog box if there are too many of them because they take up a fair amount of space and can increase the clutter. A good alternative is to group controls using a combination of static text and a static line (actually a static frame with a height of one dialog box unit). The Options dialog box in Microsoft Word, shown on page 243, is a good example. This technique also works well to organize groups of controls within a group box.

TIP Static lines and text are a good alternative to group boxes because they don't take up as much space and don't add to the clutter.

Dynamic dialog boxes

Dynamic (or unfolding) dialog boxes initially display only the most essential information and give the user a command to use to see more advanced information. The size of a dynamic dialog box changes to display the selected level of information. Dynamic dialog boxes are becoming less common as property sheets are often used instead. A good example is the Color common dialog box, which unfolds when the user clicks the Define Custom Colors button. Note that using a property sheet would not be appropriate in this case because a custom color is not an independent property.

Cascading dialog boxes

Just because you can use a property sheet doesn't mean you can't have a dialog box display another dialog box. Sometimes the best way to group controls available through a dialog box is to put them in a separate dialog box. This is especially true if the controls are used for a task that isn't often performed.

Menu Item Groupings

Organizing clearly related menu items into groups can greatly simplify menus. The following are some of the most common techniques for grouping menu items.

Menu separators

Menu separators are used to group related menu items. While this technique is simple and effective, the only trick is to make sure you don't use too many separators. Avoid creating several groups with only one item in them. For example, the File menu from Microsoft Word, shown below, has Send To and Properties in the same group even though they are unrelated. Together, they are kind of a related group of unrelated items.

Cascading menus

Cascading menus are another effective technique for grouping related menu items. Cascading menus are best used to allow the selection of one of a related set of options. Since cascading menus can be difficult to use, you should avoid employing them for frequently used commands and try to limit them to one or, at most, two levels of submenus.

Dialog boxes

If your menu structure is too complex, you might need to move some of the commands into a dialog box. As discussed earlier, a strong relationship exists between dialog box controls and menus. If your menu structure is simple, use the menus to eliminate unnecessary dialog boxes. If your menu structure is complex, you should favor dialog boxes.

Single-Choice Selection

You can present the user with a single choice in a set of mutually exclusive choices in several ways. The trade-off between these approaches involves the amount of effort required to make the choice and the amount of screen space employed to present the choices.

Radio buttons

Radio buttons should be your preferred technique for presenting the user with a single-choice selection. Radio buttons work well when you have a small set of options, typically eight or fewer, and a dialog box that isn't too cluttered. If the dialog box is cluttered, a combo box is usually better, even with only two or three options.

Combo boxes

Combo boxes allow you to present the user with a nearly unlimited number of choices in a compact form. If only a few choices are available, be sure to make the drop-down list long enough so that the user doesn't have to scroll to make a selection. The only drawback to using a combo box is that it requires the user to take an additional step to see the selections. This makes combo boxes less desirable than radio buttons in situations where user efficiency is most important.

Single-selection lists

Single-selection lists are also a possibility but are used less often because they take up a fair amount of screen space. Lists are preferable to combo boxes when it is desirable for the user to always be able to see the list of selections or when the user is constantly changing the selection. A good example, as shown on the following page, is the Category list on the Format tab of the Visual C++ Options dialog box.

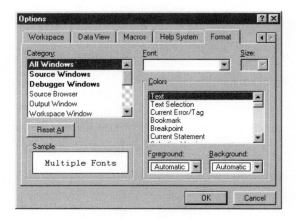

Note that combo boxes could be used in place of the Category and Colors lists, but this would result in the user constantly having to drop down the combo boxes to make selections.

Multiple-Choice Selection

To present the user with multiple choices in a set of nonexclusive choices, you also have several approaches you can take. Again, the trade-off between these approaches involves the amount of effort required to make the choices and the amount of screen space used. Note that there is no such thing as a multiple-choice combo box.

Check boxes

Check boxes should be your preferred technique for presenting the user with a multiple-choice selection. Check boxes work well when you have a small set of options in an uncluttered dialog box. If the dialog box is cluttered, a check box list is probably better.

Multiple-selection lists

A multiple-selection list is a possibility whenever you need to present a set of related choices that is so large it needs to be displayed in a scrollable list. The problem with multiple-selection lists is that they aren't visible—the user can't tell that the list supports multiple selection just by looking at it. This problem is solved with check box lists.

Check box lists

A check box list is the best alternative when you have too many choices to use check boxes. A good example is the Advanced tab of the Internet Explorer Internet Options dialog box.

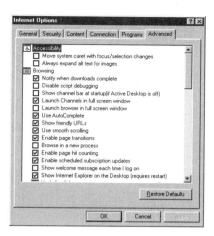

Note that a check box list is not a standard list format. You need to use an owner-draw list box control, the MFC CCheckListBox class, or the new Internet Explorer 4.0 ListView control with the LVS_EX_CHECKBOXES style.

Simplifying Window and Dialog Box Layout

You can simplify the appearance of windows and dialog boxes by applying the following layout rules.

Consistency

A window's layout should be consistent with itself, the program, and Windows standards. For example, while an individual dialog box might appear simple by itself, it adds complexity if its style is significantly different from all other dialog boxes in the program. If many dialog boxes share the same controls, try to give the controls the same name, size, location, and meaning. Of course, when controls have different meanings, make that clear by varying their appearance so that they aren't easily confused. Applying a consistent layout to controls with different meanings will mislead users.

Flow

Window layout should flow from left to right and from top to bottom. More important information should appear on the top and left, less important information on the right and bottom.

Grouping

You should try to group related items by using property sheets, group boxes, and cascading dialog boxes. Grouping related items reduces complexity by allowing the user to understand the controls as a group.

Grid

Groups of items should be organized according to some kind of grid. Using a grid simplifies the interface's appearance by providing organization and making it easier for the user to understand the relationship between items. Grids can be symmetrical, but asymmetric grids work just as well, as you can see here.

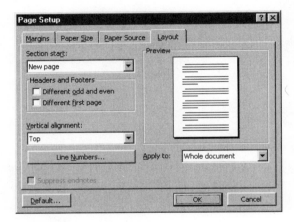

Alignment

Except for numeric text and main command buttons, items should be left-aligned. Numeric text should be decimally aligned or right-aligned, and main command buttons in dialog boxes should be right-aligned, not centered.

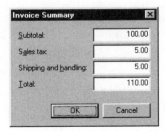

PART

III

White Space

Using white space creates "breathing room" that makes window layout easier to understand and more comfortable to view. A window jam-packed with controls can be intimidating. The spacing should appear more or less balanced and even, with no awkward gaps.

Progressive Disclosure

Progressive disclosure is the technique of presenting information only as it is needed. Place complex, advanced, or rarely used activities in separate dialog boxes. This simplifies the remaining activities and makes them easier to lay out.

Simplifying Menu Layout

You can simplify the appearance of menus by applying the following layout rules.

Consistency

Menu layout should be consistent with itself (including the menu bar and context menus), the program, and Windows standards. Use the standard menu names, and put menu items in the standard locations. For example, printing commands should go in the File menu and help commands should go in the Help menu, even if you can make a good case for putting them elsewhere. You should follow the conventions to match your users' expectations.

Flow

More important commands should appear at the top of the menu, less important commands at the bottom.

Grouping

Put related items in the same menu, and group related menu items by using separators and cascading menus. Avoid having several groups with only one item in them. Grouping related menu items reduces complexity by allowing the user to quickly perceive the items as a group.

Simplifying Appearance

When it comes to the elements that create your user interface's appearance, you can definitely have too much of a good thing. You should use restraint in designing your program's appearance. Try to limit the use of color, multiple fonts, and three-dimensional effects. Avoid unnecessarily distracting

CHAPTER 15

graphics and icons, and use animation sparingly. Note that most of these ideas are routinely violated by poorly designed Web sites. The designers of these sites must think that users find such effects attractive and that the effects will make them want to come back. But they are mistaken—such sites usually repulse viewers.

Unnecessary Three-Dimensional Effects

Take a look at the new 2-D–style toolbar (sometimes called a coolbar) used in Windows Explorer and Internet Explorer. By default, the toolbar is completely monochrome, which eliminates distraction and gives the program a cleaner and simpler appearance. As you move the mouse over a toolbar button, the button is highlighted with a 3-D border and its icon becomes colored. This technique creates the same visual impact as full-time 3-D borders and colored icons but without the distraction. Consider the alternative. While toolbars are clearly a good feature, a toolbar with permanently colored icons can be a distracting element in the program using it, attracting your attention while you struggle to keep your eyes on the document you're working on.

A common trap programmers fall into is using too many 3-D effects in their interfaces. After all, if some 3-D effects are cool, a lot of 3-D should be really cool, right? Not exactly. Look at the following dialog box.

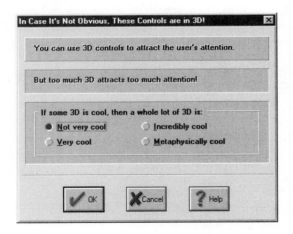

Definitely not cool. Once 3-D controls caught on, it seemed as if absolutely everything that could be 3-D was made 3-D, whether it looked good or not. Even 3-D borders were given 3-D borders just to drive the point home. Using a lot of 3-D static frame controls is usually a bad sign. The modern trend is toward a much simpler style.

A Muted Palette

When used properly, color can add a great amount of style to your program. When misused, color can make your program look ugly and amateurish. A good use of color employs a limited number of muted, coordinated colors. To understand what this really means, look at the custom color settings in the Color dialog box.

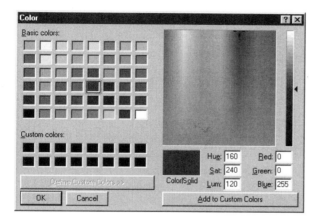

To understand these settings, it helps to understand hue, saturation, and luminosity (or HSL). Hue is the base color, such as red, yellow, green, cyan, blue, or magenta, as shown in the *x*-axis at the top of the color matrix. Saturation is the intensity of the color, ranging from brilliant (a pure color) to dull (a color mixed with a lot of gray), as shown in the *y*-axis of the color matrix. Luminosity is the lightness of the color, ranging from white to pastel to normal to dark and then to black.

A limited number of colors really means a limited number of hues. You can use a fair number of shades, though, which are obtained by changing the saturation and luminosity of the hue. A color is muted when it is not highly saturated or when it has a low luminosity. When you are limited to the standard 16 system colors, you can mute the color by dithering it with a shade of gray.

The toolbar icons used in Visual C++ show a good use of a muted palette. Note that the predominant colors are various shades of gray: white, light gray, dark gray, and black. Both yellow and blue are often used as accent colors, but whenever yellow is used in more than a few pixels it is dithered. Blue does not require dithering because it is not a harsh color; that is, the eye is physically less sensitive to blue. Lastly, green, red, purple, and brown are used sparingly when needed, and the majority of the icons use only one or two hues.

CHAPTER 15

Note that RGB values—a method of mixing red, green, and blue light to get the appearance of a particular color—while useful in programming, do not correspond to how the eye perceives color. Although it's easy to understand what changing the saturation of a color does, changing a specific RGB value is much harder to understand because its perceived effect on the color depends upon the other RGB values. For example, adding more red to a shade of red makes the color more brilliant, but adding more red to a shade of cyan makes it less brilliant. Consequently, if you are doing any color manipulation, most likely you will need to convert colors from RGB to HSL, perform the change, and then convert from HSL back to RGB.

Fonts

Using too many fonts can add unnecessary complexity to a program. You should try to use black—actually, use the system color COLOR_BTNTEXT or COLOR_WINDOWTEXT, both of which are usually black—sans serif fonts, such as MS Sans Serif and Arial, with a limited number of sizes. Both the Arial and MS Sans Serif fonts are attractive and very compact—in fact, they look almost the same—but Arial has the advantage of being a TrueType font, making it more appropriate when the user can select any font size. Tahoma, Verdana, Trebuchet MS, and Century Gothic are also good choices for a slightly different look. The default Windows font is 8-point MS Sans Serif.

Bitmaps and Icons

Graphics in user interfaces are most effective when they are simple abstractions of real objects. For example, a cartoonlike icon of a person is more effective than a realistic photo. See the Reply, Reply To All, and Forward buttons used in Microsoft Outlook, for example. The guidelines on color that I presented earlier apply to bitmaps and icons as well.

Use Simple Interactions

In addition to making sure your program has a simple appearance, you need to make sure that users can perform their tasks using simple interactions. While Windows uses many different types of interaction techniques, let's just consider two: dragging and dropping, and double-clicking.

Dragging and Dropping

As I discuss in Chapter 17, "Direct Manipulation Is Cool," I think dragging and dropping is one of the best features in Windows and I definitely want you to support it. However, it isn't always an especially easy feature to use. The first problem is that the drop target must be visible. And how do you make a drop target visible without accidentally dropping your selections at the wrong place? Try this: open a large document in Microsoft Word, select some text at the head of the document, and drag it to the bottom of the document. While Microsoft Word is nice enough to scroll automatically, the scrolling isn't easy to do. A thin region at the top and bottom of the window lets you scroll when you have a drop source, but it is especially difficult to control the scrolling when the document window is small. And if you accidentally drop the text on the desktop or the taskbar, you will be in for a real surprise. This action will create a scrap object—probably not what you had in mind.

The other problem with dragging and dropping is dragging across a long distance without scrolling. For example, try to drag an object from one corner of the screen to the opposite corner of the screen. It's difficult to move the mouse such a long distance without accidentally releasing the mouse button.

Double-Clicking

One trend in user interface design is to use single-clicking instead of double-clicking when possible. Windows 95 requires less double-clicking than Windows 3.1. For example, the Start menu and taskbar use single clicks where the File Manager and Program Manager use double clicks. Windows 98 gives the user the option to eliminate double-clicking almost entirely with the View As Web Page option. HTML pages have also helped promote single-clicking, since all hypertext links use single-clicking.

Is double-clicking really more difficult than single-clicking? Of course it is. How many times have you accidentally launched several instances of a program by double-clicking its icon on the desktop? This happens to me a lot. The problem is that when you double-click an item but don't get an immediate and obvious response, you think the double click didn't happen so you try again. If you don't perform the double click just right, Windows interprets it as two single clicks. (The wait cursor helps this problem but doesn't completely eliminate it.) On the other hand, how many times have you accidentally launched several instances of a program from the Quick Launch bar? I rarely make this mistake. This is because the single click is much easier to perform and I have confidence that I have successfully performed a single click, even if I don't get immediate feedback from the program.

Are you skeptical? Do you think these interaction techniques are really easy and I am overstating my case? If so, try testing your program with a trackball, an IBM TrackPoint or other similar pointing device, or a touch pad instead of a mouse. If you are like me, any interaction that is too complex becomes immediately obvious when you're using a trackball. In fact, everything seems more complex when using a trackball. Trackballs and touch pads are used on all laptop computers (except IBM notebook computers, which use TrackPoint), so users of these devices represent a significant portion of the market. I personally use a trackball because the Surgeon General has determined that using a mouse can be hazardous to my wrist.

 TIP Test the program using a trackball. All interactions seem more complex when using a trackball.

When testing with a trackball, I find that some interactions are just too difficult. For example, constantly having to make a selection from a cascading context menu can be especially difficult. For commands that are used often, I find providing plenty of keyboard shortcuts to be helpful.

Keeping the interaction techniques used by your interface simple, and providing alternatives to those techniques, helps your laptop users and your physically impaired users. In fact, it helps everyone else as well.

Making Trade-Offs

The world is not a simple place. Sometimes achieving one goal compromises another. Everything can't be universally simple. What do you do if making one task simple makes another task more complicated? Your goal should be to make simple tasks and the tasks users perform most often, which are generally the simple tasks, as easy as possible. Complex tasks and tasks that users perform rarely can function in a less than ideal way without harming the overall usability of your program.

 TIP Make simple things easy, complex things possible.

A Case Study: Tooltips vs. Balloon Help

Let's now look at keeping things simple by examining a real-world example. My favorite example of simplicity is a comparison of tooltips and balloon help. You are familiar with tooltips—little pop-up windows that provide brief context-sensitive help. Here's a typical example:

 PART III

Balloon help is very similar. It was developed by Apple Computer to be their context-sensitive help system for System 7.0. Here's an example:

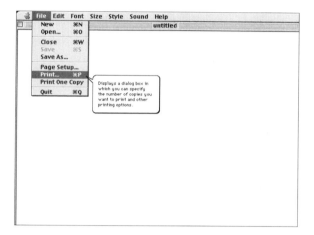

Both these features have identical objectives: to display context-sensitive help in an interactive manner. Specifically, the user receives help related to a specific screen item by moving the mouse pointer over that item. Although both approaches accomplish the same objective, most users find balloon help to be irritating while tooltips have become popular. To get a sense of why this is the case, let's compare the two features.

Tooltips

- The display of the help window is timer-based. You don't have to select a special mode for the feature to work.

- The help window is a small, simple rectangle. Its appearance is low-key.

- The text is generally short and concise, aimed primarily at inter-mediate users. The text is typically a few words or a sentence fragment.

CHAPTER 15

Balloon Help

- The display of the help window is modal—you must select balloon help mode for the feature to work. Once you activate the mode, help balloons are displayed without any delay and they pop up nearly everywhere as you move the cursor.

- The help window is a large, cartoonish thought balloon. Its appearance is hardly subtle.

- The text is generally long and detailed, aimed primarily at beginning users. The text is often several sentences long.

The difference is that tooltips require simple user interaction (moving the mouse and waiting a couple of seconds), have a simple appearance (a simple rectangle taking up very little screen space), and present simple text (usually a few words). By contrast, balloon help requires much more effort by the user, its appearance is much too "in your face," and it presents far more text than most users would want to read. In short, tooltips are successful because they are the simplest possible implementation of mouse-driven context help, and balloon help fails because of unnecessary complexity that undermines its effectiveness. While the differences between the two approaches might seem small, they make all the difference in the world.

Related Chapters

- Chapter 6—Beginning vs. Advanced Users.
  Stresses the importance of keeping the default configuration simple for beginning users.

- Chapter 11—Good User Interfaces Are Visible.
  Discusses how the most successful user interface metaphors are simple.

- Chapter 13—Learn from the Web.
  Discusses how to learn from the Web to simplify appearance, navigation, and interaction. The goal behind this approach isn't to be trendy but to make software simpler and easier to use.

- Chapter 19—Configurability Is Cool.
  Discusses the trade-off between power and simplicity and why simple configurations are usually better than powerful ones.

- Chapter 21—Tooltips Are Cool.

  Discusses the different types of tooltips, when to use them, and how to use them correctly.

- Chapter 22—Unnecessary Dialog Boxes Are Evil; Chapter 23—Unnecessary Message Boxes Are Pure Evil; and Chapter 24—Unnecessary Repetitive Tasks Are Evil.

  These chapters present specific ways to simplify user interfaces by eliminating unnecessary dialog boxes, message boxes, and tasks.

- Chapter 33—Check Your Setup Program.

  Describes the importance of simplicity in setup programs and presents several techniques for simplifying them. Many setup programs are just too complicated.

Recommended Reading

- Armstrong, Strohm. "Previewing the Common Controls DLL for Microsoft Internet Explorer 4.0, Part II." *Microsoft Systems Journal,* November 1996.

  Discusses the new ListView control, including the LVS_EX_ CHECKBOXES style.

- Capucciati, Maria R. "Putting Your Best Face Forward: Designing an Effective User Interface." *Microsoft Systems Journal,* February 1993.

  Offers many good ideas on keeping things simple.

- Cooper, Alan. *About Face: The Essentials of User Interface Design.* Foster City, CA: IDG Books Worldwide, Inc., 1995.

  Chapter 23, "Toolbars," has a good discussion about tooltips, primarily with respect to providing help for toolbars. There is also a good discussion of tooltips vs. balloon help and why tooltips are better. He describes tooltips as "one of the cleverest and most effective user interface idioms I've ever seen."

- Horton, William. *The Icon Book: Visual Symbols for Computer Systems and Documentation.* New York, NY: John Wiley & Sons, Inc., 1994.

  The ultimate resource for icon design information.

CHAPTER 15

- Howlett, Virginia. *Visual Interface Design for Windows*. New York, NY: John Wiley & Sons, Inc., 1996.

  Chapter 5, "Universal Design Principles," presents a good discussion of basic design principles that help achieve simplicity. Chapter 8, "Affordances, Realism, and Dimension," presents helpful information about visual affordance and the use of 3-D. Chapter 13, "Interface Makeovers," presents a couple of case studies of interface makeovers, including a makeover of Microsoft Encarta.

- Microsoft Corporation. *Designing for the User Experience*. Redmond, WA: Microsoft Press, 1999.

  See the discussion of menus, controls, and toolbars for useful guidelines for selecting and using controls.

- Tognazzini, Bruce. *Tog on Interface*. Reading, MA: Addison-Wesley Publishing Company, 1992.

  Chapter 28, "More Short Subjects," discusses the problems with balloon help.

CD-ROM Resources

The CD-ROM included with this book contains the following resources related to this chapter:

- The DevUI MFC Extension Library, which contains a CMcColor class for colors, including functions to convert RGB values to HSL values and back. Converting to HSL values is essential for color manipulation.

PART

IV

Design Details

16 CHAPTER

Prefer the
Standard Controls

Many programs out there
are definitely not normal. You know the programs I'm talking
about—you can spot them a mile away. They look weird, they
don't look or behave like most other Microsoft Windows programs, and they
make you feel uncomfortable when you use them.

Many of these programs acquire their strangeness by using custom
controls unnecessarily. Perhaps their developers chose to use custom controls to make these programs stand out. They succeeded. The programs
stand out because they don't look and feel right. In the worst cases, they
look unprofessional. Most mainstream programs I have seen that make
heavy use of custom controls probably shouldn't have.

To help prevent your programs from standing out for the wrong reasons, you should always try to employ the standard controls—which I
consider to be the six original basic controls and the new Win32 common

CHAPTER 16

controls—whenever you can and to reserve custom controls, whether you develop them yourself or acquire them from a third party, for unusual circumstances.

It's important to note that third-party controls can be extremely valuable in developing Windows software. They offer off-the-shelf solutions to complex problems and are available at a fraction of the cost of designing, implementing, and testing equivalent code from scratch. In fact, third-party controls are some of the most successful examples of software reuse in the field.

But standard controls have a significant advantage over custom controls simply because they are standard. The standard controls look good together and constitute a significant part of the Windows look and feel. Using them also satisfies the Designed for Microsoft Windows logo requirements, especially the accessibility requirements. Users already know how they work. Users know what they look like, can identify them easily, and know how to interact with them. They don't have to spend time figuring out the controls. With custom controls that look or behave differently, the user has to learn how to use them. It might not be a big effort for a single control—the user might only have to look at the screen and conclude, "Oh, that's just a weird radio button"—but extra effort is required. Remember that your users want to get their work done quickly and that having to expend extra effort to perform their work isn't likely to be well received.

TIP Standard controls have a significant advantage over custom controls simply because they are standard. Users already know how they work.

Of course, this is not to say that all custom controls are bad or that you should never use custom controls. It depends upon the controls and how you use them. But you should limit the use of custom controls to circumstances in which they are really needed and be careful in choosing them. Don't use custom controls just because you can. Have a reason to utilize them instead.

TIP
Don't use custom controls just because you can. Always have a reason.

Good Reasons to Use Custom Controls

I consider the following to be good reasons for employing custom controls:

- The standard controls do not provide the behavior you need. You should never assign nonstandard behavior to standard controls, so if you really need nonstandard behavior, you need a custom control.

- The standard controls do not provide the appearance you need. Note that with the custom draw feature, the new common controls give you quite a lot of control over how they are displayed, so you don't need custom controls to change backgrounds, fonts, colors, or margins, or to add icons.

- You are creating a game or multimedia program that is designed primarily to entertain, and you feel that using standard controls is too boring or you want controls to have an appearance that matches the style of the program's interface.

- You are creating a children's program or multimedia program that is designed primarily for beginning users, and you feel that standard controls are insufficient for this type of user.

I find the last two reasons to be the most interesting. Many successful games, multimedia programs, and children's programs use few standard controls. Examples include Microsoft Encarta, Microsoft Money, and Microsoft Greetings Workshop. There are several reasons for this. The first is that most multimedia applications have to compete with other alternatives. For example, Encarta has to compete with printed encyclopedias, which have extremely high production values. An online encyclopedia limited to the standard controls would not provide a comparable visual experience. The goal behind Encarta's interface is to make finding its information as pleasant an experience as possible. General productivity is not the most important goal.

16
CHAPTER

In fact, people sometimes use the product just for the fun of it and not to accomplish any specific task. Furthermore, people normally don't use Encarta all day, as they do professional applications such as Microsoft Visual C++ or Microsoft Office.

Programs like Greetings Workshop and children's programs use custom controls to create interfaces that even the most inexperienced user can immediately understand and operate. This makes using the program a pleasant experience for this level of user, and it maximizes the size of the product's potential market. Since the typical user runs this kind of program so infrequently, there is little need for advanced user interfaces to improve productivity. In Greetings Workshop, the assistant, Rocky the dog, helps make all tasks foolproof. (While I could easily live without Rocky, my two-year-old son, Philippe, loves him.) For example, while you are working on a project, Rocky presents all the tasks you are likely to want to perform so that you don't have to search for them.

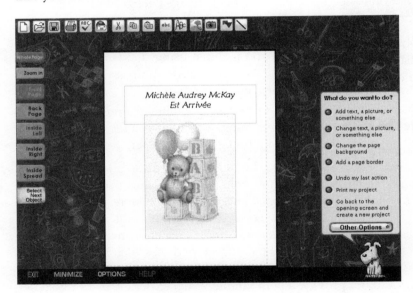

Since modal dialog boxes can confuse beginning users, Greetings Workshop helps guide the user through the process. For example, if you click outside a modal dialog box, Greetings Workshop displays a hint, as you can see in the following screen shot, to get you back on track.

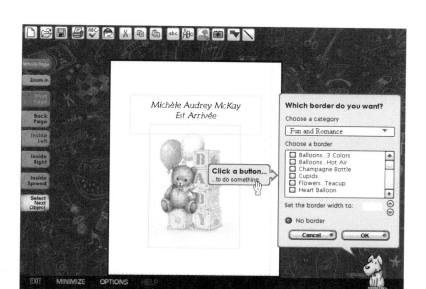

If you are creating a user interface at this level, it's fairly easy to justify using custom controls, since the standard controls simply do not provide this type of behavior.

Bad Reasons to Use Custom Controls

I consider the following to be really bad reasons to use custom controls:

- You think they are cool, but the standard controls would do the job just fine.

- You want your program to have a different look—just for the sake of being different.

- You found a really cool ActiveX control on the Internet and want to use it in your program somehow.

Whenever I use a program with nonstandard controls used for one of these reasons, I find it's as if the program is shouting, "Hey look at me! I'm not normal! I want your attention!"

A Case Study:
The Borland Custom Controls

In the bad old days of Windows 3.1 programming, dialog boxes used to look like this:

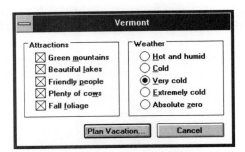

Then, in 1991, Borland International released their custom controls, which allowed you to create dialog boxes like this:

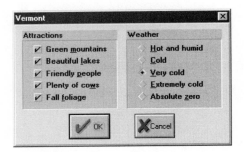

These 3-D controls were a significant improvement over the old, boring 2-D controls that were part of Windows. Without these controls, only command button controls had a 3-D appearance. With these controls, almost all controls could have a 3-D appearance and dialog boxes could have a sculptured, chiseled-steel look. All of a sudden everyone, myself included, was developing programs using these controls.

I have regretted it ever since. When I finally came to my senses, I removed them from the programs I was working on. Now I am embarrassed to show programs I developed back then because they used these controls.

Why? While 3-D controls are certainly an improvement over the 2-D controls, these controls were way too much. Too much "in your face"—having too much texture, too much 3-D, and too much color—they soon became irritating. Using them resulted in sensory overload and often drew attention to interface elements that really shouldn't receive attention. And their awkward fixed size made efficient screen layout especially difficult. What was I thinking? What was everyone else thinking? My only defense is that it seemed like a good idea at the time.

To put us back on the right track, Microsoft released the Ctl3d.dll and later the Ctl3dv2.dll control libraries. These controls allowed programmers to use 3-D controls without overdoing it to create dialog boxes like this one:

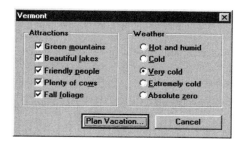

While certainly a step in the right direction, these controls can still be improved. Let's compare all these dialog boxes to one using the Win32 controls:

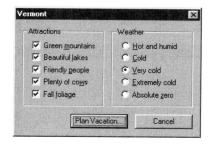

Isn't this dialog box much better? Using normal text instead of bold text creates a much cleaner and crisper look. The command buttons, check boxes, and radio buttons use very simple 3-D graphics. Note that the framing rectangle around the dialog box and command buttons isn't even black all the way around—it's black on the lower and right sides only. The use of black is minimized to give the controls a softer appearance. In short, these controls use the simplest graphics possible to convey an elegant 3-D appearance.

How to Select a Custom Control

So what should you do if you need to create or buy a custom control? My advice is to make sure that the control looks and behaves like a standard control as much as possible. Most third-party controls give you significant control over their appearance and behavior, so make sure standard appearance and behavior are among the options. The goal should be that a nonprogrammer user (that is, someone who doesn't know what is standard) can make good use of your program yet have no clue that he is using a custom control.

TIP   Choose custom controls that look and behave like standard controls. Ideally, users should have no clue that they are using a custom control.

Interestingly, if you look at the advertisements for custom controls in programmer's magazines, the ads typically go out of their way to make it painfully obvious that the control is nonstandard and looks nothing like the standard controls. This makes sense, of course, since the ad wouldn't get anyone's attention if the control looked like a standard control, but definitely don't use this marketing technique as a guide for user interface design.

When evaluating a custom control, I recommend that you ask yourself the following questions:

- Does the control look like a standard control? Does it look good? Does it look normal? Do you have significant control over its appearance? Can you set the control's fonts? Are its 3-D effects not overdone?

- Does the control behave like a standard control? Do you have significant control over its behavior? Does the control support the standard mouse and keyboard behaviors defined in *Designing for the User Experience*? Does the control work with either the mouse or the keyboard?

- Does the control use system colors and metrics? Can you change the colors? Can you select subdued colors? Does it satisfy the Designed for Microsoft Windows logo requirements, especially the accessibility requirements?

- If applicable, does the control use the standard 3-D frames? Does it use the DrawEdge API function to employ the same frame styles as the standard controls? Note that using DrawEdge is important because it makes the control look consistent with other controls now and in the future (if the DrawEdge algorithm is ever changed).

- If applicable, does the control support the standard appearances, such as normal, pressed, unavailable (disabled), input focus, option-set, and mixed-value?

If the custom control scores well on all of these points, the control is probably appropriate to use and a pleasure for your user to work with.

Recommended Reading

- Armstrong, Strohm. "Previewing the Common Controls DLL for Microsoft Internet Explorer 4.0." *Microsoft Systems Journal,* October 1996 and November 1996.

  Describes the new common control features provided by Internet Explorer 4.0 and Windows 98. These features give you significant flexibility and help eliminate the need for some custom controls.

- Howlett, Virginia. *Visual Interface Design for Windows.* New York, NY: John Wiley & Sons, Inc., 1996.

  While this book doesn't directly describe the design of the Windows 95 controls, it does describe the general motivation behind many of the Windows 95 design decisions. It contains useful information if you want to understand why Windows looks the way it does.

- Tognazzini, Bruce. *Tog on Interface.* Reading, MA: Addison-Wesley Publishing Company, 1992.

  Chapter 36, "Case Study: One-Or-More Buttons," presents a case study on how Tognazzini designed a control that allows the user to select one or more items but not none. This case study is interesting because it shows how much effort is required for talented user interface designers to design a relatively simple interface.

- The Designed for Microsoft Windows logo requirements.

  The logo requirements have guidelines and recommendations for accessibility, which the standard controls satisfy.

CD-ROM Resources

The CD-ROM included with this book contains the following resource related to this chapter:

- The Designed for Microsoft Windows logo requirements.

CHAPTER 17

Direct Manipulation Is Cool

A user is performing a task using direct manipulation when the following occurs:

- There is an object visible on the screen.
- The user can interact directly with the object, typically by using the mouse.
- There is immediate feedback that shows the current results of the interaction.

All three of these requirements are essential to direct manipulation. If any one of them is missing, the sensation of directness is destroyed. By this definition, the MS-DOS command line is the antithesis of direct manipulation. There are no visible objects on the screen except the command prompt, you have to type in each command (and the interface doesn't help you if you don't know what to type), and you receive little or no feedback so you don't know for sure whether a command you typed in worked.

In practice, direct manipulation often boils down to an even simpler definition: the ability to interact with a screen object directly by using the mouse instead of indirectly by using the keyboard, dialog box, or menu bar. It is the use of a mouse to interact with a screen object that creates the essential sensation of directness. You feel as if you are manually manipulating the object, and it's possible at times to lose your awareness that software is involved. The mouse feels like an extension of your hand. The object and what you are doing to the object seem more "real" than other kinds of interaction with a program, such as that in the MS-DOS command line example I just mentioned.

Direct manipulation has numerous advantages. It is a natural way to perform tasks in a modern graphical user interface, is easy to learn, and is quick and convenient to use. If the extent of manipulation is properly restrained, you can avoid the need for error messages. Direct manipulation is also easy to remember—once you learn how to manipulate an object directly it's unlikely that you'll forget how. Best of all, direct manipulation makes you feel as if you're directly in control of the task at hand and its continuous visual feedback makes it easy for you to decide when you have what you want. Simply put, direct manipulation makes using software fun.

TIP Direct manipulation makes using software fun. It is the ultimate form of interactivity.

In the remainder of this chapter, I'll present the alternatives to direct manipulation, the various types of direct manipulation commonly found in Microsoft Windows programs, the problems with direct manipulation, and how to solve these problems.

The Alternatives

Let's consider the alternative to direct manipulation, which, of course, would be indirect manipulation. Suppose you have a window on the screen and you want to change its size and location. The most indirect approach would be to use a dialog box such as this one:

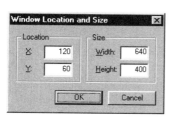

While this dialog box allows you to manipulate the window, it is anything but direct. You have to guess what numbers to use for the size and location. And, because there is no immediate feedback when you change the numbers, you have to enter some numbers and click the OK button to see and review the results. If you don't like what you get, you have to repeat the process until you get it right. Also, this interface needs error messages, because you might enter an off-screen location or sizes that are too large or too small. Note that using a property sheet with an Apply button would at least make this technique practical. The only merit to this approach is that it is easy to program, which isn't much of a consolation for the user. Happily this technique is not used in Windows.

An intermediate approach is to use the window's system menu to move or size the window, as done here:

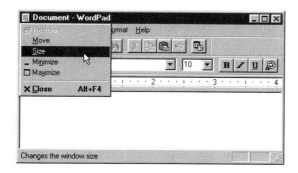

Using either the Move or Size command, you can move or size the window by using the keyboard. Note that this technique is a bit cumbersome but it does satisfy the definition of direct manipulation. You manipulate the window directly with the keyboard, and you receive immediate feedback. The interaction's cumbersomeness results from using the keyboard to do a task better suited for the mouse. One interesting detail is that once you start to move or size the window using this technique, the cursor changes its location and shape to give you a hint on how to perform the manipulation in the future using the mouse. For example, when you hit the up arrow key while resizing a window using the keyboard, the cursor moves to the top window border and changes shape to the vertical resize pointer, clearly showing that the mouse can be used directly to accomplish the window sizing.

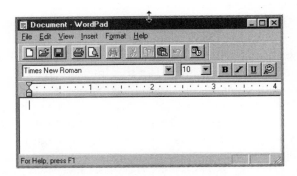

The most direct way to move the window is to click and drag its title bar; the most direct way to size it is to click and drag its border or the window corner. In both cases, error messages are unnecessary because it is impossible to move the window off the screen or to give it an unaccept-able size. Using this technique, you don't feel like you are using software to manipulate the window as you do when using a dialog box. Rather, you feel like you are actually moving the window.

As I noted, in its simplified definition direct manipulation often is the ability to interact with a screen object directly by using a mouse instead of indirectly by using the keyboard, a dialog box, or the menu bar. Are there times when manipulation by using the keyboard, a dialog box, or a menu can be considered direct? The answer is yes, as in the following cases.

For the keyboard, the first case is text entry. Word processing and numeric processing (such as when using a calculator) are common ex-amples. In this case, the keyboard isn't used to give commands but sim-ply to enter text. In fact, using a mouse to enter text would be considered indirect manipulation.

The keyboard's second case is sensible keyboard shortcuts, such as the following:

- Deleting a selected object with the Delete key
- Using the arrow keys and the Home, End, Page Up, and Page Down keys to view a document and move the cursor
- Moving the caret in a text document and then pressing the Shift key and any arrow key to select text
- In the Microsoft Visual C++ dialog box editor, typing text to set a control's label, using the arrow keys to move a control, using the Shift+arrow keys to size a control, and using the Tab key to select another control

These keyboard shortcuts are so natural for an experienced Windows user that they have a direct feel to them. You can easily determine their existence and how they work without any help. They are also easy to remember. Of course, there are exceptions. For example, you can move up one level to the previous folder in Windows Explorer using the Backspace key. This shortcut does not feel natural, so it does not have any sense of directness.

Dialog boxes can be used in direct manipulation, but not to actually perform the manipulation. A good example is a palette of controls used in a paint program or dialog box editor. Customizing toolbars in Visual C++ by using the Customize property sheet involves a dialog box. In these cases, the dialog box is used to present the available options, not to perform the manipulation itself. Another case is when the dialog box itself is what is being manipulated, such as with a calculator utility.

Lastly, context menus can present a sense of directness that a menu bar cannot. If you right-click an object and give a command or change a property by using the context menu that appears, that action feels direct. Performing the same action with a menu bar feels indirect. In this case, the sense of directness decreases as the physical distance between an object and the method of manipulation increases.

Just as there are times when using the keyboard, a dialog box, or a menu can feel direct, there are times when using a mouse can feel indirect. As I said earlier, using a mouse to enter text would be an example of indirect manipulation. In many types of games, input devices such as joysticks and steering wheels feel direct, whereas a mouse feels indirect. I think the subjective attributes of direct manipulation, such as the sense of being in control and the experience of receiving immediate feedback, are more important than the specific type of input device used. If an interaction feels direct, it's direct, regardless of how it is performed.

Types of Direct Manipulation

Direct manipulation is interesting both because of the numerous techniques for achieving it and because these techniques are often the most creative aspects of user interfaces. Direct manipulation typically involves one or more of the following forms of interaction:

- Selecting
- Dragging and dropping
- Clicking or double-clicking
- Moving or sizing
- Using a context menu
- Using tooltips
- Entering text

Let's look at some direct manipulation techniques used by Windows programs.

Windows Shell and Windows Explorer

- You can click+drag (outside objects) to select objects in Windows Explorer and the desktop.
- You can drag and drop files and folders to move, copy, or create shortcuts within Windows Explorer and between Windows Explorer, the desktop, the Start menu, and the Quick Launch bar.
- You can drag and drop files on program icons on the desktop and the Quick Launch bar to launch the program using the file. Dropping files on a printer icon prints the files using the appropriate program. Dropping files and folders on the Recycle Bin deletes them.
- You can drag and drop items within the Start menu to move their location or change their order.
- You can drag and drop items within the Quick Launch bar to change their order.
- You can drag and drop the program icon on the Windows Explorer title bar or the Address bar to create a shortcut to the currently displayed drive or folder.
- You can rename a file in Windows Explorer by selecting a filename, clicking it, and typing a new name.
- You can open, send, cut, copy, paste, rename, delete, print, and view properties by using a file's context menu.

PART
IV

- You can access the same direct manipulation capabilities of Windows Explorer from the Open and Save As common dialog boxes.

- You can use context menus to manipulate all file shortcuts and folders in the Start menu.

Windows

- You can move a window by dragging its title bar, maximize a window by double-clicking its title bar, and close a window by double-clicking its title bar icon. You can also minimize, maximize, restore, and close a window by clicking the appropriate title bar button.

- You can size a window by dragging its window border or its window corner.

Controls

- You can directly manipulate the Windows basic controls. You can click buttons, select and scroll lists and combo boxes, and modify text in edit boxes.

- You can directly manipulate the new Windows common controls. You can select and scroll list views; select, scroll, expand, and contract tree views; set the size and sort order of header controls; increment and decrement spin buttons; move the slider on slider bars; and click tabs. You can also directly select dates by using the date and time picker control.

Microsoft Internet Explorer

- You can drag and drop the document icon from the title bar or the URL icon from the Address bar to create a shortcut to the currently displayed URL. You can also drag and drop the URL icons between the Address bar, Links bar, and Web page window.

- You can click a hyperlink to see related information.

TIP Direct manipulation usually involves using a mouse, but sometimes using a mouse feels indirect. The user's subjective feel of the manipulation is more important than the specific input device used.

CHAPTER 17

Visual C++

● You can drag variables and expressions from a source window to the watch window and memory window.

● You can create Windows resources, including dialog boxes, bitmaps, icons, menus, strings, toolbars, and version resources by using direct manipulation.

● You can view variable values directly by using tooltips.

● You can create and customize toolbars directly by using the Customize property sheet. You can move items within a toolbar by dragging and dropping. You can add a new toolbar item by dragging the item's icon from the Customize property sheet to the toolbar. You can add a spacer between items by dragging the icon to the right of where you want the spacer to be. Lastly, you can remove a spacer between items by dragging the icon on the right of the spacer to the left.

Microsoft Word

● You can drag and drop text and other objects within and between documents.

● You can select whole lines of text by using the selection bar at the left-hand side of a document.

● You can change the indents, margins, column widths, and tab stop type by changing the markers on the horizontal and vertical rulers.

● You can have Word perform spelling and grammar checking and indicate questionable text directly within a document. This example is a somewhat inverted form of direct manipulation because it is the program itself that is performing the manipulation directly to the document. However, the effect is to make questionable spelling and grammar visible without the use of dialog boxes.

● You can drag selected text from Word to the desktop, Start menu, or Quick Launch bar to create a document scrap.

Microsoft Outlook

● You can use the AutoCreate feature to drag an item of one type into a folder of another type to create a new item. For example, you can drag an email message to the Contacts folder to automatically create a new contact. You can also drag an email message to the Calendar folder to schedule an appointment.

PART
IV

- You can drag and drop names between the recipient lists. For example, you can drag a name from the To: field to the Cc: field or even to the Subject: field.

- You can add columns to a table view by displaying the Field Chooser and dragging fields where you want them. You can also reorder the columns in a table view by dragging them where you want them.

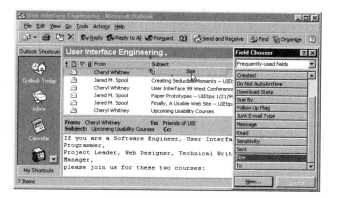

- You can drag and drop icons in the Outlook bar to rearrange them within a group or to move them to another group.

- You can drag and drop a file onto a message to attach the file to the message.

Other Examples

- You can drop a file on the title bar of a program that is a drop target, which has the same effect as dropping the file in the body of the program.

- You can use tooltips to get more information about an object.

- Using the Time Zone tab in the Windows 95 Date/Time Control Panel applet, you can set your time zone by clicking your location on the world map. Unfortunately, Microsoft decided to remove this feature from Windows 98 and later versions of Windows 95 due to political differences about national boundaries. While the combo box alone allows you to set the time zone using direct manipulation, the time zone map provides additional feedback.

CHAPTER 17

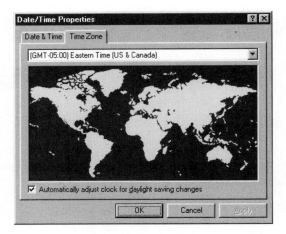

Of course, there are many other examples of direct manipulation in these programs and others. In fact, several types of programs use direct manipulation almost exclusively, such as games and painting and drawing programs. Consider how much more complex these programs would be if you had to use a dialog box or menu to perform these tasks.

Direct Manipulation Opportunities

In theory, any dialog box that is used to give a command or set a property could be eliminated by direct manipulation. In practice, there are simply too many commands and attributes to make this objective possible. However, before you create a new dialog box, ask yourself whether you can come up with a way to perform the action directly.

Before you create a new dialog box, ask yourself whether you can create a way to perform the action directly.

I've found that one specific type of dialog box is consistently a prime candidate for elimination with direct manipulation. In the above list of examples, I intentionally omitted one of my favorite forms of direct manipulation. In Windows 3.1 Help systems, Help authors used to create segmented hypergraphics (also called SHED bitmaps) of windows to allow the user to click a region on the graphic to get help. Such a Help window for a typical dialog box would look like the following:

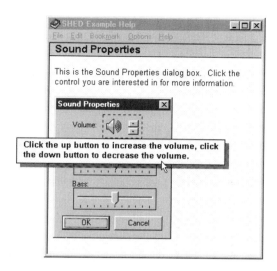

Let's think this situation through. You need help for a dialog box on the screen, so you ask for help—the Help system then covers the dialog box with a large Help window with a picture of the dialog box so that you can click the picture to get specific help. This technique doesn't make any sense. Why should the Help system display a picture of the dialog box when the dialog box is already on the screen? Why not eliminate the Help window and ask the dialog box for help directly? This is the technique used in Windows 98 with the What's This? button.

In the first example, the Help window replicates the dialog box it provides help for, but a better solution, as shown here, is to obtain the same information from the window directly. I believe this principle applies in general. Whenever the appearance of a dialog box mimics the window it supports, that dialog box can probably be eliminated by direct manipulation.

Some of the earlier mentioned examples that follow this principle are the direct file rename feature used in Windows Explorer, the toolbar editor used in Visual C++, and the table view column editor used by Outlook.

Making Direct Manipulation Visible

As I mentioned earlier, both Windows Explorer and Internet Explorer allow you to drag and drop the title bar's document icon to create a shortcut to the currently displayed disk, folder, or Web page. I think this is a really good feature, and I wish all Windows programs allowed you to do this. I'd also like to be able to drag the title bar icon to make a shortcut to the program itself. I could then add a shortcut to a running program to the Quick Launch bar with little effort.

The problem with this feature and its possible variations is that it isn't visible. As currently implemented, there is no visual indication suggesting that the title bar icon can be dragged. The cursor doesn't even change shape when it passes over the icon. Without visibility, very few users will discover this feature.

In general, direct manipulation needs the following forms of visibility:

- Before the manipulation, the interface should suggest that an object can be manipulated and perhaps suggest how to do it.

- During the manipulation, the interface should indicate that a manipulation is in progress.

- After the manipulation, the interface should indicate that the operation was successfully completed or cancelled.

Indication prior to the manipulation can be achieved in two ways—by the visual characteristics of the object itself, such as handles or grabbers, and by the shape of the cursor. Of course, both techniques are often used together. Also, sometimes an object becomes highlighted when the mouse passes over it to show that it can be manipulated. Here are some typical examples of handles:

Painting and drawing programs are famous for using the cursor to show the kind of manipulation possible in the program. The following graphic shows some typical examples of cursors that suggest the ability to manipulate:

At the very least, you should indicate that an object can be manipulated by changing the cursor.

TIP

You should indicate that an object can be manipulated by changing the cursor.

How a user interface indicates that manipulation is in progress largely depends on the type of manipulation. According to our definition of direct manipulation, the in-progress feedback needs to indicate the results of the interaction, and it needs to be immediate. Selection is always indicated by highlighting the background of the selected objects. Actions such as sizing and moving are indicated either by actually sizing or moving the object or by showing a frame that indicates the currently selected size or location. Drag-and-drop functionality is typically represented by having the cursor move a ghost image of the object (created by alternating the object's image with translucent pixels) and change shape to indicate when the object is over a drop target. If several types of manipulation are possible for an object, the interface needs to indicate which option is taking place. Windows Explorer indicates a move with a normal cursor, a copy with a cursor and a plus sign, and a shortcut with a cursor and a shortcut arrow. In

the case of dragging title bar icons, dragging a shortcut to the program could be indicated by showing the program icon with a shortcut arrow and dragging a shortcut to a document could be indicated by showing a document icon with a shortcut arrow.

A successful manipulation is typically indicated by the action completing. For example, the object changes size or shape, or the files are moved to the target and removed from the source. The indication is often obvious, but sometime it is subtle. Too subtle, perhaps. For example, when you move a file in Windows Explorer, there's about a two-second delay before the file icon in the source folder is removed. The fact that the file has been removed from the source folder is fairly clear, but you have no positive visual feedback that the target folder was the one you intended. A simple animation, such as the target folder icon opening and then closing (or even a Pac-Man-style devouring of the files), would provide even better feedback.

You can cancel a drag-and-drop operation by dropping the object back on its source or an invalid drop target or by pressing the Esc key during the drag. Windows indicates a cancellation with the Esc key by removing the ghost image of the dragged object. I find this technique works fairly well. In fact, I think it should be used whenever an object is moved back to its source to clearly indicate that method of cancellation.

Other Direct Manipulation Problems

Direct manipulation can present other potential problems besides lack of visibility. Manipulation can happen by accident, drop targets can be hard to access, the rules of manipulation can sometimes be difficult to figure out, direct manipulation is often not precise or scalable, and direct manipulation isn't especially accessible. I will address each of these issues below.

Accidental Manipulation

While direct manipulation has many benefits, it is possible for an object to be too easy to manipulate. Specifically, you want to make sure that the user intends the manipulation and that the manipulation isn't accidental. Regarding mouse movement, there's a fine line between selecting an object and dragging an object. For example, I occasionally receive the following error message when I select a folder in Windows Explorer:

In this case, I selected a folder but moved the mouse slightly during the selection, so Windows Explorer interpreted this as a move. There's also a fine line between a double click and two single clicks. To rename a file in Windows Explorer, you need to first select the filename with a single click and then click the selected filename again to enable the rename feature. But if you do this action too quickly, instead of renaming the file you launch the program associated with the file—not quite what you had in mind.

The more you support direct manipulation in your program, the more likely it is that an action of manipulation will be misinterpreted. In the most difficult situations, you might have to monitor how long the user clicks an object and the path of the mouse movement before and after the click to determine what the user is trying to do. The simpler solution to this problem is to avoid ambiguous manipulations (like two clicks vs. a double click) and to limit the objects that can be manipulated to a reasonable number so that the user can perform most tasks without fear of disturbing something. You don't want the user interface to be too fragile.

 TIP Prevent accidental manipulation. Avoid ambiguous manipulations, and limit the number of objects that can be manipulated.

Drop Target Access

While it is usually simple to select an object to drag, it can be much more difficult to access the place to drop the object. For example, when dragging and dropping text within a Word document, if you want to drop the text in a part of the document that isn't visible, you can move the cursor to the edge of the document and Word will scroll the document until you move the cursor away from the edge. This technique works well in large document windows, but in small windows the document scrolls so fast that it is impossible to scroll with precision. A better implementation would adjust the speed of the scrolling based both on how near the cursor is to the edge (that is, the closer to the edge, the faster it should scroll) and on the size of the window.

When dragging and dropping an object between programs, it can often be difficult to have both the source and target visible on the screen at the same time. The ability to drop on the title bar helps somewhat, but most users don't know about this feature. In the most awkward situations, it is easier to use the cut, copy, and paste commands than to drag and drop.

291

Direct Manipulation Confusion

Direct manipulation can be confusing when several possible actions are associated with the manipulation. The default action used is determined by the target, not by the source. For example, when you drag and drop a file using Windows Explorer, you can be moving the file, copying the file, or creating a shortcut to the file. Consider the rules related to dragging and dropping files in Windows Explorer:

- Dragging and dropping one or more nonexecutable files to the same drive performs a move.

- Dragging and dropping one or more nonexecutable files to a different drive performs a copy.

- Dragging and dropping one or more executable files creates a shortcut.

- Dragging and dropping a mixture of executable and nonexecutable files to the same drive performs a move.

- Dragging and dropping a mixture of executable and nonexecutable files to a different drive performs a copy.

- Regardless of the file types and where they are dropped, if the Control key is pressed during the drop, it performs a copy.

- Regardless of the file types and where they are dropped, if the right mouse button is used to perform the drag, a pop-up menu appears after the drop, allowing the user to choose the desired action. This is called a nondefault drag and drop.

In other words, the result of a drag and drop in Windows Explorer depends on the type of files, the number of files, and the destination. Did you know these rules? How many users understand these rules? Probably not many. The good news is that the cursor accurately indicates what is going to happen, and most of the time these rules result in what you want. Beginning users, who don't yet know the significance of the cursor hints, are often frustrated by not being able to copy an executable file by dragging it. These rules are complex for a reason, and there is no simple solution to this problem. Generally, when a user transfers files within a drive, he intends to move them instead of copy them. When dragging between drives, the user intends to copy them, as moving them is impossible. When a user drops an executable onto the desktop, the Quick Launch bar, or the

Start menu, the intention is to copy a shortcut, not to move the program. These drag-and-drop rules could be modified to copy a shortcut in these three cases and perform a move or copy in all others, but that would make the rules even more complicated than they already are.

Precision

Direct manipulation is often difficult to perform precisely. For example, it's usually much easier to set the size of a window by dragging its border than by typing its size into a dialog box. However, if you want to set a window to an exact size, such as 320 x 240, it is much easier to do this using a dialog box. Precise manipulation requires feedback. In this case, setting a precise dialog box size would be possible using direct manipulation if Windows displayed a tooltip that gave the size during the manipulation, as the Microsoft Visual Basic dialog box editor does. The Visual C++ dialog box editor gives the sizes and locations of the dialog boxes and their controls on the status bar. But window and control sizes are in pixels, which never require decimals. If you need the ability to make an object exactly 0.127 inches long, direct manipulation is pretty useless.

You can use the keyboard to help obtain precise manipulation. For example, in paint programs it is difficult to get a perfect circle or square. Microsoft Paint uses the Shift key to constrain an object's shape. An oval drawn with the Shift key depressed is a circle, a rectangle is a square, and lines are constrained to be at angles that are multiples of 45 degrees. If you really need the ability to make an object 0.127 inches long without using a dialog box, you could use Shift+arrow keys to change the size in 0.1-inch increments, Ctrl+arrow keys to change the size in 0.01-inch increments, and Shift+Ctrl+arrow keys to change the size in 0.001-inch increments. In this case, perhaps using a dialog box isn't so bad.

Scalability

Another problem with direct manipulation is that it simply isn't scalable. For example, it is very convenient to rename a few files using Windows Explorer, but it is very inconvenient to rename a thousand files this way. Using wildcards in MS-DOS is scalable, so it is no more difficult to rename a thousand files than it is to rename one. If your program performs tasks that require scalability, you will need to provide alternatives to direct manipulation.

Accessibility

Unfortunately, direct manipulation is also not especially accessible. The most common direct manipulation techniques, especially dragging and dropping, require significant manual dexterity. This makes them inappropriate for many types of users, such as young children, the physically impaired, and even those using trackballs or touch pads. In my own experience, I have found that too much direct manipulation can lead to repetitive stress injuries. Such injuries can be quite painful, and they can be especially stressful to those who depend upon using computers for their livelihood.

In addition to the ability to perform the manipulation, users also need the ability to see the objects being manipulated. For drag-and-drop functionality, users need to be able to see the objects and the drop targets, as well as the cursor hints. Screen readers are of little help for these tasks.

The lack of accessibility, as well as the other direct manipulation problems I've described, can be addressed by making sure that all tasks performed using direct manipulation can be performed using an alternative mechanism, such as a menu command, a dialog box, or the keyboard. Users can then shift back and forth between using direct manipulation and other techniques to work most efficiently. Advanced users want to keep their hands on the keyboard. Note that the easiest way to copy a file from a hard disk to a floppy disk using Windows Explorer isn't dragging and dropping but the Send To context menu command. As useful as it is, direct manipulation should not be the only way to perform a task.

Program features that effectively use direct manipulation are among the best in Windows. Direct manipulation is a quick, natural way to perform tasks that is easy to learn and remember. Direct manipulation keeps the user in control and provides continuous feedback. It makes software a pleasure to use.

While direct manipulation makes tasks simple for users, it often makes work difficult for programmers. Direct manipulation is not easy to implement, and it requires you to address many details. As noted in *Designing for the User Experience*, "Simplicity is not the same as being simplistic. Making something simple to use often requires a good deal of work and code."

Related Chapters

- Chapter 22—Unnecessary Dialog Boxes Are Evil.
  A benefit of direct manipulation is that it can eliminate the need for dialog boxes. This chapter discusses why unnecessary dialog boxes are undesirable, how to identify unnecessary dialog boxes, and how to eliminate them.

- Chapter 23—Unnecessary Message Boxes Are Pure Evil.
  Another benefit of direct manipulation: if the manipulation is properly restrained, there is no need for error messages. This chapter presents the different types of message boxes and tips on how to identify and eliminate unnecessary message boxes.

Recommended Reading

- Cooper, Alan. *About Face: The Essentials of User Interface Design.* Foster City, CA: IDG Books Worldwide, Inc., 1995.
  Chapter 17, "Direct Manipulation," describes the various forms of direct manipulation and gives details about their appearance and behavior. Chapter 18, "Drag-and-Drop," describes some of the gory details about implementing drag-and-drop functionality, including making the source, target, and drop completion visible; modal drag and drop; automatic scrolling; and "debouncing" drags so that dragging is not confused with selection.

- Microsoft Corporation. *Designing for the User Experience.* Redmond, WA: Microsoft Press, 1999.
  See the information on general interaction techniques for a detailed description of the appearance and behavior of selection, drag and drop, automatic scrolling, and direct manipulation feedback.

- Norman, Donald A. *The Design of Everyday Things.* New York, NY: Currency/Doubleday, 1990.
  Chapter 6, "The Design Challenge," describes how direct manipulation is a "first-person" interaction and indirect manipulation is a "third-person" interaction. When using direct manipulation, Norman observes that "I do think of myself not as using a computer but as doing the particular task. The computer is, in effect, invisible."

CHAPTER 17

- Shneiderman, Ben. *Designing the User Interface—Strategies for Effective Human-Computer Interaction, Third Edition.* Reading, MA: Addison Wesley Longman, Inc., 1999.

  Chapter 6, "Direct Manipulation and Visual Environments," is dedicated to direct manipulation but extends the concept to technologies such as computer-aided design, visual languages, and virtual reality. Shneiderman coined the term *direct manipulation* and is one of its leading proponents.

CHAPTER 18

Appropriate Defaults Are Cool

Good user interfaces help users get their work done by eliminating unnecessary effort through the use of appropriate defaults. Programmers often do not provide appropriate defaults, either by omission or through the mistaken belief that you can't provide defaults if you're not really sure what the user wants to do.

Defaults occur in many circumstances in a typical program, such as when a program is started, an object is created, or a dialog box is displayed. It is a bad sign when a program always starts the same way, objects are always created with the same properties, or dialog boxes are always initialized to the same settings, regardless of the user's previous input. Good user interfaces keep track of the user's input and use it to determine default values whenever appropriate. Good user interfaces also save the user's previous settings—like open documents, and window sizes and locations—and restore them when the program is restarted.

Providing appropriate defaults is just one of many techniques for achieving the ultimate goal of eliminating unnecessary repetitive tasks, a subject I'll address in detail in Chapter 24. This chapter focuses on setting defaults, most often in dialog boxes.

What Defaults Are Appropriate?

The goal of selecting appropriate defaults is to provide defaults that reduce the amount of work needed to accomplish a task. A good default doesn't have to be exactly right all the time. Being close is good enough if it reduces the amount of effort to perform a task. For example, when you create a new document in Microsoft Word and then save the document, Word creates a default filename from the text in the first line of the document—specifically, it uses all the text up to the first punctuation character. This default makes sense because the first line of a document is often the document title. While this default filename isn't always right, I find it usually takes a simple edit to get what I want. Even if it is completely wrong, the default filename is automatically selected, so all I have to do is type in the filename I want.

TIP A good default doesn't have to be right all the time.

This example is fairly unusual. Most often the best default is the last setting that the user selected. After all, if the user wanted that setting last time, most likely the user will want it next time as well. For example, when working in Microsoft Visual C++, if I selected to optimize my code by size in my last project, chances are I will want to optimize my next project by size. (Unfortunately, Visual C++ does not work this way. It always uses the same default settings.) However, as you'll see below, there are several circumstances where using the last setting is a poor choice. The best rule in general is to give the default value that is most likely to be right, given how the setting is used. Remember that just because you can't be certain what the user wants doesn't mean you can't have good defaults.

TIP Give the default value that is most likely to be right, given how the setting is used.

Actions performed automatically by a program should not affect the defaults. For example, if a program saves a file to the Temp folder, that action should not change the program's default folder. Defaults should change only as a result of user input.

TIP Defaults should change only as a result of user input.

Defaults vs. Placeholders

A good default value and a placeholder value differ significantly. While a good default value has a reasonable chance of being the right value, a place-holder value is practically never right. For example, when you create a new document in Word, a placeholder name is used until you save the file. Saving the file establishes the filename you choose. Until then, the placeholder name makes it clear that the name hasn't been set. It is fairly certain that placeholder names like "Document1" or "New Folder" are not what the user wants. Using placeholders is appropriate when either you want to draw attention to the fact that a value hasn't been set or it is impossible to deter-mine a default value with even a chance of being right.

TIP Use placeholders to make it clear that a value hasn't been set.

Default Examples

Let's look at some examples.

Open and Save As Common Dialog Boxes
The Open and Save As common dialog boxes are notable for how often their default values are handled incorrectly. The Open dialog box ordinarily should use the last folder and file type (that is, file extension) entered by the user in the program as the default values. Some programs use the pro-gram path as the default folder for opening and saving files. This default is almost certain to be wrong, since the program's path is a poor choice for saving user files. Defaults like this are clearly chosen for convenience to the programmer, not the user.

18

Interestingly, my suggestion is in conflict with the Designed for Microsoft Windows logo requirements. Specifically, the logo requirements suggest that all user files should be saved to the My Documents folder or one of its subfolders. (This can be easily programmed by initializing the lpstrInitialDir member of the OPENFILENAME structure to the path returned by calling the SHGetSpecialFolderPath function with the CSIDL_PERSONAL flag. Setting the default folder for the Open dialog is demonstrated later in this chapter in the section titled "Example Code.") This way, it is easier for the user to find files, since they can be found in a centralized location regardless of what program created the file; to access files, since a shortcut to the My Documents folder is on the desktop; and to back up files, since they are all stored in one place.

Unfortunately, rigid adherence to this recommendation ignores one small detail—the user. The very first time a program is run, using the My Documents folder as the initial default folder makes perfect sense. But if the user isn't storing his documents in the My Documents folder, why use this folder as the default? If you set the last folder used as the default, you are providing the user a default folder based on his actual behavior, not his ideal behavior. Following the user's actual behavior is always the right thing to do.

TIP Provide defaults based on the user's actual behavior.

While using the last folder as the default is simple enough, it isn't always the right thing to do. You have to think about how the program is used. Consider the WinDiff utility included with Visual C++, which is used to compare two files. To compare files, you have to open the first file with an Open dialog box and then open the second file with another Open dialog box. But how is such a program typically used? Whenever I use it, I compare files in one folder to files of the same name in another folder. While I sometimes compare two files in the same folder, that situation is rare. Although comparing files in different folders is common, you would never know it from using WinDiff. When selecting the first file to compare in WinDiff, instead of using the previous first file folder, the WinDiff Open dialog box defaults to the previous second file folder, which is never right. Furthermore, it never supplies a default filename, even though the second filename is likely to be the same as the first. Consequently, comparing several files using WinDiff is infuriating—and only because of its poorly chosen defaults. Every time you compare another pair of files, you effectively have to start over completely.

For the Save As common dialog box, programs that save only a single file type can safely use the last folder and file type for default values as well. However, programs that save several file types should save the last folder used for each file type and select the default folder for a new document based on its file type. Why? Because the folder to which a user saves a file can correspond closely to the file type. For example, in a software project, I generally save the .CPP, .H, and .RC files to the project folder; .BMP and .ICO files to the RES subdirectory; .DOC files to the documentation folder; .RTF files to the help folder; and .HTML files to the Web site folder. The fact that I saved my last file to the help folder is irrelevant if my new file is a .CPP file. Again, using this technique is safe for the logo requirements because no harm is done if the user always saves his files to the My Documents folder.

Handling Default Groups

Usually settings can be handled individually, but sometimes it makes more sense to handle them as a group. That is, the value of one setting can determine the default values for several other settings. Consider a personal finance program that helps you write checks, such as Microsoft Money. The check's date should default to the current date (as all date fields should), but the default values for all other fields should depend upon the information in the Payee field. Even though you can't know for sure what the amount field should be set to, it is likely to be close to the amount of the last check to the same payee. For mortgage, auto loan, or insurance payments, the amount is likely to be exactly the same for each check to the same payee. For this type of program, selecting default values individually wouldn't make any sense. The amount of the last check is almost certain not to be the amount of the next check.

Using Defaults to Make Features Visible

An interesting use of defaults is to make certain program features visible when a program is first installed. For example, Word defaults to Page Layout mode instead of Normal mode to help the user discover this mode. Word also defaults to having the Office Assistant on so that new users will know this help facility is available. Similarly, Visual C++ defaults to having the Tip Of The Day feature turned on to help new users learn about

303

the program. Lastly, the Windows Paint utility uses the transparent copy mode by default so that users will be aware of it. All users understand what the opaque copy mode does, so initializing to transparent copy mode is a simple way to make the feature visible.

In all these cases, users would have required much more time to learn that the features were available had they not been operational by default. These defaults make important features visible without getting in the way.

TIP Make carefully selected features visible by turning them on by default when the program is first installed.

Shut Down Windows Dialog Box

For another simple example, take a look at the Shut Down Windows dialog box:

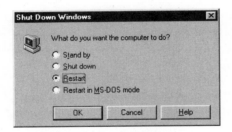

This dialog box always uses the last value selected by the user as the default. I don't think this is necessarily the best choice. It makes sense for the Stand By option, since someone that uses the Stand By option is likely to choose that option often. However, if the user restarts Windows, what is the likelihood that the user will want to restart it the next time? I think the best default for all other modes is the Shut Down option.

Saving Files by Default

Lastly, let's examine a default that doesn't have anything to do with settings in a dialog box. Consider software that allows the user to modify files. Using a program that modifies files is unlike any other life experience. For example, when you fly across the country, you are not presented with a choice like that in the following dialog box:

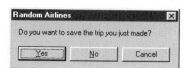

If commercial aviation worked like software, clicking the No button would instantly return you to where you departed from. But if you use Word to edit a file for eight hours and click the document's close button, you will be presented with the same choices. Why? While this confirmation gives equal weight to the yes and no options, it is almost certain that the user will want to save the changes. After all, if the user didn't want to save the changes, he wouldn't have made them in the first place. If the user accidentally clicks the No button, he is going to be pretty upset. This problem begs the question: is it really necessary to ask?

Of course, software uses this file model for some particular reasons. The first reason is that this is the way software works. All changes are in memory and are not saved until they are saved to disk. Another reason is that requiring an explicit save means that the user can experiment without fear since any disastrous or otherwise unwanted changes can be easily abandoned. But since this file model is so unusual, beginning users have a difficult time with it. Advanced users probably don't care one way or the other.

Some programs do directly save changes. If you accidentally blast a setting in the registry using RegEdit, you are out of luck. This makes major registry changes using RegEdit a bit scary. (Where is the vital Undo command?) Similarly, any changes you make in Microsoft Outlook are saved to disk when the program exits.

If you want your program to use a more natural file-handling model, you can make two simple changes. First, your program should always save files by default. It is essential to eliminate the file save confirmation because the unnecessary confirmation is the problem. Don't bother asking; just do it. Second, your program needs an Abandon All Changes command so that in those rare cases in which the user does want to abandon changes, the program can simply reload the original document. Everything else in the program, including the typical Save and Save As commands, can remain as is.

Consider automatically saving file changes by default. Provide an Abandon All Changes command to allow users to revert to the original document.

CHAPTER 18

Don't Surprise the User

While you want to minimize the effort required of the user, make sure you do so in a way that the user expects. The Print Setup common dialog box is a good example of when not to change the default settings to the last selection. Although you certainly want to use the last printer selected and the last page orientation, you should never change the default number of copies to print or the default page range. Your typical user will want to print one copy of all pages unless he explicitly selects otherwise. While he may have printed 47 copies of a document last time, this is almost certain to have been an anomaly. Also, safety should be a consideration. Defaulting to a single copy is risk free, but defaulting to 47 copies is not.

TIP

Consider safety when selecting default values. Never use a default value that would surprise the user.

For another example, suppose you are designing a stock-trading system where the user enters trades and then submits them. A trade action command allows the user to either buy or sell, and it has a simple dialog box that might look like this:

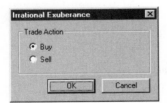

You could argue that once an initial selection is made, the only thing the user can do with this dialog box is toggle between the buy and sell options. Instead of setting the default to the current option, you could set the default to the opposite of the current option. That way if the user had initially entered a trade to sell 1000 shares, the next time the dialog box is used you could select the buy option by default. Then the user could select OK to change the trade action or Cancel to leave it as is. If the default setting were set to the current option, the user would always have to explicitly change the selection, requiring extra effort.

While this technique would save the user a little effort, it definitely isn't what the user expects. The user expects that clicking the OK button

PART

IV

without explicitly making any changes is the same as clicking Cancel. During a panic sell, the user might display this dialog box accidentally and press OK to dismiss it. Now instead of selling 1000 shares, the user has bought 1000 shares. Surprise! Furthermore, if the user really did want to buy, the user expects that clicking the Cancel button in an unmodified dialog box should result in the state indicated by the dialog box. Since the dialog box is initialized to a buy, the user expects clicking Cancel to result in a buy, not a sell. Handling a dialog box this way will completely confuse the user.

TIP Dismissing an unchanged dialog box with the OK button should have the same effect as dismissing it with the Cancel button.

Make sure that an activity that has significant consequences requires explicit selection from the user. While this might require extra work, an explicit selection makes the change obvious. Potentially destructive or disastrous actions should never result from the default. The default command button on a dialog box or message box should never result in an action that is irreversible or destructive. Such defaults are neither cool nor appropriate.

TIP Make sure that an activity that has significant consequences requires explicit selection from the user. Disastrous actions should never result from the default.

This same concept also applies to property sheets. Property sheets, as well as dialog boxes that are effectively property sheets in that they show the state of an object, should always reflect the actual state of an object, not what you expect the user to want to change it to. While it is appropriate to save the user effort by creating a new object with default values that are based on previous input, dialog boxes and property sheets that show the existing state of an object must always be initialized to its actual state—regardless of the user's previous behavior. This is what the user expects.

TIP Property sheets should always reflect the actual state of an object.

CHAPTER 18

Example Code

All this is easier said than done, so let's look at some example code that sets defaults. The following MFC code excerpt shows how the Open dialog boxes should have been handled in WinDiff. It also shows how a Find common dialog box should be initialized.

```
class CUIBookApp : public CWinApp
{
public:
    // Default values
    CString  m_OpenPath1;
    CString  m_OpenPath2;
    CString  m_OpenFileName;
    CString  m_FindString;
    BOOL     m_MatchWholeWord;
    BOOL     m_MatchCase;
    BOOL     m_SearchDown;
    ⋮
};

// Given a file (with path), returns its extension
CString GetFileExt(const CString &filepath);

// Given a file (with path), returns its path
CString GetPath (const CString &filepath);

CUIBookApp theApp;

BOOL CUIBookApp::InitInstance()
{
    // Change the registry key under which our settings are stored.
    SetRegistryKey(_T("UI Book"));

    // Set My Documents path.
    TCHAR myDocumentsPath[MAX_PATH];
    SHGetSpecialFolderPath(NULL, myDocumentsPath, CSIDL_PERSONAL,
                           FALSE);

    // Get the default values.
    m_OpenPath1     = GetProfileString(_T("Defaults"),
                        _T("OpenPath1"), myDocumentsPath);
    m_OpenPath2     = GetProfileString(_T("Defaults"),
                        _T("OpenPath2"), myDocumentsPath);
    m_OpenFileName  = GetProfileString(_T("Defaults"),
                        _T("OpenFileName"), NULL);
    m_FindString    = GetProfileString(_T("Defaults"),
                        _T("FindString"), NULL);
    m_MatchWholeWord = GetProfileInt(_T("Defaults"),
                        _T("MatchWholeWord"), FALSE);
```

```
   m_MatchCase        = GetProfileInt(_T("Defaults"), _T("MatchCase"),
                         FALSE);
   m_SearchDown       = GetProfileInt(_T("Defaults"), _T("SearchDown"),
                         TRUE);

   ⋮
   return TRUE;
}

int CUIBookApp::ExitInstance()
{
   // Save the default values.
   WriteProfileString(_T("Defaults"), _T("OpenPath1"),
                      m_OpenPath1);
   WriteProfileString(_T("Defaults"), _T("OpenPath2"),
                      m_OpenPath2);
   WriteProfileString(_T("Defaults"), _T("OpenFileName"),
                      m_OpenFileName);

   WriteProfileString(_T("Defaults"), _T("FindString"),
                      m_FindString);
   WriteProfileInt    (_T("Defaults"), _T("MatchWholeWord"),
                      m_MatchWholeWord);
   WriteProfileInt    (_T("Defaults"), _T("MatchCase"),
                      m_MatchCase);
   WriteProfileInt    (_T("Defaults"), _T("SearchDown"),
                      m_SearchDown);

   return CWinApp::ExitInstance();
}

void CMainFrame::OnFileOpen()
{
   CString filters, ext;

   // Set filters.
   ext = GetFileExt(theApp.m_OpenFileName);
   if (!ext.IsEmpty())
      filters.Format(_T("Last file (*.%s)|*.%s|All files "
                     "(*.*)|*.*||"), (LPCTSTR)ext, (LPCTSTR)ext);
   else
      filters = _T("All files (*.*)|*.*||");

   // Open first file.
   CFileDialog open1(TRUE, NULL, (LPCTSTR)theApp.m_OpenFileName,
    OFN_FILEMUSTEXIST | OFN_HIDEREADONLY, filters, this);
   open1.m_ofn.lpstrInitialDir = (LPCTSTR)theApp.m_OpenPath1;
   if (open1.DoModal() != IDOK)
      return;

   // Set filters.
```

(continued)

CHAPTER 18

```
        ext = GetFileExt(open1.GetFileName());
        if (!ext.IsEmpty())
            filters.Format(_T("Last file (*.%s)|*.%s|All files "
                            "(*.*)|*.*||"), (LPCTSTR)ext, (LPCTSTR)ext);
        else
            filters = _T("All files (*.*)|*.*||");

        // Open second file - use first file as default file.
        CFileDialog open2(TRUE, NULL, open1.GetFileName(),
         OFN_FILEMUSTEXIST | OFN_HIDEREADONLY, filters, this);
        open2.m_ofn.lpstrInitialDir = (LPCTSTR)theApp.m_OpenPath2;
        if (open2.DoModal() != IDOK)
            return;

        // Save user input for future defaults.
        theApp.m_OpenFileName = open1.GetFileName();
        theApp.m_OpenPath1    = GetPath(open1.GetPathName());
        theApp.m_OpenPath2    = GetPath(open2.GetPathName());
    }

void CMainFrame::OnFind()
{
    if (m_pFindDlg == NULL)
    {
        DWORD flags = 0;

        // Set flags.
        if (theApp.m_MatchWholeWord)
            flags |= FR_WHOLEWORD;
        if (theApp.m_MatchCase)
            flags |= FR_MATCHCASE;
        if (theApp.m_SearchDown)
            flags |= FR_DOWN;

        // Allocate, create and show the Find dialog box.
        m_pFindDlg = new CFindReplaceDialog;
        m_pFindDlg->Create(TRUE, theApp.m_FindString, 0, flags, this);
    }
    else
        m_pFindDlg->SetFocus();
}

LONG CMainFrame::OnFindReplace(WPARAM, LPARAM lParam)
{
    LPFINDREPLACE lpfr = (LPFINDREPLACE) lParam;

    if (lpfr->Flags & FR_FINDNEXT)
    {
        // Save the user's input for future defaults.
        theApp.m_FindString      = m_pFindDlg->GetFindString();
```

```
    theApp.m_MatchWholeWord = m_pFindDlg->MatchWholeWord();
    theApp.m_MatchCase      = m_pFindDlg->MatchCase();
    theApp.m_SearchDown     = m_pFindDlg->SearchDown();
    :
}

// If the Find dialog is being closed destroy it.
if (m_pFindDlg->IsTerminating())
{
    m_pFindDlg->DestroyWindow();
    m_pFindDlg = NULL;
}
return(1L);
}
```

This code is fairly routine. The default values are stored in the application class, but they could be global variables as well. They are initialized by reading their values from the registry in InitInstance. Note that the My Documents path is used until the user explicitly changes the path, as suggested by the Designed for Microsoft Windows logo requirements. The default values are then saved to the registry at program exit in the ExitInstance function.

The OnFileOpen function sets the default files, paths, and filters and saves any changes back to the default values. Setting the file filters string is interesting. It filters out all files that do not satisfy the filter (of course), so setting the proper filter is important to the usability of the dialog box. However, the file extension of the default file isn't fixed, so the filter string has to be created from the default file's extension each time it is used.

Note that the only extra work required for handling the defaults is to load, save, and update their values. Actually, using the defaults isn't difficult at all. If you don't want to bother setting defaults, you will have to come up with a better excuse than it being too difficult to do.

The overall significance of default settings depends upon how often a task is done. If a task is performed once or twice, it probably doesn't make much difference. But if a task is performed many times, providing appropriate defaults can make a significant difference in the usability of your program.

Related Chapters

- Chapter 24—Unnecessary Repetitive Tasks Are Evil.
  Presents many ways to eliminate unnecessary repetitive tasks—for example, by monitoring user input, saving and restoring user settings, designing dialog boxes properly, and other techniques.

311

Recommended Reading

- Bickford, Peter. *Interface Design: The Art of Developing Easy-to-Use Software*. Chestnut Hill, MA: Academic Press, 1997.

  Chapter 7, "Preferences," is subtitled "Preferences, Persistence, and the Soft Machine." Although this subtitle might seem a bit strange, it's quite meaningful. Hardware (a hard machine) has mechanical switches and settings that maintain their state after the power is switched off (although, technically, few switches used in consumer electronics are still mechanical). Software (a soft machine) has a tendency to reset its state whenever it is restarted. The idea in this chapter is that software is improved if it models the behavior of hardware in this respect. This concept applies well to preferences because a program that persistently saves user settings requires fewer explicit user preferences.

- Cooper, Alan. *About Face: The Essentials of User Interface Design*. Foster City, CA: IDG Books Worldwide, Inc., 1995.

  Chapter 8, "Load of the Files," includes an interesting discussion of the problems with the file system–based programming model used by most software. Chapter 11, "Orchestration and Flow," describes how programmers confuse possibility with probability and, as a result, ask the user questions (usually through unnecessary dialog boxes) even when it's almost a given what the answer will be. Chapter 14, "The Secret Weapon of Interface Design," covers how to eliminate unnecessary user input by remembering previous input.

- Microsoft Corporation. The Designed for Microsoft Windows logo requirements, "Save Data to the Best Locations."

  Provides requirements and recommendations for saving data. You can find the logo requirements on the CD-ROM included with this book and in the MSDN library.

- Microsoft Corporation. *Designing for the User Experience*. Redmond, WA: Microsoft Press, 1999.

  See the information on secondary windows for useful guidelines on selecting default command buttons for dialog boxes.

CD-ROM Resources

The CD-ROM included with this book contains the following resources related to this chapter:

- The Designed for Microsoft Windows logo requirements.
- The DevUI MFC Extension Library, which contains a CMcWindowPlacement class to help save and restore window sizes and locations.

CHAPTER 18

CHAPTER 19

Configurability
Is Cool

Configurable programs recognize the fact that not all users are the same. Different users have different personalities, work styles, and requirements, and configurable programs adapt to the user instead of forcing the user to fall into line with the program.

Users like configurable programs, and the ability to customize a program has a strong impact on how a user feels about the program. Consider Microsoft Windows itself. Users can change the Start menu contents and appearance, colors, fonts, wallpaper or background pattern, items on the desktop, taskbar System Tray, quick launch programs, screen saver, and many other details. Add-on programs such as Microsoft Plus! 98 and the Microsoft Tweak UI Control Panel applet are especially popular. As a challenge, quickly compare all the different Windows configurations used in your workplace and try to find two that are even close to being configured the same way. You probably won't be able to.

Configurability vs. Design

As important as it is, the need for configurability should not be used as an excuse to avoid making design decisions. Users don't want the ability to configure absolutely everything, since there is an obvious trade-off. While having more options makes a program more configurable, it also makes it harder to configure. The logic that if some configurability is cool, a whole lot of configurability should be really cool doesn't hold. Having dozens of unnecessary options makes it harder to find the options that are really worthwhile. Configurability isn't the answer to all problems.

In Windows, all of the configurable items I mentioned earlier have a clear purpose, and users routinely configure all of them. Gratuitous options have been avoided. For example, you cannot customize the way menus are drawn, change the look of the caption bars, or change the look of the standard controls. A Windows program looks more or less the same on everyone's computer—there isn't so much configurability that programs are not recognizable. But Windows includes enough configurability to accommodate different personal tastes, work styles, and accessibility requirements. Considering the amount of functionality in Windows, the designers of Windows used a fair amount of restraint in its configurability.

When faced with a user interface design decision, your first reaction shouldn't be "Oh well, let's just make it configurable." The mere possibility that somebody might want to configure a feature isn't a good enough justification. Rather, consider how the feature is going to be used. Is there really a need for configurability? Is it really impossible to accommodate most users in one way only? If the feature were configurable, would anyone bother to configure it? If so, go for it—make it configurable. If not, you should design the feature one way for all users.

TIP While having more options makes a program more configurable, it also makes it harder to configure. Avoid providing options that aren't useful.

While this might sound harsh, the fact is that good constraints are also an important user interface quality. A good user interface guides the user through complex tasks, carefully balancing the need to keep the user in control with the need to prevent the user from screwing up. Constraints are especially important for beginning users. Probably the ultimate restrained user interface is a wizard. In a typical wizard, the user has very little control—the user can select from among a fixed group of settings and then choose either to continue to the next step or to cancel. Yet there is no better way to guide a user through a complex task. By contrast, probably the ultimate unrestrained user interface is the MS-DOS command line. Enough said.

Note that accessibility issues are an exception to this line of thinking. The goal of accessibility is to create software that everyone can use. Where accessibility is concerned, accommodating most users isn't good enough. You want to accommodate all users, so you need to make sure that the user can configure attributes like colors, fonts, system metrics, sounds, and timings. Fortunately, Windows itself provides most of this configurability, so all your program has to do is honor it. The Designed for Microsoft Windows logo requirements are an excellent resource for accessibility information.

Provide configurability to make your program accessible to all users.

Types of Configurability

There are two fundamental types of configurability: implicit and explicit. Explicit configurability is when the user explicitly sets options in a property sheet that was obtained through an Options or Properties command. Implicit configurability is when the user makes choices by directly manipulating objects on the screen—the program then preserves those choices. For example, in Microsoft Visual C++, you can directly configure the toolbar by selecting the toolbars you want displayed from the toolbar context menu, moving the toolbars around by clicking their gripper bars, and positioning individual toolbar items by Alt+clicking on them. This type of configuration eliminates—or, in this example, reduces—the need for choosing options with a dialog box.

Implicit configurability has all the advantages of explicit configurability without any of the drawbacks. The user selects what he wants, and the program honors it by making that selection the default setting. Implicit settings don't add any complexity to the user interface, so they are much easier to justify than explicit settings. They are also more enjoyable to use. You should prefer implicit configurations whenever they are possible.

Prefer implicit settings (that is, direct manipulation with persistence) to explicit settings (that is, property sheets or dialog boxes) whenever possible.

Power vs. Simplicity

Once you've decided what to make configurable, you need to determine how to configure it. For explicit configurations, this usually involves some type of property sheet. The Options property sheet used in Microsoft Word is fairly typical:

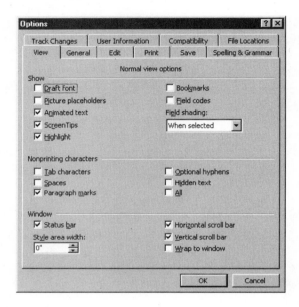

This property sheet is notable in that it reaches just about the right limit for the maximum amount of complexity you want in a single property sheet. Any property sheet with more than two rows of tabs is clearly too complex.

Another interesting example is the Internet Options property sheet in Microsoft Internet Explorer 4.0 (at the top of the next page). This property sheet is unusual in that few options are set directly in the property pages themselves. Rather, the typical page has buttons that display other dialog boxes and property sheets, many of which have buttons that display still more dialog boxes and property sheets. While this technique reduces the number of tabs in each dialog box, it also makes it difficult to tell what the settings are. You have to visit a lot of dialog boxes to review all the settings. This technique works for Internet Explorer only because the program has so many options and they are not homogeneous. Putting all of them in a single property sheet would not be practical. However, you should probably avoid this approach in your programs.

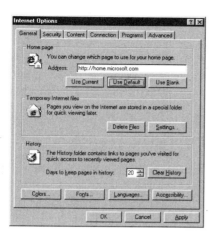

Yet another interesting example is the Project Settings property sheet used by Visual C++. The project settings are so complex that in addition to a multiple-tab property sheet—with so many tabs it needs a scroll bar!—it also needs a combo box and a list control just for the user to select which object to display. (This complexity is necessary for the program, however, so the mechanism isn't as bad as it sounds.) The Visual C++ Project Settings property sheet will be discussed in detail later in this chapter, in the section titled "Case Study: Visual C++ Project Settings."

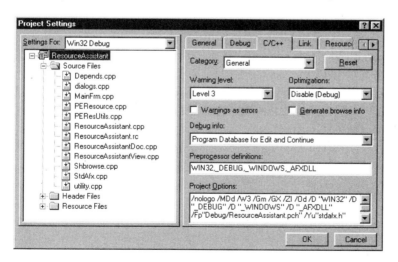

When selecting a user interface for your program options, the most important thing to keep in mind is the unavoidable trade-off between power and simplicity. While power is nice, simplicity is always better. Why?

Because simple configurations get used and complex ones do not. Unless your program is intended exclusively for advanced users, you should favor simplicity over power.

TIP

Simple configurations are better than powerful ones.

Managing Configurability

If your program really needs a complicated configuration, provide functionality to help the user manage it. The following sections describe some configuration management techniques that you should consider using.

Consider Group Settings

If a program has many options, it is often helpful to gather related options into coordinated groups so that the user can deal with the options at a group level, greatly simplifying the configuration.

Let's look at some examples. Windows allows the user to use and define schemes for the desktop appearance (that is, all the system colors, fonts, and metrics) and for sounds. Windows also allows the user to set the regional settings using a single locale selection instead of having to select the individual numeric, currency, time, and date settings. In all these cases, the user can change individual settings but is more likely to change the complete set. For one last example, Word allows the user to combine a collection of text styles into a document template and apply them as a group.

Consider Previews and the Apply Button

The Background, Screen Saver, and Appearance settings in the Windows Display Options property sheet are especially useful because they give the user a quick preview of what the settings will look like. Additionally, the Apply button allows the user to see what the changes will actually look like. This two-level approach helps the user select the desired settings with a minimum amount of effort.

TIP

Always implement the Apply button in property sheets.

Consider Configuration Maintenance Features

For especially complex configurations, it is helpful to provide the user with commands to save, restore, compare, print, and lock configuration settings. Ideally, this information should be stored to a text file so that the user can directly review the information by reading the file. Such functionality would be a great help in routine configuration management, and it would be especially helpful for technical support. Users could then back up, copy, and test their configuration settings.

For example, suppose you have two Visual C++ projects, but one works and the other doesn't and you suspect the problem is in the project settings. To compare the two projects, you are forced to go screen by screen and visually compare each setting. A bit primitive, don't you think? A far better approach would be to have the program itself do the grunt work. I would especially like the ability to create a project template for various types of projects so that I don't have to remake all the same settings every time I create a new project. Then, once everything is set up the way I want it, I would like to be able to lock the configuration to prevent accidental changes.

I have never seen this type of maintenance ability provided, and I am at a loss to explain why. (OK, it would take a fair amount of work, but this is a feature for complex applications.) I think such features would be extremely helpful for programs like Windows, Internet Explorer, and Visual C++.

Consider a Settings History

If the configurations are used in such a way that individual settings are constantly changed among a small set of values, then providing a history list (typically through a combo box) is very useful. Not only does a history list make it easier for the user to make changes, but it also reduces the chance of error.

Consider Restoring Original Settings

Providing configurability carries a certain amount of risk. Windows again is a good example. The user can easily select options that make Windows inoperable. If the user selects the wrong display settings, such as the wrong video adapter, refresh rate, or monitor type, Windows may become unusable. Windows 98 allows the user to restart in Safe Mode to help diagnose and correct such configuration problems, and Microsoft Windows NT allows the user to restore the last known good configuration. Users shouldn't have to completely reinstall the program to correct an accidental configuration change.

CHAPTER 19

While your program might not have settings that are quite as risky as some of those in Windows, you can give users a greater level of comfort by providing a Reset, Restore Original Settings, or Restore Defaults command. Such a command would restore the configuration either to the "factory" settings or to a configuration that is known to work for the specific computer. Beginning users as well as your technical support staff will especially welcome such a feature. Such a command is especially useful in times of panic. You need to provide the user a means to restore the original options without having to resort to a drastic measure such as completely reinstalling the program.

TIP   Consider providing a Restore Original Settings command to return the program to a configuration that is known to work.

Configuration Command Interface

You also need to consider where the configuration commands appear in the user interface. Should you put all the configuration options in a single property sheet that is accessed from a single Options menu? Alternatively, should you have separate menu options for each type of configuration, such as Search Options, View Options, Format Options, and so forth? With the exception of Print Setup, which is always separate by convention, I don't like the separate menu option approach at all. When I want to set options, I want to set options—and I don't want to figure out which type of options I want to set beforehand. I want all the settings to be in one place. Separate configurations result in a kind of configuration safari, where you have to hunt down the right command. Visual C++, for example, includes three configuration commands: Project | Settings, Tools | Customize, and Tools | Options. I use Visual C++ a lot, but I make more mistakes trying to figure out which configuration command to use than I make using all the other Visual C++ commands combined.

The user should also be able to set the options for a specific item by displaying its Properties property sheet from the item's context menu. Sometimes it's also handy to be able to access a Properties property sheet directly from a dialog box. For example, in Word, you can access the Spelling & Grammar property sheet directly from the Spelling And Grammar dialog box by clicking the Options button. This approach is especially convenient for modal dialog boxes; otherwise, the user would have to dismiss the modal dialog box, change the options, and then redisplay the modal dialog box.

The contents of the main Options property sheet can consist mostly of property pages for the individual objects in the program. I like this approach when it makes sense—it doesn't make sense if there are too many configurable items—because it allows the user to find, change, and review all the settings from a single location.

Case Study: Visual C++ Project Settings

For a specific example of configurability, let's take a detailed look at the Visual C++ Project Settings property sheet. This is a good example because it is about as complex as a configuration property sheet can get. And there's also plenty of room for improvement!

Multilevel Configuration

The Project Settings property sheet is a good example of a multilevel configuration user interface. It has three levels of configuration. At the highest level, you select the project configuration, typically Debug, Release, or All Configurations. At the next level, you select the specific items you want to change—typically the entire project, Source Files, Header Files, Resource Files, or any combination of these. The Project Settings property sheet then displays all the property pages that are common for the items you selected. Finally, you can change specific settings in each of the property pages.

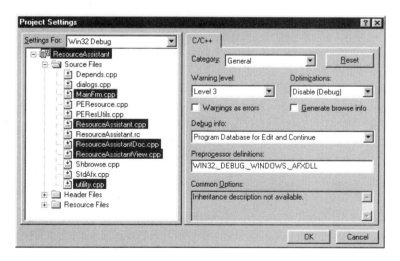

While there are many different ways of handling multilevel configurations, this particular approach is effective because it is visible. That is, you can readily tell what you are doing by looking at what you have selected on the screen. By contrast, I once used a Brand B compiler that used a completely different technique. It let you determine settings for the project as a whole from the menu bar and settings for specific items from a context menu. While this technique doesn't sound all that bad, the problem is that it took me quite a while to realize that this was the way it worked. (Admittedly, this was a long time ago, before context menus were a standard Windows interface.) The program provided a subtle hint that the settings for an individual item were an override of the project settings, but somehow that didn't register immediately. As a result, I used the context menu to change what I thought were the project settings only to be confused when the changes I thought I made to the project didn't take effect. By putting the project settings and the individual item settings together in a single property sheet, the Visual C++ Project Settings makes this confusion impossible.

TIP Make multilevel configurations visible. Put related configurations in a single property sheet.

Multi-Item Changes

Of course, the real objective behind the Project Settings property sheet is to be able to change settings, and having the ability to change settings for several items at a time is a valuable feature. When you select multiple items, the property sheet displays the property pages that are common to those items. Within each property page, each control shows the settings that are common as well. Check boxes are checked if all the items are checked, not checked if none of the items are checked, or displayed in a mixed-value appearance if the settings are mixed. The edit boxes display all the settings that are common to the selected items. Similarly, the combo boxes display a setting if all the items have the same setting; otherwise, they are blank.

This arrangement makes it easy to change multiple items at one time. Just select the items you want to change, and change them. A default-with-override scheme is used to make it easy to change settings at the project level. For example, if you set one file to compile at warning level 2 and then set the project to compile at warning level 4, the file retains the warning level 2. Ordinarily, this is what you want, but you will be in for a surprise if you select the entire project, change a setting, and think that you changed all the items in the project. In fact, you changed the default value only, and all the individual items with overrides maintained their overrides. If you want to change all items, you have to explicitly select the project and all the relevant items in the project before you make the change.

PART
IV

Displaying the common settings in an edit box is a powerful feature. If you select multiple source files, you can change a preprocessor definition common to all the files simply by changing the common setting. This technique has an interesting side effect. Since the edit box displays only what is common to the selected items, you can change only those settings that are common to those items. For example, let's say you want to completely clear the preprocessor definitions for a group of files that do not have completely common settings. The only way to do it is by clearing the items individually.

I find these rules interesting, and they allow the Project Settings property sheet to work more or less the way the user expects. The only problem I have is that these rules aren't explained anywhere. The Source File Options box helps somewhat by clearly indicating when a value is an override. However, I think there should be a help context for the entire property sheet to explain how the rules work.

TIP   If you set rules for using an interface, you need to explain them.

Room for Improvement

While the Visual C++ Project Settings property sheet is pretty good, I think room for improvement definitely exists. As mentioned earlier, I think the Project Settings property sheet could benefit by providing commands to save, restore, compare, print, and lock configuration settings. By saving the settings to an easily editable text file, the user could bypass the Project Settings property sheet in situations where it gets in the way, such as when making many changes to a large project. Again, I would like the ability to create a project template so that I don't have to remake all the same settings every time I create a new project. I would also like the ability to easily gather all my settings, including those for my toolbar and window layout, and transfer them to other computers. This capability would save me a lot of time.

The Project Settings property sheet has a Reset button that works on the granularity of a single property page. When you click the Reset button, you get the following confirmation:

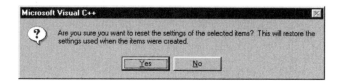

While this is a nice touch, I would usually prefer to restore the settings used before the property sheet was displayed. True, I can obtain that result by simply canceling the property sheet, but that technique isn't so attractive if I've just spent 15 minutes making a bunch of changes and botched the last one. Consequently, I would prefer a message box that looks like this:

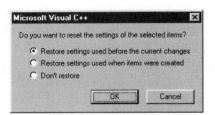

One interesting problem I find with the multilevel settings technique used by the Visual C++ Project Settings property sheet is that the settings' visibility doesn't mean that the user has actually seen them. Has the following ever happened to you? You need to add a library to the link, so you display the Project Settings property sheet and add the library file to the link. You then link, and everything is fine. So far, so good. Now you change to a release build and discover that you added the library to the Debug configuration only. While I completely understand this problem, I always seem to make this mistake. The fact that you can make settings like this without even looking at the selected project configuration doesn't help.

The Project Settings property sheet uses the current project configuration as the default. Ordinarily this is a good thing, but some settings, such as the library files, usually need to be set to the All configuration. I rarely need to add a library to just the Debug or Release configuration. I can think of several solutions to this problem, but they all make the general case much less efficient. The only solution I can think of that doesn't affect the general case is to identify the settings that are typically applied to the All configuration and warn the user when he's made a change without explicitly choosing a project configuration.

The Visual C++ Project Settings property sheet is about as complex as a configuration gets. Despite the shortcomings I've mentioned, I find that it works quite well. In fact, I used it for years without fully understanding exactly how it works. The fact that you can use it and get it to do what you want without really understanding exactly how it works is evidence that the feature is effective.

Related Chapters

- Chapter 15—Keep It Simple.

  Offers tips on reducing the complexity of property sheets and dialog boxes.

- Chapter 17—Direct Manipulation Is Cool.

  Offers several techniques for implementing direct manipulation.

- Chapter 18—Appropriate Defaults Are Cool.

  Describes the importance of having defaults, and presents suggestions on how to implement them. Defaults implement implicit configurability based on user actions and persistence.

- Chapter 20—Previews Are Cool.

  Presents several techniques for previewing settings.

Recommended Reading

- Bickford, Peter. *Interface Design: The Art of Developing Easy-to-Use Software*. Chestnut Hill, MA: Academic Press, 1997.

  Chapter 7, "Preferences," is subtitled "Preferences, Persistence, and the Soft Machine." Although this subtitle might seem a bit strange, it's quite meaningful. Hardware (a hard machine) has mechanical switches and settings that maintain their state after the power is switched off (although, technically, few switches used in modern consumer electronics are still completely mechanical). Software (a soft machine) has a tendency to reset its state whenever it is restarted. The idea in this chapter is that software is improved if it models the behavior of hardware in this respect. This concept applies well to preferences because a program that persistently saves user settings requires fewer explicit user preferences.

- Cooper, Alan. *About Face: The Essentials of User Interface Design*. Foster City, CA: IDG Books Worldwide, Inc., 1995.

  Chapter 32, "Installation, Configuration and Personalization," presents some interesting ideas about configuration, especially relating to the problem of disturbing navigation by configuring a program in a way that removes fixed reference points in the user interface.

CHAPTER 19

- Microsoft Corporation. The Designed for Microsoft Windows logo
requirements, "Accessibility and User Interface."

Gives useful information for providing configurability for accessibility. You can find the logo requirements on the CD-ROM included with this book and in the MSDN library.

CD-ROM Resources

The CD-ROM included with this book contains the following resource related to this chapter:

- The Designed for Microsoft Windows logo requirements.

C
H
A
P
T
E
R

20

Previews Are Cool

In post–World War II Japan, many foreigners had an interesting problem whenever they went to restaurants: they had no idea what they were ordering. Dishes like teriyaki, tempura, and sushi were not yet well known outside of Japan. By the 1960s, some restaurant owners realized that if they displayed plastic models of their dishes, their foreign customers would better understand what they were ordering and would be more satisfied with their choices. This practice continues today, and you often see sample dishes displayed in the front of Japanese restaurants, both in Japan and here.

Although I've never found the glazed plastic models of food displayed in Japanese restaurants to be especially appetizing, they do give you an effective preview of what to expect when you make a selection. In software, some of the text used to describe selections may as well be in a foreign language, as it is often meaningless or difficult to understand. For example, what are Albertus, Andy, Bertram, Chiller, Edda, Ginko, Nadianne, and Thunderbird? If you have done a fair amount of word processing, you might recognize these as names of typefaces. Do you have any idea what they look like? How much work would it take for you to find out? Previews can help you understand such choices with little effort.

Previews are most effective in the following circumstances:

- You need to present a list of choices to the user and the meaning of the choices isn't clear, such as a list of typefaces in a word processing program.

- You need to present several choices that are hard to differentiate and compare, such as a list of different document styles in a word processing program.

- You need to present a combination of choices and the user cannot effectively make a choice without being able to see its impact on other choices, such as when selecting a color scheme.

- You need to present several choices that are time-consuming to perform, such as a list of special effects in an image-processing program.

- You provide a command that is costly to do incorrectly, such as printing a document.

Previews range in accuracy from simple fixed-icon representations to exact replicas, but they serve to give immediate visual feedback. Previews give the user the ability to quickly and easily determine the results of a selection without having to make the selection. They make features self-explanatory and easy to understand, reducing the need for documentation, and also make the user more productive by reducing the chance of making bad choices. Best of all, they help make using software an enjoyable experience by helping the user focus on the task and not on the software.

TIP Previews help users make choices and verify results by giving immediate visual feedback before the user makes a selection.

Types of Previews

While there are many kinds of possible previews, most previews fall into the following general categories:

- **Iconic previews** A preview using a fixed bitmap that abstractly shows the results of a selection. This bitmap never changes, regardless of other selections or the specific user data.

PART

- **Abstract previews**   A preview using a variable bitmap that abstractly shows the results of a selection. This bitmap changes to show the results of this selection and perhaps its combination with other selections. This bitmap does not reflect the specific user data.

- **Sample previews**   A preview of sample data that accurately shows the results of a selection. The sample data can be fixed or can reflect specific user data.

- **Approximate replica previews**   A preview of the specific user data that gives an approximate representation of the results of a selection. This technique is used when creating an exact replica would be too time-consuming or would take up too much space.

- **Exact replica previews**   A preview of the specific user data that gives an exact representation of the results of a selection.

The order of these preview types roughly corresponds to both their accuracy and the difficulty of their implementation. Generally, the more accurate a preview is, the more difficult it is to implement. The type to use depends upon how much accuracy you need to effectively indicate the results of a selection. I recommend using the simplest preview type that does the job. There's nothing wrong with the more abstract preview types—they can be quite effective. When the user needs visual feedback to make an informed decision, a simple preview is better than no preview at all.

The type of preview to use depends upon how much accuracy you need to effectively indicate the results of a selection. Use the simplest preview type that does the job.

Iconic Previews

An iconic preview uses a fixed bitmap that abstractly shows the results of a selection. This bitmap never changes, regardless of other selections or the specific user data. For example, several of the icons used on the Formatting toolbar in Microsoft Office are, in effect, a preview of their results.

CHAPTER 20

Another typical example is a tool palette, such as the Tool Box in Microsoft Paint.

In this case, the icons clearly show a preview of what you can do with the tool.

You can also use icons in a dialog box to show the results of the various options, as in the Microsoft IntelliPoint Mouse Control Panel applet.

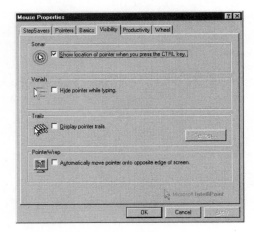

Abstract Previews

An abstract preview uses a variable bitmap that abstractly shows the results of a selection. The bitmap changes to show the results of the selection and perhaps its combination with other selections. The bitmap does not reflect the specific user data. A good example is the Microsoft Plus! 98 Desktop Themes Control Panel applet.

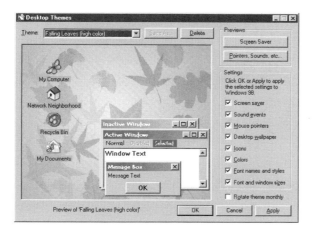

This dialog box shows a realistic abstraction of the desktop using the currently selected theme. This approach to showing color and font selections is also used in the Appearance tab of the Display Control Panel applet.

Microsoft Word has several dialog boxes that display a preview of the user's selections. The Table Of Contents tab of the Index And Tables property sheet is a typical example. Note that the preview is determined by the combination of all the settings on the tab.

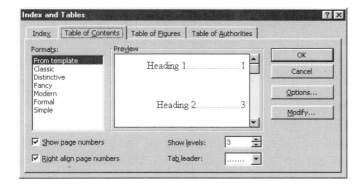

Another example from Word is the Borders And Shading property sheet, shown on the following page. Again, the preview is determined by the combination of all the settings on the tab. In this case, the preview is also interactive since you can click the individual borders to turn them on and off. Here each Setting selection is in effect a radio button that has a preview. Note how much more effective this preview technique is than the standard radio button graphic. In this case, the Shadow setting is selected, although it can be difficult to tell in the black-and-white screen shot.

CHAPTER 20

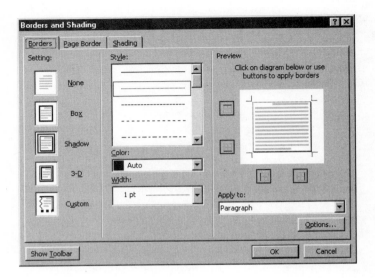

Finally, I find the Visual C++ AppWizard uses especially effective abstract previews. Just looking at changes in the preview makes it easy to figure out the significance of the various selections and reduces the need for reading online help or other documentation.

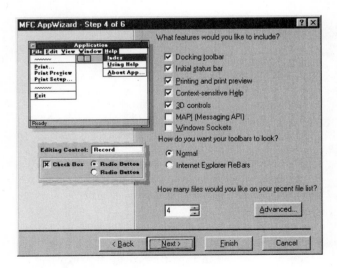

Sample Previews

A sample preview uses sample data that accurately shows the results of a selection. The sample data can be fixed or can reflect specific user data. For example, the Font property sheet from Word displays a preview of the combination of all the settings on the tab. However, unlike an abstract preview, this preview shows actual user text using the selected format rather than an abstract representation.

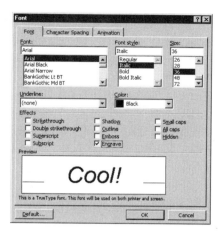

The Style combo box on Word's Formatting toolbar is a classic example of a sample preview. It shows the name of each style using that style, along with its point size, justification, and type on the right-hand side of the list. Interestingly, the Font combo box does not have a preview in Microsoft Word 97, which it badly needs. Happily, this feature has been added to Microsoft Office 2000.

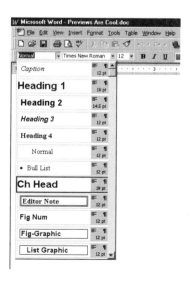

One last example of a sample preview, also from Word, is the WordArt Gallery. This preview shows sample text using several effects. Note how much easier it is to select an effect by its preview than it would be by a text description of the effect.

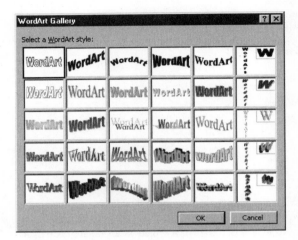

Approximate Replica Previews

An approximate replica preview uses the specific user data to give an approximate representation of the results of a selection. This technique is used when creating an exact replica would be too time-consuming or would take up too much space. This type of preview is a good choice when saving time or space is more important than accuracy.

Thumbnails are a classic example of this type of preview, as with the Microsoft Clip Gallery. (But don't use these owner-draw tabs as a model of good user interface design. Yuck!)

The Screen Saver tab in the Display Control Panel applet is an interesting example, since a small-scale version of the screen saver actually plays in the preview window. This technique is very effective and shows that the best way to preview animation is to display the animation in the preview.

TIP

Preview animations with animation.

PART

IV

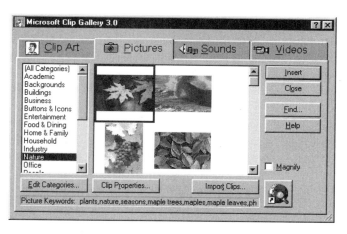

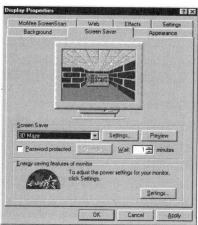

For one last example of an approximate replica preview, consider the preview used for many of the special effects in the Microsoft Photo Editor shown on the next page. Since it can take a fair amount of time to process some special effects, this preview processes only a small section of the image, which is selected by moving the black square in the full preview on the left-hand side. An alternative technique used in other special effects programs is to perform the special effect on a thumbnail. This processing takes much less time, but it is also a less accurate preview of the results.

20
C
H
A
P
T
E
R

Exact Replica Previews

An exact replica preview uses the specific user data to give an exact representation of the results of a selection. This type of preview is often used when previewing an entire document. For example, both Microsoft Outlook and Outlook Express allow the user to preview a message just by selecting an item in the message list.

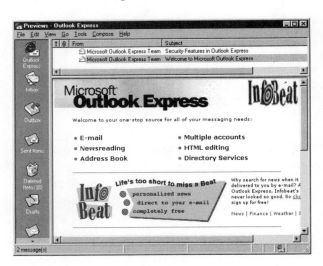

Of course, a print preview is the classic example of an exact replica preview. The print preview is used to determine how the document will look when printed without having to print it. This is an excellent feature that saves a lot of time and paper. Users typically use the print preview to check the individual page layouts and the page breaks. This kind of usage makes accuracy essential for the preview to have any value.

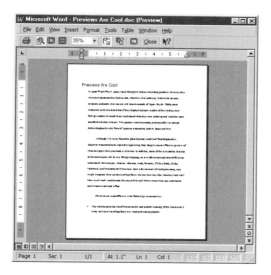

A simple variation of the print preview is the Style Gallery selection dialog box used in Word, which allows the user to select a style template. Having an accurate preview makes it easier to make the right selection.

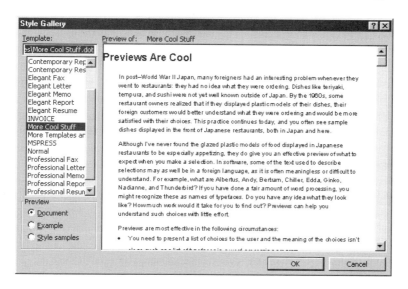

20

The old saying "a picture is worth a thousand words" isn't always true in user interface design, as anyone faced with a couple dozen indecipherable toolbar icons can attest. However, previews are one case in which visual communication is much more effective than textual descriptions. Previews are an excellent way to show the results of a selection. They are a relatively safe feature to use, since not many things can go wrong. Just make sure that the previews are reasonably fast, that they have an appropriate level of accuracy, and that they make sense. Whenever possible, don't explain a feature—show it with a preview.

TIP Don't explain a feature—show it with a preview.

Related Chapters

- Chapter 10—Good User Interfaces Are Visible.

  Presents a discussion on why visibility is important and gives several specific techniques for making Windows programs more visible. Previews are a good way to make a user interface visible.

- Chapter 12—Learn from *The Design of Everyday Things*.

  Presents the types of feedback and why previews are an excellent way to provide visible feedback.

- Chapter 19—Configurability Is Cool.

  Discusses how previews help the user make the right selections when configuring a program.

- Chapter 31—Check Your Printing.

  Discusses the advantages and implementation of print previewing.

Recommended Reading

- Cooper, Alan. *About Face: The Essentials of User Interface Design*. Foster City, CA: IDG Books Worldwide, Inc., 1995.

  Chapter 27, "New Gizmos," discusses the advantages of *visual gizmos*, which is Cooper's term for previews. His advice: "Show; don't tell."

PART

IV

- Horton, William. *The Icon Book: Visual Symbols for Computer Systems and Documentation*. New York, NY: John Wiley & Sons, Inc., 1994.

  While this book is primarily about icon design, it will also help you learn how to communicate visually. These are important skills when designing iconic and abstract previews.

- Prosise, Jeff. *Programming Windows with MFC, Second Edition*. Redmond, WA: Microsoft Press, 1999.

  Chapter 13, "Printing and Print Previewing," has a detailed description of how print previewing is implemented in MFC.

CHAPTER
20

CHAPTER

21

Tooltips Are Cool

Tooltips are little pop-up windows that provide brief context-sensitive help. The great thing about tooltips is that they require almost no effort from the user. To get help for a screen element that has a tooltip, the user just moves the mouse cursor to that object and then does nothing. After a brief delay, the tooltip appears. To remove the tooltip, the user either moves the mouse from the object or does nothing at all, and the tooltip is removed after about a 10-second delay. What could be easier? Tooltips are definitely cool.

Tooltips were originally developed to address the problem of making toolbars more usable. The problem with toolbars is that while they are useful, it is often difficult for users to figure out and remember what a toolbar button does just by looking at the icon—often, the meaning of the icon isn't especially obvious. While using a combination of icon and text is possible (and is the method of choice for utilities), always displaying text on a toolbar is an ineffective use of space. Tooltips provide the best of both worlds—a combination of icon and text, but you see the text only when you want to.

To fully appreciate the power of tooltips, consider the alternative. Before tooltips were invented, Microsoft Windows programs provided context-sensitive information to the user through the status bar. Of course, this method is still used to give help for menus, but it suffers from at least two significant problems. The first problem is that it requires the user to move his eyes from the top of the window where the toolbar is to the bottom of the window to view the status bar, requiring significant effort and making this approach distracting. The second problem is that the changes in the text on the status bar are so subtle that beginning users (who need the most help) often don't notice that help is being offered on the status bar. And making the status bar text more obvious would also prove distracting during the user's normal activity.

While tooltips were originally designed as context-sensitive help for toolbars, they are such a powerful mechanism that their use has been expanded to the following applications:

- **Title tips**   Used to display truncated items within lists and tree controls.

- **Scroll bar tips**   Used to display the scroll bar location. A good example is the document scroll bar tips in Microsoft Word 97, which show the page number and page content's heading as you move the scroll bar.

- **Data tips**   Used to display more information in a document window. A good example is the Microsoft Visual C++ debugger data tips, used to interactively display variable values as you move the mouse cursor over the source code.

There will eventually be other applications as well. In fact, you could no doubt devise a way to use tooltips for just about everything in your interface, but the world would probably be a better place if you didn't.

Tooltips are best used when they accomplish any of the following goals:

- Making your software more visible by providing helpful information to the user

- Eliminating the necessity for dialog boxes by making data more accessible

- Saving screen space, allowing you to create better screen layouts

- Requiring less effort from the user

You should avoid using tooltips that don't accomplish goals like these. One of the reasons tooltips are effective is that they appear fairly infrequently. If tooltips appear in your program every time the user moves the mouse, most likely the user will regard them as an annoyance. Tooltips definitely lose their value if there are too many of them.

TIP Tooltips lose their value if there are too many of them.

Title tips are an excellent mechanism for creating better screen layouts and eliminating work for the user. Suppose you are using a tree view as a primary mechanism for accessing information, as with Windows Explorer or the Visual C++ Workspace window. If you make the tree window too narrow, the tree is difficult to use because the user has to do a lot of scrolling to see the choices. If you make the tree too wide, it takes up too much space on the screen, requiring more work to view a document once it's been selected. Title tips offer an excellent compromise and let you make the tree view a size that works well most of the time. When the user needs to see information that is too long for the available space, he can use the title tip rather than having to scroll.

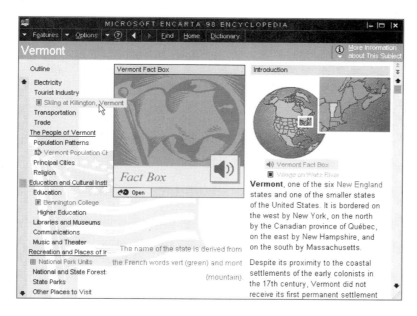

CHAPTER 21

Scroll bar tips help overcome the problem with using scroll bars in large lists and documents. Suppose you have a dictionary list that contains 100,000 items. Without scroll bar tips, using the scroll bar to navigate such a list is ineffective because the user has no idea where he is in the list until he releases the scroll bar thumb. If the user doesn't end up where he wants to be, he has to take another shot in the dark. While it is possible to update the screen while the user scrolls, this approach only works well if the updating is responsive, which is typically not the case with large lists and documents. Scroll bar tips solve this problem elegantly by providing the user with feedback, but in a way that can be updated responsively.

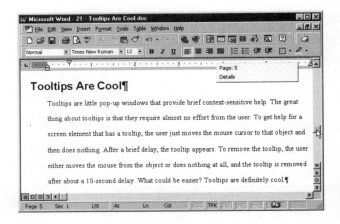

Data tips help make your document interactive by truly implementing the "information at your fingertips" concept. If the user wants more information about an object in a document, he simply moves the mouse over the object. Of course, the text you display in the data tip depends upon the specific information in the document, so it is hard to characterize in general. Unlike the other types of tooltips, data tips must be configurable so that the user can select what information he wants to see and how the information is displayed. If the information displayed in a data tip is complex, you should not automatically remove the data tip after 10 seconds, since the user might need more time to view the information. Anyone who has used the data tip variable watch feature in the Visual C++ debugger never wants to go back to the old approach of having to select data and view a dialog box. Data tips are much easier to use.

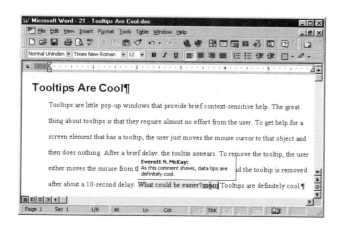

And now for the bad news: there is currently no direct support for scroll bar tips or data tips in the Windows API or in MFC. If you want to add such functionality to your program, you are on your own for now. One note of caution: I have often seen tooltips described as a yellow pop-up window. Of course, this isn't true, since the color of the tooltip text and background are system colors that can be set by the user. If you write custom tooltip code, be sure to use the GetSysColor API function with the COLOR_INFOBK and COLOR_INFOTEXT indices.

Details

Tooltips add significant value to a program, but they can be misused. The most common misuse that I have seen is to provide tooltip text that isn't helpful. Your tooltip text should avoid stating the obvious. For example, don't give a toolbar button with a printer icon a tooltip that says *Print*. Please tell me something I don't necessarily know. For example, on my computer, the tooltip text that Microsoft Word 97 gives is *Print (HP DeskJet 820C Series Printer)*. I find this useful—now I don't have to view the Print Options dialog box to know where my document will be printed. Of course, your tooltip text can provide much simpler types of useful information. Note that Visual C++ gives shortcut keys in tooltips—for example, *Go (F5)* instead of *Go*, and *Stop Debugging (Shift+F5)* instead of *Stop*. You can also indicate that further input is required to perform a command with an ellipsis, such as *Find... (Ctrl+F)*. By simply adding a word or two, you can often make your tooltip text much more helpful.

CHAPTER 21

On the other hand, try to keep the tooltip text brief. Note that the text in the previous examples is short and easy to read. One of the main reasons tooltips are so effective is that the text is brief, which invites the user to actually read the text. Presenting a paragraph or even a sentence is less effective because the user is less likely to read it.

TIP Make your tooltip text informative yet brief. Avoid stating the obvious.

If you are using tooltips to provide help, aim the level of the help at intermediate and advanced users. Tooltip help aimed at beginning users grows tiresome quickly. And, again, don't overdo it. Provide tooltips only when they are really helpful. I would just as soon not have every dialog box control have a tooltip. Using tooltips for screen elements like status icons is welcome when their meaning isn't especially obvious, but you don't have to have tooltips for every screen element. Windows 98, I believe, has taken tooltips too far in this respect. Tooltips aren't necessary for the Minimize Window, Restore Window, and Close Window boxes, for example. These kinds of tooltips are too much in your face; no doubt many users would appreciate a way to turn them off.

TIP Aim tooltip text at intermediate to advanced users.

Finally, don't use tooltips as an excuse to make your software less visible. While tooltips help clarify the meaning of your toolbar icons, tooltips don't mean that you don't have to create good icons. Likewise, MFC makes it easy to add tooltips, but this doesn't mean you can stop thinking.

Related Chapters

- Chapter 10—Good User Interfaces Are Visible.
  Describes how tooltips are an excellent way to give visible feedback and how they are essential in making toolbars visible.

- Chapter 15—Keep It Simple.
  Compares tooltips to balloon help and discusses why tooltips are much better.

- Chapter 17—Direct Manipulation Is Cool.

  Includes tooltips as one of the forms of direct manipulation. Tooltips are an excellent way to manipulate an object to discover its properties.

Recommended Reading

- Armstrong, Strohm. "Previewing the Common Controls DLL for Microsoft Internet Explorer 4.0, Part II." *Microsoft Systems Journal,* November 1996.

  Describes the new tooltip features provided by Internet Explorer 4.0 and Windows 98. These features include custom drawing; the ability to have the tooltip track along with the mouse (probably not a good idea); and the ability to set margins, maximum width, and text and background colors.

- Cooper, Alan. *About Face: The Essentials of User Interface Design.* Foster City, CA: IDG Books Worldwide, Inc., 1995.

  Chapter 23, "Toolbars," has a good discussion about tooltips, primarily with respect to providing help for toolbars. There is also a good discussion of tooltips vs. balloon help and why tooltips are better. He describes tooltips as "one of the cleverest and most-effective user interface idioms I've ever seen."

- Jack, Roger. "Tiptoe Through the Tooltips with Our All-Encompassing ToolTip Programmer's Guide." *Microsoft Systems Journal,* April 1997.

  Provides useful information on how to implement tooltips, data tips, and title tips using MFC.

- Krzeminski, Damian. "Tooltips for Any MFC Window." *Windows Developer's Journal,* June 1997.

  Presents an MFC class to add tooltips to any MFC window.

CD-ROM Resources

The CD-ROM included with this book contains the following resource related to this chapter:

- The DevUI MFC Extension Library, which contains a CMcTooltip class to help you create any kind of tooltip with any contents or format.

21
CHAPTER

2 CHAPTER

Unnecessary Dialog Boxes Are Evil

When your program needs additional information to perform a command, often the easiest solution is to present a dialog box and have the user tell the program what to do. This is also sometimes the best approach, but it isn't always. In fact, usually it is the best approach only when all other alternatives fail.

The idea that dialog boxes are undesirable might come as a surprise to you. After all, dialog boxes are fundamental to modern user interfaces. A well-designed dialog box is easy to understand and use, and dialog boxes are also relatively easy to program. Dialog boxes are all over the place in good Microsoft Windows programs. But while in general dialog boxes are an effective user interface, they become harmful when used in situations where they aren't necessary. Necessary dialog boxes are good, but unnecessary ones should be avoided.

In this chapter, I'll look at when dialog boxes are necessary and when they are unnecessary. I'll also present some common ways to eliminate unnecessary dialog boxes. Note that most of this discussion pertains to modal dialog boxes, as modeless dialog boxes typically are not a problem. One type of unnecessary dialog box that I won't discuss is the unnecessary message box, which is the subject of the next chapter.

Unnecessary Dialog Boxes

Alan Cooper likes to compare displaying a dialog box to going to another room. I think this is a perfect analogy. Consider a kitchen. In a kitchen, you want to have everything you need to prepare a meal within easy reach. It would certainly be awkward to have to go to another room just to get a spoon. If you had to go to another room, this would be a poorly designed kitchen, unless, of course, the spoon in question is a family heirloom or is part of a rarely used silver service. In this case, it would be entirely appropriate to find such an item in a different room, since this isn't something you need to access often.

In this example, the type of task being performed (that is, getting a spoon) isn't the factor deciding which room the task should be performed in. Rather, the frequency of the task is. Of course, there are cases when the type of task alone is enough to warrant a separate room. For example, while you might need to use bathroom facilities while you are in a kitchen, no one would suggest that such facilities belong in the kitchen. The tasks performed in a kitchen and a bathroom are completely unrelated, so performing them in separate rooms is appropriate and desirable. For everyone's benefit, I will stop the analogy here, but as Cooper says, "A dialog box is another room. Have a reason to go there."

The reason dialog boxes are undesirable is that they break the flow— that is, the user's train of thought. Dialog boxes require extra effort to use, both physically and psychologically. When I am performing a task without using a dialog box, I feel as if I am telling the program what I want it to do. The program is serving me. When a modal dialog box appears, the program is interrupting what I am doing to ask a question. Furthermore, it is very insistent and won't do anything more until it gets an answer. Now I feel as if I am serving the program and have to stop whatever I am doing to make it happy.

TIP   Dialog boxes break the user's flow.

The psychological effort to use a dialog box is probably more significant than the physical effort. For example, in Microsoft Visual C++ you can
search for a string using either a modal dialog box or the toolbar. If you
were to count the number of actions required to perform a typical search
using each technique, it would come out to be about the same. (It takes
three by my count.) If you were to time how long it took to perform each
task, the modal dialog box method would probably come out ahead since
you can do it entirely with the keyboard whereas I usually perform the
toolbar approach using the mouse. (Note that Visual C++ supports keyboard
access using Ctrl+D.) Yet the toolbar approach seems faster and more
convenient. For the dialog box, you have to stop what you are doing, give
the command to display the dialog box, review the dialog box, fill in the
required information, click the Find Next button, and then resume your
work. By contrast, the toolbar approach feels like much less effort, like
you're just doing the task without fooling around. Also, there's less of a visual
impact since nothing changes significantly on the screen. The dialog box
approach breaks (or at best suspends) your train of thought and removes
your sense of being in control, whereas the toolbar approach feels much
more direct.

TIP The psychological effort to use a dialog box is probably more significant than the
physical effort.

Necessary Dialog Boxes

When is a dialog box necessary? Of course, that depends on the dialog box
and how it is used. Dialog boxes are often necessary for the following
situations:

- **Making a feature visible**   A well-designed dialog box with instructive labels and with controls organized to clearly show their
  relationships is a very visible mechanism for performing commands. Dialog boxes are also an excellent teaching tool, especially for beginning users. A good dialog box conveys what the
  command is, what the options are, and what input is needed to
  perform the command. However, once the command has been
  mastered, such a dialog box can become the user interface equivalent of training wheels—cumbersome and restrictive—when there
  are more efficient alternatives.

- **Making a feature invisible**   You can hide advanced features that you don't want beginning users to see by placing them in a separate dialog box. The typical user won't bother clicking a command button labeled *Advanced...* until he feels comfortable with the program.

- **Gathering information required to perform a task**   Dialog boxes are effective for gathering input, especially complex input. Although there are other interfaces for making simple selections, dialog boxes are often the best way to get text and numeric data to perform a task.

- **Showing and changing properties**   Dialog boxes (actually property sheets) are the standard way to show and change properties in Windows.

- **Selecting infrequently used settings and commands**   Dialog boxes are a good choice for infrequently used settings and commands, allowing you to separate them from the frequently used settings and commands.

- **Performing a task unrelated to the task at hand**   Dialog boxes are a good mechanism for performing an unrelated task. Combining unrelated tasks into a single window is confusing.

- **Performing a hazardous task**   The fact that a modal dialog box has a Cancel button is significant because it gives the user the ability to bail out. A modal dialog box should always be used for a potentially hazardous task like formatting a hard disk.

These are all good reasons to use dialog boxes, but the best programs strive to make sure that you don't need dialog boxes for routine commands. Consider Microsoft Word. It has dozens of dialog boxes, yet for normal word processing you don't need to use any of them except for the Open and Save As dialog boxes. For example, Word has a Font dialog box that allows you to select a font's typeface; its size; whether it is regular, bold, italic, or underlined; its color; and its various other attributes, such as superscript, subscript, small caps, or hidden. However, since the most useful of these attributes are also on the toolbar, I almost never use this dialog box. Surprisingly, the same can be said for most of the other dialog boxes found in Word. If the user constantly has to access a dialog box to perform a routine command, this is a sign of an unnecessary dialog box.

PART IV

TIP Having to constantly access a dialog box to perform a routine command is a sign of an unnecessary dialog box.

Eliminating Unnecessary Dialog Boxes

You can eliminate unnecessary dialog boxes in several ways. The most commonly used techniques are

- Combining multiple dialog boxes into a single dialog box.
- Direct manipulation.
- Incorporating the dialog box into the window.
- Appropriate defaults.
- Automatic processing.
- Toolbars.
- Status bars.

Let's look at each of these techniques in detail.

Combining Multiple Dialog Boxes into a Single Dialog Box

The goal behind this technique isn't to eliminate all dialog boxes used to perform a command but to have fewer of them. Instead of using multiple related dialog boxes or cascading dialog boxes, combine them into a single dialog box. Such a dialog box could be a property sheet or a dynamic dialog box. Similarly, you could just combine two simple related dialog boxes into one larger dialog box, assuming that the resulting dialog box isn't too large or complicated. A good example is the new Page Setup common dialog box in Windows, shown on the following page, that incorporates the settings found in the old Print Setup dialog box and the old Page Setup dialog box. Why use two dialog boxes to set up your printer when one will do?

TIP Consider combining several related dialog boxes into a single dialog box.

22 CHAPTER

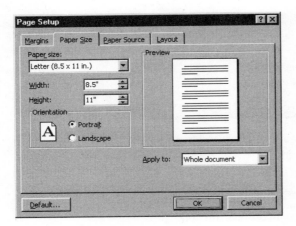

As another example of dialog boxes that might be combined, have you ever run the ScanDisk utility and received a problem report such as this?

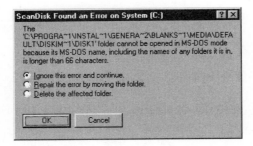

Receiving one or two problem reports like this isn't a problem, but it's a bit much when you receive hundreds of such messages, which is possible for the particular problem being reported. Such dialog boxes are definitely unnecessary. A far better approach would be for the ScanDisk utility to report problems as they are found using a list view control, similar to the way that the Find utility displays the files it finds.

Direct Manipulation

Direct manipulation is when an object is visible on the screen, the user can interact directly with the object, and immediate feedback is given showing the results of the interaction. The most common direct manipulation techniques used in Windows are selection, dragging and dropping, clicking or double-clicking, moving or sizing, context menus, tooltips, and text entry. I find that dragging and dropping and tooltips are especially effective in eliminating the need for dialog boxes. For example, the tooltips used in the Visual C++ debugger allow you to obtain a tremendous amount of information simply by moving the mouse around.

Windows Explorer provides a good example of eliminating a dialog box that works through selecting, clicking, and text entry. To rename a file or folder in Windows Explorer, you select the item, click it to make it editable, and then type in the new name. This approach is much more graceful than using a dialog box to rename a file.

While direct manipulation is an excellent way to perform many commands, it does have drawbacks. For instance, sometimes it isn't obvious that an object can be manipulated, making direct manipulation a poor choice for beginning users. This suggests that you might need to provide a dialog box in addition to the manipulation to accommodate beginning users. Interestingly, Windows Explorer also provides a menu command to rename a file or folder. Selecting the Rename command just makes the item editable, but the menu command is more visible than the direct technique. The other problem is that direct manipulation isn't especially accessible, so again you might want to consider providing a dialog box as an alternative for those who prefer it.

Incorporating the Dialog Box into the Window

One simple technique for eliminating dialog boxes was inspired by the Web: incorporating information that would otherwise be in a dialog box directly into the window. For example, if you want to search for text in a message when using Microsoft Outlook, the search screen is incorporated directly into the window, as you can see in the graphic on the following page.

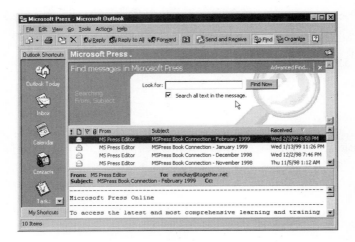

Another good example is Windows Explorer in View As Web Page mode. The most important information about the selected file is displayed on the left-hand side of the Files window, largely eliminating the need to view a file's property sheet. Interestingly, although Windows Explorer displays useful information about selected files and folders, it doesn't do the same for selected drives. It would be useful to see the drive information displayed on the General tab of a drive's property sheet.

Appropriate Defaults

Alan Cooper observes that questions are not choices; questions demand answers now, whereas choices can be made as desired. One example of presenting choices instead of questions is with direct printing, which is used by the Print toolbar button in Microsoft Office and supported by MFC. Instead of demanding that the user indicate which printer to use, the number of copies, the page ranges, and so on, direct printing prints one copy of all pages to the currently selected printer. Direct printing allows the user to not bother with the Print dialog box except when necessary.

Another common technique of using appropriate defaults can be seen in just about any HTML editor, such as the Microsoft FrontPage Editor. An image in HTML can have several properties, such as a type, size, text description, and hyperlink. However, when you insert such an object, the editor uses default properties. It doesn't demand this information immediately; rather, you can set the properties when you want to. Consider how much harder it would be to have to set properties every time you inserted an object. In this case, the dialog box itself is necessary, but it isn't necessary to display it every time the user inserts an object.

Create objects using appropriate defaults to free the user from having to set properties.

Automatic Processing

Another way to eliminate unnecessary dialog boxes is to have certain tasks performed automatically. A good example is the spelling and grammar check feature in Word. Word displays wavy red lines under suspected spelling errors and wavy green lines under suspected grammatical errors. The standard approach (still used by the Spelling and Grammar menu command) is to present a dialog box that displays one problem at a time and to give a variety of message boxes along the way. The visual feedback method of underlining provides the same functionality yet eliminates numerous dialog boxes and message boxes.

Automatic processing is also performed by the IntelliSense features used by Word, including the following:

- The AutoCorrect feature, which automatically fixes common spelling errors.

- The AutoFormat feature, which automatically capitalizes the first word in a sentence, automatically creates numbered and bulleted lists when you start a list with a number or an asterisk, and automatically carries out similar functions.

- The AutoComplete feature, which automatically suggests the rest of the word or phrase that you are typing.

Since these features are performed automatically, no dialog boxes are necessary.

Toolbars

Toolbars are functionally equivalent to modeless dialog boxes, but they are far more convenient. When a toolbar is docked to the program frame, it has the advantage of not obscuring the document window. If you undock a toolbar, it behaves exactly like a modeless dialog box, and it has a distinct visual appearance that makes it impossible to confuse with a modal dialog box. The advantage of a toolbar over a modal dialog box is that it doesn't break the flow, as discussed earlier in the Font dialog box example.

In Visual C++, you can search for text by using either a modal dialog box or the toolbar. All the options available in the dialog box version are also available in the toolbar version. However, since toolbar space is limited, most users put only the search options that they use often on the toolbar. Then the dialog box version is required only for unusual searches.

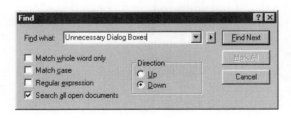

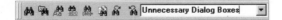

The Visual C++ Find in Files toolbar button uses an interesting technique that eliminates the need for a dialog box. The Find In Files toolbar button remains depressed during a search that is still active. If you are performing a search that is taking a long time and you decide to cancel, you can click the toolbar button again to cancel the search. This technique eliminates the need to display a progress dialog box with a Cancel button.

TIP Use the toolbar to cancel toolbar commands.

Status Bars

Clearly, status bars are good only for displaying status-related information, but using a status bar to display such information is much more effective than using a dialog box. Try to display something more useful than *Ready* on your status bar, which is what is displayed by default in MFC programs.

Related Chapters

- Chapter 13—Learn from the Web.

  One interesting fact about HTML is that it doesn't have the notion of a dialog box, since everything is an HTML page. While HTML pages are often used as a substitute for dialog boxes, better Web designs tend to integrate the equivalent of a dialog box directly into the page, making the dialog box unnecessary.

- Chapter 17—Direct Manipulation Is Cool.

  Describes the various types of direct manipulation and gives many examples. Also discusses some of the problems with direct manipulation and their solutions. Direct manipulation is one of the best ways to eliminate unnecessary dialog boxes.

- Chapter 23—Unnecessary Message Boxes Are Pure Evil.

  Discusses the different types of message boxes and gives tips on how to identify and eliminate unnecessary ones.

- Chapter 24—Unnecessary Repetitive Tasks Are Evil.

  Presents many ways to eliminate unnecessary repetitive tasks by monitoring user input, saving and restoring user settings, properly designing dialog boxes, and other techniques. Unnecessary repetitive tasks often use unnecessary dialog boxes.

CHAPTER 22

Design
Details

Recommended Reading

- Cooper, Alan. *About Face: The Essentials of User Interface Design.*
  Foster City, CA: IDG Books Worldwide, Inc., 1995.

  In Chapter 7, "Windows-with-a-Small-w," Cooper compares windows to rooms and contrasts unnecessary rooms with necessary ones. He then points out how some bad programs have a confusing mess of windows, which he calls "windows pollution." Chapter 11, "Orchestration and Flow," describes how direct interaction is better than using dialog boxes, the advantage of keeping often-used tools close at hand, how good orchestration can be used to eliminate unnecessary user interface elements, how programmers confuse possibility with probability and tend to ask questions with dialog boxes even when the answer is almost certain, and how asking questions differs from offering choices. Chapter 14, "The Secret Weapon of Interface Design," describes how to eliminate unnecessary dialog boxes by remembering previous input and using direct manipulation. Chapter 21, "Dialog Boxes," again describes how dialog boxes are like rooms and how dialog boxes break the flow.

PART
IV

CHAPTER 23

Unnecessary Message Boxes Are Pure Evil

Unnecessary message boxes are a variation of unnecessary dialog boxes, but they are even more irritating and far more common. A simple way to turn a good interface into an unusable one is to ask the user to confirm every action he does. Unnecessary message boxes are pure evil.

Programs have unnecessary dialog boxes and unnecessary message boxes for significantly different reasons. Unnecessary dialog boxes are used primarily because the alternatives, such as direct manipulation, are fairly hard to implement. The alternative to unnecessary message boxes is often to do nothing at all, which is clearly easier. One of the reasons programmers create unnecessary message boxes is that they think they are doing the user a favor.

A good example of an unnecessary message box is one confirming a program exit. While it might seem like a good idea to make sure the user wants to exit the program, doing so is nothing but irritating. Such message boxes exist because programmers are afraid that users will exit the program accidentally and become upset that they have to reload the program to continue their work. Let's consider the benefit of this confirmation. Suppose I accidentally exit Microsoft Visual C++. On my computer, it takes about 10 seconds to load Visual C++ the first time but only about three seconds to reload it. Furthermore, Visual C++ is one of my slowest loading programs. Microsoft Internet Explorer takes about a second to reload.

Now let's consider the cost of this confirmation. The user has to read the message, think it over for a second (not having to think it over is a clear indication of a useless message), possibly move his hand from the keyboard to the mouse, move the mouse cursor to a message box button, click the button, and then resume his work. This whole process may take several seconds and completely disrupts the user's train of thought. This is why users hate unnecessary message boxes.

If you assume that the user correctly selects the exit command far more often than he incorrectly selects it, this is a very poor trade-off. A far better solution to this problem is to ask the user to save any unsaved work (which you should be doing anyway), save the current program state (which you should be doing anyway if that state is difficult to re-create), and exit the program without further user interaction. Instead of making it difficult to exit, a good program makes it easy to pick up where the user left off.

Types of Message Boxes

Messages boxes occur in the following varieties:

- **Notifications** A notification provides the user with information about the results of a command. Usually implemented with the Information message box type.

- **Flash Boxes** Same as notifications, except that a flash box removes itself after a couple of seconds. Doesn't have buttons.

- **Confirmations** A confirmation alerts the user to a condition or situation that requires the user's input before proceeding. Usually implemented with a Warning message box type.

- **Error messages** An error message informs the user of a problem that requires correction before work can continue. Usually implemented with a Critical message box type.

Each type of message box is used in different ways and therefore has different implications, which I will discuss in the following sections.

Notifications

A notification message box can be eliminated if the information it provides isn't significant or could be replaced with some type of visual feedback. You could make the argument that most notifications are unnecessary. After all, if the user executes a command, it usually goes without saying that the command has executed successfully unless some form of error message is displayed. Notification message boxes should be used only when the successful completion of a command isn't obvious and there is no alternative way to provide feedback.

Let's look at some examples. The typical Find command that finds text in a document needs to inform the user when it has reached the end of a document without finding any more occurrences of the specified text. If the command loops back to the beginning of a document without informing the user, there is a risk that the user will make several passes through the document without realizing that he has reached the end. The Find command in Visual C++ solves this problem by displaying the text *Passed the end of the file* on a blue background on the status bar. While this takes a little getting used to at first, it is far more convenient than a message box. Interestingly, Microsoft Word displays a message box that states *Word has finished searching the document.* I assume the status bar approach isn't used in Word because its target audience is much broader than the Visual C++ audience is.

TIP Consider using the status bar to eliminate notification message boxes.

The Find utility in Microsoft Windows indicates its status by enabling and disabling buttons and displaying an animated icon. When the Find utility is searching for something, the animation clearly shows that it is searching, the Find Now button is disabled, and the Stop button is enabled. When the search is finished, the animation stops, the state of the buttons is reversed, and the number of files found is displayed on the status bar. This visual feedback keeps the user fully informed without using message boxes at all.

TIP Consider using control enabling and animation to eliminate notification message boxes.

CHAPTER 23

Flash Boxes

Flash boxes are fairly new to Windows, so they aren't used often. A good example is the flash box shown when Microsoft Outlook shuts down.

Flash boxes are an ideal way to eliminate many notifications. They provide the user with obvious feedback but don't require any acknowledgement. This makes them ideal for feedback that isn't essential for the user to know. Of course, flash boxes are most effective when their text is short and easy to read.

TIP
Consider using flash boxes to provide feedback that isn't essential for the user to know.

Confirmations

If you want users to hate your program, just sprinkle a bunch of unnecessary confirmations throughout it. This will make your users scream. You shouldn't confirm a user action just because the user might make a mistake.

How do you decide when a confirmation is necessary? I recommend using trade-off analysis similar to that used for analyzing the program exit confirmation. If the accumulated cost of the confirmations exceeds the benefits, or if it takes less than about 10 seconds for the user to recover, most likely the confirmation isn't necessary.

You also need to understand that using too many confirmations completely undermines your objective of protecting the user. The natural user response to a flurry of message boxes is to get rid of them as quickly as possible. Most likely, the user will just click the OK or Yes button without even reading the text. Even if one of those confirmations says *Click OK to lose all information*, most likely the user will click OK without reading the text.

Any action that can be easily undone should not be confirmed. If you have many actions that aren't easy to undo, you should consider putting the burden on your program instead of on the user by providing an undo command. Good examples are the Undo and Redo commands in Microsoft Office and Visual C++, as well as the Recycle Bin in Windows.

TIP Consider providing an undo command to eliminate confirmations.

Of course, any action that cannot be easily undone should definitely be confirmed. For example, do ask the user to confirm destroying an unsaved document and to confirm before erasing or formatting a hard disk. But your first choice should be to add enough functionality to make the confirmation unnecessary.

One confirmation that I find especially bothersome is when a program asks me if I want to save changes to a document when I didn't make any changes in the first place. If I didn't make any changes, why would I want to save them? The answer to this questions is always no, so why bother asking me? A program should ask the user to save changes only when the user explicitly made a change. This problem occurs in Outlook when you view an attachment to a message using Microsoft Word. Changes created automatically by a program, like changes to pagination created by Word when it loads a document, should not be considered worthy of bothering the user.

TIP Don't confirm saving changes unless the user actually made changes.

Note that in all other cases the user is far more likely to want to save a document than destroy it but has only a fifty-fifty chance of selecting the right button in the confirmation. If the user accidentally presses the wrong button, it's possible that several hours of work may be lost. If the user chooses not to save the document and the document isn't too large, you might want to do the user a favor and save the document anyway to a temporary folder. This way, if the user made a mistake, nothing is lost and your user is grateful. To implement this feature properly, you will need to make sure that the user is aware of it (ideally with a flash box, as shown below) and periodically delete the old files in the temporary folder so that they don't take up too much space.

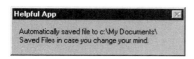

CHAPTER 23

By the way, while modal dialog boxes almost always have OK and Cancel buttons, confirmations are almost always better with Yes and No buttons. For example, the world's most confusing message box—

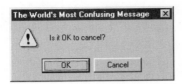

is at least comprehensible when it uses Yes and No buttons instead:

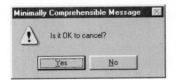

Error Messages

Presenting the user with many error messages is often a sign of a shortcoming in your program. Your goal should be to provide enough functionality to make most error messages unnecessary by preventing the user from making errors in the first place. It is always better to prevent an error than to report it. The most common ways of preventing errors are

- **Disabling invalid menu commands and controls** The user should never be able to select a menu command or control that will only result in an error message.

- **Preventing invalid user input** Use constrained controls whenever possible. In other words, avoid using edit boxes for anything other than unconstrained text and numeric input. For constrained input, use other controls such as combo boxes, lists, sliders, and spin boxes. Use the date and time picker control for dates and times. Edit boxes should be your last choice control, but, if necessary, confirm the user's input immediately instead of waiting until the user clicks the OK button. Ideally, invalid input could be automatically corrected or indicated with some visual feedback.

Prevent invalid input to eliminate error messages.

- **Providing appropriate defaults**   Appropriate defaults reduce the need for input, thus reducing the possibility of error. Furthermore, default values make the format of valid input visible. For example, a date field that has today's date as a default value is less likely to result in an error since it makes it clear what date format is expected.

- **Using direct manipulation**   Direct manipulation eliminates the need for error messages by restraining the manipulation to acceptable limits.

What if you can't prevent the error? Another possibility is to fix the problem automatically. This is a good approach if

- You can be fairly sure what the user really wants to do.
- You can make the automatic change obvious.
- You can give the user the ability to override the automatic change.

For example with Microsoft Word, if I type *hte*, Word automatically replaces it with *the*. It is fairly safe to assume that the user doesn't want to create a document with typos in it, so you can be sure this is what the user wants to happen. It is obvious when the automatic change occurs because the user can see the text change. If correctly implemented, there should be a fixed time lapse between the typo and the change so that the change is obvious even on the fastest computer. Lastly, the user can easily override the change. If the user then replaces *the* with *hte*, Word leaves it alone. Alternatively, the user can override the change with the Undo command. If the user never wants to do this change at all, he can remove this word from the AutoCorrect list.

If you fix problems automatically, make it obvious.

If you don't satisfy these three requirements, you run the risk of automatically "fixing" problems incorrectly and with potentially disastrous consequences.

Use automatic features to help the user, but leave the user in control.

---

23 CHAPTER

Details

You should consider the following issues when creating message boxes.

Present Only One Message Box

A variation of the unnecessary message box problem is to present a necessary error message with several variations of the same problem in separate message boxes. For example, suppose you are developing a program that accesses a CD-ROM, but the wrong CD-ROM is in the drive. The user should receive a single error message, not three or four, like *Can't access CD-ROM*, *Can't open file*, and *Can't open document*. One error message is enough.

Of course, this is easier said than done. The problem is that often such error handling is distributed across many low-level modules. The solution is to avoid displaying error messages in low-level modules but to pass back status information and let the calling module decide how to handle the error.

Present It Just Once

Whatever you do, don't keep asking the same question over and over again. Have you ever been low on disk space? If so, Windows 95 presents you with this dialog box:

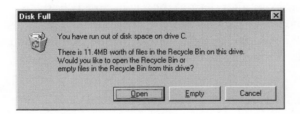

If you click the Cancel button, guess what happens? A few minutes later you will receive the same message again. Even though you have explicitly told Windows not to bother you with this problem, it continues to remind you until you finally submit and empty the Recycle Bin. This message would be improved either by waiting several hours between messages or by giving the user an option not to display the message in the future.

Another good example of an annoying message box comes from the Windows 95 ScanDisk utility. When I run ScanDisk on my computer, I get the following error message:

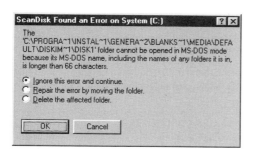

Unfortunately, the one option I really want is

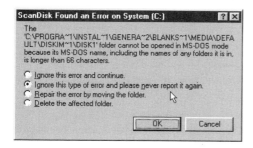

I don't care about this error because I will never attempt to access anything in this folder in MS-DOS mode. This error practically renders ScanDisk useless to me because I have hundreds of such folders on my computer and would prefer not to press the OK button a few hundred times to check my hard disk. Fortunately, Windows 98 has solved this problem by providing a Report MS-DOS Mode Name Length Errors option that I can turn off in the Advanced Options dialog box.

One last example: copying a group of files using Windows Explorer. If one of the files you are copying already exists in the target folder, you receive the following message:

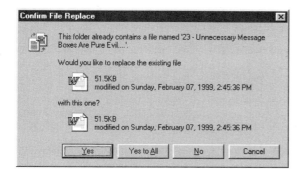

The Yes To All option is especially nice, since it allows you to complete the operation without having to respond to possibly many message boxes. However, note that answering No is also a sensible thing to do, so this message box could be greatly improved by adding a No To All option. If you are copying a thousand files, you shouldn't have to click No a few hundred times.

Consider Message Box Time-Outs

While message boxes are sometimes a pain to use, they are even more painful when you don't use them. Have you ever prepared a large project build or a large print job to run overnight and then come back the next morning only to find a confirmation like this one?

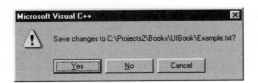

Without a response, the program is essentially locked up forever.

Since Visual C++ does occasionally crash and burn during a compile, I truly appreciate having Visual C++ save my files before it compiles, so this is clearly a necessary dialog box. However, I would prefer that Visual C++ not save a file rather than wait forever for me to respond.

The solution? Use a time-out, as is done in the following example from Outlook. If you have a message box whose response is optional (typically if the issue is trival or if there is an appropriate default response) and the lack of response will prevent your program from doing important work, the message box should time-out after a few minutes. Without a time-out, even a necessary message box can be pure evil.

When in Doubt, Make It Configurable

When in doubt about a message box, make it configurable. I don't mind using a program that confirms an exit as long as I have the ability to turn this confirmation off. Provide the user the ability to not display certain types of messages, either from program options or from the message box itself, as with the following example:

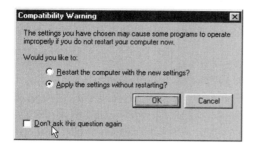

If you provide an option like this, you should also provide a mechanism to undo this action, preferably through an options property sheet.

Case Study: Error Moving File

Let's look at a classic message box that is completely unnecessary. Have you ever selected a folder in Windows Explorer and received the following error message?

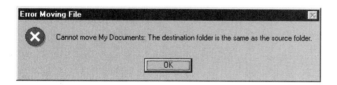

Over the years, I have received this error message hundreds of times. You get it when you select a folder in the All Folders pane of Windows Explorer and move the mouse slightly before you release the button, which is interpreted as an attempt to drag the object onto itself instead of as a selection. However, not once did I actually intend to perform this action. Doing so wouldn't make any sense.

Why is this error so bad? The text is certainly easy to understand. The problem is that the message is completely unnecessary—there shouldn't be a message at all. Rather, Windows Explorer should simply treat a folder being dragged onto itself as an accident and should only select the folder. Feedback isn't necessary, since if I really did intend to copy a folder to itself, no action would be required.

Related Chapters

- Chapter 4—Establish a Consistent User Interface Style.

  The Sample User Interface Guidelines section presents several useful guidelines for message boxes and error messages.

- Chapter 12—Learn from *The Design of Everyday Things*.

  Discusses feedback interfaces and gives several examples. Of the feedback interfaces, message boxes are the most obtrusive.

- Chapter 22—Unnecessary Dialog Boxes Are Evil.

  Discusses why unnecessary dialog boxes are undesirable, how to identify unnecessary dialog boxes, and how to eliminate them.

- Chapter 30—Check Your Error Messages.

  Gives a list of useful items to check to make sure that your error messages are necessary, helpful, informative, and easy to understand.

Recommended Reading

- Cooper, Alan. *About Face: The Essentials of User Interface Design*. Foster City, CA: IDG Books Worldwide, Inc., 1995.

  Chapter 13, "Overhead and Idiocy," describes how software often has unnecessary overhead, which he calls excise since it doesn't contribute to performing the task at hand. Idiocy is how Cooper describes it when a program stops a task to ask a stupid question with an unnecessary message box. As Cooper puts it, "The typical error message box is unnecessary. It either tells the user something that he doesn't care about or demands that he fix some situation that the program could usually fix just as well." Chapter 28, "The End of Errors," presents a thought-provoking discussion about message boxes, particularly error messages. Cooper's theory: "I believe that, with proper design, all error messages and confirmation dialogs can be eliminated." While I don't agree with this theory, and I don't know anyone else who does either, most of the ideas presented are worth serious consideration. Chapter 29, "Managing Exceptions," introduces the "inverted meta-question," which "tells a dialog to go away and not ask again. In this way, a user can make an unhelpful dialog box stop badgering him, even though the program mistakenly thinks it is helping."

- Microsoft Corporation. *Designing for the User Experience*. Redmond, WA: Microsoft Press, 1999.

  See the chapter on secondary windows for guidelines on message box types, title bar text, message box text, and button text. Essential information.

- Tognazzini, Bruce. *Tog on Interface*. Reading, MA: Addison-Wesley Publishing Company, Inc., 1992.

  Chapter 28, "More Short Subjects," presents a discussion and guidelines on when to use time-closure dialog boxes.

CD-ROM Resources

The DevUI MFC Extension Library on the CD-ROM included with this book contains the following resources related to this chapter:

- A McMessageBox function that provides a message box with options for customizable button text, customizable icons, HTML tagging in the text, an option to not display the message box in the future, and an automatic timeout.

- A McDetailsBox function that provides a message box with options for a Details button to show additional information, customizable button text, customizable icons, HTML tagging in the text, an option to not display the message box in the future, and an automatic timeout.

- A McFlashBox function that provides options for customizable icons and HTML tagging in the text.

- A CMcProgressDialog class to display a progress dialog box.

- A CMcProgressStatusBar class to display progress on the status bar.

CHAPTER 23

CHAPTER 24

Unnecessary Repetitive Tasks Are Evil

Many programs have tasks that require unnecessary repetition. You know what I mean. To use these programs, you have to go through the same steps over and over again. You have to move and resize the same windows, select the same settings, and enter the same input in dialog boxes. You have to go through the same sequence of steps to perform a task that could be replaced by a single step or even performed automatically. Using these programs is a real grind. It's no fun to have to repeat the same unnecessary steps to get your work done.

Whenever you notice that you or any of your users are repeating the same steps over and over, ask yourself whether there's a way to eliminate the repetition. There usually is, either by adding functionality or by monitoring the user's input. The user shouldn't have to start completely over every time he runs the program or performs a task. Users are telling your program how they want to use the program while they are using it. All your program has to do is listen.

CHAPTER 24

Some Examples

Suppose you are developing an MDI program. Whenever you run the program, you always maximize the main window first. Then you usually load the last document that was accessed. And then you maximize the document window to fill all the available space within the MDI frame. Now suppose that not just you but all of your users typically follow a similar sequence of actions when they start your program. Why? Should it be necessary to perform these steps every time?

Now suppose that your program performs these three steps by default or, better yet, if these steps were performed the last time the user ran the program. Now the program is launched maximized and the last document accessed is automatically loaded into a maximized window. You've done the user a big favor. But what is the downside? The downside is that the user might occasionally use the program in a slightly different way from what you expect. In this example, probably the worst case is that the user will have to close a window he really didn't want to use. Assuming the document loading process is fast, this is not a significant drawback.

TIP A program should restore itself to the state it was in when last quit.

Let's look at a variety of techniques used by Microsoft Windows programs to eliminate unnecessary repetitive tasks.

General Windows

● Automatically saving and restoring user preferences.

● Automatically saving and restoring window sizes and locations.

● Automatically saving and restoring the last document used or all previously opened documents, and possibly restoring the previous scroll positions.

● Maintaining a list of the most recently used documents.

● Automatically selecting appropriate defaults in dialog boxes to reduce the effort required to use them.

● Automatically displaying the last page used in a property sheet.

● Providing property sheets with an Apply button. The Apply button eliminates the user having to display a properties dialog box, making a change, clicking the OK button, checking the results, and repeating the process until satisfied.

- Making lists and combo box drop-downs that are long enough to eliminate unnecessary scrolling. If a list or combo box has only a few items that can easily be viewed all at once, the control should be long enough to not need the scroll bar.

- Automatically expanding an unexpanded node in a tree control when you drag and hold an object over the node for more than two seconds.

- Quickly finding files by providing shortcuts to the My Documents folder.

- Providing file browse buttons so that the user doesn't have to type in the name and path of existing files.

Microsoft Word

- Automatically checking for spelling and grammatical errors as you type, eliminating the need to perform these checks manually. Microsoft Word makes the bold assumption that users want to write documents without errors.

- Automatically placing the most recently selected fonts at the top of the Font combo box, eliminating the need to perform a lot of scrolling to find a font.

- Providing the Format Painter feature to copy the format of text or an object and directly apply it to other text or another object. Totally cool!

- Providing the AutoCorrect feature to automatically fix many common spelling errors, such as replacing *hte* with *the*. AutoCorrect even detects accidental usage of the Caps Lock key. For example, if Caps Lock is on, Word replaces *tHE* with *The* and turns off Caps Lock. I really like this feature because my usage of Caps Lock, as well as Num Lock and Scroll Lock, is always accidental.

- Providing the AutoFormat feature to automatically capitalize the first word in a sentence, automatically create numbered and bulleted lists when you start a list with a number or an asterisk, automatically create borders when you type three or more consecutive hyphens in a row and press Enter, automatically format ordinal numbers and fractions (for example, 1st becomes 1st and 1/4 becomes ¼), automatically turn networks and Internet paths into hyperlinks, and automatically convert "+----+----+" patterns into tables with a column for each pair of plus signs.

CHAPTER 24

- Providing the AutoComplete feature to automatically suggest the rest of the word or phrase that you are typing. To accept the suggestion, you press Enter and Microsoft Word makes the substitution.

- Providing templates and document wizards to save time in creating many common types of documents.

- Using the first line of a document as the default filename when the document is first saved.

- An example of where Microsoft Word fails to eliminate an unnecessary task: Every time I create a new document, I select the default font to be 10 pt. Arial, not 10 pt. Times New Roman. I do this every time—I have to since Word isn't smart enough to give it to me by default. Yes, I know, I can change the default font by changing the default document template, but Word ought to be smart enough to at least ask me if that is what I want to do and then do it automatically.

Two important details contribute to the successful implementation of the automatic features supported by Microsoft Word. First, you can turn the features off or fully customize them. While the features help most users in most situations, of course there are situations in which they get in the way. Second, these features monitor the user and perform a correction only once. To use my earlier example again, if I type *hte*, Word automatically replaces it with *the*. But if I then replace *the* with *hte*, Word leaves it alone. Alternatively, I can have Word bail out of any automatic change with the Undo command. Word's automatic features are intended to help the user, but ultimately the user, not the program, is in control. (This is where the designers of HAL 9000 really blew it!)

TIP Allow the user to fully customize automatic features and include the ability to turn them off.

TIP Use automatic features to help the user, but leave the user in control.

Microsoft Visual C++

- The AppWizard automatically creates boilerplate program code that allows you to create a baseline working program quickly.

PART

IV

- The ClassWizard automatically creates new classes and performs routine maintenance such as adding and removing member functions and member data.

- The WizardBar simplifies many repetitive tasks, such as finding class and function definitions and defining new functions and message handlers. The WizardBar allows you to perform all of these activities directly from the toolbar.

- The WizardBar Action menu is especially useful in routine tasks, such as finding a function declaration from its definition, finding a function definition from its declaration, adding message handlers, virtual functions, and member functions, creating new classes, and opening any include file used by the active source file. You can also define a default action—for example, you can find the declaration of a function simply by clicking on the WizardBar Action button.

- The IntelliSense feature provides Statement Completion, which provides quick access to valid member functions or variables, including globals, via the Members list for the Win32 APIs, MFC, and ATL.

- The resource editors automatically define resource IDs.

- The Variables window in the debugger automatically displays variables used in the current statement and in the previous statement, as well as the return values when you step over or out of a function. This approach often eliminates the need to select variables to watch during debugging.

- While debugging, the source windows display variable values using tooltips. This is an incredibly useful feature that eliminates the need to use dialog boxes to view variables.

- The Windows menu can optionally sort the windows in most recently used order. This feature is useful since the user is more likely to want to see a recently used file than one used hours ago. (Unfortunately, there seems to be something of a bug in that the program considers a file used if Visual C++ itself uses it. It would be much more useful if a file were considered used only if it had been activated directly by the user.)

Microsoft Outlook

- Providing the ability to view the contents of a new message directly without opening a separate window.

24
CHAPTER

- Providing options to automatically check the names of message recipients, have names the user replies to automatically added to the Address Book, to have messages automatically removed from the Deleted Items folder on exit, and to have many other tasks automatically performed according to the user's personal preferences.

- The Rules Wizard allows you to create many different types of complex actions to perform when a message arrives, such as to automatically move, delete, forward, flag, categorize, reply to the message, or notify you, all based on various parameters you select.

- You can use the AutoCreate feature to drag an item of one type into a folder of another type to create a new item. For example, you can drag an email message to the Contacts folder to automatically create a new contact. You can also drag an email message to the Calendar folder to schedule an appointment.

- Automatically checks for spelling errors before you send a message so that you don't forget. (Although it would be even better if it were to check for spelling errors as you type, as done with Word.)

Windows Explorer

- The Back and Forward toolbar buttons have a drop-down list of choices so that you can view previously visited folders quickly.

- Providing the ability to change the attributes of several files at a time with a multifile property sheet.

- Remembering the column widths and sort orders for individual folders in Windows 98.

- Providing the Enable Thumbnail View folder property to allow a Thumbnail view in Windows 98, which displays thumbnails for the graphics files. This feature eliminates the need to open a graphics file to view its contents.

Microsoft Internet Explorer

- The Back and Forward toolbar buttons have a drop-down list of choices so that you can view a previously visited page directly instead of pressing the Back and Forward buttons several times.

- The URL address box simplifies entering URLs in several ways. It includes a drop-down list with the recently entered URLs. It includes the AutoComplete feature—if you enter a partial URL, it suggests a complete URL if the partial URL matches the URL of a previously visited site. The address box also automatically prepends the protocol, so you only have to type in *www.microsoft.com* instead of *http://www.microsoft.com*. And you can drag and drop a URL by selecting the icon next to the address and dragging it anywhere that accepts a URL, such as the Favorites list, the taskbar, or the desktop.

- The Explorer bar gives you quick access to the Favorites menu and to recently visited sites in the History list. The History list is hierarchically organized by the base URL so that the list is easy to navigate.

The Find Utility

- Continuously monitors the files it finds for changes, such as file-name changes or deletion.

- The Open Containing Folder command in the File menu makes it easy to find a file in Windows Explorer.

Hardware

- The Microsoft IntelliMouse mouse wheel eliminates having to move the mouse to the edge of a window to scroll.

- Printers that turn on automatically whenever a document is printed.

- Computers that turn off automatically whenever Windows is shut down.

- Plug and Play hardware that automatically installs itself.

These features have a tremendous range—some are very simple, some are very complex, but they all have one thing in common. They are all totally cool because they help users get their work done without fooling around. Features like these are among my favorites.

These features all show different ways that a program can eliminate unnecessary repetitive tasks. By performing tasks automatically, they all run a slight risk in performing a task in a way that the user doesn't want, but this risk is small and the advantages greatly outweigh the disadvantages. They also demonstrate another important principle: good programs go out of their way to help users get their work done.

Design
Details

TIP The best programs go out of their way to help users get their work done.

Case Study: A Find Dialog Box

Now let's apply these ideas to a fairly typical example. Let's design a Find dialog box that searches for text strings in a file, similar to the Find command in Visual C++. The goal of the design is to eliminate as much unnecessary repetition as we can.

The first design is a simple dialog box, with an edit box to type the search text, a Find Next default button to find the next occurrence of the string, and a Cancel button to close the dialog box. The input focus is initially on the Find Next button, and the input focus moves from the Find Next button to the Cancel button to the edit box.

While this dialog box is completely functional, the user has to enter the complete search string every time he uses it. The dialog box has no recollection of any past usage. While the user will often completely change the text, it is likely that the user will want to search on the previous search string or a string similar to it. Let's eliminate the need to reenter the last entered text by saving it and automatically initializing the edit box to the last searched string.

Now if the user wants to search for the last string, all the user has to do is click the Find Next button or press the Enter key. What if the user wants to change the text? The user has to select the existing text, clear it, and then enter the new text. We can eliminate this unnecessary step by setting the input focus to the edit box by default and selecting the entire search string. While we're at it, let's also disable the Find Next button whenever the search string is empty to eliminate the need for an error message.

PART
IV

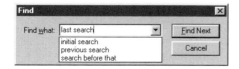

Now if the user wants to search for the last string, this dialog box requires the same effort as before—the user has to click the Find Next button or press the Enter key. However, if the user wants to search for a different string, the user just has to type the new string and press Enter.

Let's reconsider the first design attempt that didn't initialize the edit box to the last search string. Giving the Find Next button (or, as in most modal dialog boxes, the OK button) the initial input focus is a poor choice. Why? Because it is impossible for the user to use this dialog box by simply pressing the Enter key. By setting the initial focus to the control that the user is most likely to interact with first, you can eliminate an unnecessary step. Furthermore, since the default button can be pressed with the Enter key (by definition), there is simply no reason to give the default button the initial input focus.

TIP Assign the initial input focus to the control that the user is most likely to interact with first.

This last design is functional and easy to use, and it would be suitable for a utility. However, for an application like Visual C++ or Microsoft Word that a user might use for several hours a day, there is still room for improvement. The problem is that while searching for the last word is easy, searching for any other previous input requires the user to completely reenter the string. The worst case is when the user alternates searching between two words. In that case, the user has to do a lot of typing.

The next improvement is to use a combo box with a history list of the recent searches. With the history list, the user can search for any recent search simply by dropping down the history list and making a selection. Of course, such a list is most effective when its contents are saved and restored between instances.

Is this as good as it gets? Well, there is room for one last improvement. What is the sort order of the history list? If the order is alphabetical or any order other than the most recently used order, it's possible that the user will have to do quite a bit of scrolling to find a previously entered item in the list. The user is far more likely to want to search for a recently entered string than one entered hours ago, so placing recently entered strings at the top of the list will make them easier to find and eliminate unnecessary scrolling. With this last refinement, this Find dialog box design is now similar to the Find dialog box in Visual C++. Note how small differences make a big difference in the usability of the dialog box.

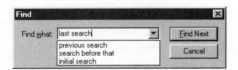

To wrap up this case study, consider these few additional details:

- Pay attention to how a dialog box is used when you assign tab order. For example, in Visual C++ 4.0, the Replace dialog box (shown below) tab order went from the Find What edit box to the Find What regular expression button (to the right of the edit box) to the Replace With edit box to the Replace With regular expression button. Although this tab order follows the dialog box layout, it doesn't follow how the user will use the dialog box. If the input focus is on the Find What edit box and the user presses the Tab key, it is almost certain that the user wants to enter the Replace With text, not select a regular expression. Visual C++ 5.0 fixed this problem by moving the regular expression buttons after the edit boxes in the tab order.

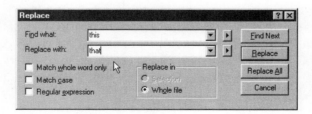

- Consider using the toolbar for activities that the user performs often. For example, with Visual C++ you can set up the toolbar to have all of the Find dialog box capabilities. Using the toolbar eliminates having to display and close the dialog box. Since the toolbar is modeless, using the toolbar also allows the user to perform any other activity while searching for text whereas a modal dialog box does not. Furthermore, the toolbar version requires less effort than the modal dialog box, both physically and psychologically, as I discuss in Chapter 22, "Unnecessary Dialog Boxes Are Evil."

● Visual C++ eliminates the need to type a search word altogether by searching for the word that the caret is in or for selected text. This approach is effective when the text the user wants to search for is likely to be displayed somewhere on the screen, which is less likely in most other programs. I think this feature could be improved by giving the user a way to bypass it when desired and default to the last search string instead.

● Consider using keyboard shortcuts to eliminate having to use a dialog box. For example, repeating the last search is a likely action, so Visual C++ and most other programs provides a Find Next command with an F3 keyboard shortcut. Unfortunately, Microsoft Word provides a nonstandard Ctrl+PgDn keyboard shortcut that isn't displayed in the main menu, so it isn't obvious that the shortcut exists. However, Word does provide an interesting alternative with the Select Browse Object button with the Next Find and Previous Find buttons on the scroll bar. Note that the tooltip gives the shortcut key.

Do you always have to do all this work for every dialog box you do? Fortunately no. As I suggested previously, the depth of the functionality needed to eliminate unnecessary repetitive tasks should match how repetitive those tasks are. Simple utilities probably don't need such functionality since users typically don't do enough searching for the repetition to be a problem. Such functionality is warranted for user interface features that are constantly used.

24
CHAPTER

Guidelines

Now that we've reviewed many techniques for eliminating unnecessary repetitive tasks, let's look for patterns. Let's first outline some general objectives and then the specific techniques.

General Objectives

- When evaluating your program, constantly monitor the user's behavior and look for repetitive behavior. Tasks that are always done should be performed by default. Commonly used multistep tasks should be consolidated into a single command.

- Any input worth asking for is probably worth saving. Don't throw away the user's input as soon as you are done with it. Save it and use it for future default settings.

- Monitor user interaction for trends, and use the most common interaction as the default behavior.

- When possible, have the program perform tasks automatically rather than having the user perform them manually.

- Eliminate unnecessary dialog boxes.

- Eliminate unnecessary typing.

- Make automatic features customizable, and allow the user to turn them off.

- While performing tasks automatically is helpful, make sure the user is ultimately in control of the program.

Specific Techniques

- Save and restore the program state. Save the user preferences, windows sizes and locations (using GetWindowPlacement and SetWindowPlacement functions), open documents, and so on, and restore them when possible.

- Restored windows sizes and locations might need to be adjusted for changes in the screen resolution. Never restore a window to a size larger than the screen (minus the taskbar) or position the window off the screen.

- Use history lists, and sort them in most recently used order.

- Use an autocomplete feature when possible to eliminate unnecessary typing.

- Optimize dialog boxes by using appropriate defaults. The dialog box controls should be initialized to the selections the user is most likely to make. Edit boxes should be initialized to the most likely input, often the last text entered. Dialog boxes that always use the same fixed default values regardless of user input require unnecessary repetition.

- Some property sheets are more convenient when initialized to the last tab used, especially Options property sheets. Property sheets should also support the Apply button so that users can experiment with settings easily.

- Dynamic dialog boxes should be initialized to the last mode they were in.

- The Open and Save As common dialog boxes should remember where the user last opened or saved a file. If the program uses different file types and those different types are often saved to different folders, the program should keep track of the last folder used for each file type.

- Set the dialog box tab order strategically.

- Set the dialog box initial input focus strategically. Assign the initial input focus to the control that the user is most likely to interact with first.

- Reroute input focus strategically. For example, suppose you have a dialog box with an editable list and several command buttons, such as Add, Delete, and Rename. If the user selects an item in the list and clicks the Delete button, the input focus should return to the list to eliminate a step. Leaving the input focus on the Delete button has no value since the user cannot delete anything until another item is selected. The next action will probably require selecting something in the list, so give the list the input focus.

- Provide shortcut keys for commonly used tasks.

- Provide drag-and-drop capability for commonly used tasks.

- When possible, make windows and controls large enough to eliminate scrolling.

- When possible, prefer using the toolbar and direct manipulation instead of dialog boxes.

- Use tooltips to allow the user to obtain more information about an object by using the mouse instead of relying on dialog boxes.

CHAPTER 24

Related Chapters

- Chapter 18—Appropriate Defaults Are Cool.

  Having to make the same selections in dialog boxes over and over again is one of the most unnecessary repetitive tasks there is. This chapter discusses how to select appropriate defaults so that the user has to do the least amount of work.

- Chapter 22—Unnecessary Dialog Boxes Are Evil.

  Dialog boxes that aren't really necessary are the worst type of unnecessary repetitive task. This chapter discusses how to identify unnecessary dialog boxes and how to eliminate them.

- Chapter 29—Check Your Dialog Boxes.

  Presents rules on assigning the default button and initial input focus in dialog boxes.

Recommended Reading

- Cooper, Alan. *About Face: The Essentials of User Interface Design*. Foster City, CA: IDG Books Worldwide, Inc., 1995.

  Chapter 11, "Orchestration and Flow," has an interesting discussion of how programmers confuse possibility with probability, and as a result ask the user questions (usually through unnecessary dialog boxes) even when it is almost certain what the answer will be. Chapter 13, "Overhead and Idiocy," discusses how to recognize and eliminate many unnecessary tasks. Chapter 14, "The Secret Weapon of Interface Design," includes a good discussion about how to eliminate unnecessary user input by remembering previous input.

- DiLascia, Paul. "C/C++ Q & A." *Microsoft Systems Journal*, March 1996.

  Describes why the GetWindowPlacement and SetWindowPlacement API functions are necessary for saving and restoring window sizes and locations. Presents a C++ class to read and write this information to the registry.

PART
IV

CD-ROM Resources

The DevUI MFC Extension Library on the CD-ROM included with this book contains the following resources related to this chapter:

- The McGetProfileStringList and McSetProfileStringList functions to get and set string lists to the registry to help manage settings and user preferences.

- A CMcWindowPlacement class to help save and restore window sizes and locations.

- A CMcMRUList class to help manage MRU lists.

CHAPTER
24

25 CHAPTER

Speed Is a User Interface Issue

How do you ruin a user interface? Let me count the ways.... You make it ugly, nonstandard, inconsistent, and confusing. You make the features invisible and hard to find. You clutter the windows and lay out the dialog boxes poorly. You pester the user with many unnecessary dialog boxes and message boxes. But even if you avoid these pitfalls and do things right, you can still end up with a bad user interface if the program is slow. While a program's performance is generally not considered a user interface issue, it should be. Slow software simply isn't usable.

General Techniques

In this section, I'll describe several general ways to improve performance, none of which should be especially surprising. The most important factor in determining a program's performance is to make sure that it uses efficient data structures and algorithms to accomplish time-consuming tasks. For the many tasks that are not time-consuming, the best data structures and algorithms are usually those that are easiest for you. Interestingly, of the common collections of linked lists, arrays, and hash tables, linked lists are by far the least efficient. The problem is that they allocate a separate piece of memory for each node, which leads to poor memory usage (poor locality of reference) and possible page faults. When the CPU must retrieve data from virtual memory stored on your hard disk, page faults are pure evil in terms of performance. A modern CPU can execute about a million instructions in the time it takes to handle a page fault, so an "efficient" binary search that results in page faults can be far slower than an "inefficient" linear search that doesn't. Check "Tips for Improving Time-Critical Code" in the Microsoft Visual C++ documentation for more information.

Profiling is an important technique for finding inefficiencies in your programs. In my distant past, my experiences with profiling were a big waste of time—the information I obtained was totally misleading. Either the profiling tools have improved or my luck has changed, but all of my recent attempts at profiling have been worthwhile. I find the profiling in Visual C++ easy to do and the results valuable. If you have had bad luck with profiling in the past, try it again. Maybe your luck will change as well.

You should always ship a release version of your program that is optimized and has the debug information removed. Note that the debug version of a program is not optimized at all. In fact, debug code is the opposite of optimized—it is terribly inefficient. While shipping the release build might seem like an easy and obvious thing to do, there is a catch. Most programmers do their development and quality assurance (QA) using the debug version. Since you must test the program you ship, you need to make the transition in the QA process from testing the debug version to testing the release version. Whatever you do, don't assume that you don't need to test the release version if you have carefully tested the debug version—although they share the same source code, they are not the same program. A test of the release version might reveal bugs not present in the debug version. Also note that not all optimizations are safe, especially aggressive speed optimizations. If you are concerned about optimization safety, optimize for size instead. You can obtain significantly better performance by optimizing for size than by not optimizing at all, and small code is generally fast code. All executable files that come with Microsoft Windows are optimized for size.

Lastly, here's an assortment of miscellaneous performance techniques to consider:

- Perform time-consuming operations on an as-needed basis. For example, don't create a complex object or read a large file until you need to. If possible, load large objects incrementally.

- Use file caching when accessing data from a slow network or CD-ROM.

- Offer the user previews of the results of time-consuming operations. For example, good special effects programs show thumbnails of the results of the different effects so that the user doesn't have to waste time viewing an effect only to decide he doesn't like it.

- Avoid performing unnecessary tasks in any functions that are frequently called, such as the MFC CWinApp::OnIdle and CWinApp::PreTranslateMessage functions.

- Use timers strategically. For example, suppose you have a list box with a list of options and selecting an option from the list results in an action that takes several seconds to perform. If you perform the action every time the user changes a selection, scrolling the list will be torture. Instead, use a timer and perform the action only after the user hasn't made a change for a few seconds.

- Don't do all your testing on hardware that is significantly better than your average target user's. Evaluating your program's performance using state-of-the-art hardware might cause you to draw misleading conclusions.

Improving the Perception of Speed

Speed, responsiveness, and the perception of speed are different. When the user issues a command, speed relates to the time it takes to complete the command, responsiveness is the time it takes to respond to further user input, and the perception of speed is determined by how much the user notices each of these.

You can often improve responsiveness by using multiple threads of execution. (Note that multithreading does not improve the speed on a single CPU computer, just the responsiveness.) A good example is the print spooler in Windows. When you print a large document, Windows spools the document to a metafile and returns to the program quickly, even though it might then take several minutes to print the document. Another example is Windows Explorer's handling of the display of program icons. For program files, Windows Explorer reads a program's resources to extract the program icon, which can take a fair amount of time for hundreds of files. Yet if you display the Windows system folder (which typically has hundreds of executable files) using Windows Explorer, the program is immediately responsive. This is because the program icons are loaded in a separate thread on an as-needed basis. While multithreading can be useful, you should use

399

it sparingly since using it adds to the complexity of the code and can introduce bugs that are next to impossible to reproduce while debugging. A simple alternative to multithreading is to perform processing during idle time, such as with the MFC CWinApp::OnIdle function.

You can improve the perception of speed in several ways. One common way is to change the order in which windows are drawn by using the UpdateWindow function. For example, if a command results in four windows being repainted—one that is slow and three that are fast—the repaint will seem faster if the fast windows are redrawn first. Similarly, a command will be perceived as slow if a window remains invalidated for a long period of time. The command will be seen as faster if the window is repainted first and then the command is performed.

Another way to improve the perception of speed is to give progress feedback using something other than a wait cursor. For example, if you copy many files using Windows Explorer, you get this progress dialog box:

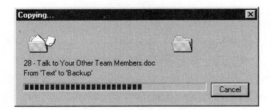

This progress feedback has several advantages: it indicates how long the command will take, it shows how much work has already been done, it confirms that progress is being made, and it gives the user the opportunity to stop the command. Most of all, it is engaging enough to help the time pass faster. Note that the wait cursor has none of these benefits. Also note that displaying this progress dialog box would be overly distracting for quick commands, so it appears only if the copy takes more than about five seconds.

Loading

The time it takes for a program to load is certainly part of the perception of speed. Nobody likes to wait 20 seconds or more for a program to load. While a user might load an application only once per session, a user might load a utility many times in a session, so load time is especially important for utilities.

Load time can be especially slow when a program uses many dynamic-link libraries (DLLs). Consider what Windows has to do to load such a program. First Windows loads the executable file itself, and then it goes through the list of dependent DLLs and loads one DLL at a time into the program's address space. Each DLL has a preferred base address from which all internal code and data has a relative offset. The DLL can load fairly quickly if it can load at its preferred address. However, if there is already something loaded at that address, Windows has to assign another base address and effectively relink the DLL to reset all the internal references to code and data. This process takes a far greater amount of time and results in the infamous *LDR: Dll example.dll base 00600000 relocated due to collisions with c:\projects\example.exe* message you see when you run the program from the debugger. Finally, once all the DLLs are loaded, Windows has to resolve all the external linkages by calling the GetProcAddress function for each imported DLL function.

One simple technique you can use to make loading faster is to ensure that your DLL files are easy for Windows to find. Windows (with the LoadLibrary function) searches directories in this order when looking for a DLL file:

1. The directory from which the program loaded.
2. The current directory.
3. The Windows system directory.
4. [Windows NT] The 16-bit Windows system directory.
5. The Windows directory.
6. The directories that are listed in the PATH environment variable.

Clearly, any DLL file found in the Windows directory or from the PATH environment variable is going to take longer to find than a DLL file in the program directory. Furthermore, note that the Designed for Microsoft Windows logo requirements recommend against installing your own DLLs in the Windows system directory. This prevents bloating the system directory with files that don't need to be there. It also avoids DLL version conflicts caused by DLLs shared between programs, at only a small cost of hard disk space. Once your DLL files are easy to find, much of the remaining loading activity can be eliminated by properly building your program. You can run the Rebase utility that comes with Visual C++ to process all your program's DLLs and set their base addresses so that they do not collide. Once the DLLs have base addresses that do not change when the DLL is loaded, you can then run the Bind utility on all the program's executable files,

CHAPTER 25

eliminating the need for the GetProcAddress function call by storing all the actual addresses of imported functions within the executable. There is no risk in doing this, since the binding process saves the timestamps of the DLLs to make sure the right file is used. If your program loads with a different DLL than the one that was bound, the linker uses the GetProcAddress technique instead. Note that you must always run Rebase before you run Bind.

TIP   Use the Rebase and Bind utilities to reduce your program's load time.

If you properly rebase and bind, even large programs that use many DLLs can load quickly. All executable files that come with Windows NT are bound.

Drawing

Poor drawing performance not only slows down your program and gives it a sluggish appearance but also is very obvious to the user. The following techniques can help you improve drawing performance.

The first technique is to eliminate unnecessary redrawing. While there are many ways to accomplish this goal, the most important is to understand how Windows does painting and let it do its job. The designers of Windows intentionally gave paint messages a low priority. With the exception of timer messages, paint messages have the lowest priority in Windows. In fact, paint messages are not stored in the application message queue but are synthesized when the application message queue is empty. While painting windows is vital to a program, giving it a low priority allows other tasks, such as computation, to take place first. Since the window has to be painted eventually, it might seem like the trade-off doesn't accomplish much. However, a region in a window can become invalid many times before a task is completed. Because the paint messages are delayed, the window will be painted once instead of multiple times. This makes the results much more efficient and eliminates flashing. You should allow Windows to use this process to optimize painting. You should not call the UpdateWindow function to force an immediate paint unless it's necessary (which isn't unusual). If your program has some windows that are repainted over and over again, unnecessary calls to the UpdateWindow function are probably to blame.

TIP Let Windows automatically optimize drawing by not calling the UpdateWindow function unless really necessary.

You indicate to Windows that a portion of a window needs to be redrawn with the InvalidateRect and InvalidateRgn functions. With InvalidateRect, you need to specify a pointer to a rectangle containing the area that needs to be updated. You can also pass NULL to update the entire region. To eliminate unnecessary drawing, you should avoid passing NULL unless you really cannot determine the size of the invalid area. When supplying an update rectangle, you should try to invalidate as little as possible. For example, a list view will redraw much more efficiently if several individual rows or columns are invalidated instead of an entire range of rows or columns.

TIP Optimize drawing by passing the InvalidateRect function an invalid rectangle whenever possible. Try to invalidate the smallest area possible.

Let's look at a good example of how not to handle redrawing. If you have ever used the standard list box control, you know that before you add items to the list you have to call *SetRedraw(FALSE)* to disable drawing. If you don't, the list will redraw itself every time an item is added. When you have finished adding list items, you then have to call *SetRedraw(TRUE)* to enable drawing. The problem is that every call to the CListBox::AddString or CListBox::InsertString function invalidates and updates the list box, resulting in a flash. As you now know, this approach is completely wrong. The correct approach is to invalidate the individual rows that change when an item is added instead of calling the UpdateWindow function. This way, Windows will automatically repaint the list window when the message queue is empty or the programmer can force a repaint when needed by calling the UpdateWindow function.

When you invalidate a window with the InvalidateRect or Invalidate-Rgn function, be careful with the erase background parameter—erase the background only when necessary. Note that this parameter is TRUE by default in MFC. When is it necessary to erase the background? The background needs to be erased when it is both invalid and visible. For example, if you paint the same text in the same location, the background doesn't need

25
CHAPTER

to be erased because the background isn't invalid. If you paint different text, you need to erase the background; otherwise, the old text will show through. But painting transparent objects like text is the worst case. If you are drawing opaque objects like bitmaps, you never need to erase behind the bitmap because the background is never visible. If you draw the entire area, you never need to erase the background.

TIP Avoid erasing the background unless really necessary.

Note that erasing the background is an all-or-nothing deal when the paint actually occurs. If you call the InvalidateRect function 10 times without indicating that the background should be erased and then call it once indicating that it should, the entire background will be erased when the paint message is processed. If you have a large region that doesn't need the background erased and a small region that does, it is more efficient to invalidate the large area, call the UpdateWindow function to force the window to be painted, and then invalidate the small area. A lot of flashing is a symptom of unnecessary background painting.

Another technique is to make sure that your windows are registered with the correct class styles. A window needs the CS_HREDRAW and CS_VREDRAW styles only if changing the size of the client area requires a complete redraw. This is true when something in the window is centered, but most windows do not center anything, so they don't need these class styles. If you are using MFC, note that MFC uses these styles by default, so you need register your own class in the window's constructor to remove these styles. You should consider doing this for all MFC views or other windows that can be resized.

TIP Use the CS_HREDRAW and CS_VREDRAW styles only when necessary.

If you are displaying an object that takes a significant amount of time to render, you should consider rendering the object into a bitmap and blitting the bitmap to the screen in one step. Using a bitmap improves the perception of speed and eliminates flashing since you never see the background being erased. In fact, you don't need to erase the background when you use this technique, since the foreground and background are both contained in the bitmap. This technique isn't difficult—just create a

PART
IV

memory device context and a bitmap, select the bitmap into the memory device context (DC), clear the background, call your normal painting function with the memory DC instead of the window DC, and then blit the resulting bitmap into the window DC. From this point on, you can repaint just by blitting the bitmap until the object or window changes.

Consider rendering to a bitmap instead of rendering directly to the screen.

Lastly, if your drawing code spends a relatively large amount of time creating and selecting Graphical Device Interface (GDI) objects—profiling will indicate this by showing a lot of time in functions like CreateSolidBrush, CreatePen, and SelectObject—you can improve drawing performance by keeping the GDI resources in memory and selecting the GDI objects only when necessary. If necessary (and it usually isn't), you can use the CS_OWNDC class style to help maintain the selected GDI objects across paint messages.

Scrolling

Efficient scrolling is important for achieving good performance with scrollable windows, especially with document-based programs. The key to efficient scrolling is to not draw the entire contents of a window every time a paint message is received (which is usually what is done in sample code), but to draw only the portion of the window that is invalid. You can determine the invalid area by looking at the rcPaint rectangle in the PAINTSTRUCT or with the CDC::GetClipBox function in MFC. (If you are using MFC, note that scrolling is usually accomplished by changing the view's window origin. You need to subtract the window origin from the clip box to get the invalid region relative to the top of the document.)

Improve drawing and scrolling performance by redrawing only the invalid area.

How you determine exactly what part of the document to draw given an invalid rectangle is the difficult part, and it is completely dependent upon the document you are drawing. Let's take drawing a simple HTML page as an example. The screen shot on the next page shows an HTML page in Microsoft Internet Explorer with H1, H2, and H3 headings and some text.

405

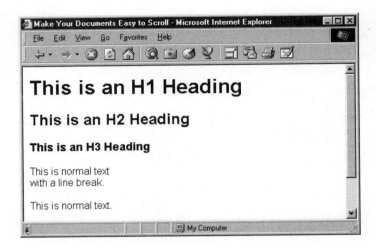

If you look carefully, you will notice that each item displayed is an integral number of normal text lines in height. For example, the H1 and H2 headers are twice the size of a normal text line, and all spacing between headings and paragraphs is the size of a normal text line. If you maintain this simple relationship between formatted HTML text and its position on the screen, it's easy to determine the lines that need to be painted. In general, avoid designing documents and views where there is not a simple relationship between the document and its view.

Recommended Reading

- Bickford, Peter. *Interface Design: The Art of Developing Easy-to-Use Software*. Chestnut Hill, MA: Academic Press, 1997.

  Chapter 11, "Speed and Feedback," describes the difference between real speed and perceived speed and gives suggestions on how to improve both.

- Pietrek, Matt. "Remove Fatty Deposits from Your Applications Using Our 32-bit Liposuction Tools." *Microsoft Systems Journal*, October 1996.

  Presents very useful information on avoiding address space collisions using the Rebase utility and on resolving the addresses of imported functions using the Bind utility. Using both techniques greatly improves the load time of programs that use many DLLs.

The article also includes code optimization information and a useful Liposuction32 utility that finds easily correctable inefficiencies in executable files.

● Prosise, Jeff. *Programming Windows with MFC, Second Edition.* Redmond, WA: Microsoft Press, 1999.

Chapter 2, "Drawing in a Window," presents useful information about scrolling in general and efficient scrolling using MFC. Also discussed is the fact that while the CScrollView class was designed for the MFC document/view architecture, you can use it on its own without any problem (unless you want to support print previewing). This information is extremely useful, since CScrollView is quite powerful on its own.

25
CHAPTER

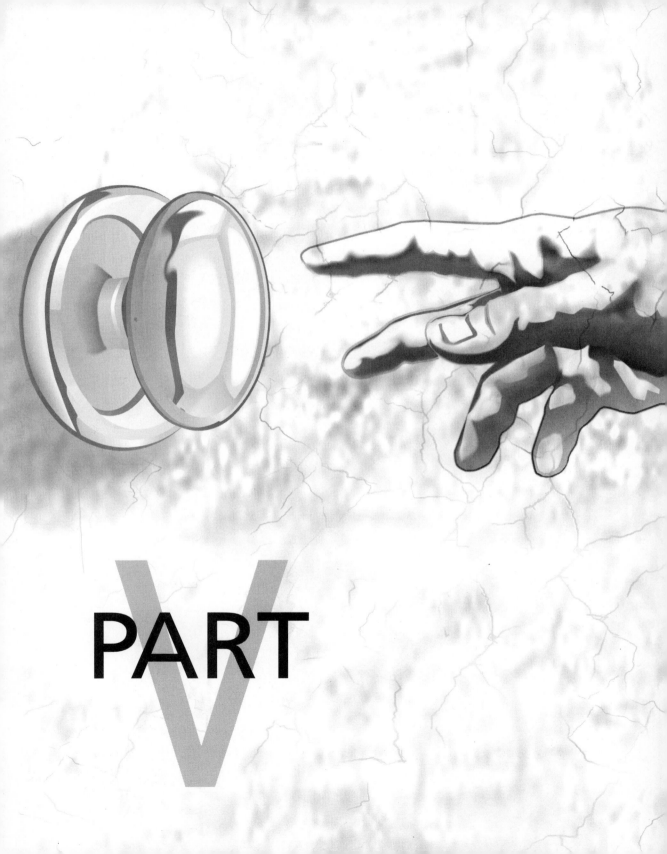

PART V

Testing and QA

26 CHAPTER

Programmer Testing

I believe that programmers are primarily responsible for software quality. This is true even if your company has a formal quality assurance (QA) process. In fact, it is especially true if you have a formal QA process. Once programmers are not responsible for quality, quality has nowhere to go but down. Software QA is not some magic process. No amount of QA testing can possibly turn bad software into good software. At best, it can turn bad software into less bad software. It's important to understand that the QA process itself does not create quality software. It is the programmer's job to write quality code and perform the appropriate testing to verify that the code works as expected. Rather, the QA process verifies that quality is there and provides the feedback necessary to help ensure that quality.

 TIP The programmer is primarily responsible for software quality.

CHAPTER 26

A significant portion of the problems found during the testing and QA process are user interface–related. While many of these problems can be found through QA testing and possibly user testing, you should make your best effort to find as many problems as you can before QA and user testing. Why? One reason is that programmer testing is more cost-effective, since there is little overhead when you find problems on your own. Another reason is that you can obtain better coverage than QA and user testing because you are working directly with the source code and user interface resources. The last reason is that there are some user interface problems that are difficult, if not impossible, for other testers to find.

There are three specific types of user interface testing that programmers can perform effectively:

- **User interface implementation testing**   Checking for specific implementation-related user interface problems that are difficult to find using other types of testing.

- **Usability testing**   Checking for general usability problems by using a list of design principles that are known to be effective in finding usability problems.

- **Demo testing**   Performing demos and looking for implementation and usability problems during the demos.

In all cases, your ability to find user interface problems will be significantly enhanced by changing your perspective from being a programmer to being a user. I'll explore each of these ideas in the remainder of this chapter.

Changing Your Perspective

Conventional wisdom says that programmers are incapable of testing their own user interfaces. My experience is different. I believe that programmers can and should test their own user interfaces, but doing so requires them to learn how to change their perspective.

A common argument is that programmers are so familiar with the user interface they've created that they are blind to its problems. I believe this argument is only partially true. For example, if you have just developed your first Microsoft Windows user interface, you probably are unaware of the interface's shortcomings because of your lack of experience. But the real reason programmers have difficulty testing their own user interfaces is that they need to learn to change their perspective. You need to stop testing your program as a programmer and start testing it as a user. Try to use the program as a user would. Stop thinking about the problems you already know about. Stop doing those same old tests over and over again, using the same old test data. Rather, pretend you are a first-time user who is trying to accomplish the basic tasks that the program provides. It's essential that you test the program by doing real tasks, not by using features. Explore the program as a user would. Try to figure out how to use the program just by looking at it. Try to respond only to what you see on the screen—if it's not on the screen, it doesn't exist. Try to do new or unusual things. You'll be amazed at how many problems you can find if you simply change your perspective.

TIP   The key to successful programmer testing is to change your perspective and use your program like a user.

User Interface Implementation Testing

Programmers are able to find certain types of user interface problems better than other testers because they have a better understanding of how their code works and far better tools at their disposal for testing and debugging. Some problems are much easier to find by reviewing the source code and resource files directly.

A programmer can easily discover problems that are literally impossible for other testers to find. For example, a surprising number of programs don't use the system colors correctly. Instead of using system colors, many programmers mistakenly hardwire their pens and brushes to use various shades of gray, such as light gray for dialog boxes and button faces, white for 3-D highlights, and dark gray for 3-D shadows. However, these default color assignments can be changed by the user and are not used by all color schemes. Programs with these problems look absolutely awful using such color schemes. This problem is easy to detect if you develop using a color scheme that doesn't use any of the default colors with the possible exception of black text. You can also scan the source code for the incorrect use of pen and brush colors. But the important point I want to make is that this is the only way to detect this problem reliably. It's practically impossible to detect a problem like this during user testing. Such a problem could possibly be found during QA testing but only if the QA testers explicitly check for this problem or just happen to use a color scheme that has nondefault colors.

Most of the remaining chapters in this part of the book describe the important user interface problems that programmers are best at uncovering. Here is a brief summary of these problems:

- **Dialog box problems**   Typical dialog box problems include not displaying correctly in all video modes, not assigning the correct tab order, not using the group property correctly, and not assigning unique assess keys to all the interactive controls. These problems and more are described in detail in Chapter 29, "Check Your Dialog Boxes."

- **Error message problems**   Typical error message problems include poorly worded, unhelpful text, incorrectly constructed error message text, and missing error messages. While programmers often have trouble finding such problems, they have the advantage of knowing what all the error messages are. These problems and more are described in detail in Chapter 30, "Check Your Error Messages."

- **Printing problems**   Typical printing problems include not handling printer errors, not handling all paper sizes, not handling all printer resolutions, not handling both landscape and portrait modes, and not handling color printing correctly. These problems and more are described in detail in Chapter 31, "Check Your Printing."

- **Setup program problems**   Typical setup program problems include making the installation process too complicated, making the setup results too complicated, asking unnecessary questions during setup, and copying files to the wrong folders. These problems and more are described in detail in Chapter 33, "Check Your Setup Program."

- **System color problems**   Typical system color problems include using hardwired colors instead of system colors, mismatching system colors, and not responding to system color change messages. These problems are described in detail in Chapter 34, "Use System Colors."

PART

V

- **Video mode problems**   Typical video mode problems include windows and dialog boxes that do not display correctly in all supported video modes, window layouts that do not work well in all supported video modes, and using graphics that do not scale well. These problems are described in detail in Chapter 35, "Handle All Video Modes."

- **Spelling errors**   You can quickly find spelling errors by extracting your string resources and running them through a spelling checker.

Once you get in the habit of checking for these types of problems, I think you'll discover that they are fairly easy to find and correct.

Usability Testing

In addition to finding the previously mentioned user interface implementation problems, you can also test for usability problems. What is the difference? What I'm calling an "implementation problem" is a problem related solely to the implementation of the user interface and not to its design. Theoretically, you could find all of these problems by inspecting the source code and resource files directly. On the other hand, usability problems relate to the user's ability to actually use the program. To find these problems, you have to test the program using real tasks.

You could find many usability problems by reviewing your program with a checklist of possibly hundreds of low-level attributes that good user interfaces have. In fact, the Sample User Interface Guidelines presented in Chapter 4, "Establish a Consistent User Interface Style," could be used as a basis for such a list. I like to review such lists when testing a program because I always seem to find a couple details that I overlooked.

Instead of trying to review hundreds of low-level attributes, an alternate approach is to check for usability problems by using a list of high-level design principles that are known to be effective in finding such problems. The technical term for this type of testing is *heuristic evaluation*. A *heuristic* is an approach to problem solving that uses self-education to obtain the desired results. In other words, we can develop our own knowledge of effective user interface design to find usability problems instead of (actually, in addition to) direct user testing. Of course, you can use this technique at any time during the software development process, especially during the design phase. Clearly, waiting until the program is just about to ship is too late.

26 CHAPTER

There is a standard process for heuristic evaluation recommended by usability experts, and that process has two significant attributes. The first is that you should perform the design review using a group of usability experts—the more usability experts the better. (What a surprise!) The second is that the usability evaluators should work independently, since independent points of view are more likely to uncover different problems. After all, there is no advantage to having more than one person find the same problem. Just in case you don't have a crew of usability experts at your disposal, you might want to try to use the same evaluation process with your team members. Use this technique to get early feedback on the user interface design from everyone involved in the project, including users, testers, graphic designers, technical writers, and managers. As you shall soon see, these design principles used during heuristic evaluation are not difficult to understand and apply, as long as you make the appropriate change in perspective.

TIP Evaluate the usability of your program with your team members by using a short list of high-level design principles.

A Usability Roadmap

Jakob Nielsen recommends using the first 10 of the following design principles in Chapter 5, "Usability Heuristics," of *Usability Engineering*. The remaining four principles are from *Designing for the User Experience*. I'll give a brief description of each principle as well as references to the chapters in my book that relate to that principle. You should be able to use this list as a usability roadmap.

Simple and natural dialog

Good user interfaces are simple; have natural mappings; and use good arrangement, flow, and grouping. In this case, "dialog" refers to all interactions between the user and the interface, not just dialog boxes.

Chapter 15, "Keep It Simple," gives suggestions on how to achieve simplicity, particularly how to simplify a window's layout and appearance. Chapter 13, "Learn from the Web," describes how to take advantage of Web-based technology to make programs that are simpler and easier to use and features that are easier to find. Chapter 12, "Learn from *The Design of Everyday Things*," discusses how to create natural mappings to make a clear relationship between what the user wants to do and the mechanism for doing it. Chapter 4, "Establish a Consistent User Interface Style," and Chapter 29, "Check Your Dialog Boxes," give guidelines on how to organize windows to obtain good arrangement, flow, grouping, and such.

Speak the user's language

Good user interfaces use words, phrases, concepts, and graphics that the user understands. Appropriate metaphors can be used to express unfamiliar concepts in the user's language.

Chapter 3, "Establish Consistent Terminology," discusses the importance of establishing consistent terminology in eliminating confusion. Chapter 30, "Check Your Error Messages," describes how to phrase error messages in a way the user can understand. Chapter 12, "Learn from *The Design of Everyday Things*," discusses natural mappings, particularly in how they eliminate the need for translation. It also discusses some of the problems with using metaphors. Chapter 19, "Configurability Is Cool," Chapter 34, "Use System Colors," and Chapter 35, 'Handle All Video Modes," help you speak the user's language by having your program adapt to the user rather than the other way around.

Minimize the user's memory load

The user should not have to memorize anything to use your program. The information required to use the program should be contained within the program itself.

Chapter 10, "Good User Interfaces Are Visible," describes how to make your user interfaces visible, so that users can figure them out just by looking at them. Chapter 12, "Learn from *The Design of Everyday Things*," describes how to use constraints so that the knowledge required to use an object is contained within an object itself. It also discusses affordance, which allows the user to determine how to use an object just by looking at its visual clues. Chapter 13, "Learn from the Web," describes how Web pages compensate for not having help by putting detailed instructions in the user interface itself. Chapter 17, "Direct Manipulation Is Cool," discusses the advantages of direct manipulation, which is one of the easiest forms of interaction to use.

Consistency

Good user interfaces use consistent terminology, have windows with a consistent appearance, and have commands with consistent behavior. Such programs are consistent within themselves and with other programs.

Chapter 1, "Know the Standards," discusses the importance of knowing and following the standards, which will make your program consistent with others. Chapter 3, "Establish Consistent Terminology," discusses the

CHAPTER 26

importance of establishing consistent terminology in eliminating confusion. Chapter 4, "Establish a Consistent User Interface Style," gives sample user interface guidelines to help you achieve consistency. Chapter 16, "Prefer the Standard Controls," describes the advantages to using standard controls, the most important being that users already know how to use them.

Feedback

Good user interfaces use feedback to indicate to the user that a task is being done and that it is being done either correctly or incorrectly. Your program needs to inform the user what it is doing. Without feedback, the user is giving commands without any knowledge of their results. Feedback completes the loop. Since the user needs to know when an action cannot be done or is being done incorrectly, error messages are also an important form of feedback.

Chapter 10, "Good User Interfaces Are Visible," describes when to give feedback and how to make it visible. Chapter 12, "Learn from *The Design of Everyday Things*," describes the attributes of good feedback and compares the different forms of feedback. Chapter 20, "Previews Are Cool," and Chapter 21, "Tooltips Are Cool," describe two excellent forms of feedback. Since good feedback is immediate, Chapter 25, "Speed Is a User Interface Issue," gives some tips on how to improve both the actual and perceived speed of a program. Chapter 30, "Check Your Error Messages," describes how to phrase error messages in a way that provides useful feedback.

Clearly marked exits

Good user interfaces allow the user to recover from mistakes quickly, either by exiting an undesired window quickly or by returning to a known location. Such actions should not require the user to jump through any unnecessary hoops.

Chapter 12, "Learn from *The Design of Everyday Things*," describes visible navigation, which has an attribute of having a clearly marked exit. Chapter 13, "Learn from the Web," discusses the value of home pages and the advantages of the Web Browser Navigation Model. Chapter 22, "Unnecessary Dialog Boxes Are Evil," discusses the problems with unnecessary confirmations, such as confirming a program exit.

Shortcuts

Good user interfaces accommodate advanced users by letting them get their work done efficiently. Advanced users appreciate features like toolbars, context menus, keyboard shortcuts and access keys, and direct manipulation.

Chapter 4, "Establish a Consistent User Interface Style," gives guidelines on when to provide shortcuts and access keys. Chapter 6, "Beginning vs. Advanced Users," and Chapter 7, "Using Applications vs. Utilities," describes

PART
V

the features that are appropriate for advanced users and applications. Chapter 18, "Appropriate Defaults Are Cool," and Chapter 24, "Unnecessary Repetitive Tasks Are Evil," discuss ways to eliminate unnecessary repetition by providing appropriate defaults and by keeping track of the user's input. Chapter 17, "Direct Manipulation Is Cool," gives many examples of direct manipulation, which is a good shortcut for advanced users.

Good error messages

Good error message text must provide enough information so that the user can understand the problem and know what to do about it. Typically, an error message needs to provide a notification that indicates a problem occurred, an explanation that explains why the problem occurred, and a solution that suggests how to solve the problem. Furthermore, good error message text is brief, clear, consistent, and specific.

Chapter 30, "Check Your Error Messages," describes how to phrase error messages that give a notification, explanation, and solution in a way that is brief, clear, consistent, and specific.

Prevent errors

The best error message is often no error message at all.

Chapter 23, "Unnecessary Message Boxes Are Pure Evil," gives suggestions on how to eliminate unnecessary error messages. Chapter 12, "Learn from *The Design of Everyday Things*," describes how to use constraints to eliminate error messages by making it impossible for the user to make a mistake. Chapter 17, "Direct Manipulation Is Cool," discusses how direct manipulation eliminates the need for error messages when the manipulation is properly restrained.

Help and documentation

Good user interfaces shouldn't require the user to read any external documentation, but good programs should provide short, task-oriented help when the user needs it. While users don't read Help unless they have to, when they do read it they want it to answer their questions. If Help doesn't answer their questions, they are not happy.

Chapter 32, "Check Your Help System and Documentation," describes the attributes of good Help, how to prepare your program for Help, tips on how to work with technical writers, and how to find problems in the documentation.

User in control

Good user interfaces keep the user in control of the software, rather than the other way around. This means that the user should determine what the program does, in terms of both interaction and appearance.

419

CHAPTER 26

Chapter 22, "Unnecessary Dialog Boxes Are Evil," shows how unnecessary modal dialog boxes force the user to react to the program and how such dialog boxes can be eliminated. Chapter 19, "Configurability Is Cool," Chapter 34, "Use System Colors," and Chapter 35, 'Handle All Video Modes," help make sure that the user has control over the program's appearance.

Direct manipulation

Direct manipulation is a natural way to perform tasks in a modern graphical user interface that is easy to learn, and quick and convenient to use. You feel like you are directly in control of a task and the continuous visual feedback makes it easy for you to decide when you have what you want. Direct manipulation makes using software fun. It is the ultimate form of interactivity.

Chapter 17, "Direct Manipulation Is Cool," discusses the advantages of direct manipulation and gives several examples.

Forgiveness

Good user interfaces allow the user to explore the program by using trial and error. Your user interface needs to warn users when they are about to perform a function that is potentially destructive or difficult to undo. You should consider putting the burden of correcting mistakes on your program instead of the user by providing an Undo command.

Chapter 11, "Good User Interfaces Are Invisible," discusses the importance of forgiveness. Chapter 23, "Unnecessary Message Boxes Are Pure Evil," gives guidelines on what actions need to be confirmed and what actions don't.

Aesthetics

Lastly, the visual appearance of a user interface plays an important role in the program's ability to communicate to the user and the user's overall satisfaction with the program. Good user interfaces keep the user informed without being distracting.

Chapter 4, "Establish a Consistent User Interface Style," presents sample user interface guidelines that help you get "le look." Chapter 11, "Good User Interfaces Are Invisible," gives suggestions on how to make sure your program doesn't draw unwanted attention. Chapter 22, "Unnecessary Dialog Boxes Are Evil," describes how to prevent unnecessary dialog boxes, which can be very distracting. Chapter 28, "Talk to Your Other Team Members," gives tips on how to take advantage of the talents of a good graphic designer.

PART
V

Demo Testing

I highly recommend that you give lots of demos during the development process, since they always seem to reveal problems. Many people are baffled why this occurs, but the explanation is quite simple. The reason you always find bugs when you give a demo is that you are using the program as a user, not as a programmer. Demos force you to make the critical change in perspective I've emphasized throughout this chapter. You are presenting the program to your audience to show how the user will accomplish various tasks, which is not what you normally do during development. Furthermore, your audience will ask questions and want to do tasks that never occurred to you. They will be confused by user interface elements that you think are obvious. Of course, a program in development always has to crash at least once during a demo. Demos never seem to go as planned.

Another advantage to giving demos is that having people watch you use your program makes you extra self-conscious. Features that are slow seem to take forever during a demo. Interactions that are cumbersome or unnecessary become especially apparent, even though they didn't bother you much during development. Features that you implemented months ago that you thought were obvious and straightforward seem to have somehow disappeared from the user interface or become confusing. And details that you thought were cool, like flaming logos, start to look a little dorky. The size of small mistakes and inconsistencies grows by at least an order of magnitude when others are watching. Every little glitch in your demo should be considered a sign of a user interface problem.

Giving demos is an easy, cost-effective way to obtain valuable feedback. You can give a demo at any time, even at the earliest stages of development, since you are in total control of the program and can talk your way through missing features. Be aware of the problems that arise, and be sure to take notes. I believe demos are a critical part of the testing process, and I recommend that you try to give as many as you can. If nobody is asking you for a demo, just grab anyone that makes the mistake of walking by your office.

TIP   Give a lot of demos to obtain valuable feedback, especially early in the development process.

You Can Do This!

Be honest—do you really need somebody else to tell you that this message box below doesn't make any sense? You can find problems like this. Your QA testers are a valuable resource, so you should save them for problems that are truly difficult to find.

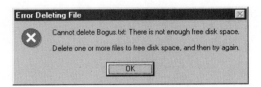

Most of the remaining chapters in this part of the book, "Testing and QA," present different user interface issues that need your attention during the development and testing process. You should make an effort to address as many of them as you can. Remember that making quality software is your responsibility.

Related Chapters

- Chapter 4—Establish a Consistent User Interface Style.

  The "Sample User Interface Guidelines" section presents guidelines that can help you find user interface problems during programmer testing. Although this list is primarily intended for the design and implementation phases, you might find selected items useful in the testing phase as well.

- Chapter 27—User Testing.

  Describes how to perform user testing and gives a specific procedure to make sure you get good feedback.

Recommended Reading

- Apple Computer. *Macintosh Human Interface Guidelines*. Reading, MA: Addison-Wesley Publishing Company, 1992.

  Chapter 1, "Human Interface Principles," extends the list of design principles presented in this chapter to include metaphors, see-and-point, perceived stability, modelessness, know your audience, and accessibility.

- Arlov, Laura. *GUI Design for Dummies*. Foster City, CA: IDG Books Worldwide, 1997.

    Chapter 19, "Other Paths to Enlightenment," gives a brief description of the heuristic evaluation process and some suggestions on how to perform a user interface review using a checklist.

- Microsoft Corporation. *Designing for the User Experience*. Redmond, WA: Microsoft Press, 1999.

    See the chapter on design principles and methodology for discussion of many of the design principles given in this chapter.

- Nielsen, Jakob. *Usability Engineering*. Chestnut Hill, MA: AP Professional, 1993.

    Chapter 5, "Usability Heuristics," presents a detailed description of the design principles given in this chapter along with a detailed description of the standard heuristic evaluation process. For a challenge, you might want to check the heuristic evaluation of a paper mock-up interface given in Appendix A.

CD-ROM Resources

The CD-ROM included with this book contains the following resources related to this chapter:

- A copy of the sample user interface guidelines presented in Chapter 4 in Microsoft Word format that you can customize for use in the testing process.

- Resource Assistant, a utility that checks the resources in an executable, and Resource Assistant for VB, a utility that checks the resources in a Visual Basic program. Both programs verify that dialog boxes will fit on the screen in all video modes, static text controls and buttons (command buttons, radio buttons, and check boxes) are large enough to display their text in all video modes, the tab order of the controls has been set, the tab stop and group properties of the controls have been set, and control access keys are unique. Resource Assistant also extracts all resource strings so that you can check for spelling errors, and Resource Assistant for VB does the same for string resources, forms, and menus.

26 CHAPTER

CHAPTER 27

User Testing

User testing is when you witness real users operating your program to perform realistic tasks. User testing can be performed in a formal usability lab equipped with a test room and an observation room separated by a one-way mirror and soundproof walls, with the test user's every action recorded with multiple video cameras. Or user testing can be performed in any room equipped with a table, a computer, and a couple of chairs. The environment doesn't matter that much. What is important is that a real user is testing the program and someone is watching.

In Chapter 8, "Users Aren't Designers," I pointed out that there is a limit to what users can do to help you in the design process. Users can't tell you how to design your software, but they can tell you if a design has usability problems. They can tell you whether they understand the software, whether they can perform tasks with it, and whether they are confused or don't know what to do next while using it. They can also tell you if they enjoy using the program. User testing is the best way to obtain this information during the development process.

TIP
Users aren't designers, but they can tell you if a design has usability problems.

User Testing vs. Other Testing

User testing is just one of many types of testing that can occur during the development process. Let's compare user testing to some of the alternatives.

- **Programmer testing**   Programmer testing is a cost-effective way to find common user interface errors, some of which are described in the remaining chapters of this book. There are several practical techniques that you can use to find routine usability problems. While I believe that programmers can find usability problems by testing their programs from the user's point of view (by performing real tasks and responding only to what they see on the screen), the problem is that programmers already know how their programs work and sometimes there are usability problems that they simply cannot detect without having a fresh perspective.

- **Demo testing**   Demo testing is also a cost-effective way to find common user interface errors and involves giving demos to colleagues, customers, or even random bystanders. The advantage to demo testing is that it forces you to use the program as a user, since when demo testing you typically show how to perform tasks instead of how to use specific features. You are also self-conscious during a demo, so problems that seemed minor during programmer testing tend to seem much worse during a demo. Furthermore, during a demo people typically ask questions and make requests that you never anticipated—you're also able to get a quick reality check to see whether people react to your program in the manner you expect.

- **QA testing**   QA testing is a vital part of the testing process, but typically QA is focused on finding bugs and puts less emphasis on more subjective problems like usability. I believe this is wrong—QA testers should be encouraged to find usability problems. Unfortunately, QA testers lose value over time because as they become more familiar with the program they, like programmers, have a difficult time seeing some usability problems.

- **Beta testing**   While beta testing is performed with real users, you have no control over what they test and you are not able to witness them using the program. If a beta tester struggles to complete a task, there is no guarantee that you'll get this feedback. Furthermore, if you do get this feedback, you probably won't get specific information that helps you determine why there was a problem. You won't be able to determine what the user was thinking or what specifically the user found confusing.

Each of these types of testing can be effective and provide valuable information. Each has its advantages and plays a strategic role in the development process. But none of them have the critical combination of testing your program with real users and directly observing the testing. This combination makes user testing the most realistic indicator of how users will react to the program. You can't just give your program to people and ask them to go off and use it and then tell you what they think. You have to watch them struggle.

TIP User testing is the most realistic indicator of how users will react to your program. You have to watch real users struggle to use your program.

If user testing is the most realistic form of testing, why bother with the others? For two reasons. First, user testing finds mostly usability problems and is unlikely to find bugs. The second reason is economic. Although user testing doesn't have to be expensive or time-consuming, user testing is more difficult to do than programmer testing, demo testing, or QA testing. If you can find usability problems by using these other methods, it's more cost-effective to try them first.

The Best Is the Enemy of the Good

Jakob Nielsen's *Usability Engineering* is considered by many to be the best guide to user testing. Nielsen understands that developers don't have unlimited budgets or time, so they need to use testing techniques that are quick and cost-effective. As Nielsen puts it, "Unfortunately, it seems that 'Le mieux est l'ennemi du bien' (the best is the enemy of the good) to the extent that insisting on using only the best methods may result in using no methods at all." Clearly, some user testing is better than none. The inability to perform every type of user test in an ideal manner should not be used as an excuse to avoid user testing altogether. You shouldn't feel guilty for employing user testing techniques that are less than ideal. This concept is a major theme of this chapter.

TIP Some user testing is better than none. Don't feel guilty for using user techniques
that are less than ideal.

User Testing on the Cheap

You can perform user testing cost effectively. Nielsen calls this goal "discount
usability engineering," whereas Bruce Tognazzini calls it "user testing on
the cheap." But whatever you call it, the fact is that you do not need an
expensive soundproof usability lab with one-way mirrors and Ph.D. psy-
chologists in white lab coats. If these resources were true requirements, few
organizations would be able to perform user testing. You can do effective
user testing with bare-bones facilities. What really matters is setting realistic
goals and giving proper instructions to the test user. Of course, you should
use such resources if you have them lying around.

User Testing Goals

The key to successful user testing is having practical, realistic goals, so the
first step is to understand exactly what you want to accomplish. You also
need to decide how much time and money you want to spend. Let's look
at some practical and impractical user testing goals.

Practical User Testing Goals

For a given task, you can perform user testing to determine whether your
program has the following attributes (as outlined by Nielsen):

- **Learnability** Can the user figure out how to perform the task
  without assistance? Can the user perform the task at all? If so,
  did the user find it difficult or easy? Does the user's conceptual
  model of how the program works correspond to the way it actually works?

- **Efficiency** Can the user perform the task in an acceptable
  amount of time? This is often referred to as *time to task*. The standard user testing technique of *thinking out loud*, described later,
  affects the time it takes to perform a task, so relative times (that
  is, comparing the efficiency of two different interfaces) are more
  likely to be meaningful than absolute times (that is, the time it
  takes to do a task using a single interface).

 PART V

- **Few errors** Can the user perform the task without making an unacceptable number of mistakes? How error-prone is the task? How serious are the errors?

- **Memorability** Can the user remember how to perform a task after a period of time?

- **Satisfaction** Did the user enjoy using the program? Did the user find using it a pleasant experience?

You can use these attributes to evaluate a single user interface design or you can compare two different designs by testing for any of these attributes and comparing the results.

Impractical User Testing Goals

I consider the following to be impractical user testing goals:

- **To find design problems not related to usability** Since user testing is focused on performing tasks, it is unlikely that users will find design problems that are not task-related. A mediocre yet usable design will perform well in user testing.

- **To find bugs** Since user testing is focused on performing tasks, it is unlikely that users will identify implementation problems. User testing is to find usability problems. It is not a substitute for QA.

- **To test usability for advanced users** Since user testing is usually focused on beginning users, it's difficult to predict how advanced users will respond to the program and to test advanced features that require a significant amount of experience.

- **To discover repetitive tasks** Since user testing focuses on having a user perform a task once or maybe twice to check memorability, it is difficult to determine whether a task is unnecessarily repetitive.

- **To obtain complete coverage** Unless your program is fairly simple, it's unlikely that you can test all its features. You have to select specific tasks for the user to perform, and user testing is unlikely to find problems with features that are not associated with those selected tasks. For example, you cannot find problems with your setup program during user testing unless you explicitly make it part of your test plan.

- **To determine program usefulness** Since you are the one selecting the tasks in the test and not the user, it's unlikely that the user would be able to determine the overall usefulness of the program by performing those tasks.

CHAPTER 27

- **To determine marketability** You cannot determine whether the user would buy the program or whether the program will be competitive.

Given all of this, what should your goals be? Of course this depends upon the type of information you want to obtain. Although you can design tasks to measure all of these attributes, in general I think it makes more sense to focus on learnability. Perform user testing to determine whether users can figure out how to use your program. If users are able to learn how to use the program quickly, chances are they will also find it easy to remember and make few mistakes. They're also likely to enjoy using the program. However, efficiency is a totally separate issue. A task that is easy to learn isn't necessarily efficient. For example, a task that is performed using a wizard is likely to be easy to learn but inefficient, whereas a task performed using keyboard shortcuts isn't learnable but is efficient. Consequently, tasks that are performed often should also be tested for efficiency. Such efficiency tests might require experienced users, since it is unlikely that a first-time user is going to become a proficient user during the test.

TIP Focus user testing on learnability. If users find the program easy to learn, chances are they will find it efficient, not error-prone, and enjoyable as well.

You also need to select the specific tasks to test. Tasks that are performed often, that are essential to the basic functionality of the program, or that involve features that have unusual or complex user interfaces are obvious candidates. Tasks that are rarely performed or that involve features that have user interfaces similar to other successful programs are less likely to result in serious usability problems.

Types of User Testing

There are two fundamental types of user testing:

- **Design check** A test made to check the usability of a user interface design during the design process. Such a test typically uses some kind of prototype, such as a paper prototype, a resource prototype, or a functional prototype. A design check is a good way to get early feedback to make sure that a difficult or unusual user interface design is going to work.

- **Product check**   A test made to check the usability of production code as it nears completion as part of the testing and QA process. This type of test is best suited for fine-tuning a user interface by finding small problems. Programmer testing and QA testing should be performed before this test to remove any obvious problems.

Do not use the placement of this chapter within this book as a guide for when you should perform user testing. You can perform user testing as needed at any time during the development process, not just toward the end. Typically, you'll need to perform user testing during the design phase and the QA phase.

While I've mentioned in Chapter 8, "Users Aren't Designers," and Chapter 14, "Prototype with Caution," that I have reservations about the effectiveness of functional prototypes, I am convinced that the only way to get useful information from a functional prototype is through user testing. You have to actually witness users trying to perform tasks with a functional prototype for it to have any value.

Selecting Users

User testing is testing with real users. So, who is a real user? Clearly, *you* are not a real user, nor is anyone else on your development team. The ideal real user is a target user, the specific type of user that the user interface was designed for. A target user has specific needs and goals as well as a specific background. I discussed target users in detail in Chapter 8.

Usability testing typically focuses on first-time users performing a task once. This makes sense because testing for learnability is such an important goal, as I discussed earlier. There are usually more intermediate and advanced users than beginning users for a typical program in the real world, and thus most user testing misses a significant portion of the user base. However, beginning users are more likely to reveal problems.

 TIP   Testing with beginning users is more likely to reveal problems.

It can be difficult to find suitable test users. For example, beginning users don't stay beginners for long, so you can't use an individual test user as a representative beginning user for more than one set of tests. It is even more difficult to test advanced users, since it is unlikely that a test user is going to use the program long enough to be a representative advanced user. If the program is new, you'll have to create advanced users yourself, since they don't exist yet, by giving some users sufficient exposure to the program. The difficulty in finding suitable test users is yet another reason why you need to perform programmer testing and QA testing before user testing. You don't want to "waste" users on easy-to-find usability problems.

What about user testing with colleagues that are not on your development team? Most usability experts recommend against this, since colleagues have different backgrounds, biases, expectations, and knowledge about the program than real users. However, target users are usually not readily available and colleagues are. I've tested with colleagues and found that it works quite well. I find application engineers make good test subjects. In keeping with the idea that some user testing is better than none, I think that testing with colleagues is far better than no user testing at all. After all, testing with colleagues is a waste of time only if they can't find any problems. If they are confused by a feature or can't perform a task, their input is probably just as good as that of target users.

On the other hand, some types of target users have no substitutes, such as:

- Noncomputer users

- Children

- Physically impaired users

- Highly trained specialists

For these types of users, everything you know is wrong. You must test with these specific target users to obtain useful information. If you're writing software for brain surgery, you had better test with brain surgeons.

How many users should you test with? For a design check of a typical mainstream program, testing with three beginning-level users is about the minimum. If you want to also test experienced users, you should test with at least three experienced users as well. Of course, the more complex your program is and the larger the market, the more users you should test with. Nielsen has found that you can get good coverage with as few as three test users per iteration. For a product check, you might want to use more than three test users to get broader coverage.

User Testing Procedure

Once you have set your goals and selected test users, you're ready to start the process. The following procedure gives the basic steps for performing user testing on the cheap.

Prepare a Test Plan

You first need to prepare a test plan, which needs to address the following issues:

- **Select the tasks that the test users will perform**   Again, these tasks should be essential to the basic functionality of the program or involve features that have unusual or complex user interfaces. Note that you need to test tasks, not features, since it is meaningful to ask a user to perform a task but it doesn't make any sense to ask a user to use a feature. If your goal is to test specific features, test tasks that incorporate those features. Try to select realistic tasks that are likely to happen in the real world rather than contrived tasks designed solely to test specific features.

- **Determine whether the Help system is part of the test**   If a test user is confused, he might try to use the online Help. This should be part of the test only if the Help system is developed enough to actually be helpful. You don't need to perform user testing to conclude that poorly developed, incomplete Help isn't helpful.

- **Determine the length of each test**   While some user tests can take several hours, I recommend keeping most tests to under an hour. Two hours should be the maximum. If a test tasks more than two hours, you should divide it into parts and have different users test different parts. Each test user doesn't have to do every test.

- **Determine the number of test users required**   Again, three test users are usually the minimum.

- **Determine the equipment and materials you need to perform the test**   You'll need a furnished room, a computer (except for paper prototypes), and the program you want to test. You'll certainly need a notebook to take notes. You might choose to use a video camera or an audio recorder to record the test. You might also want to prepare a questionnaire for the test users to fill out after the testing is finished.

- **Determine who will run the tests**   As I'll discuss later in this chapter, it may not be a good idea to have the programmers responsible for the user interface run the tests—they might not be receptive to bad news.

- **Schedule the users for the test**   Select test users, and make sure that their background matches the program's target users as much as you can. Be sure to document their background, since this information will help you evaluate the test results. For scheduling, be sure to leave enough time between each test for the test user instructions and wrap-up, each of which I'll describe later.

Consider a Test Run

If you plan to do a lot of testing, you should consider doing a test run. You need to make sure that the test makes sense and that the selected tasks accomplish what you want them to. You need to work out any problems beforehand.

Now you are ready to test with the real test users.

Give the Test User Instructions

Before you start testing, give the test user instructions about the test. These instructions are very important, as they can significantly affect the results of your tests. They will help you get as much information out of the testing process as possible. Take these steps before beginning user testing:

- **Introduce yourself**

- **Introduce the program that the user is going to test**   Explain what the program is for. You should explain the state of the program, that is, whether the test user is testing a prototype, a nearly finished program, or something in between. But regardless of the program state, you need to make it clear that everything is changeable and that you would be happy to throw away what isn't good. The test user should not feel reluctant to make suggestions because the program appears to be in an advanced state.

- **Explain that you are looking for problems in the software**   You are especially looking for problems where the program is difficult to use. The test user shouldn't feel bad if he can't complete a task. That's the program's fault, not the test user's, and that is the kind of information you are looking for. The goal is to find problems, not to complete tasks. Make it clear that you are testing the software, not the test user. Lastly, explain that since the goal is to find problems, the test user won't hurt anyone's feelings by criticizing the program.

PART
V

- **Give an overview of the testing process**   Explain what tasks the test user is to perform and roughly how long it will take.

- **Explain that the test user should not worry about harming the computer**   Test users should use the computer exactly as if it were theirs. For example, if a task requires saving a file, the user should go ahead and save the file. Test users shouldn't worry about harming the computer or leaving test files. Also, the test user should feel free to make any adjustments to the monitor, keyboard, mouse, chair, or anything else to be more comfortable. Obviously, you should select a computer for testing that the test user really can't harm. You probably shouldn't use your development computer. This step obviously doesn't apply to paper prototypes.

- **Have the test user sign any forms**   You might choose to have the test user sign a consent form, as I describe later. If the program you are testing reveals anything you don't want made public, you should also have the test user sign a nondisclosure agreement.

- **Explain that participation in the test is voluntary and the test user can leave at any time**   Explain to the test user that if the test makes him feel uncomfortable or if he prefers not to continue, he can stop the test for any reason. The last instruction is especially interesting. Although it might seem as if asking a test user to try a couple tasks with a computer program is no big deal, there have been some tests performed on people that are now considered highly unethical if not illegal. The most famous of such tests is Stanley Milgram's "Obedience to Authority" tests conducted in the late 1950s. In these tests, a test subject was told that he, "the teacher," and another subject, "the learner," were going to perform a test on learning behavior. The subject was to ask the learner a series of questions involving word pairs. If the learner missed a question, the teacher was to deliver an electric shock, starting at 15 volts and going all the way up to 450 volts in 15-volt increments, and repeat the question until the learner got it right. As the learner missed more and more questions, the teacher would apply ever-increasing jolts and the learner would beg the teacher to stop. Only a few did. In reality, the learner was really an actor and there weren't really any electric shocks applied. The point of the test wasn't to test learning behavior but to test the participant's willingness to follow the instructions of an authority figure, even to the harm of others.

CHAPTER 27

There are now laws on the books as a result of such testing. While I know you would never apply electric shocks to your test users, you need to understand that user testing is serious business. Some users find the testing process to be very emotional, especially if they are not able to perform the tasks. Some companies require test users to sign a consent form that states that the test user has agreed to participate and that gives you permission to use the test results, including any audio tapes or videotapes. You might want to ask your company's legal counsel for advice on this matter.

Ask the Test User to Think Out Loud

You should now ask the test user to think out loud. This is the most important instruction you can give. Thinking out loud is when the test user verbalizes all his thoughts while performing a task. Having the test user think out loud helps you understand exactly what the user is doing and thinking. It helps you know if the user is confused or has made incorrect assumptions. Most importantly, it helps you understand why. Having the test user think out loud helps you get into the test user's head. You don't need to guess what the user is thinking.

TIP Ask the test user to think out loud, that is, to verbalize all thoughts while performing a task.

Since most people are unfamiliar with this concept, explain to the test user what thinking out loud is. You should then demonstrate how to think out loud by performing a simple task, such as changing the desktop's wallpaper. This example will make what is a fairly abstract concept easier to understand. You can use the following instructions: "We find the tests are more helpful if the participants say what they are thinking while they are using the program. Just say what you are thinking—whatever comes to mind. For example, if you are thinking about clicking a button, say why you think you need to click that button and what you expect to happen once you click it. To help you understand what I have in mind, let me give you a quick demonstration…" Some test users find thinking out loud difficult to do. If the test user starts staring quietly at the screen for a while, just ask "So, what are you thinking now?" to get the test user going again.

The only time I would not recommend asking the test user to think out loud is when it undermines what you are trying to test. For example, if you're trying to test how efficient an order entry system is by timing how long it takes to perform the task several times, thinking out loud would make any time measurements less accurate since it forces the user to work at the speed at which he can talk or find the words to describe what he is thinking.

Avoid Giving the Test User Assistance

Another important instruction you need to give is that you will only be watching the test user perform the tasks and will not be able to answer any questions about performing those tasks. You should explain that it is important to make the test as realistic as possible and real users do not have expert users standing by to answer questions. The goal of the test is to determine the user's ability to use the software, and this goal will be undermined if you tell the user how to do it. However, since you want the test user to think out loud, explain that you want the test user to ask any questions he may have—you just won't be able to answer them. You should also tell the test user that you would be happy to answer any questions once the test has completed.

TIP Avoid giving the test user assistance during the test. Encourage the test user to ask any questions—you just won't be able to answer them.

Despite these instructions, the test user may get stuck while performing a task. Do not explain this to the test user, but in this case you'll have to give the test user some help to keep the test going. If the test user is really stuck, give hints at first and more helpful information only as needed. You can answer questions the test user asks with counterquestions. For example, if the test user asks, "What happens if I click on this?" you can answer, "What do you think will happen?" Resist the temptation to give help at the first sign of struggle. Give the test user sufficient time to solve the problem before you start giving hints.

Perform the Tests

Now you are ready to roll. Ask the test user if he has any questions before you start. Perform the tests in their order of importance in case you run out of time, but make sure that the first task is fairly easy so that the test user will gain confidence. For each task, describe the task and its goal, but be careful not to suggest how the task should be accomplished. Then have the test user perform the task. Keep your eyes and ears open and your mouth shut. Never laugh at a test user's mistakes. Take good notes. At the very least, keep track of the specific user interface elements that the test user is having trouble with and what the user was thinking at the time.

During the test, keep your eyes and ears open and your mouth shut.

Wrap Up

After the testing is complete, you should wrap up the test with an appropriate selection of the following steps:

- **Ask if the test user has any questions**   Now that the testing is complete, you can answer any questions that the test user has that you were unable to answer during the testing. Providing this opportunity makes the testing process more satisfying for the test user.

- **Discuss any events that occurred during the test that you would like the test user to explain further**   You might want to have the test user clarify some statements or questions that were made while thinking out loud. You might want to explore some of the test user's actions further.

- **Ask for the test user's opinion of the program**   While you have to carefully interpret such feedback (since the test user may be trying to be nice), this information can be helpful. Don't try to defend the program when you receive negative feedback. You can ask questions to get more information, but defending the program discourages feedback.

- **Ask the test user for any comments or suggestions**   Up to this point, you've been running the show. The test user might have some interesting ideas that he would like to express.

- **Consider having the test user fill out a questionnaire**   Create a questionnaire if you have specific questions that you'd like test users to answer. Questionnaires are a good way to determine satisfaction with the program.

- **Provide access to a suggestion box**   People are often reluctant to say something in person if they are afraid it might hurt someone's feelings. A suggestion box allows test users to provide such feedback anonymously. It also gives them a means to provide additional feedback at a later time. The "suggestion box" may simply be a self-addressed, postage-paid envelope with a feedback form inside.

PART
V

438

- **Thank the test user**   Test users can feel discouraged at the end of the test, especially if they had difficulty performing the tasks. Reiterate that your objective was to find problems in the software, so they have helped you accomplish what you set out to do.

- **Show your appreciation for the test user's time**   Show test users that you value their time by giving them something of value for their effort. Test users like to receive items such as free software, T-shirts, gift certificates, and even cash.

Interpret the Results

Once a round of testing is done, you need to interpret the results since you can't necessarily take them at face value. Look for trends. If nobody has a problem performing a task, that of course is a good sign. One test user having a problem with a feature isn't necessarily significant, but multiple test users having the same problem is a clear sign of a usability problem.

When asking test users for their opinion, it's important to understand that most people want to be nice. Even if test users absolutely hate the program, to be diplomatic they often say something like, "Well, so far so good, but it clearly needs more work." Translation: "Yuck! We hate it! Better try again." I have seen this happen. Don't expect test users to list all the problems they have with a program. Some users might, but many users won't. Users' natural preference to emphasize the positive can be counterproductive in the feedback process.

TIP   Users want to be nice, so you can't always take what they say literally.

You also need to carefully interpret the test users' suggestions. If a test user's suggestions make perfect sense, you know what to do. However, if the suggestions don't make sense, try to understand why. For example, users are much better at determining problems than designing solutions, but they often phrase problems they find in terms of a suggested solution. I call this phenomenon QA Gefahren, which I discuss in detail in Chapter 36.

Interpretation of the results is necessary, but I am not suggesting that you don't take the results seriously. If you think a task is easy to do and users find it difficult, they are right and you are wrong. Don't dismiss this feedback or try to defend the feature—just fix it. The computer industry has a bad reputation for quickly dismissing feedback. For example, suppose a nuclear reactor has a meltdown because an operator accidentally pushed the wrong button. Further suppose that the reason the operator pushed the wrong button is that all the buttons on the power plant's control panel look the same. Ordinarily, one would assume that a mistake like this would be a clear sign of a design problem—the ultimate user test. In fact, such problems are often readily dismissed as operator errors or training problems, not design problems. Peter Neumanns' *Computer-Related Risks* is full of examples of design problems leading to "operator errors." Any mistake a test user makes is an indication that the user interface can be improved. Blaming test users for incorrectly using a poor interface prevents you from making this realization.

Fix the Problems and Try Again

If the testing process revealed significant usability problems, you need to fix the problems and do another round of testing. Keep going until you get it right.

Issues to Consider

Here are a few more issues you should consider in the user testing process.

Egoless User Testing

You need to decide whether you should personally perform user testing on your own user interface designs. The problem is that there is a natural conflict of interest: the goal of user testing is to reveal problems in a user interface, whereas your natural tendency is to defend your work. If you want to be a successful user interface designer, you have to learn to accept criticism. That said, it can be a humiliating experience to watch someone trash your work. It might be better to have someone else conduct the user testing for your user interfaces. At least until you get used to it.

TIP It can be a humiliating experience to watch someone trash your work. Consider having someone else conduct the user testing for your user interfaces.

Attitude

Whether or not you personally run the tests, you're going to receive feedback and most of that feedback isn't going to be good. After all, the goal of user testing is to find problems. Your response to criticism is primarily a question of attitude. Remember, if test users find problems in your user

PART
V

interface, they are doing you a big favor. Look at the bright side: It's better to have a couple of random people know about your mistakes than the whole world. Users are going to test your interfaces one way or another.

TIP

Lighten up! Test users are doing you a big favor when they find problems in your user interfaces.

If test users find problems with your user interface, it isn't their fault. User interfaces are for users. If users can't use them, it is the user interface that has failed, not the user. Don't blame the problems on the test users.

Videotaping

Should you bother to videotape the testing? That depends upon who is present during the testing and who needs to review the testing. If you're not using a usability lab with a one-way mirror, only one person should directly witness the testing. After all, you don't want a gang of people standing over the test user's shoulder. For egoless user testing, you might not want that person to be one of the developers, but the developers do need to see the results. There is nothing quite like the experience of watching test users struggle with an "intuitive" user interface to make it clear that the interface needs more work. Making a videotape of the test is a cheap and easy way to make a record of the test that you can review at any time. While you probably won't watch the entire tape if you witnessed the test, there may be times when you need to go back and review the tape to check for missing details.

On the other hand, if you have been through the user testing process several times and developed a thick enough skin to conduct the tests directly, you can simplify the testing process by not using a video camera. It is less work for you, and test users will find it easier to relax without a video camera present.

If for any reason you want to record the tests but you can't use a video camera, note that an audio tape recorder also works reasonably well. Just make sure that the test users think out loud, and the audio tape will contain useful information.

User-Testing the Setup Program

As I discuss in Chapter 33, "Check Your Setup Program," you should consider the setup program's user interface to be part of your program's user interface. Unless installing the program is unusually time-consuming or the

CHAPTER
27

program is one that the test user wouldn't normally install (such as network software), you should consider testing the setup program by making the program setup the first task in the test.

Take the Challenge

If you have never tried user testing before, take the challenge and try it. Identify three or so features in your program that you are most concerned about and create a quick test with tasks that use those features. Get three test users (try to get target users, but take anybody you can get—don't worry too much if they're not target users), and follow the procedures outlined in this chapter. Don't bother with videotaping, question forms, or any nonessential detail. Try to do the whole process in an afternoon. Greet any problems found with extreme enthusiasm. Then draw your own conclusion about the effectiveness of user testing.

Remember, some user testing is better than none.

Related Chapters

- Chapter 8—Users Aren't Designers.

  Presents the concept that users aren't designers and their feedback needs to be carefully interpreted.

- Chapter 12—Learn from *The Design of Everyday Things*.

  Presents conceptual models and why it is a really good idea to do user testing when you choose one.

- Chapter 14—Prototype with Caution.

  Discusses various techniques for prototyping, the problems with prototyping, and tips on how to get the most out of prototyping. User testing plays an important role in the prototyping process and can be the difference between obtaining useful feedback and wasting your time.

- Chapter 26—Programmer Testing.

  Discusses the importance of programmer testing in the testing process and how programmers can improve their ability to find problems by changing their perspective. This chapter also explains how to find problems by giving demos and why things never go as planned during a demo. Lastly, it describes a technique called heuristic evaluation, with which you can find many common usability problems by checking a list of usability principles.

- Chapter 36—Learn How to Play QA Gefahren.

  Discusses how to deal with feedback that doesn't appear to be especially good and turn it into useful information.

Recommended Reading

- Arlov, Laura. *GUI Design for Dummies*. Foster City, CA: IDG Books Worldwide, Inc., 1997.

  Chapter 17, "A Cookbook for Testing with Users," gives a good overall description of the user testing process and a detailed test script. It also gives useful information on how to handle difficult situations, such as what to do when a test user gives up on a task or decides to quit. The chapter also has useful information about creating test tasks.

- Bickford, Peter. *Interface Design: The Art of Developing Easy-to-Use Software*. Chestnut Hill, MA: Academic Press, 1997.

  Chapter 27, "Guerrilla Usability Testing," gives a brief summary of the user testing process. It also discusses the need to carefully interpret the results.

- Howlett, Virginia. *Visual Interface Design for Windows*. New York, NY: John Wiley & Sons, Inc., 1996.

  Chapter 3, "The Process for Designing Visual Interfaces," presents a brief design process based on prototyping and user testing.

- Microsoft Corporation. *Designing for the User Experience*. Redmond, WA: Microsoft Press, 1999.

  See the chapter on design principles and methodology for a concise description of usability assessment in the design process.

- Neumann, Peter G. *Computer-Related Risks*. Reading, MA: Addison-Wesley Publishing Company, 1995.

  This book is based on the data gathered for ACM's International Risks Forum. From the point of view of user interface design, the most significant (and disturbing) trend is how often problems resulting from bad design are blamed on user error.

CHAPTER 27

- Nielsen, Jakob. *Usability Engineering*. Chestnut Hill, MA: AP Professional, 1993.

  Chapter 6, "Usability Testing," gives a comprehensive description of the user testing process. It discusses all the issues raised here but in much more depth. This is *the* book on user testing.

- Shneiderman, Ben. *Designing the User Interface—Strategies for Effective Human-Computer Interaction, Third Edition*. Reading, MA: Addison-Wesley Longman, Inc., 1999.

  Chapter 4, "Expert Reviews, Usability Testing, Surveys, and Continuing Assessments," gives a good overview of user testing as well as other forms of user feedback such as surveys, acceptance tests, user interviews, focus groups, suggestion boxes, and newsgroups. The chapter contains a complete sample user satisfaction questionnaire.

- Tognazzini, Bruce. *Tog on Interface*. Reading, MA: Addison-Wesley Publishing Company, Inc., 1992.

  Chapter 14, "User Testing on the Cheap," does an excellent job of condensing the user testing process recommended by Apple's usability experts to a mere six pages. This chapter also presents an excellent case study of user testing in action.

- Weinschenk, Susan; Jamar, Pamela; and Yeo, Sarah C. *GUI Design Essentials*. New York, NY: John Wiley & Sons, Inc., 1997.

  Chapter 5, "Usability Testing," presents a detailed description of the user testing process. Among the subjects covered are the myths of user testing, identifying the scope of the test, planning the test, conducting the test, and analyzing the results.

CHAPTER 28

Talk to Your Other Team Members

Talk to your other product development team members. Or, more specifically, talk to your other product development team members who aren't programmers. They have valuable input and different points of view that you need to seriously consider. This is especially true if you are not experienced in creating user interfaces. If your other team members are experienced, undoubtedly they have seen the common mistakes before. In this chapter, I'll describe the nonprogrammer team members you should work with and how their input is valuable in developing user interfaces.

A typical product development team can include programmers, user interface designers, graphic artists, technical writers, technical support staff, quality assurance testers, and management. These team members might be part of the general development process, or they might all be active members of the design team. Either way, taking full advantage of your team's input should not be confused with anything resembling a design-by-committee approach to software development. If you prefer to design using a team effort, use a design team. If you prefer to design with one or two designers, design that way. Regardless of how many people actively participate in the actual design, everyone involved in the project should participate in evaluating the results and providing feedback. This way everyone understands the product direction and is able to make a contribution.

Involving Team Members in the Process

When you ask nonprogramming team members for their input, I can already tell you what they will say: they want to be involved early in the development process. Of course, this doesn't mean that they have to attend every design meeting and have a say in every design decision. At the very least, what it means is that they need to review the preliminary designs and the early prototypes and demos. They need to know what is going on so that they can make their contribution early in the process—when it can make a significant difference—rather than later in the process when it is often too late. The last thing you want to do is plop the finished program on their desk a week before it ships and say, "Here it is, what do you think?" At that point, their input won't count for much and they will be fully aware of that fact.

TIP Your other team members want to be involved early in the development process.

Make an effort to make sure that the other team members understand that their input is wanted. Many people in these other roles do not take this for granted. In fact, they often preface their opinions with something like, "Well, I'm just a tech writer, but I think that...." Make it clear you want their input, and always give it a warm reception, even though it might be critical of your work. User interface design is not for the fainthearted.

TIP Make sure that the other team members understand that their input is wanted.

Do not use the placement of this chapter within this book as a guide for when and the degree to which you should involve other team members in the development process. In fact, this is true for all the other chapters in the "Testing and QA" portion of this book. All of these chapters present issues that need to be addressed during the entire development process, but a logical presentation in the book requires that they be toward the end, regardless of when the issues are important during the development of a user interface.

The Team Members

In the following sections, I'll describe the roles of your nonprogramming team members in the user interface development process.

Management and Marketing

Management and marketing's biggest contribution to user interface design is to make sure that the product includes the necessary features required for it to sell (which is the ultimate business goal of commercial software products) or to satisfy the customer (which is the ultimate business goal for contract work or in-house development). They are your connection to the marketplace and the customer, so their input is critical to the success of the project.

The biggest problem I have experienced with managers and marketers is their fascination with vaporware. They seem to be enthralled with the concept of being able to tell their customers that they can completely satisfy all their needs without knowing whether the software they're promising can actually be developed. Consequently, the biggest challenge with working with management and marketing is to make sure that they are not creating unrealistic customer expectations and that they are countering unrealistic expectations that do exist with honest facts. With so much vapor, sometime you need to nail their feet to the floor to keep them from floating off into space.

Graphic Designers

You should take advantage of the talents of a good graphic designer whenever possible. At the very least, you should have a graphic designer create the program bitmaps, icons, and animations and review user interface designs. In some cases, you might want a graphic designer to create the entire look of the program. Since the amount of time required to do these designs is small compared to the time it will take you to implement them, graphic designers can make a significant contribution to the overall product without significantly affecting its cost.

The first time I worked on a project with graphic designers, I was certain a graphic designer wasn't necessary since the task didn't involve anything even remotely graphic. In fact, the program worked entirely with text and very simple text at that. However, I found working with graphic

CHAPTER 28

designers to be an enlightening experience. Their contribution added a certain snap to the product that it never would have had without their help.

Of course, everyone has their strengths and weaknesses, and graphic designers are no exception. Good graphic designers focus on visual communication (especially visual affordance, through which a user can determine how an object is used just by looking at its visual clues), whereas not-so-good graphic designers focus on visual decoration. The not-so-good graphic designers are under the impression that if each visual element of the user interface uses a metaphor, has a textured background, is in 3-D, and has an icon associated with it, then for sure the user interface is a good one. While it's possible that this approach will result in a good-looking user interface, a program's visual appearance is only a small part of its overall usability. A lot of cheesy CD-ROMs and Internet sites are like this. They look great, but their functionality and usability are poor. By contrast, the visibility of the program's functionality—the degree to which the user can figure out how to use it just by looking at it—is a significant part of the overall usability. Work with graphic designers to increase your program's visibility—visibility rather than pure aesthetics is what you really want from graphic designers.

TIP Use graphic designers to improve your program's functional visibility and its visual appeal.

Technical Writers

Technical writers are in a unique position: their job is to describe in a reasonably concise and coherent way what your program does. If a user interface feature doesn't make sense or is difficult to use, your tech writer will surely know it. Technical writers are especially good at recognizing nonstandard user interface designs, overly complex user interfaces, inconsistencies in the user interface or the terminology, commands that are missing or hard to find, and poor or misleading error messages. I find the feedback from good technical writers to be extremely valuable in discovering user interface problems.

TIP Technical writers are in a unique position to find user interface problems.

Of course, the interesting question is what should you do when a technical writer discovers an interface problem. Should you fix the problem or only document it? Unless you are dealing with extraordinary circumstances,

PART
V

450

you should always prefer to fix the bug. To make this policy practical, make sure that the technical writing process starts early enough so that there is time to respond to such problems. You also need to make this policy clear so that your technical writer will know to report bugs instead of documenting them.

TIP Don't document problems; fix them.

QA Team

The QA team needs to be involved early in the design process to review the design and make sure that the project is on track. After all, there is no point in implementing a user interface if the design isn't any good. Members of the QA team might also be part of the user interface design team. At a minimum, they need to review the design documents and evaluate any demos and prototypes.

It's important to make sure that QA testers check for usability problems. Often testers tend to focus on objective issues, such as missing features, incorrect or inconsistent behavior, and crashes, and not on subjective issues such as usability and performance. If a tester has trouble figuring out how to perform a command or if the tester finds a dialog box poorly laid out or confusing, the problem should result in a bug report. In fact, it usually makes more sense to focus on usability issues first and then look for more objective bugs. If a dialog box is hopelessly confusing and needs to be completely redone, I would rather receive that as the first bug report for that dialog box rather than the last. There is no point in fixing a bunch of details if the dialog box needs to be completely reworked anyway.

As far as usability testing is concerned, more information is almost always better than less. Testers should feel free to submit bug reports on all usability and performance issues, even those concerning the smallest details. On several occasions when I've found a usability problem with a program I was working on, I've said to a tester, "I just found a silly bug that has apparently been in the program for quite a while." Very often the response is, "Oh, I've seen that. I thought it was weird, but I assumed that it was supposed to be like that." By encouraging bug reports on all usability issues, you, not the testers, can be the judge of what is important.

Technical Support

Your technical support team will have many concerns that you as a programmer rarely think about. You need to understand that developing software for technical support is different from developing quality software.

451

CHAPTER 28

You can create a program that is "bug-free" but that is still difficult to support because it is difficult to install or configure. Discuss with your technical support team what the biggest technical support problems are now and in the past and see if there are ways to avoid them in the future.

Your technical support team will likely be concerned about the following issues:

- Setup and uninstall
- Upgrading
- Error messages

Using a good, well-tested setup program is the single most important step in reducing technical support calls. This is not an exaggeration. The reason is simple. While your program's advanced features might be its selling point and what gets all the attention, if a user has a problem with an advanced feature, maybe you'll get a technical support call and maybe you won't. But if the user cannot install your program, you will get a support call. Guaranteed. And if technical support isn't able to solve the problem, most likely you will get a product return. What good is a program that you can't install?

If the program is an upgrade to a previous release, you also need to address upgrade issues. Does the upgrade install over and replace the existing version or can the user run old and new versions of the program simultaneously? For example, note that you can install Microsoft Visual C++ 6.0 while keeping Visual C++ 5.0 on your system. This is made possible by maintaining completely different sets of configuration information in the registry that is keyed on the version number, as recommended by *Designing for the User Experience*. It is made practical by having the setup program automatically use all applicable user settings from the previous version so that the user doesn't have to input all of these settings manually.

Lastly, you should encourage your technical support team to review all of your program's error messages to make sure that they are clear, concise, consistent, and informative. Imagine what it would be like if someone you didn't know called you up, read you the error message, and asked you what to do. This is what your technical support staff faces every day. They need to understand the error messages and their significance well before the program ships, not after.

The Designed for Microsoft Windows logo requirements include many useful items to check to make sure that your program installs, uninstalls, and upgrades well.

Related Chapters

- Chapter 10—Good User Interfaces Are Visible.

  Describes program visibility and visual affordance. These goals are why you need to consider using a graphic designer.

- Chapter 32—Check Your Help System and Documentation.

  Presents many suggestions on working with technical writers.

- Chapter 33—Check Your Setup Program.

  Describes many of the problems found in a typical setup program and recommends solutions. You should review these issues with your technical support team.

- Chapter 36—Learn How to Play QA Gefahren.

  Describes how to deal with feedback that doesn't appear to be especially good and turn it into useful information.

Recommended Reading

- Howlett, Virginia. *Visual Interface Design for Windows*. New York, NY: John Wiley & Sons, Inc., 1996.

  Part 1, "Foundation," presents useful information about the members of a user interface development team and how they should work together.

- Microsoft Corporation. The Designed for Microsoft Windows logo requirements, "Logo Requirements, Recommendations, and Best Practices."

  Presents information of particular interest to technical support.

- Microsoft Corporation. *Designing for the User Experience*. Redmond, WA: Microsoft Press, 1999.

  See the chapter on integrating with the system for useful information about integrating with Windows, installing programs, and using the registry.

- Tognazzini, Bruce. *Tog on Interface*. Reading, MA: Addison-Wesley Publishing Company, 1992.

  Chapter 11, "Three Key Players," describes working with user interface designers, graphic designers, and tech writers.

28

- Weinschenk, Susan; Jamar, Pamela; and Yeo, Sarah C. *GUI Design Essentials*. New York, NY: John Wiley & Sons, Inc., 1997.

  Presents guidelines for assembling analysis and design teams.

CD-ROM Resources

The CD-ROM included with this book contains the following resource related to this chapter:

- The Designed for Microsoft Windows logo requirements.

PART
V

CHAPTER 29

Check Your Dialog Boxes

I've discussed many of the issues related to creating good dialog boxes in other chapters. This chapter focuses on finding common dialog box problems that often slip between the cracks. But before we look at problems, let's review some dialog box navigation basics and the rules for setting the default button and the control with initial input focus.

Dialog Box Navigation Basics

Many dialog box problems have to do with keyboard navigation. Dialog boxes in Microsoft Windows provide substantial keyboard support so that the user can use a dialog box without using the mouse. Early versions of Windows needed this ability because not all computers included a mouse. Although all computers do include a mouse today, providing keyboard support offers many advantages, including the convenience of not having to constantly remove your hand from the keyboard and the improved accessibility for users who have trouble using a mouse.

The order in which the controls are listed in a dialog box template is referred to as the tab order. When the Tab key is pressed, the next control in the tab order that has the tab stop attribute (WS_TABSTOP) receives the input focus. The previous control in the tab order that has the tab stop attribute receives input focus when Shift+Tab is pressed. In Microsoft Visual C++, all controls that can receive input focus, except radio buttons, have the tab stop property set by default.

Note that while a control that doesn't take input focus (such as a static text control or a group box) can have the tab stop attribute set, no visual cue indicates when it receives input focus. When such a control has input focus, it looks as if the input focus has disappeared from the dialog box. Consequently, controls that do not take input focus should never have the tab stop attribute set. Aside from this, the most common dialog box tab stop problem is forgetting to assign the tab order.

The group attribute (WS_GROUP) is used to determine the behavior of the arrow keys. It is usually used to delimit a group of radio buttons. The group attribute identifies the first control of a group of controls, so the first radio button must have the group attribute and all the other radio buttons in the group must not. The first control in tab order that isn't in the group must have the group attribute to indicate the end of the group and the beginning of the next group. In Visual C++, only static text controls have the group attribute set by default. Note that if the control grouping is not done properly, the arrow keys will "leak out" of the radio button group to other controls or get stuck on the last control in the group rather than cycling back to the top of the group.

Also note that the group attribute works for all controls, not just radio buttons. For example, you could create a group of check boxes with the first check box having the group attribute and the remaining check boxes not. This would allow the user to use the arrow keys to navigate between the check boxes. There is no official guideline for the group attribute for nonradio buttons, so if you consider this behavior desirable you might want to group all controls that receive input focus, which is something I do.

Access keys allow the user to directly move to a control or push a button from the keyboard. An access key is identified by a label with an underlined character, as with

The user can then access the help button directly by pressing Alt+H. Note that while buttons have their own captions, most other controls do not. To assign access keys to controls that do not have captions, you can assign an access key to a static text label and place the label just before the control you want activated in the tab order. In the example on the previous page, the edit box is activated when the user presses Alt+N if the *Enter Name* static text precedes that edit box in the tab order. Common access key problems include missing access keys, access keys assigned to items that don't have input focus (such as static text not used as labels), access keys not assigned uniquely, and the tab order assigned incorrectly so that an access key in a static text label doesn't activate the correct control.

Lastly, the Enter, Esc, and Spacebar keys also play an important role in keyboard navigation. The default command button is the button that is activated when the Enter key is pressed. Default status is assigned to the command button with the Default button style (BS_DEFPUSHBUTTON) (obviously, only one command button should have this style) or to the first command button in tab order if no command button has been given the Default button style. The Default button style is visually indicated by a bold outline around the button's border. The Esc key is used to dismiss a modal dialog box and requires no special handling. The button with input focus is activated when the Spacebar key is pressed; button input focus is visually indicated with a dashed outline around its caption. Note that the default command button and the button with input focus are independent for all controls except for command buttons—the command button with input focus is always the default button, regardless of the Default button style—so they may or may not be the same control.

If you don't test specifically for keyboard support, you will find some actions will be impossible to do with the keyboard alone. Keyboard problems are generally easy to fix once detected.

Rules for the Default Button and Initial Focus

You need to assign the default button and the control that has initial focus carefully. Generally, you want to assign these controls to eliminate unnecessary effort for the user. For example, in the case study in Chapter 24, "Unnecessary Repetitive Tasks Are Evil," I show how strategically assigning the initial input focus eliminates unnecessary effort. On the other hand, some of your program's functions might be destructive, so you don't want them to be too easy to do—you want to prevent the user from making catastrophic errors by accident. There is a fine line between protecting the user and pestering the user, so I'll try to help you make that distinction.

In Chapter 4, "Establish a Consistent User Interface Style," I gave the rule that irreversible or destructive actions should never be the default. This works well as a basic rule, but let's look specifically at how you should assign default buttons. For a normal, nondestructive dialog box, the rule is simple: assign the default button to the command the user is most likely to choose, usually the OK button or its equivalent. This rule makes the dialog box more convenient to use.

For dialog boxes with nondestructive actions, assign the default button to the command the user is most likely to choose.

In the case where the action performed by the dialog box is destructive (such as deleting a file), I like to use what I call the one-mistake rule. That is, the user should be able to make any single mistake without serious consequences.

For dialog boxes with destructive actions, assign the default button so that the user can make any single mistake without serious consequences.

In the case where the action performed by the dialog box is catastrophic (such as formatting a disk), I like to use the two-mistake rule. That is, the user should have to make two explicit mistakes in a row before there are serious consequences. I consider clicking the wrong button to be an explicit mistake, whereas pressing Enter is an implicit mistake.

For dialog boxes with catastrophic actions, assign the default button so that the user has to make two explicit mistakes in a row before there are serious consequences.

Let's look at a couple examples. If I use Windows Explorer to delete a file, I get the following confirmation:

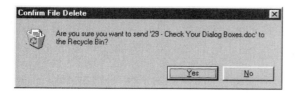

Having the Yes button as the default is correct in this case, even though it is a destructive action. Why? Suppose that I deleted the file by accident. Pressing the Delete key would be my first mistake and then pressing Enter accidentally to confirm would be my second mistake, so I would have had to make two mistakes in a row to accidentally delete a file. Any single mistake can be corrected. Since deleting a file isn't catastrophic (especially since I can undo the action by using the Recycle Bin), this is the correct assignment of the default button.

Now if I use Windows Explorer to format a floppy disk, I get the following dialog box:

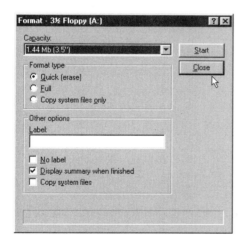

In Windows 98, the Close button is the default, which is correct since accidentally formatting a floppy can be catastrophic (although you can undo a floppy format by using special software). In this case, I need to make two explicit mistakes in a row to accidentally format a floppy: I need to accidentally select the Format command and then accidentally press or click the Start button. I cannot format a floppy by mistakenly pressing the Enter key after my first mistake. If this were a command to format a hard disk, I wouldn't mind an additional confirmation after selecting the Start button. This way; formatting a hard disk by accident would require three mistakes in a row. After all, I don't format hard disks every day, so an additional

CHAPTER 29

confirmation here isn't exactly a burden. Happily, most dialog box actions are not destructive, so you can apply the first rule of assigning the default button to the command that the user is most likely to choose most of the time.

The initial input focus can be set to any noncommand button control independently of the default button. The input focus rule is simple: assign the initial input focus to the control the user is most likely to interact with first. Note that since the default button moves to the command button with input focus, you never have to worry about destructive actions when assigning the initial input focus if you follow the previous rules.

TIP Assign the initial input focus to the control that the user is most likely to interact with first.

How to Find Problems

With the basics out of the way, I'll now list a number of issues related to dialog boxes to help you avoid most dialog box problems.

General Appearance

- **Check the dialog box sizes**   When displayed in VGA mode (640 × 480), a dialog box should be no larger than 640 × 460 (saving 20 pixels for the taskbar) so that it can be displayed in all video modes.

- **Check the arrangement and flow**   In Western cultures, people read from left to right and from top to bottom, so make sure that the more important information is on top and to the left. The upper left corner receives the most attention.

- **Check the alignment**   In general, left alignment should be used to make user interface elements easier to scan. Decimal alignment or right alignment should be used for numeric text. Avoid center alignment and right alignment for nonnumeric text. Everything doesn't have to be centered or made symmetrical. Prefer having white space on the right side and bottom instead.

- **Check the grouping**   Related user interface elements should be grouped to show relationships. Related information should be displayed together and controls should be placed near the objects acted upon. White space, group boxes, lines and labels, or other separators should be used to group related user interface elements.

- **Dialog boxes used as secondary windows should not have title bar icons, menu bars, toolbars, and status bars** Secondary windows must not appear on the taskbar, since clicking on a primary window taskbar button also activates any secondary windows. Secondary windows should not have the complexity to warrant a menu bar, toolbar, or status bar. Title bar icons are used as a visual distinction between primary windows and secondary windows. Also, the default Windows icon (the flying window icon) should never be used as a window icon.

- **Check the title text** Ellipses should not be used in dialog box title text. For example, a dialog box that is displayed as the result of choosing the Print Options… command should have the title *Print Options*. An exception is to indicate that a command is in progress, such as with "Connecting To The Internet…" The title of a Properties property sheet should include the word *Properties*.

General Usability

- **Check the defaults** Are there appropriate default values for the fields in the dialog box? Having default values makes the dialog box easier to use and makes it less likely that the user will make mistakes. The default value that is most likely to be right should be used based on how the setting is actually used. Often the best default is the last setting that the user input. A dialog box with many empty controls is tedious to use.

- **Make sure modal dialog boxes are really modal** Make sure that all modal dialog boxes that have parent windows supply the correct parent window handle instead of a NULL handle. (Note that the correct parent handle is automatically supplied when using MFC.) If the parent window handle isn't supplied, the parent window is still active, so the dialog box really isn't modal.

- **Check the default button** Is the default command button selected correctly? The default button should not be one that initiates an irreversible or destructive action, unless the user has another way to correct mistakes.

- **Check the input focus** Make sure that the initial input focus is on the control that is most likely to be used first.

CHAPTER

29

- **Check the Help**   Review the online Help for helpfulness. Does the Help explain the dialog box? Does it answer any questions you have? Is there a Help button? Do the F1 and Shift+F1 keys work?

Navigation

- **Check the keyboard navigation**   Test the dialog box using the keyboard alone. Is it easy to use? Does the Tab key move among the controls in a sensible and orderly manner? Is the tab stop attribute assigned to all controls that should have it? Is the tab stop attribute not assigned to controls that shouldn't have it? Do the arrow keys move among controls in a sensible order? Do the arrow keys get stuck on a control or leak out of a group?

- **Check using the mouse**   Test the dialog box using the mouse alone. Is it easy to use? If the dialog box has edit boxes, could they be replaced with other controls that don't require typing, such as spin boxes, combo boxes, lists, and radio buttons?

- **Check the access keys**   Try accessing all controls with access keys. Does each control that could possibly be accessed with an access key have one assigned? Are the access keys unique? Are access keys assigned that don't do anything? Is the tab order correct so that each static text label access key activates its associated control? If possible, avoid assigning an access key to a lowercase *g*, *j*, *p*, *q*, or *y*, or to a character immediately preceding or following one of these characters. The underline doesn't look right against the character's descender.

Main Command Buttons

- **Check the command button separation**   Are the main command buttons separated from the main body of a dialog box? Main command buttons are command buttons such as OK, Cancel, Close, Help, Stop, Hide, and other related buttons. This separation makes the main command buttons easier to find and identify.

- **Check the dialog box orientation**   In Western cultures, people read from left to right and from top to bottom, so main command buttons are easier to find if they are on the bottom or right. The dialog box orientation chosen should make the aspect ratio of the dialog box more similar to the aspect ratio of the screen, which is typically 3 units high to 4 units wide. This makes the dialog box appearance more comfortable and easier to position on the screen. Position the command buttons on the bottom if they have different sizes.

- **Check the command button alignment** Are the main command buttons placed on the bottom right-aligned? Right-aligned main command buttons follow the left-to-right flow. You might want to make an exception by centering the main command button when there is only one.

- **For modal dialog boxes, check the OK and Cancel buttons** For modal dialog boxes, are OK and Cancel buttons provided? To use a dialog box, the user needs to be able to easily identify how to move forward (with the OK button) and backward (with the Cancel button). The OK button can be replaced with a more specific command, but never replace Cancel in a modal dialog box, except with Stop to indicate that the effect of an operation in progress cannot be cancelled.

- **For modeless dialog boxes, check the Close button** For modeless dialog boxes or dialog boxes used as primary windows, is a Close button provided but not OK and Cancel buttons? Using OK and Cancel for a modeless dialog box or primary window makes the dialog box appear to be a modal dialog box. Furthermore, OK and Cancel are not meaningful when used in a modeless context. Use Close instead to eliminate any confusion.

- **Check the button order** Is the OK button first, Cancel second, and Help last? OK or its equivalent should always be the first main command button. Cancel should be to the right of or below OK. The OK and Cancel buttons should be placed next to each other. The Help button should be the last button. If there is no OK button, the Cancel button should be just before the Help button. This makes the main command buttons easier to find and identify.

- **Make sure the OK and Cancel buttons are labeled correctly** The OK button should be labeled *OK*, not *Ok* or *OK*. The Cancel button should be labeled *Cancel*, not *Cancel* or *CANCEL*.

- **Make sure the Cancel button really cancels** The program state should be exactly the same as it was before a modal dialog box was displayed. If not, the Cancel button should be replaced with a Stop button. Make sure that the Cancel button in the body of a modal dialog box has the same effect as the Close button on its title bar. Property sheets are an exception, since the Cancel button doesn't cancel or undo changes that have already been applied.

465

Controls

- **Check the control sizes** Are the controls consistently sized, especially the command buttons? Command buttons with text labels should have a minimum width of 50 dialog units (1095 twips in Microsoft Visual Basic) and a standard height of 14 dialog units (375 twips in Visual Basic). The static text control sizes should be large enough so that they can display their text in all video modes.

- **Make sure invalid controls are disabled** Make sure controls that don't apply in the current program state are disabled.

- **Check for unnecessary scroll bars** Will scroll bars be eliminated from list boxes, edit boxes, or combo boxes if you make the control slightly larger? If so, making the control larger will make it easier to use.

- **Always give combo boxes, list boxes, list views, tree views, edit boxes, and sliders labels** Labels are necessary to identify what the control is for.

- **Check for bold text** Bold text should be used sparingly. Bold text was used in Windows 3.1 dialog boxes to draw disabled text on old video hardware (that is, dithered gray). Since modern video hardware can draw gray text without dithering, Windows now uses normal text in dialog boxes for a much cleaner look. Bold text should be used only for emphasis. Most dialog boxes should not use any bold text.

- **Check that edit box widths suggest the size of the expected input** The width of an edit box should be a visual clue of the expected input. For example, if the user is entering an address, a State field that is about two characters wide clearly suggests entering a two-character state abbreviation. If the expected input has no particular size, a width that is consistent with other edit boxes or controls should be used.

- **Check the static text labels for colons** Colons should be used to clearly indicate that the static text is a control label. Labels used to give supplemental information about a control should not have a colon, such as labels used to interpret a slider control. Colons are also used as a clue by screen readers.

- **Check the justification of static text labels** Left justification gives the labels an organized look and makes them easy to scan.

PART
V

- **Check the use of ellipses** An ellipsis in a command indicates that more information other than a simple confirmation is required to carry out the command. An ellipsis does not mean that a dialog box follows.

Details

- **Check the error handling** Enter invalid input when possible. Is there feedback? If there is an error message, does it make sense? Is it necessary? Could the interface prevent the error from happening? Could different control types be used to prevent invalid input?

- **Review the dialog box templates** Are the window styles, such as WS_POPUP, WS_CAPTION, and WS_SYSMENU, applied consistently? Is the same font used consistently?

I admit that there's a lot to check in this list. However, once you master this list you can make sure your dialog boxes are correct while you create them, enabling you to review them rather quickly during the QA process.

Related Chapters

- Chapter 4—Establish a Consistent User Interface Style.
  Provides additional items to check for property sheets, wizards, and specific controls.

- Chapter 15—Keep It Simple.
  Offers suggestions on how to simplify dialog boxes.

- Chapter 18—Appropriate Defaults Are Cool.
  Describes the importance of having defaults and presents suggestions on how to implement them. Also presents a case study of a find dialog box that shows how strategically assigning the initial input focus eliminates unnecessary effort.

- Chapter 22—Unnecessary Dialog Boxes Are Evil.
  Explains why unnecessary dialog boxes harm an interface and presents some suggestions on how to eliminate them.

- Chapter 23—Unnecessary Message Boxes Are Pure Evil.
  Describes dialog box time-outs and when they should be used.

CHAPTER 29

- Chapter 35—Handle All Video Modes.

  Presents suggestions on how to make dialog boxes resolution-independent and how to find video mode problems.

Recommended Reading

- Capucciati, Maria R. "Putting Your Best Face Forward: Designing an Effective User Interface." *Microsoft Systems Journal*, February 1993.

  Presents a good discussion of basic design principles and gives several examples of how not to design a dialog box.

- Cooper, Alan. *About Face: The Essentials of User Interface Design.* Foster City, CA: IDG Books Worldwide, Inc., 1995.

  Chapter 21, "Dialog Boxes," and Chapter 22, "Dialog Box Etiquette," present a good discussion on how to design dialog boxes and tell you specifically what to check to make sure you have done it right.

- Microsoft Corporation. *Designing for the User Experience.* Redmond, WA: Microsoft Press, 1999.

  See the information on secondary windows for a good discussion of navigation, default buttons, and validation of input, property sheets, and common dialogs.

- Prosise, Jeff. *Programming Windows with MFC, Second Edition.* Redmond, WA: Microsoft Press, 1999.

  Chapter 8, "Dialog Boxes and Property Sheets" (in the section "The Dialog Box Keyboard Interface"), includes a discussion of dialog box keyboard navigation.

CD-ROM Resources

The CD-ROM included with this book contains the following resources related to this chapter:

- Resource Assistant, a utility that checks the resources in an executable, and Resource Assistant for VB, a utility that checks the resources in a Visual Basic program. Both programs verify that dialog boxes will fit on the screen in all video modes, static text controls and buttons (command buttons, radio buttons, and check boxes) are large enough to display their text in all video modes, the tab order of the controls has been set, the tab stop and group properties of the controls have been set, and control access keys are unique. Resource Assistant also extracts all resource strings so that you can check for spelling errors, and Resource Assistant for VB does the same for string resources, forms, and menus.

CHAPTER

29

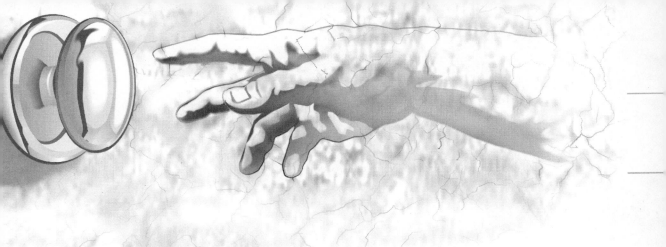

30 CHAPTER

Check Your Error Messages

Errors happen. In an ideal world, your program would work perfectly and your users would never make mistakes. In the real world, neither is true and error messages play an important role in handling what goes wrong. While programmers don't want to give error messages (and we need to make sure we don't give unnecessary error messages) and users certainly don't want to receive them, an error message had better be helpful when you've decided that the error message is necessary. The helpfulness of an error message is an important part of a program's user interface.

Why Error Messages Are Poorly Done

Unfortunately, error messages are often poorly done. Sometimes the message doesn't make any sense. Other times the message identifies a problem but gives no clue how to solve the problem. Occasionally the error message is completely wrong or misleading. Reasons for these problems include the following:

- Crafting quality error messages is not a priority during program development. Just as receiving an error message while using a program breaks the user's train of thought, writing an error message while programming breaks the programmer's train of thought. As a result, programmers often write an error message as quickly as possible without giving it much thought.

- Making sure that an error message is helpful is not a priority during quality assurance. QA testers try to find bugs and perhaps make sure that the program includes error messages when necessary, but, interestingly, finding problems in error messages doesn't receive much attention.

- A good error message is simply hard to write. A good error message notifies the user that there is a problem, explains why the problem occurred, and recommends how to solve the problem. The message is clear, consistent, and specific. A good error message is also brief so that the user will bother to read it. Writing an error message that has all these attributes can be quite a challenge.

- While modern exception handling makes it easy to detect problems—in fact, C++ exceptions don't give you a choice since they can't be ignored—it is often much harder to determine the true cause of the problem. While it is fairly easy to put a try statement around a block of code, it's often difficult to know all of the different exceptions that the code can receive and their significance. This difficulty often results in generic error messages that basically say, "I know I can't perform the command you gave, but I have no idea why."

- The ability to create good error messages isn't highly regarded. It doesn't make good résumé material.

In the remainder of this chapter, I'll explore the attributes of a good error message, give you tips on how to make your error messages helpful, and give some examples of typical error message problems.

Attributes of a Good Error Message

A good error message has a surprising number of attributes. The most important attribute is that the error message must be necessary. The best error message is no error message at all. Your first choice should always be to prevent the problem in the first place. Your second choice should be to try to work around the problem without bothering the user. A good third choice is to notify the user in a way that doesn't require the user to respond, such as putting information on the status bar. See Chapter 23, "Unnecessary Message Boxes Are Pure Evil," for a detailed discussion of avoiding unnecessary error message boxes.

An error message must provide enough information so that the user can understand the problem and know what to do about it. Typically this means that the error message needs to provide:

- **A notification**   The user needs to know that a problem occurred.
- **An explanation**   The user needs to know why the problem occurred.
- **A solution**   The user needs to know how to solve the problem.

Providing this information makes error messages complete and self-explanatory. However, providing all of this information does not necessarily mean that a good error message is long and involved. If you can present the user with the information in a single short sentence, by all means do so. Users don't want to read long error messages. Rather, the error message should be:

- **Brief**   Make the message as short as possible but no shorter. Use progressive disclosure when necessary (as described later).
- **Clear**   Make sure that the user can understand the message. Use plain language and terminology that your target user understands. Avoid meaningless error numbers and technical mumbo jumbo.
- **Consistent**   Make sure that error messages within the program are consistent and their terminology is consistent with the rest of the user interface.
- **Specific**   Vague wording is a common problem in error messages. Give the specific names and locations of the objects involved in the error.

Provide Necessary Error Messages

While it is important not to give unnecessary error messages, it is equally important to give necessary error messages. This might seem incredibly obvious, but not reporting errors with error messages is an easy trap for programmers to fall into. Assertions and TRACE statements are largely to blame. Perhaps you've seen code that looks like this:

```
if (!SaveFile(filename,…))
   TRACE("Can't save file");
```

Now suppose that this code is in a text editor and an error occurs while the user is saving a file. Since no error message is provided, the user will assume the file was saved, only to find out later—the hard way—that the information has been lost. I know—you would never do such a thing. Maybe so, but other programmers do, since I see code like this all the time.

Regarding the TRACE statement itself, the most important thing to understand with this example is that this use of a TRACE statement is totally inappropriate. You should use assertions and TRACE statements only to help you debug and to report erroneous execution. Erroneous execution is the result of a bug in your program. The inability to save a file isn't a bug; it is abnormal execution, which is the result of a situation beyond the program's control. Any abnormal execution that cannot be handled by the program requires an error message.

Assertions and TRACE statements are not error messages and should never be used as a substitute.

TIP Never use assertions or TRACE statements as a substitute for error messages.

Error Messages Are for Users, Not Programmers

Have you ever used a program and come across a totally bizarre error message? For example, have you ever seen an error message like this one?

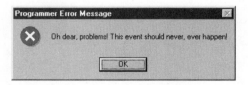

Of course, the event did happen, and the user is very puzzled by such a message. In fact, the user can do absolutely nothing in response to this error message except panic.

The problem with this error message is that it isn't intended for the user. Rather, it was intended for the programmer to debug a problem and unfortunately was left in the release version of the program. There are four ways to prevent this problem:

● Use an assertion instead.

● Use a TRACE statement instead.

PART
V

474

- Use a debug report instead.

- If really necessary, use an error message that is conditionally compiled for only the debug build (that is, use #ifdef _DEBUG … #endif) like the TRACE and ASSERT macros.

This observation makes the converse of my conclusion in the last section true. Error messages are not assertions or TRACE statements and should also not be used as a substitute.

Don't use error messages as a substitute for assertions or TRACE statements.

Use Clear, Consistent Messages

An error message isn't helpful if the user doesn't understand it. What kind of error messages can the user understand? Of course, this depends upon the user. Consider common programming terms like *syntax error, integer, Boolean, reboot,* and *contiguous.* If you are developing software for programmers, these terms are appropriate for error messages. If your software isn't for programmers, terms like these are totally inappropriate for an error message. Stop for a minute and consider what it would be like to be a first-time computer user and receive an error message telling you to reboot your computer. Reboot? Do computers have boots? And if they do, how exactly do you reboot it? You must do your best to make sure that the words you use are in the user's vocabulary.

Consistency is important. Make sure that the terminology used in the error message matches the terminology used elsewhere in the program. If the terminology doesn't match, it will definitely confuse the user.

I realize that coming up with a clear, consistent error message while you are in the middle of programming isn't easy to do. It's tempting to write a quick-and-dirty error message and move on. Nonetheless, I strongly recommend that you make an effort to write the best error messages you can while you are programming. If for any reason the error message isn't good, tag it and come back to it later. The visibility of your tagging scheme should depend upon how structured your development process is. For example, you could tag messages that need improving with text such as *[Bad message— improve later!]*, but this technique isn't such a good idea if there's a chance you might ship the program with those tags. In this case, a safer approach might be to tag such error messages by appending a tab character to the end of the string. Using this method, the tag isn't visible to the user and at

า appropriate time, you or another team member can review the tagged
essages and improve them. Ideally, your technical support staff and tech-
...cal writers should review all the error messages as well.

Be Specific

Make your error messages as specific as possible, even if this eliminates
some unimportant options. For example, this error message is famous for
causing technical support problems:

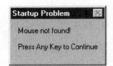

Why is this message a technical support problem? The problem is that many
users call tech support to ask where the "Any Key" is. Since it doesn't matter
which key the user presses, why not be specific and choose one?

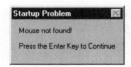

On the other hand, don't be so specific that you eliminate important options. For example, consider the infamous critical error message in
Microsoft Windows:

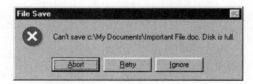

This is possibly the most hated error message ever created. Windows allows you to provide your own message for critical errors by calling the
SetErrorMode API function with the SEM_FAILCRITICALERRORS parameter, which is automatically done in MFC but not when you are programming using the Windows API directly. One program handles the critical error
with this error message:

PART

V

Does this error message bother you? It certainly bothers me. While the Abort, Retry, and Ignore options are as awkward as they get, I can always abort the command and save my file elsewhere, such as another hard disk or a network drive. With the "improved" version, I no longer have this choice or, at least, I no longer appear to. What if I am using a laptop without a floppy drive? What if my file is too large to fit on a floppy disk? Now I have two options: I can lose my file, or I can lose my file. Definitely not cool! The real way to improve the critical error message is to present the specific options the user really has—which are to retry the save, select a path on another drive, or cancel the save—and to give these option in plain English:

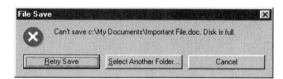

TIP

Make the error message as specific as possible. There is no harm in eliminating unimportant options, but never eliminate important ones.

Being specific also means providing different error messages for the different causes of a problem. For example, if there are several reasons why a file cannot be saved or an object cannot be created, provide a specific message for each condition that the user can understand. (You don't need to give specific explanations that the user is not able to understand.) Avoid using generic, catchall error messages, since such error messages don't help the user understand the problem.

TIP

If an error can occur as the result of several conditions, provide a specific error message for each condition.

CHAPTER

Lastly, try to provide the specific names and locations of the objects involved in an error. For example, once while I was trying to install a program on an old computer of mine, the setup program indicated that it couldn't install because it needed at least 8 MB of hard disk space. I was installing to the C: drive, so I checked that drive and, sure enough, I didn't have enough space. I freed some space and tried again but got the same error message. I freed 20 MB and tried yet again but still no luck. At this point, I was about to call technical support when I realized what the problem was. While I was installing to the C: drive on my old multidrive computer, my system folder was on my E: drive, which didn't have 8 MB free. Had the error message said that it was drive E: that needed at least 8 MB of hard disk space, there wouldn't have been a problem. Note how unhelpful the error message I received was and how easy it would have been to make it helpful by simply making it a bit more specific.

Keep It Short

An error message should be clear, consistent, and specific, but you also want to keep it as brief as possible. Why? Because you want the user to read it, and users don't like to read long, involved error messages. The most effective error message is a short error message.

Let's look at a typical example. Suppose while renaming a file a user types in an invalid filename character, such as a colon. You could issue the following error message:

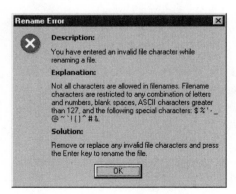

Aside from being incredibly long, this error message accomplishes all the other goals we have outlined so far. Its information is technically accurate, and it completely informs the user what the problem is and how to correct it. But it's way too much. Do you want to read it? I don't. An error message like this begs not to be read.

PART
V

478

Now let's look at a much better error message used by Windows Explorer:

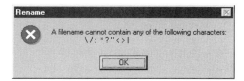

This error message is much more to the point, and it also accomplishes all our goals, including being very specific. This error message makes it clear that the user entered an invalid character and implies a solution to fix the problem by removing the invalid characters. Note that this message also avoids typical technical terms such as *error* or *invalid*. Lastly, note that this example shows that if it is awkward to describe valid input, it might be easier to describe invalid input. (The opposite is also true.)

Aside from their length, there is another significant difference between these two error messages. The first error message tries to train the user about filenames, and the second version doesn't bother. Interestingly, of the many attributes of a good error message, the message's ability to train the user isn't one of them. Why? Because this goal would be in direct conflict with keeping the message short. Also, attempting to train the user with an error message is doomed to failure anyway. When a user receives an error message, his immediate objective is to solve the problem and get back to work. The user isn't likely to be in the mood to take time out for a lesson on how to use the software.

Use Progressive Disclosure

What should you do if you can't create an error message that meets all the requirements I've described earlier in a small amount of text? It's important to understand that you don't have to display absolutely everything in a single error message. The technique of presenting information only as it is needed is called *progressive disclosure*. Instead of displaying a simple error message that isn't too helpful, like this one:

30
C
H
A
P
T
E
R

or displaying a complete but overwhelming error message like this:

you can balance simplicity and completeness by displaying an error message that uses progressive disclosure, such as this one:

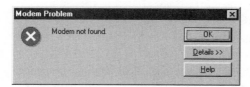

While you can present any text as the message box text, details text, and Help text, a good general technique is to present a summary of the error and its solution in the message box text, a detailed explanation in the details text, and the full solution in the Help text. In the example above, if the user presses the Details button the message box will look like this:

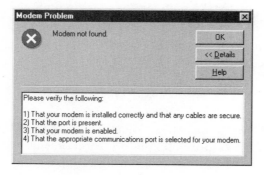

The information in the help file can be significantly more detailed than the information you put directly in the message box itself. For example, there is nothing wrong with putting training information in the Help text, since the user doesn't have to read it. You could present the same solution text presented previously (in the complex message box example) in a Help file, but for this particular problem an even better solution is to link the Help button to the Windows 98 Modem Troubleshooter:

PART

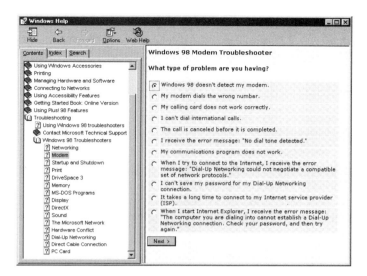

TIP Use the Windows Troubleshooters for solutions to system problems.

Variations of progressive disclosure for this example would also be effective, specifically using only a Details button or using only a Help button. Whatever approach you choose, your goal should be to provide the necessary information without overwhelming the user.

TIP Use progressive disclosure for complex error messages.

Construct Messages Carefully

Although displaying error messages with simple strings is fairly foolproof, you need to be careful when constructing error message strings at run time. Specifically, you need to make sure that the string parameters are never blank. For example, consider the follow error-handling function:

```
void DisplayGenericObjectError(HWND hParentWnd, LPCTSTR action,
                               LPCTSTR object)
{
   TCHAR buffer[LARGE_SIZE];
   _stprintf(buffer, _T("Can't %s on %s."), action, object);
   MessageBox(hParentWnd, buffer, AppName, MB_OK);
}
```

Suppose you call this function when both *action* and *object* are empty strings. This will result in the following error message:

Pretty useless, don't you think? As silly as it is, this type of mistake happens fairly often. Not surprisingly, the solution to this problem is to make sure it doesn't happen. For example, the above function could be changed to provide a generic error message whenever the *action* or *object* strings are empty:

```
void DisplayGenericObjectError(HWND hParentWnd, LPCTSTR action,
                              LPCTSTR object, LPCTSTR genericError)
{
   TCHAR buffer[LARGE_SIZE];
   if (*object != _T('\0') && *action != _T('\0'))
      _stprintf(buffer, _T("Can't %s on %s."), action, object);
   else
      _tcscpy(buffer, genericError);
   MessageBox(hParentWnd, buffer, AppName, MB_OK);
}
```

Alternatively, you could handle such an error by assigning generic names to the action or object:

```
void DisplayGenericObjectError(HWND hParentWnd, LPCTSTR action,
                              LPCTSTR object)
{
   TCHAR buffer[LARGE_SIZE], objectBuf[LARGE_SIZE],
      actionBuf[LARGE_SIZE];

   if (*object != _T('\0'))
      _tcscpy(objectBuf, object);
   else
      _tcscpy(objectBuf, _T("unknown object"));
   if (*action != _T('\0'))
      _tcscpy(actionBuf, action);
   else
      _tcscpy(actionBuf, _T("perform unknown action"));
   _stprintf(buffer, _T("Can't %s on %s."), actionBuf, objectBuf);
   MessageBox(hParentWnd, buffer, AppName, MB_OK);
}
```

Now if the parameters are empty strings, the error message is:

While the resulting error message isn't especially helpful, at least it is understandable. It also isn't as embarrassing.

TIP Make sure that the string parameters to error message text constructed at run time aren't empty.

Consider Internationalization

If there is a chance that your program will be distributed in non-English-speaking markets, you should consider internationalizing your error messages. Internationalization is the process of developing a program whose design and code doesn't make assumptions based on a single language or locale and whose source code simplifies the creation of different language editions. Localization is the process of actually adapting and testing a program for a specific market. If you plan to sell in other markets, you need to internationalize your code now, but you can delay the localization to other markets until later.

The last version of the DisplayGenericObjectError function, shown on the previous page, is a good example of how not to write internationalized error messages. How many problems can you find? Although the function does use the right data types, function calls, and macros to support Unicode, it has two critical flaws:

●   All strings that can be seen by the user should be in resources, not in the source code.

●   Error messages created by combining strings should not use functions such as CString::Format or _stprintf. The problem is that the order of the components in the string can change in different locales. For example, in French, many adjectives follow the nouns they modify. In German, verbs are often at the end of a sentence. To solve this problem, use the FormatMessage function instead, which allows you to change the order of the string parameters by changing the format-control string.

Here is an internationalized version of DisplayGenericObjectError written using MFC:

```
void DisplayGenericObjectError (const CString &action,
                                const CString &object)
{
   CString buffer, objectBuf, actionBuf;

   if (!object.IsEmpty())
      objectBuf = object;
   else
      objectBuf.LoadString(IDS_UNKNOWN_OBJECT);
   if (!action.IsEmpty())
      actionBuf = action;
   else
      actionBuf.LoadString(IDS_UNKNOWN_ACTION);
   buffer.FormatMessage(IDS_GENERIC_OBJECT_ERROR, actionBuf, objectBuf);
   AfxMessageBox(buffer);
}
```

In this case, if IDS_GENERIC_OBJECT_ERROR is "Can't %1 on %2.", the results will be the same as before. By using FormatMessage, you can now change the order of the text without changing the code. For example, you could set IDS_GENERIC_OBJECT_ERROR to "Can't use %2 to %1." and, if the parameters are empty strings, the error message will be

> For internationalization, always put the error message strings in string resources, and construct strings at run time using FormatMessage.

Using MFC significantly helps writing internationalized code. Not only is the CString::FormatMessage function much easier to use than the ::FormatMessage API function, but CString::LoadString and other resource functions automatically handle resource-only DLLs so that you can local-ize a program just by changing its resource DLL. Furthermore, using CStrings eliminates having to select fixed sized buffers that are large enough to handle translated text.

The most important observation to make about this example is that internationalizing your error messages doesn't take much additional effort if you do it from the beginning of your project. Do it at the end, and it is a real pain in the neck.

Keep the Recommended Solutions Practical

While you should try to provide the user with a solution, don't bother unless you really know what the problem is. Whatever you do, don't give silly or impractical solutions. Here are some of my favorites:

Yeah, right.

Sounds good. Wait a minute—what if I *am* the network administrator?

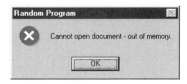

OK, except I have 100 MB of free memory.

How much do you want to bet that the problem isn't with the hard disk but with the program reporting the error?

The first two error messages give solutions that aren't especially practical. In fact, they are not solutions at all. Basically, they say, "I don't know what is wrong and you don't know, so go ask somebody else." The third error message is a catchall that is unlikely to be right given the amount of free memory. An object couldn't be created and the problem was blamed on insufficient memory, but most likely the real problem is something else, such as an invalid input parameter, a missing file, a bad registry setting, or an unregistered COM object.

The last error message is by far the worst. What is wrong with this message? While a system disaster is possible, it is unlikely to be correctly diagnosed by a typical program. It's far more likely that the program itself has a serious bug and at this point doesn't know up from down. Instead of admitting to the bug, the program is suggesting that the user take draconian measures to solve a critical system problem that is most likely misdiagnosed. You should avoid blaming the system for problems and especially avoid recommending solutions like performing ScanDisk, reformatting the hard disk, reinstalling software, upgrading hardware, or contacting the computer manufacturer unless you really know what you are doing. Blaming program bugs on the system and suggesting that the user perform all sorts of drastic measures isn't going to score any points. Instead, it is likely to freak out the user. Many users are naïve enough to believe that error messages like this actually mean something.

Never propose a solution that isn't likely to be right. If you really don't know what is wrong, just say so. This is far better than having the user rebuild his system for nothing.

TIP

Keep the recommended solutions practical. Never propose a solution that isn't likely to be right.

Bad News Is Never OK

Now suppose that you are writing a utility that continuously checks for hard disk errors, so you really do know if there is a hard disk problem. If the utility finds such an error, whatever you do, don't give an error message like this one:

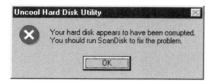

What's wrong with this message? While programmers are used to such error messages, users are not. They read messages like this carefully and think, "No, it's not OK that I have a corrupted hard disk!" Using an OK button to report such bad news is a particularly poor choice since it has a tendency to make users want to scream. A better approach is to report the problem by asking a question (and preferably one that helps the user solve the problem), such as:

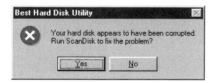

If asking a question isn't practical, at least use different text on the button:

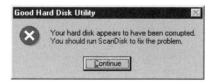

Talk to Technical Support

You should encourage your technical support team to review all of the program's error messages to make sure that they are clear, concise, consistent, and informative. Imagine what it would be like if someone you didn't know called you up, read you an error message, and asked you what to do. This is what your technical support staff faces every day. Make sure that all error messages satisfy tech support's requirements.

Tips

In the following sections, I'll offer miscellaneous tips that I hope will help you create good error messages.

Error Message Appearance

- **Carefully select the right message box type**   Use the Warning message box with Yes, No, and possibly a Cancel button to ask a question or alert the user to a condition or situation that requires the user's input before proceeding. Use the Critical message box to inform the user of a problem that requires correction before work can continue.

- **Do not use the Question message box type**   The question mark symbol (MB_ICONQUESTION) is no longer recommended for message boxes because it is now used consistently within Windows 98 to signify context-sensitive help.

- **Ask questions with yes or no answers**   When asking the user a question, use the Yes and No buttons instead of the OK and Cancel buttons. Using these buttons make the question easier to understand. Unlike in dialog boxes, the OK and Cancel buttons are rarely used together in message boxes.

- **Make sure the message box option buttons match the text**   For example, never give Yes and No as responses to nonquestions. Also, don't give multiple option buttons that have the same effect. For example, don't give both No and Cancel button options unless they have different results. The No button should perform the operation, whereas Cancel should cancel the operation.

- **Carefully select the default button**   Make the safest or most frequent option the default button. For more information on selected default buttons, see Chapter 29, "Check Your Dialog Boxes."

- **Avoid unhelpful help**   Don't provide a Help button unless you can provide additional information that really is helpful. Don't supplement a meaningless message box with meaningless help.

PART
V

- **Consider using system-modal message boxes for critical errors** Use system-modal message boxes to notify the user of serious, potentially damaging errors that require immediate attention. A system-modal message box is the same as an application modal message box except that the message box has the WS_EX_TOPMOST style. Unlike in 16-bit Windows, being system modal has no effect on the user's ability to interact with other programs.

Error Message Text

- **Establish high standards** Try to establish high error message standards at the start of the project. If the early error messages are poorly written, it is easy to justify continuing to create new messages of poor quality.

- **Avoid error numbers** Never give error numbers unless the user can actually do something useful with the number.

- **Avoid blaming the user** Avoid using the words *you* or *your* in the error message text. If necessary, use the passive voice when referring to user actions. It's better to say the equivalent of "mistakes were made" than the equivalent of "you screwed up."

- **Avoid offensive language** Avoid violent terms such as *fatal, execute, kill, terminate,* and *abort.*

- **Avoid hostile language** Avoid using the terms *bad, caution, error, fatal, illegal, invalid,* and *warning* in the error message text. Try to use more specific, descriptive terms instead. Try to explain what exactly is wrong.

- **Use plain English in the error message text** Be brief, clear, consistent, and specific. Never use words with all uppercase letters unless the word is an acronym. This makes it look like you are shouting at the user. Use full sentences and the simple present or past tense. Avoid abbreviating words.

- **Explain unusual meanings** If the error message option buttons (that is, OK, Cancel, Yes, and No) have unusual meanings, explicitly describe those meanings in the text. For example:

- **Avoid trying to be funny or clever in the error message text** Users do not find error messages funny, and any attempt at humor will not be well received.

Presentation

- **Consolidate error messages** A single problem (for example, a bad network connection) should result in only a single error message. A good solution to this problem is to handle all errors at the highest level code, such as where the commands are handled, and have lower level routines detect problems but not report them.

- **Report a single problem just once** Don't report the same error over and over again.

- **Allow the user to suppress noncritical error messages** For noncritical errors that occur often, give the user an option to suppress the error message in the future.

Resources

- **Use string resources** The entire process of creating error messages is simplified if all error message text is in string resources.

- **Consolidate error message resources** Assign all error message resource IDs together so that they are easy to review.

Final Example

Let's look at one last simple example regarding error message text. To the user, this error message

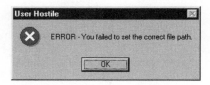

is very similar in tone to this error message:

490

A far better error message is something like this one:

Why is this message better? Take a moment and come up with all the reasons. I think it's a better error message for these reasons:

- It is more specific (in that it gives the filename and folder).
- It doesn't blame the user (for example, "You failed…").
- It uses the passive voice to avoid blaming the user.
- It doesn't use technical terms (such as *file path*).
- It doesn't use any words with all capital letters.

These small changes make a big difference.

Related Chapters

- Chapter 3—Establish Consistent Terminology.

  Presents guidelines on what needs to be named and how to name. Also stresses the importance of establishing names early in the development process. Consistency is important to helpful error messages.

- Chapter 23—Unnecessary Message Boxes Are Pure Evil.

  Discusses the different types of message boxes and tips on how to identify and eliminate unnecessary ones.

Recommended Reading

- Cooper, Alan. *About Face: The Essentials of User Interface Design.* Foster City, CA: IDG Books Worldwide, Inc., 1995.

  Chapter 28, "The End of Errors," and Chapter 29, "Managing Exceptions," present a thought-provoking discussion about message boxes, particularly error messages. But I definitely wouldn't use the proposed solution for error messages—it is way too much.

30 CHAPTER

- Ezzell, Ben. *Developing Windows Error Messages*. Sebastopol, CA: O'Reilly & Associates, 1998.

  Discusses everything you ever wanted to know about error messages. While the first two chapters do a good job of identifying common error message problems, I wouldn't use the proposed solutions presented in the remainder of the book.

- Kano, Nadine. *Developing International Software for Windows 95 and Windows NT*. Redmond, WA: Microsoft Press, 1995.

  Chapter 4, "Preparing the User Interface for Localization," presents everything you need to know about internationalizing software.

- Microsoft Corporation. *Designing for the User Experience*. Redmond, WA: Microsoft Press, 1999.

  Presents guidelines for message box types, title bar text, message box text, and button text. Essential information.

- Microsoft Corporation. "Error and Event Message Guidelines." MSDN, January 1999, Platform SDK, Windows Programming Guidelines, Programming Tips and Techniques.

  Presents several useful guidelines for creating clear and useful error messages.

- Microsoft Corporation. *Microsoft Manual of Style for Technical Publications, Second Edition*. Redmond, WA: Microsoft Press, 1998.

  Provides useful guidelines for all aspects of documentation, including error messages.

- Microsoft Corporation. *Microsoft Press Computer Dictionary, Third Edition*. Redmond, WA: Microsoft Press, 1997.

  A good source for making sure you are using the right term.

CD-ROM Resources

The CD-ROM included with this book contains the following resources related to this chapter:

- An electronic version of the *Microsoft Manual of Style for Technical Publications, Second Edition*.

- The DevUI MFC Extension Library contains a McMessageBox function that provides a message box with options for customizable button text so that you can use something other than *OK* to report bad news.

PART
V

3 1 CHAPTER

Check Your Printing

You should consider printing as part of your program's user interface, even though the user doesn't interact with printouts in the usual sense. Providing a print preview does make printing a more obvious part of the user interface. In fact, printing code is often derived from the display code—MFC's document/view architecture encourages this—and it has many similar types of problems. But the problems unique to printing include:

- Handling printer errors, such as the printer being turned off or being out of paper
- Handling all paper sizes, not just 8½-by-11-inch paper
- Handling all printer resolutions
- Handling landscape and portrait modes
- Handling the printing of single pages vs. complete documents
- Handling color vs. black-and-white printing

In this chapter, I'll explore useful printing features you should consider providing and offer some tips on how to test for printing problems.

Direct Printing

A Microsoft Windows program typically provides the user the following print commands:

- **Page Setup or Print Setup**   Displays the Page Setup or Print Setup dialog box but doesn't actually print.

- **Print Preview**   Shows what the printed pages look like on the screen so that you can see the results without printing.

- **Print**   Displays the Print dialog box and then prints the document.

- **Direct printing**   Prints a single copy of all the pages of a document to the currently selected printer directly without displaying the Print dialog box.

Direct printing is a valuable feature since it eliminates what is often an unnecessary dialog box. Once the user selects his preferred print settings with the Page Setup dialog box or Print Setup dialog box, the program has all the information it needs to print a document. The Print dialog box allows the user to select the printer, page range, and number of copies, but almost always the user wants to print a single complete copy to the currently selected printer. As a result, the normal response to this dialog box is to click OK.

How do you distinguish between normal printing and direct printing? Microsoft Office and Microsoft Internet Explorer perform normal printing from the menu but direct printing from the toolbar. This is a natural distinction, since the toolbar is intended to be a shortcut and the menu can clearly indicate when more information is required by displaying an ellipsis. Interestingly, Microsoft Visual C++ performs normal printing in both cases.

TIP   If your program has a toolbar, provide direct printing.

Print Previewing

Print previewing is a totally cool feature. It is implemented in the MFC document/view architecture by creating two device contexts (DCs)—one for the printer and one for the screen. The printer DC is used to get the

PART

V

various metrics required for printing, such as the page size, printer resolution, the printable region, and so on. While the printing code is called to output the document, the screen DC is used for rendering the view to the screen. From the programmer's point of view, the print preview process is completely invisible. There is no distinction between a preview DC and any other DC in MFC—OK, there is a CDC::IsPrinting function to allow you to determine what kind of DC you have—and the printing code is executed as if the output were to the actual printer. Darn clever, don't you think?

The good news is that if you are using MFC document/view, you can provide print previewing with almost no effort. The bad news is that if you are using MFC but not document/view, or if you are not using MFC at all, providing a print preview isn't especially practical. You might want to consider this when you are designing your program.

One little-known fact is that you can make print previews interactive. Print previewing disables the document, so the user isn't able to interact with the document directly, but any menu or toolbar command that modifies the document can be used during the preview.

Make your print previews interactive when possible.

You should provide print previewing when you can. It helps your users and, as you'll see in the next section, it also helps you.

How to Find Problems

Most printing problems occur when you make incorrect assumptions about the printer or the printing process. Some typical false assumptions include:

- All paper is 8½ by 11 inches.
- All pages have the same margin size.
- All printers print at 300 dpi (dots per inch).
- All print jobs are in portrait mode.
- All print jobs print the complete document.
- All print jobs are printed to completion.

First check your printing source code, since it is easy to find incorrect assumptions by looking at the code directly. Are there any assumptions made about the printer? About the resolution? About the paper? About the size of text? About the mode? Large constants in print code are usually a bad sign. Rather, the layout should be determined by information returned by the GetDeviceCaps and GetTextMetrics API functions. GDI objects should also be sized relative to this information as well. Don't use fixed width pens or draw with pixels, since such drawing is resolution-dependent and will be hard to read when printed on higher-resolution printers.

TIP You can find many types of printing problems by checking for incorrect assumptions in your printing source code.

How does your code print individual pages? Can it render any page by itself? Does the code know where any page starts and ends? Do any variables require printing all pages to be set correctly? Are all GDI resources correctly created and destroyed? For color printing, note that popular color printers usually dither colors, so using the StretchBlt function is probably a bad idea. Graphics should be rendered to the correct size and drawn using the BitBlt function instead. Lastly, if your program prints page numbers, note that the first page typically does not have a page number.

If your program supports print previewing, you can use the print preview feature to perform most of your print testing. This technique saves you a lot of time and paper. With print preview, you can check all the pages, review output in both portrait and landscape mode, print individual pages, and print using different paper sizes. Don't have any A4 paper to test with? No problem—just select A4 paper from the Page Setup dialog box or Print Setup dialog box and test using the Print Preview command.

TIP Use print previews to find many types of printing errors.

However, you can't find all printing problems using the print preview. Problems involving printer resolution, individual pixels, precise alignment, or even using the wrong device context and fonts (that is, using a display device context or fonts instead of the printer device context or fonts) will not show up in a print preview. So, now with real paper, you can finish testing. I recommend at least the following tests:

- Print in portrait mode using a 300-dpi color printer.
- Print in landscape mode using a 600-dpi black-and-white printer.
- Print the last two pages of a document.

PART

V

498

- Cancel a print job.
- Print using a printer without paper.

If your program makes assumptions about the printer status, printer resolution, page orientation, and number of colors, it will not print correctly in any of the above situations.

Related Chapters

- Chapter 21—Tooltips Are Cool.

  Describes how to make tooltips helpful. The tooltip for the Print toolbar button can be improved by showing the currently selected printer, which makes it easier to understand the results of direct printing.

- Chapter 22—Unnecessary Dialog Boxes Are Evil.

  Discusses why unnecessary dialog boxes are undesirable, how to identify unnecessary dialog boxes, and how to eliminate them. Providing direct printing is a good way to eliminate an unnecessary dialog box.

Recommended Reading

- Cooper, Alan. *About Face: The Essentials of User Interface Design*. Foster City, CA: IDG Books Worldwide, Inc., 1995.

  Chapter 11, "Orchestration and Flow," presents an interesting discussion on the Print command vs. the Print Setup command and the importance of direct printing from the toolbar. Other ideas about printing are sprinkled throughout the book.

- Microsoft Corporation. *Designing for the User Experience*. Redmond, WA: Microsoft Press, 1999.

  See the chapter on secondary windows for a discussion of the Print, Print Setup, and Page Setup dialog boxes. It recommends the Page Setup dialog box over the Print Setup dialog box. I believe this is a good recommendation, since the Page Setup dialog box presents more useful settings than the Print Setup dialog box. However, note that currently the MFC document/view architecture doesn't give you a choice.

CHAPTER 31

● Prosise, Jeff. *Programming Windows with MFC, Second Edition*. Redmond, WA: Microsoft Press, 1999.

Chapter 13, "Printing and Print Previewing," describes printing in Windows in general, printing specifically with MFC and document/view, print previewing, and printing tips and tricks. It includes a detailed description of how print previewing is implemented in MFC. I always review this chapter when I write printing code.

CHAPTER 32

Check Your Help System and Documentation

The Help system and documentation are part of the user interface, and they should definitely be reviewed during the QA process. As a programmer, you probably are not responsible for writing Help or documentation since a technical writer will perform that work, but you're likely to be responsible for providing the information upon which Help and documentation will be based. You might also be responsible for reviewing them for completeness and accuracy and for integrating Help into the program.

In this chapter, I'll give you suggestions for working with a technical writer, integrating Help into your program, and specific items to check to make sure that Help is done correctly. I'll focus primarily on online Help since that is what you're most likely to be working on directly as a programmer. With a few exceptions, most of the information I present in this chapter also applies to printed documentation.

While in theory it might be possible to obtain the services of a technical writer, explain everything you want, and have the tech writer go off and create excellent and accurate documentation with no further interaction, I have never seen this happen. You shouldn't expect it to happen. Delivering quality Help and documentation requires significant programmer input and review. Tech writers and QA testers play a significant role in this process, but they can't do it all without your assistance. Remember that at this point in the development process you are the only one who really knows how the program works.

Help Should Be Helpful

Let's start by understanding the true goal of documentation. After all, users don't like reading documentation, and we certainly don't like writing it. So why bother? Users need documentation to help them get their work done. Although users don't read it unless they have to, when they do read it they want it to answer their questions. If it doesn't answer their questions, they're not happy.

Software developers want good documentation because they want happy users and they want to have small technical support departments. Bad documentation means a lot of technical support calls. To minimize technical support calls, you need to address documentation issues in the following order:

- **Improve the software**   Your first choice should always be to improve the software so that documentation isn't required.

- **Add to the documentation**   If improving the software can't solve the problem, you need to document the problem for the user.

- **Add to the readme file**   The readme file is your last defense against a technical support call.

However, the above goals can be consolidated into a single, simple goal. The ultimate goal of Help and documentation is summed up by this tip:

TIP   Help should be helpful.

This goal would go without saying were it not for the fact that much Help out there isn't helpful! Software documentation sometimes looks as if it has been written by someone who understands Microsoft Windows but who knows nothing about the particular program. And sometimes it looks as if it has been developed with little thought, simply as an obligation that nobody really cares about.

And what is helpful? Let's start by first looking at what *isn't* helpful:

- **Giving basic information on how to use Windows**   Your Help shouldn't spend time explaining how to use the mouse,

PART

504

what a menu is, how to select items in lists, how to double-click, and so on. If your users are beginners, you might want to refer them to the Help that comes with Windows or the appropriate sections in the Windows user's manual, *Getting Started with Windows 98*.

- **Describing the screen, menus, or toolbar**   The user already knows what the screen, menus, or toolbar looks like. Generally, such descriptive Help isn't helpful.

- **Covering what is obvious by looking at the screen**   Nothing makes me want to scream more than asking for help and being told what should be obvious to a complete idiot.

- **Providing a tutorial that teaches a procedure without explaining the significance of its action**   Tutorials that show how to select various menus, dialog boxes, controls, and so on but don't say why you'd want to do this teach little.

Given what isn't helpful, what is? Whenever I use Help, I'm generally looking for the following Help topics that *are* helpful:

- Providing an overall description of the program and a quick tutorial if the software is complex and unfamiliar to me.

- Explaining how to perform specific tasks.

- Clarifying the significance of the choices in a dialog box.

- Telling me what to do when I receive an error message I don't understand.

- Providing tutorials that present information the way you would present it if you were training someone to use the program. You wouldn't train someone by saying "First click this button, and then click that button." Rather, you would explain what the feature does, when and why you would use it, and what the significance of the various options are.

If your documentation accomplishes all of the above, you're on the right track.

Modern Help Systems

In case you haven't been keeping up with the latest trends in Help systems, this section outlines the style of Help recommended by *Designing for the User Experience*. Modern Help systems should have the following characteristics:

- Help topics are generally short and task-oriented. Large Help subjects are divided into smaller tasks to make them easier to read.

505

- Help windows are small so that the user can look at the program while he is reading the Help.

- Help hyperlinks connect only to useful, relevant information. There is no obligation to link to another topic simply because you can.

- Screen windows and dialog boxes are not described with Help topic windows but with mouse-driven context-sensitive Help using the What's This? command.

This is in sharp contrast to the old-style Help, now referred to as reference Help. Reference Help was typically displayed as a near-full screen window, and it included so much information that the user really had to be motivated to want to read it. Large Help topics are intimidating and tend not to be read. Also, obviously, it took up too much screen space for the user to be able to read the Help and view the program at the same time. Often the Help text contained a screen shot of the program window that the user was already looking at, which makes no sense at all. Modern task-oriented Help systems are much more helpful to the user and much less oppressive.

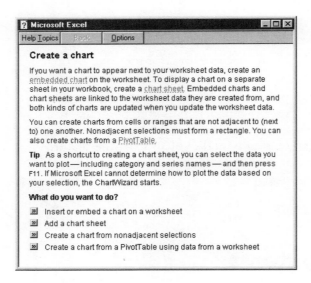

Task-oriented Help corresponds much more closely than other forms of help to how and when users need help while using a program. For example, a user might want to know how to copy an image to the clipboard but is unlikely to ask, "How does the Copy command in the Edit menu work?"

PART

V

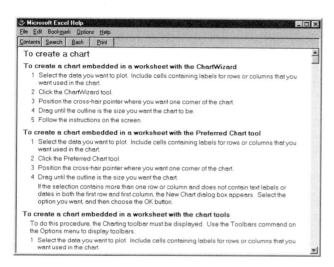

 TIP   Prefer task-oriented Help.

Printed Documentation

The trend is toward online Help and away from printed documentation. As user interfaces improve and become more standardized, the need for printed documentation decreases. It's been years since I have bought a software product from Microsoft with much more than 100 pages of printed documentation. I haven't missed it much. Since printed documentation is fairly expensive and difficult to modify quickly, you might want to follow this trend. Of course, providing printed documentation is a good idea in several cases:

- **If your customers need it**   You might have a product or be in a market that requires printed documentation. Note that beginning users are more likely to miss printed documentation than advanced users.

- **If your customers expect it**   You might have a custom or expensive product, in which case your customers might expect printed documentation.

- **If your software needs it**   Your program might be so complicated that it requires an introduction, tutorial, or other form of help that is significantly better when printed. The more reading the software requires to get the user going, the more the software needs printed documentation. It's more convenient to spend several hours reading a printed manual than reading online Help.

- **If your software needs a competitive advantage** Printed documentation adds to a product's perceived value. It can be shocking to pay several hundred dollars for a product and receive only a disk or a CD-ROM. A printed manual makes the product seem much more substantial.

Many tools on the market can help you create Help and printed documentation from the same content. You might not want to bother. Although this approach certainly promotes consistency, it scores poorly in helpfulness. Needing help, looking it up in the online Help, not finding the information you need, looking it up in the printed documentation, and finding exactly the same useless information is extremely annoying. What's the point?

TIP Having exactly the same help online and in the printed documentation isn't helpful.

Preparing the Program

Perhaps the most difficult question to answer is when to start developing the documentation. If you start too early, the documentation will be wrong because too much of the software will have changed, leading to a lot of wasted effort. If you start too late, the documentation might not be finished in time or receive sufficient review. You also want to have time to fix any user interface problems that are revealed during the documentation process. A good time to start is when the user interface is fairly stable and the most basic features are near completion. It's better to start too early rather than too late, but starting before this time is probably too early. When in doubt, ask your technical writer.

The next step is to make sure that all screen elements and program activities have descriptive names that are used consistently throughout the program. The screen elements that need names are all windows, dialog boxes, and nonstandard interface objects. You need to have names for the data used by the program, names for the tasks the user performs with the program, and of course the program itself should have a name. Consistency is extremely important. Using several different names to describe the same object confuses everybody and makes the program difficult to document. I discussed what, when, and how to name in Chapter 3, "Establish Consistent Terminology."

PART
V

Another useful step is to find a model for the Help system. Find an example Help system that you like and that meets most of your goals and use it as a reference point. Try to determine what you like about it and what changes you'd like to make to it. A good model helps you express your ideas with specific examples to your technical writer.

The last step is to prepare a preliminary design of the Help system. Of course, the design of the Help system is something you will negotiate with the tech writer, but you should prepare a preliminary design on your own so that you can express your ideas when you meet with the tech writer. The last thing you want to do is not express your ideas and then be dissatisfied with the results. To prepare the design, review the program and make an outline of the program features. You should highlight the features that need special attention. Such features might be complex or advanced, or they might not be visible directly from the interface.

You need to consider the level of context-sensitive Help you want to provide. While each dialog box should have context-sensitive Help, you have several options in how to implement it. Should there be a Help context for every control accessed through the What's This? button or the Shift+F1 key, as suggested by *Designing for the User Experience*? Should each dialog box have a single Help context accessed through a Help button or F1 key? Should you support both methods? For property sheets, should there be a single Help context for the entire property sheet, or should there be a Help context for each page?

You should also consider what Help features you plan to support. Will the program support shortcut buttons? Does it need to have troubleshooters? Should it have Tips and Tricks? Note that such help might require support from the program to display a specific dialog box or a specific page on a property sheet.

Lastly, I recommend creating a *quick tips* list. Whenever I read printed documentation, I highlight the information most interesting and useful to me so that I can quickly review it later. Typically, this information is only a small portion of the total documentation. Since the user cannot highlight online documentation and isn't likely to read it "cover to cover," I like to consolidate the most useful information into a Help topic or set of Help topics and give the user direct access to this information from the program's Help menu.

Programming Context-Sensitive Help

If you plan on having context-sensitive Help for all individual window elements and dialog box controls, note that this will result in hundreds or thousands of context-sensitive Help topics. To manage the integration of context-sensitive Help, you need to assign the Help context IDs in a systematic manner. You can give your tech writer the responsibility of assigning the IDs, but you are the one who is going to have to integrate the context-sensitive Help so you should be the one who decides how it is done.

Since the Help compiler has several restrictions on header files (for example, it doesn't support *#ifdef* and *#endif* statements, and it can't handle arithmetic in *#define* statements), you should create a separate header file just for the Help context IDs that you can share with the tech writer. If you assign the context IDs using consistent prefixes (such as HIDC_), the Microsoft Help Workshop can automatically verify that the IDs defined in the header file exist in the Help file. This technique helps you make sure that all Help topics actually have help. If you are using Microsoft Visual C++, you can have the dialog box editor automatically assign context IDs for controls by selecting the Help ID check box in the control's Properties dialog box. The context ID values are based on a combination of the dialog box ID and the control ID. Alternatively, you can use the MakeHm utility to automatically generate the context IDs.

If you are using context-sensitive Help for dialog boxes, be careful in how you assign control IDs in the dialog box templates. Note that when users need Help for a control, sometimes they click the control directly and other times they click the control label. The good news is that you can give context-sensitive Help to static text labels simply by giving them a control ID of −1 (that is, IDC_STATIC) and ensuring that the control with the desired Help context is directly after the label in the tab order and has the tab stop attribute set. Now if the user clicks the label, WinHelp will recognize the control as a label and use the desired Help context instead. The bad news: WinHelp does this for all controls, not just static text labels, so you need to assign control IDs other than −1 for any control that should not have context-sensitive Help. Lastly, you need to discuss with your tech writer whether group box controls should have context-sensitive Help, since it might make sense in certain cases, such as when you're using the group box as a label for one or more controls.

You provide WinHelp the information it needs to map from the selected control ID to the desired Help context ID by using an array of DWORD pairs, where the first DWORD is the control ID and the second DWORD is the Help context ID. This array is terminated with two NULLs so that WinHelp can find the end of the array. All controls in the dialog box with a control ID other than −1 need to be in this array, even if they do not have a Help context. In this case, the Help context ID should be −1. Let's look at some typical code:

```
LRESULT CALLBACK ExampleDlgProc (HWND hDlg, UINT uMsg, WPARAM wParam,
                                 LPARAM lParam)
{
    // The array of control IDs and context IDs
    Static DWORD helpIDs [] =
    {
        ID_CONTROL1, HIDC_CONTROL1,
        ID_CONTROL2, HIDC_CONTROL2,
        0, 0
    }

    switch (uMsg)
    {
        case WM_HELP:
            WinHelp((((LPHELPINFO)lParam)->hItemHandle,
            _T("helpfile.hlp"), HELP_WM_HELP, (DWORD)(LPVOID)helpIDs);
            break;

    }
    return FALSE;
}
```

Given all these requirements, let's quickly summarize the rules for assigning control IDs and Help context IDs:

- **For a normal control with a Help context**   Assign a control ID other than −1 and a context ID other than −1 and put the mapping in the Help ID array.

- **For a normal control without a Help context**   Assign a control ID other than −1 and a context ID of −1 and put the mapping in the Help ID array.

- **For a static text label of an enabled control**   Assign a control ID of −1 and assign its tab order just before the control with the desired Help context. Do not put the mapping in the Help ID array.

- **For a static text label of a disabled control**   Assign the label a control ID other than −1 and a context ID to the desired help context and put the mapping in the Help ID array. Unfortunately, the mechanism for assigning context IDs doesn't work if the associated control is disabled.

Preparing the Technical Writer

When I first learned to program, I created programs by walking up to a computer, turning it on, and writing some code. What I didn't do is design. I had no idea how to design. How do you turn a blank sheet of paper into software? I didn't feel comfortable thinking about code without a keyboard

511

under my fingers. This is not just a problem with programmers, because some technical writers use basically the same approach. They work with no design, no outline, and, remarkably, no real understanding of the program. They learn how to use the program as they write the documentation.

Does this make sense? Remember that the ultimate goal is to make the Help system helpful. How helpful can documentation be when written by someone, no matter how talented, who doesn't understand the program? The tech writer must become an experienced user before writing in detail. The goal isn't to write documentation for experienced users. Rather, the tech writer needs to understand how to use the program better than the typical user reading the documentation.

What is the best way to achieve this objective? I like to use the following process:

1. Give a demo.

2. Give an outline.

3. Get an outline.

4. Get a demo.

When you first meet with the technical writer, you should start off with a demonstration of the program. Be sure to point out the features that are likely to give users problems. Then present the model Help system you selected and discuss why you think it is an appropriate model. Then present the outline of your preliminary design and get the tech writer's feedback.

At this point, you will give the technical writer a copy of the program and plenty of time to become familiar with it. However, before the tech writer starts writing, I suggest that you have another meeting. You should ask for an outline of what the tech writer wants to write. Review the outline for accuracy and completeness. I also suggest that you ask the tech writer to give you a demonstration of the program and to discuss the specific details of the Help system design while giving the demo. Ask the tech writer difficult questions about the program and how the Help system is going to handle such questions. If the person is struggling to use the program or you don't agree with the proposed approach, you'll know immediately and can take the appropriate action.

Working with the Technical Writer

Once the ball is rolling, working with the technical writer generally requires keeping the technical writer informed of significant changes to the program and reviewing intermediate results.

PART

I have to admit that I find reviewing documentation one of the most tedious tasks. It's no fun, and it seems to take forever. Is there an alternative? Unfortunately no—you have to suffer through it. Although you might be able to have QA testers do some of the reviewing, it's ultimately up to you to make sure that the documentation is accurate and complete.

I find it most convenient to use the change-tracking feature in Microsoft Word. You can set up Word to use revision bars and highlight changes to clearly indicate what changes have been made. The comment feature is also very helpful, since you can embed any comments you have within the document itself. The comment feature is especially helpful in a group project in that it lets you see the comments made by all the other team members.

If for any reason I can't track changes using Word, the next best alternative is to mark up hard copy. When I am done reviewing the documentation, I go over it with the technical writer and keep a duplicate of the marked hard copy for my records. That way, when I get the next release I don't have to start completely over. Rather, I can focus on the areas that I found needed work. The last thing I want to do is completely read every draft.

Unless the user interface is stable, I recommend against making screen shots until the end of the process. Constantly updating screen shots is a fair amount of work with little benefit. After all, the people reviewing the Help at this point already know what the program looks like.

How to Find Problems

In the following sections, I'll list problems to check for while you are reviewing documentation. If you don't personally check all of these items, make sure that someone checks the items you don't.

General

- Is the Help accurate? Is it complete?

- Is the Help consistent? Does it use terminology consistently? Does the terminology used in the Help match the program?

- Is the Help helpful? When you have a question about the program, does the Help answer it? Does the Help spend too much time describing the obvious? Does it describe the program details well?

- Are the Help topics an appropriate size? Do you find them too long? Are they easy to read? Do you have to do a lot of scrolling?

- Is the Help window conveniently sized and located? Can you work with the program while viewing the Help?

- Is the Help easy to access? Try to find help using the Help button and the F1 key. If supported, try to find help using the What's This? button or the Shift+F1 key. Try to find help using the Contents, Index, and Find tabs of the Help Topics browser dialog box.

- Are the step-by-step instructions accurate? Beginning users are especially disturbed when following instructions that say something is on the screen (either through a screen shot or text) when it isn't. This makes the user think that he either doesn't understand what is going on or that he has made a mistake. Any likely discrepancies should be noted in the text. Have a beginning user review all instruction-based help and documentation and make sure that the user can accurately reproduce all the steps described with the program.

Details

- Does the Help explain one way to accomplish a task or several ways? To keep the text simple, the Help should describe a single, standard way to accomplish a task. For example, if you can accomplish a task by using the menu bar, context menu, or keyboard, just explain the menu bar approach.

- Do all the windows have context-sensitive Help? Do all the dialog boxes? Is the right Help context always used? Do static text controls such as group boxes, static rectangles, lines, bitmaps, and icons have Help contexts when they shouldn't? Do the labels of disabled controls have the correct Help context? Note that the labels of disabled controls require special handling and are likely to have the wrong Help context.

- Does the Help contain screen shots? Are those screen shots really necessary? Are they helpful?

- Do the indices use plural forms of nouns? For example, there should be an entry for *dialog boxes*, not *dialog box*. Are the terms indexed in all the variations that a user is likely to look for them? For example, a Compile tab of an Options dialog box should be indexed as *Compile tab*; *Options dialog box, Compile tab*; and *dialog boxes, Options, Compile tab*. Do different level users use different terms? If so, make sure the Help indexes the terms used at all levels.

- Are hyperlinks used effectively? Do the hyperlink topics present relevant information?

PART
V

514

- Is the spelling correct? Don't assume that using a spelling checker means that the Help does not have spelling errors.

The Readme File

Unlike most other documentation, the readme file is one document that is most likely to be the programmer's responsibility. In the bad old days of MS-DOS software, readme files were an essential part of a program. You actually had to explain how to install a program, what the name of the setup program was (it wasn't always Setup.exe), how to type it in, and what to do if the installation didn't work, which it often didn't. The readme file was an essential starting point in the installation process.

Today, you don't even have to look at the installation disk or CD-ROM. Just pop it in the drive, run Setup.exe, perhaps restart Windows if a file was already in use, and you're ready to go. CD-ROM–based programs with an AutoPlay program that launches the setup program when necessary are especially good. Today, the setup program does almost everything for the user. No more modifying the Config.sys and Autoexec.bat files. No more setting environment variables. No more loose ends that need to be tied up.

Does this mean that the readme file is obsolete? I don't think so. The readme file is best regarded as your last defense against technical support calls. You should always provide an informative readme file that gives users tips on how to solve technical support–related problems. Although there are no guarantees, many desperate users give the readme file a chance before picking up the phone.

TIP   The readme file is your last defense against technical support calls.

But where does this information come from? As a programmer, you should be able to anticipate many problems based on your knowledge of the program. My favorite source of readme file information is the QA process itself. Keep track of the various issues that arise during the QA process and look for themes. If testers are having problems, most likely your users will, too. Any issues that are not adequately addressed in the program, the installation, or the documentation are prime candidates for readme file material. Since the installation process is so important, it is also a good idea to repeat important setup information even if it is adequately addressed elsewhere. Your QA team should be able to help you gather this information.

Lastly, like anything else, your readme file should be usable. A huge random collection of mostly useless information is unlikely to be read and will accomplish nothing. A good rule of thumb is that if you can't stand to read it, your users won't be able to either. Try to present the most useful information in an organized manner.

Although I've suggested a number of ways in which you can help your technical writer create excellent documentation, don't interpret this to mean that tech writers aren't capable of doing their jobs. They are. Almost all of the tech writers that I've worked with have been professional, knowledgeable, and hardworking. If a tech writer disagrees with some of your objectives or ideas, have an open mind because that person is likely to be right. But, like anyone else, your technical writer is going to need help to do the best work possible.

Related Chapters

- Chapter 3—Establish Consistent Terminology.

    Presents guidelines on what needs to be named and how to name it. Also stresses the importance of establishing names early in the development process.

- Chapter 28—Talk to Your Other Team Members.

    Describes why technical writers are in a unique position to find user interface problems and how to work with technical writers to take full advantage of their feedback.

- Chapter 33—Check Your Setup Program

    Describes the role of the readme file in the installation process.

Recommended Reading

- Horton, William K. *Designing and Writing Online Documentation: Hypermedia for Self-Supporting Products.* New York, NY: John Wiley & Sons, Inc., 1994.

    A highly regarded resource for designing and creating online help systems. Also covers other related subjects, such as error messages and menus.

- Microsoft Corporation. *Designing for the User Experience.* Redmond, WA: Microsoft Press, 1999.

  See the chapter on user assistance for a good discussion on writing task-oriented Help, Help window design, and the Help topics browser. Also presents useful information on context-sensitive Help, tooltips, status bar text, and Help buttons in dialog boxes.

- Microsoft Corporation. *Microsoft Manual of Style for Technical Publications, Second Edition.* Redmond, WA: Microsoft Press, 1998.

  Provides useful guidelines for all aspects of documentation.

- Microsoft Corporation. *Microsoft Windows 95 Help Authoring Kit.* Redmond, WA: Microsoft Press, 1995.

  Appendix A, "Windows 95 Help Style Guidelines," presents an excellent discussion on modern, task-oriented Help; the motivation for the Windows 95 Help system design; guidelines for writing Help; Help window design; and many other Help-related topics. It gives useful information on how to integrate context-sensitive Help into your program. It also gives useful strategies for testing and debugging Help.

- Nielsen, Jakob. *Usability Engineering.* Chestnut Hill, MA: AP Professional, 1993.

  Chapter 5, "Usability Heuristics," presents an interesting study of online help that found that 23 percent of the time help requests found no useful information at all. In the cases where users did find help information, the users considered it useful only 35 percent of the time. Although it might seem obvious that Help should be helpful, it cannot be taken for granted.

CD-ROM Resources

The CD-ROM included with this book contains the following resource related to this chapter:

- An electronic version of the *Microsoft Manual of Style for Technical Publications, Second Edition.*

CHAPTER 32

CHAPTER

33

Check Your
Setup Program

The setup program is an essential part of your software, yet it's often overlooked in the development process. You should regard the setup program as a critical component of your program's user interface. Why? For starters, it is the first software the customer sees. It helps form the all-important first impression—the "out of the box" experience. Painless installations make a good first impression. Difficult installations do not. And these first impressions last a long time.

Consider how you would react to a program that didn't install easily or, worse yet, didn't install at all. The setup program is the direct link between your distribution media and the user's computer. If the setup fails, the program is worthless. Setup problems lead to product returns, lost sales, high technical support costs, and dissatisfied customers. In financial terms, poorly implemented setup programs have a direct impact on the bottom line.

Yet in spite of their importance, setup programs traditionally do not receive the attention they deserve during the development and QA process.

Programmers often perceive them as somebody else's problem and try to avoid the issue. As a result, setup programs are often created late in the process and are not given sufficient review to make sure that they are effective and reliable.

Installing Microsoft Windows programs becomes more complex as time goes on. Clearly, this isn't desirable in itself, but it isn't an indication of a failure of Windows. Rather, it's an indication of its progress. Windows programs need to have better system integration to give users more power and flexibility. The system needs to know more about programs—their location, icons, document types, and services. With this information, the system can give the user the ability to create new documents, to print documents, and to link and embed documents. These capabilities are essential to making Windows document-centric instead of application-centric.

Furthermore, users have higher expectations than before. In the early days of Windows, each setup program could behave differently and developers could depend upon readme files and technical support to tie together any remaining loose ends. This approach no longer works. Users have more programs to deal with than before. Instead of a couple of dozen programs, a typical user today might have hundreds. Users now expect to be able to manage their desktops and their hard disks more efficiently. They now want to be able to uninstall unused programs easily—without using third-party utilities. Administrators now want to perform automated installation across their networks.

In practical terms, one clear implication of this increased complexity and greater emphasis on efficiency is that it's almost impossible to write your own setup program from scratch. The proper setup process is simply too complex. However, even if you are using a fabulously wonderful commercial setup program, there are still plenty of ways to do the setup wrong. It is not by accident that nearly a quarter of the Designed for Microsoft Windows logo requirements deals with setup-related issues.

In the remainder of this chapter, I'll describe the typical problems with setup programs, how to satisfy the user's goals when installing a program, and how to improve and simplify a setup program's user interface. You'll also get some advice on being logo-compatible and tips on how to avoid common setup problems.

Setup Goals

Now is a good time to establish what the various goals are for a good setup program. Let's look at the setup goals from the point of view of installation, the user, the administrator, and the programmer.

The Basic Installation Goals

The basic Windows software installation process requires that the setup program copy the desired files from the distribution media to the user's hard disk, make the appropriate registry entries, and then create a default configuration so that the user can use the program immediately. The setup program also needs the ability to completely remove the program by removing all program files, references in the Start menu, registry entries, and the setup program itself. Somewhat simplified, there are two basic installation goals:

- A successfully completed installation should result in a functional program, without harming any previously installed programs.
- A successfully completed uninstall should remove all traces of the program except for files created by the user.

The User's Goals

Beyond the basic installation goals, users have some additional goals, which when met make the installation process a more satisfactory experience.

- Users want to have control of the desktop. Users don't want unnecessary setup artifacts to appear on the desktop without permission, such as program shortcuts on the desktop and at the top of the Start menu, and taskbar System Tray icons.
- Users want to have control of the hard disk. Although users have ever-increasing hard-disk capacity, users are also installing more and more programs. Setup programs should ask the user where to install the files, and those that install several megabytes of files should give the user options to select which files to install. The larger the hard-disk footprint, the more important it is to offer the user a choice.
- Users want to perform installations quickly and with a minimal amount of effort. They want to make a couple of simple selections, click a few buttons, and go. Users don't want to have to learn anything, gather or enter information, or call technical support. Users don't want to have to jump through hoops just to install a program. They want to use the program immediately once it has been installed.

The Administrator's Goals

Beyond the user's goals, administrators are faced with installing software on dozens, possibly hundreds, even thousands, of computers. Consequently, administrators have additional goals.

- Administrators want the option to run programs from a network server. This requires the ability to install the program on both the server and all the clients.

- Administrators want the option to perform the installation by using the network instead of dealing with individual computers.

- Administrators want the option to perform automated installation and removal so that they don't have to baby-sit the entire process.

- Administrators want the option to have diagnostic logging so that they can easily handle installations that fail.

The Programmer's Goals

Of course, programmers have quite a different set of goals.

- Programmers want to create fully functional setup programs without much effort.

- Programmers would prefer to have someone else deal with the setup program.

- Programmers want to reduce technical support costs for their company and perhaps even for their customers. (You have this goal, don't you?)

These goals are not trivial. For example, about the only bad thing I can say about the Microsoft Developer Network is that it has traditionally been a pain to install (requiring you to uninstall any existing versions first) and uninstall (not restoring the original Microsoft Visual C++ online Help once removed), although recent versions seem to be better. Poorly designed setup programs can be a real hassle—for everyone.

Happily, the goals I've mentioned do not necessarily conflict. For starters, everyone's goals can be accomplished by simplifying the setup process as much as possible.

Keep It Simple

The most common problem that setup programs have is that they are just too complicated. Some setup programs have too many screens, ask too many questions, offer too many options, and require too much effort to use. Another common problem is that the resulting desktop configuration and file system often have too much clutter.

To realize how bad these problems are, we have to break away from our current way of thinking about setup programs. As Alan Cooper points out, "Some clever vendors have developed a market selling installation-program-making tools. These have tended to institutionalize the drawbacks of bad installation procedures. The dreary sameness of most installation programs somehow lends an unwarranted credibility to them." I think this observation is right on target. Setup programs all look the same. They are all too complicated. They are indeed dreary.

Consider the User Experience

Installing your software should be a pleasant experience. It shouldn't be regarded like a trip to the dentist. Let's first look at the installation process from the point of view of the user's experience.

Simplifying the User Experience During Setup

Don't make the user jump through hoops during the setup process. Consider the following:

- For large, complex programs, offer different levels of installation (usually Typical, Compact, and Custom) and carefully explain their differences in terms of functionality and disk space. (The user isn't going to discover the differences the hard way because the user is only going to install once.) The Typical installation should do what is best for most users. Assume that most users will make this selection. The Compact installation should provide the most basic setup when disk space is at a premium. The Custom installation should select what is installed by the Typical installation by default. Most likely a user will select the Custom installation to add or remove options from the Typical installation, using it as a baseline. The Custom installation shouldn't make the user guess what the required files are.

- A setup program should let the user know how much disk space is needed to perform the installation and the amount of disk space available on the selected drive.

- Avoid situations in which the user has to abandon the setup process to gather information. If the user needs critical information to complete the setup, ask for it at the beginning of the setup, not in the middle.

- If the user has to enter a password, a serial number, or a registration number to perform the setup, ask for it once. Don't ask every time the setup is run.

- Avoid having the user restart Windows during setup. For most program installations, the only reason to restart Windows is if an

523

CHAPTER 33

installed file was in use by another program. Notice that you do not have to restart Windows to install a driver. If the setup program cannot install a file because it is in use, explain this to the user and give the user another chance to quit the running programs before requiring a restart. Or, better yet, have the setup program offer to close the running programs automatically.

TIP   Avoid restarting Windows during an installation.

Notice how the Microsoft Office setup automatically detects when other Office applications are running and suggests that you quit them before continuing the installation.

Simplifying the User Experience After Setup

Once the setup is complete, don't make the user jump through hoops to use the program. Consider the following:

- Provide an option to automatically launch the program after setup.

- Present an initial welcome screen or product introduction screen that briefly explains how to use the program and where to get more information. Provide just one window of this type. Don't pile up a bunch of welcome windows—this is far more confusing than it is welcoming.

- Choose the default program configuration carefully. If your program has a lot of functionality, let users grow into it at their own pace. You don't need to show every feature in the beginning— let the user choose to display these other windows when they are ready. Favor default options that help beginners, such as tips, agents, and wizards.

- If your program has optional components, make it easy to add or remove components after the initial installation. Such a setup should detect that the program is already installed and offer the option to add or remove components. Don't make the user completely reinstall to add a component. Worse yet, don't make the user uninstall and reinstall to remove a component.

- Make the program easy to upgrade. The upgrade should maintain all the user's current settings. An upgrade shouldn't require the user to start completely over.

- Make the program easy to uninstall. Always provide an uninstall program, and don't require the user to insert the source media to uninstall.

Simplifying the Start Menu

Suppose that your program consists of the following items: the program itself, its help file and help contents file, the setup program and uninstall utility, an online tutorial, a readme file, release notes, a technical support document, and several data files. How many of these items should be in the Start menu? The answer is one—the program itself. Putting the other items in the Start menu adds clutter and doesn't help the user at all. How many times have you launched a program's help file from the Start menu? How many times have you done this for the readme file? For most users, the answer is never. It makes sense to use the Start menu to help the user get his work done, not for dealing with installation and technical support.

Help the user clean up the Start menu and make your program easy to find. The user shouldn't have to wade through a bunch of unused icons to find your program in the Start menu. Instead of using the Start menu to tie all these items together, use the program itself. Use the program's Help menu to provide access to all the help and technical support files. The uninstall utility needs to be registered with Windows and is accessed using the Add/Remove Programs applet in the Control Panel (and possibly the program's Help menu as well), not the Start menu. Rarely used auxiliary programs and utilities should be moved to a submenu to make the main program stand out.

TIP

Reduce Start menu clutter by not adding installation, documentation, and technical support–related files to the Start menu.

33
CHAPTER

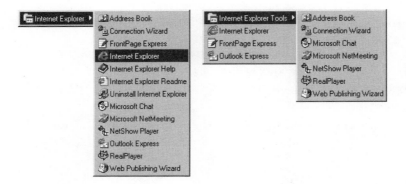

Simplifying the Desktop

The setup program can help the user clean up the desktop as well. Don't add icons to the desktop, Quick Launch bar, or taskbar System Tray without asking. These system resources have a limited amount of space, so the user will want to reserve them for the most commonly used programs. Don't take it for granted that your program is one of these. Let the user choose.

Status-only System Tray icons should be optional and off by default. For notifications, it's better to dynamically add and remove icons to notify the user of an event than to permanently keep an icon and just change its appearance. For example, a mail icon that appears in the System Tray only when there is new mail is more effective than an icon that is always there and changes its appearance when new mail is received.

Note that adding an icon to the desktop or the Quick Launch bar is very simple, since you can drag and drop an icon directly from either Windows Explorer or the Start menu. Having to add an icon to the desktop is at worst a minor inconvenience.

TIP

Reduce desktop clutter by not adding icons to the desktop, Quick Launch bar, or taskbar System Tray without asking permission.

Respect the user. Put the need of the user to maintain control of his desktop and hard disk over your need to promote your programs and your company. Don't install things like promotional material and demos without asking permission. Don't use unnecessarily long titles for items in the Start menu, since each menu is adjusted to be long enough to display the longest item. You'll make an impression if you don't respect the user, but it probably isn't the kind of impression you want to make.

PART

V

The two basic installation goals I discussed earlier were to provide the ability to successfully install and uninstall the program. But the best setup programs don't just install and remove the software; they go out of their way to help the user control his system. This is the ultimate goal for setup programs.

TIP The best setup programs go out of their way to help the user control his system.

Eliminate Unnecessary Setup Screens

A typical setup program has a collection of fairly standard screens. Some of these screens perform an essential function; others do not. Let's take a look at each type of setup screen and consider if it is necessary.

The Welcome Screen

The welcome screen introduces the user to the setup program. It serves to clearly identify what the setup program is about to install. It also "strongly recommends" that the user quit all other Windows programs before continuing. This is good advice, since Windows cannot overwrite a file while it's in use, so quitting all other programs eliminates the need to restart Windows when the setup is complete. However, this isn't much information for an entire screen. This screen can be eliminated.

The End-User License Agreement

Many setup programs display the familiar end-user license agreement, which says something to the effect that the user doesn't actually own the software (just a license to use it), that the user can't make illegal copies, and that the user can't sue the vendor if it doesn't work right. By the user clicking the Yes button or the I Accept button, the theory is that this is supposed to create a legally binding contract between the user and the vendor.

My recommendation is that if you are truly concerned about protecting your company, you should speak to a lawyer for advice on creating an enforceable end-user license agreement. I wouldn't take it for granted that the typical license agreement in a setup program would hold up in court, although there is currently proposed legislation that would make them enforceable. The problem is that the "agreement" usually occurs after the financial transaction takes place. Include this screen if you or your council feels you must, but don't do it because you think everybody else does. This screen can be eliminated.

CHAPTER
33

The Readme File

In the bad old days of MS-DOS and Windows programs, the readme file played a critical role in the installation process. It explained the entire process to the user and helped the user solve any problems—and there were usually problems. Readme files also contained any changes to the documentation added after it was printed.

Today, things are different. The setup program has the responsibility of guiding the user through the installation process and handling any loose ends. Any instructions necessary to perform installation should be in the setup user interface itself or its Help file. Most documentation is online, so there is no excuse for asking the reader to view the readme file for the latest changes because you couldn't update the documentation in time. Consequently, the role of the readme file has changed. The readme file is best regarded as your last defense against technical support calls. So now the key question: does the user need to see the readme file during the installation process? The answer is clearly no. The user is not interested in this information unless the installation process failed. You shouldn't overexpose the readme file during the setup process. This screen can be eliminated.

TIP

Don't overexpose the readme file during the setup process.

User Information

This screen asks the user his name, company, and serial or registration number. Notice that the user name and company information is readily available in the registry. This screen can be eliminated unless a serial or registration number is required. At the very least, use registry settings to provide defaults for this screen.

Choosing the Destination Folder

This screen displays the default destination folder and gives the user the ability to choose another folder instead. If the default destination folder is well chosen, there is little reason to change it. Surprisingly, I find that the default folder is often poorly chosen. Common mistakes include using 8.3 filenames, not using a Program Files subfolder, and using awful-looking names like *Expl Flder* or *EXAMPLE FOLDER*. Another good reason to change the default destination folder is to install to another hard disk. Since it's important for the user to have control over his hard disk, this screen is required.

PART

V

Choosing the Setup Type

This screen allows the user to select the type of installation. The choices are usually Typical, Compact, or Custom. As hardware improves, the exact meaning of Typical and Compact should probably change with time. With disk space costing pennies per megabyte, there's really no need to give the user options to save 100 KB of disk space. Laptops are now just as powerful as desktops, so there is no longer a reason to have a distinct setup type for laptops. Furthermore, CD-ROM drives have much better performance now, so there is less of a need to bother the user about caching files for CD-ROM-based programs. However, the larger the footprint of the program, the more important these choices are. Again, since it's important for the user to have control over his hard disk, this screen is required for large programs.

Selecting the Start Menu Program Folder

This screen gives the user the opportunity to select the name of a new Start menu program folder or to select an existing program folder. By installing to an existing program folder, users can eliminate some of the clutter in the Start menu. Since it's important that the user have control over the desktop, this screen is helpful.

Summary of Current Settings

This screen summarizes the current settings and gives the user a last chance to change them before copying files. However, unless the user is performing a complex custom install, the user simply hasn't made enough choices for such a verification to be necessary. This screen can be eliminated.

Setup Completion

This last screen indicates that the installation was successful and typically gives the user options to display the readme file or immediately launch the program. As I noted previously, if the program was successfully installed, the user should have little need for the readme file at this point. Of course, the reason users install programs is to use them, so if the program were to automatically launch immediately after installation, that would be a clear indication that the installation was successful. This screen can be eliminated.

Setup Failed

This alternative last screen indicates that the installation failed and gives the reason why. Now is the time to give an option to display the readme file. This screen is required.

Online Registration

Many setup programs have online registration as a bonus screen once the program has been installed. The most interesting observation about online registration is that it benefits the vendor, not the user. The user would just as well not fill in another form. I rarely perform online registrations. When I do, it is because the vendor has made an effort to present a clear and compelling benefit to registration. Saying something like *Register to Win!* or *Register for Free Support* usually does the trick.

An Alternative Approach

Now that we have gone through all the screens included in typical setup programs, let's see what's left. Clearly, more complex programs require a more complex setup program, so a giant 50 MB program can easily justify a multiple-step process with the options for full customization. But smaller, simpler programs do not need such complexity. All that is really needed is to select a destination folder, a Start menu program folder, and perhaps a couple of options. In this case, it isn't necessary to have a single screen to gather each piece of information. Why not use a setup program that looks like this:

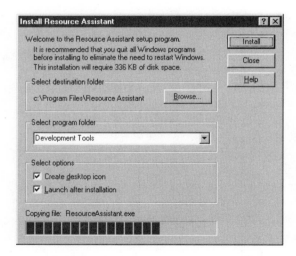

This setup program gives users all the options they need with a simple, one-click install. Don't you think that this user interface is much better? It's certainly easier to use.

Don't Ask Questions If You Don't Really Need the Answers

One of the reasons a typical setup program has so many unnecessary screens is that they spend too much time asking unnecessary questions. These unnecessary questions often relate to getting information that the setup program should already have, getting information that the setup program should be able to figure out by itself, or providing setup options that the user doesn't need.

The accuracy of this assessment became especially clear to me recently when I upgraded my computer to Windows 98. Along with the Windows 98 upgrade CD-ROM, I received a *Microsoft Windows 98 Upgrade Guide* from Dell Computer Corporation. While these instructions are specific to Dell, I'm sure other computer manufacturers have similar upgrade instructions. I believe these instructions provide a remarkable indication of the complexity of setup programs. For example, in the "Running the Windows 98 Setup Program" section, the first 10 of 19 steps (with the commentary and other miscellaneous text removed) read roughly as follows:

Turn on your system.
Insert the Microsoft Windows 98 Upgrade CD into the CD-ROM drive.
Click Yes.
Click Continue.
Click the I Accept The Agreement button, and then click Next>.
Enter the product key, and then click Next>.
Click the Yes (Recommended) button, and then click Next>.
Modify the network information as necessary, and then click Next>.
Change the location setting as necessary, and then click Next>.
Click Next>.
And so on…

The remainder of the booklet contains similar instructions for upgrading the various system drivers for Windows 98. Do you find these instructions interesting? I find them fascinating. Why? Because the only real accomplishment of these instructions is to remove all choice from the user. None of the instructions in this 19-page booklet read like, "If you want this objective, click this; otherwise, click that." Rather, they just say "Click this." You could argue that this is a good sign, indicating that the default selections are always correct, which simplifies the installation process. But you could also argue that many of the selections are completely unnecessary. Apparently Dell, which has to pay for technical support for such upgrades, doesn't think they are necessary. But what I find really interesting is the fact that this booklet exists at all. The fact that Dell believes that such a booklet is

33
CHAPTER

necessary indicates that these setup programs have failed. Dell decided it
was better to provide detailed documentation than to have users deal with
the setup programs directly. This is a bad sign about the usability of these
setup programs. Users should not need to have instructions like these.

TIP

Avoid presenting unnecessary setup options.

Now take another look at the alternative setup user interface that I
proposed earlier. If software using this setup program were shipped by Dell,
the upgrade guide would read:

Click Install.

Enough said.

Don't Ask Questions If You Don't Really Want the Answers

Long ago, when it was still feasible for a programmer to develop an acceptable Windows setup program on his own, I developed a setup program based on the sample code given in Jeffrey Richter's *Windows 3.1: A
Developer's Guide*. One of the many gory problems that a Windows 3.1 setup
program had to deal with was how to install a file that currently existed
but was in the wrong location on the user's machine. Richter recommended
using the following dialog box:

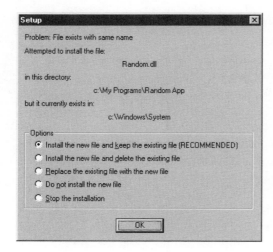

This dialog box certainly seemed reasonable at the time. After all, it offers all the possible options—the user just has to pick the right one. However, as our technical support department would attest, this turned out to be a very bad idea. If the user is computer-savvy, providing all the options works well. If not, the user either panics and immediately calls technical support or makes the wrong choice, botches the installation, and then panics and calls technical support. (OK, we really didn't get that many technical support calls, but a surprising number of them were related to users having problems with this dialog box.) Notice that clearly identifying the recommended choice, making it the first choice, and making it the default choice wasn't enough to fix the problem.

Never ask the user a question unless you really want to know the answer.

In fact, the problem wasn't with the choices or the presentation of the choices. Rather, the problem was asking the question in the first place. There is a significant practical problem with asking the user a question like this. Of these options, the only safe choice is to install the new file and keep the existing file. The copy and delete choice and the replacement choice are potentially disastrous. A setup program should never offer the user a choice that could lead to a bad installation.

All user choices should result in valid installations. Never offer the user a choice that could lead to a bad installation.

(Please note: The particular problem described here applies to Windows 3.1 and no longer exists in Windows 98 or Microsoft Windows NT. The Designed for Microsoft Windows logo requirements clearly state that a file that isn't shared should be copied to the program's folder and that shared program files should be copied to the \Program Files\Common Files\companyname folder. Only system files should be copied to the Windows system folder. This installation technique eliminates the file location problem at the cost of using slightly more disk space.)

CHAPTER

33

Guidelines for Asking Setup Questions

Since many setup problems result from asking unnecessary or confusing questions, it's useful to summarize the guidelines for asking setup questions. When asking a question in a setup program, consider the following:

- Don't ask a question if you already know the answer.

- Don't ask a question if you can determine the answer. The setup program shouldn't have to ask any questions about the user's system, for example.

- Don't ask a question if the user isn't likely to know the answer. Don't assume the user has read anything before running the setup program. Don't assume the user knows anything about his system configuration.

- Don't present responses or options that are invalid or that will lead to an invalid installation. In such cases, the setup program should automatically make the selections that result in a valid installation. With the exception of invalid serial numbers, registration numbers, and folders, all user input should lead to a valid installation.

- Carefully explain the significance of any responses or options. Make sure the user has enough information to make an informed decision.

- Clearly indicate the recommended response or option and make it the default selection.

- Provide acceptable default values whenever possible. The user should be able to perform all steps that do not require text input by pressing the Enter key or clicking the Next button.

- Verify all input when it is entered. Don't wait until it is used to discover that it is invalid.

- All input folders and file paths should have a browse button.

- If necessary, provide online help to further explain what the user needs to do. But don't assume that the user is going to read it.

Consider Eliminating Installation

The installation process is best regarded as a necessary evil. But is it really always necessary? Programs that require a CD-ROM to run (such as multimedia programs, games, kids programs, demos) are interesting because they are the only programs that require the user to insert the distribution media to run them. In this case, it's possible to have AutoPlay launch the program and to have the program install itself and then uninstall itself when the user quits.

I have several Windows computers and one Apple Macintosh. My two-year-old son Philippe loves to play with a computer whenever his father is working, so I set up the Macintosh for him to use when the other computers aren't available. This is one situation where having a single-button mouse is a good idea. The children's CD-ROMs we have are all multiplatform. I've noticed that while most of the Windows versions require installation, none of the Mac versions do. You just pop in the CD-ROM, double-click the program icon, and go. You don't know how cool this is until you've tried it.

Is it possible for a Windows program to eliminate installation? Well, it depends. Browser-based, thin-client programs routinely avoid the need for installation. There are several recent developments that make it possible to eliminate installation:

- **Improved CD-ROM performance** Currently, the best CD-ROM drives run at 40x and even the cheapest drives run at 20x. There is no longer a need to copy read-only files (such as executables and data files) to the hard disk to improve performance.

- **The new Visual C++ /DELAYLOAD linker switch** This linker switch, which delays loading a DLL until it is called, means that programs that depend upon DLLs can load, determine which DLLs need to be installed, install them, and then run. The /DELAYLOAD switch also allows programs to unload a DLL when it is no longer needed, so a program could also uninstall its DLLs before quitting.

On the other hand, there is at least one recent development that makes eliminating installation more difficult:

- **COM** Since COM components must be registered, the idea of registering components that are on removable media isn't especially attractive.

To summarize an installation-free process: After the user inserts a CD-ROM, AutoPlay could launch the program immediately. The program could have an installation function that could install and register any components that are needed before running the main program. Temporary files can be written to the Temp folder, as usual. When the user quits the program, the reverse process could be performed to remove the program. The only trace remaining would be any user settings in the registry. Since this whole process is temporary, there is no need to ask the user where to copy the files, what Start menu name to use, or whether there should be a shortcut on the desktop.

CHAPTER 33

If you have a CD-ROM-based program, consider eliminating the need for installation. You will be doing your users a big favor. When possible, the best setup user interface is no user interface at all.

TIP Consider eliminating the need for installation of CD-ROM-based programs.

Setup Settings vs. Program Settings

Users want to be able to use a program immediately once it has been installed. For the program to work, it may need to have some basic settings made. Should these settings be made within the setup program or within the main program itself? Of course, it depends on the type of setting. If a setting requires access to the distribution media, make it part of the setup. If a setting is required for the program to run at all, it should also be part of the setup. Otherwise, use default settings and let the user make changes from within the program itself as needed. This approach simplifies the setup process and gives the user the opportunity to understand which settings he wants to make.

TIP If a setting requires the distribution media or is required for the program to run, make it part of the setup. Otherwise, make it part of the program itself.

Top Dozen Setup Tips

The following sections describe my top dozen setup tips.

Use a Commercial Setup Program

Back in the bad old days of Windows 3.1 programming, I used to write my own setup programs. The advantage to this approach was that the setup process was fairly simple back then and I could get the setup program to do anything I wanted without fooling around with the limited capabilities of the commercial setup programs available at the time. That situation is no longer true. As I noted earlier, the setup process required by Windows is now so complicated that it isn't practical to write your own setup programs anymore. Do yourself a favor and do your users a favor: use a commercial setup program. Let somebody else deal with the gory details.

PART
V

When choosing a commercial setup program, I would place more emphasis on reliability than on other considerations such as popularity, price, or advanced features. The single worst technical support problem you can have is dealing with a setup program that crashes. Nothing is more useless than a setup program that crashes. Whatever you do, don't assume that using a commercial setup program means that you don't have to test your setup program. Making this assumption can be a costly mistake.

Make the Setup an Early Deliverable

Let me put it another way: do a ton of user testing. Instead of making the setup a late deliverable, make it an early deliverable. The ideal time to create the setup program is to have it in time for alpha testing so that the setup program is part of the testing and QA process. You have to do it anyway, so why fool around?

Your goal should be to expose the setup program to as many different users and as many different system configurations as possible. Users will do the most amazing things with a setup program if you give them the opportunity. You'll probably have to make several user interface changes so that users can get through the process without problems. And, again, you shouldn't assume that using a commercial setup program means that the setup program will be trouble-free. Setup programs do crash, and when they do, it's a disaster. The result of the setup must be a functioning program. A setup program that installs correctly on one system might not on another.

When your testers are able to install your program without any problems, without any help, and without crashing, you might actually have a usable setup program. But if you try to pull this off at the last minute, chances are you won't make it.

Consider Setup as Part of the User Interface

You should consider the setup user interface to be part of your program's user interface. It's certainly not any less important. This means that you should apply the same user interface objectives described in this book to the setup program. You want to make sure that the setup program uses consistent terminology; that it can be used and understood by beginning users; that its features are visible and simple; that it uses appropriate default values; that it doesn't have any unnecessary dialog boxes or message boxes; that the error messages are clear, consistent, and specific; that it works in all video modes; and that the Help system is helpful. If you perform user testing, consider making the program setup part of the test.

You need to instruct your testers to look for setup problems. Don't take it for granted that they will; my experience indicates otherwise. Any

537

setup problems found during testing should result in a program change of some kind. Ideally, you should be able to change the setup program or the main program to eliminate the problem. At the very least, you should document the problem in the readme file so that users have a chance to deal with the problem on their own. For example, suppose during testing you discover that your program is incompatible with a certain type of video card. Your first effort should be to change your program to make it compatible. If that's not possible, your next effort should be to have the setup program check for that video card and report the incompatibility during installation. Lastly, you should at least document the problem in the readme file. If you do none of these steps, you are certain to get a technical support call from every user that has that video card.

Understand the Logo Requirements

As I discussed in Chapter 1, the logo requirements were created to help you make sure that your program conforms to what the user expects. They are not arbitrary hoops you need to jump through. Although using a commercial setup program will make it easier for you to create a setup program that conforms to the logo requirements, you should still understand the logo requirements and what they are trying to accomplish.

To quickly summarize the logo requirements, your program must use new Microsoft installer technology, which makes it easy to meet the other install/uninstall requirements. Your setup program must provide a graphical 32-bit setup that works in an attended and/or silent scenario, detects software versions, creates working shortcuts, supports CD-ROM AutoPlay, supports Add/Remove Programs, and checks operations in advance. Your setup program must provide and register a fully automated uninstaller that appears in Add/Remove Programs and that when run, removes all program files, references in the Start menu, registry entries, and removes itself as well.

Let's look at some of the more interesting setup logo requirements and recommendations.

Use Microsoft installer technology (required)

The Microsoft installer technology greatly facilitates satisfying the logo requirements for Windows 98 and Windows 2000. The Microsoft installer technology is supported by the major commercial setup program vendors.

Provide attended and/or silent installation and provide a fully automated uninstaller (required)

Automated network installation provides administrators the ability to perform the installation by using the network instead of dealing with individual computers.

Detect versions when installing (required)

The setup program must be able to detect the Windows version and install the appropriate program version.

Maintain user settings across version changes (best practice)

User settings must be maintained across upgrades. Furthermore, the user should be able to install multiple versions of your program. Installing a new version of a program should not conflict with or break other versions. Providing the user the ability to run multiple versions of a program is why the program's version number should be part of the path for its registry settings.

Support AutoPlay of CD-ROMs (required)

Programs distributed on CD-ROM must use the AutoPlay feature to begin setup or to launch the program the first time the program is run. It's up to you whether AutoPlay is enabled on subsequent insertions of the CD-ROM.

Register uninstaller and make it appear in Add/Remove Programs (required)

The uninstaller must be properly registered and must appear in the Add/Remove Programs applet in Control Panel.

Remove all program files during uninstall (required)

All files and folders copied to the hard disk must be removed, including .fts and .gid files generated by the help engine. User data files and resources that other programs might use, such as sharable DLLs, sharable fonts, and sharable registry entries, should remain on the hard disk.

Remove all references from the Start menu during uninstall (required)

The uninstaller must remove all shortcuts placed anywhere in the Start menu by the setup program.

Remove registry entries during uninstall (required)

The uninstaller must remove all registry entries created by the program, with the exception of entries that might be shared by other programs.

Remove uninstaller during uninstall (required)

The uninstaller must remove itself. The Microsoft installer technology simplifies this problem since it is a system component and must not be removed.

Do not write to Windows system directories (recommended)

The setup program should not write anything to the Windows system or system32 directories. In particular, it should not place shared DLLs or executables in the Windows system directories. Instead, use the \Program Files\Common Files\companyname folder for shared program files, and use Microsoft update packs for system files.

CHAPTER 33

Use Microsoft update packs to upgrade system components (recommended)

If the program requires updated system DLLs or other core components, ship a self-extracting executable provided by Microsoft that handles installation of these components. Microsoft distributes new DLLs by means of component update packs only. You should distribute these self-extracting executables from Microsoft rather than the latest DLLs themselves.

Do not decrement or remove core components during uninstall (required)

The uninstaller must not decrement or remove any core component, in particular MFC DLLs, Open Database Connectivity (ODBC), and Data Access Objects (DAO) DLLs.

Do not add to Win.ini or System.ini (required)

Your program must not add information to Win.ini or System.ini.

Do not register hard-coded paths (best practice)

Installers and programs should make use of the registry REG_EXPAND_SZ string type; the %SystemDrive%, %SystemRoot%, %windir%, %ProgramFiles%, %Temp%, and %UserProfile% environment variables; and the API function ExpandEnvironmentStrings. Do not hard-code paths to the Windows system root or to the drive containing Windows in the registry because users can remap their drives under Windows NT.

Install programs to the Program Files directory (required)

Your setup program's default installation directory (or directories) must be in the Program Files folder. Do not install executables or DLLs in the root directory.

Query the registry for directory names (required)

Your program should not assume that directory names such as My Computer will be in English or will be unchanged by the user. Your program should query the registry directly to obtain the proper language-specific directory names.

Don't Overlook the Uninstall

A guide to Mount Everest once pointed out that you are not done when you get to the summit. In fact, you are at most halfway done, assuming you want to get home alive. Similarly, installation is only half the battle—safely uninstalling is the other half. And, from the point of view of system robustness, it is the critical half. After all, it's pretty difficult to corrupt Windows by incorrectly adding a file (assuming it is a newer version), but it's very easy to corrupt Windows by incorrectly deleting a file.

PART

V

Be sure to provide an uninstall, make sure the uninstall satisfies the logo requirements, and be sure to test it as part of the QA process. Your users will appreciate it.

Check the Minimum System Requirements

All programs have minimum system requirements. Installing a program to a computer that doesn't satisfy the minimum requirements means that either the performance will be less than satisfactory or the program flat out will not run at all. The setup program should verify that the user's system satisfies these minimum requirements before performing the installation so that the user can know about any problems ahead of time. Ideally, the program itself should also check for system-related problems that might arise after installation, such as running in an incompatible video mode or missing hardware.

Some system requirements are showstoppers. If the system is running the wrong version of Windows, is missing required software or hardware, or doesn't have enough free hard disk space to copy the program files, the setup program should identify the problem, explain how to solve the problem, and allow the user to fix the problem or stop the installation.

A common setup mistake is to start the installation when there is insufficient disk space. There's nothing more annoying than having a setup program chunk away for 10 minutes only to report that it failed due to insufficient disk space. Let the user know ahead of time. If there is not enough hard disk space, the setup program should suggest that the user stop the installation rather than forcing the user to stop the installation. Why? Because sometimes it can be difficult to know how much space is required to complete an installation. For example, suppose that the user has enough space to install a program and nearly completes the installation process but abandons it at the end to fix some problem. If the user tries to install again, there will still be enough space to complete the job but the reported free disk space will have dropped because of the abandoned setup. The user should still be able to install and ignore any warnings at this point. If not, the user will have to uninstall before reinstalling. This is not fun.

For less serious problems, the goal should be to notify the user of the problem but not prevent the installation. For example, suppose that the system is currently using an incompatible video mode. No problem, since this is a temporary, easily correctable problem. Go ahead and install the program, but notify the user to change video modes before using the program. Of course, the program itself should insist on this as well.

Manage Your Version Resources

An important step in making sure that your software components are properly configured is to make sure all the components you create and use have properly managed version resources. Make sure that all executable files you create have version resources, and be sure to advance the version number with each release.

Use the Registry, not Initialization Files

Although the standards have recommended using the registry instead of initialization files ever since the registry became part of Windows, I have to admit that it took me a while to understand why. After all, initialization files are easy to understand, modify, and program, whereas the registry is significantly more complicated. Here are some of the benefits of using the registry:

- Windows supports multiple users, and the registry allows different users to have different system configurations and each user to have multiple configurations.

- The registry can be remotely administered.

- The registry supports a multilevel hierarchy, whereas initialization files have a fixed hierarchy.

- The registry supports several different data types (including the powerful REG_EXPAND_SZ type), whereas initialization files just support strings.

- The registry has better tools, especially network system management tools. The registry is easier to back up, restore, and modify. For example, it's much easier to search for registry settings by using RegEdit than it is to search for initialization file settings.

- The registry has no size restrictions.

- The registry supports Unicode.

Given all these benefits, it's difficult to justify continuing to use initialization files.

Consider Technical Support

Using a good, well-tested setup program is the single most important step in reducing technical support calls. This is not an exaggeration, and the reason is simple. While your program's advanced features might be its selling point and what gets all the attention, if a user has a problem with an advanced feature maybe you'll get a technical support call and maybe you won't. But if the user cannot install your program, you will get a support

PART

V

call. Guaranteed. And if technical support isn't able to solve the problem, most likely you will get a product return. What good is a program that you can't install?

You should discuss the setup program with your technical support staff and determine whether they need any special functionality. One technique that I have used successfully is to provide a special technical support mode in the setup program, accessed by pressing a function key on the first screen. This mode gives technical support access to additional setup features that you don't want regular users to see. Without such a mode, having the setup program limit users to safe choices also limits your technical support options as well.

Don't Use a Full Screen Setup

This is a personal preference, but I find setup programs that take over the whole screen to be a little old-fashioned and annoying. The typical bad setup program takes over the whole screen, including the taskbar, and then immediately recommends that you quit all other programs. By covering the taskbar, it prevents the user from being able to see whether any programs are running and being able to quit them easily. I know, you can still use the Application key (the one with the Windows logo on it) or use Alt+Tab, but most users don't know this.

Beeping Is OK When Installing from Multiple Disks

As I pointed out in Chapter 4, there's no such thing as an absolute rule in user interface design. Beeping is one of the worst things a user interface can do, but it is appropriate when installing software from a series of disks. Why? Because in this situation, the user doesn't want to be shackled to the computer while the setup program is running. Most likely the user will want to do something else and will appreciate being beeped when it's time to change disks.

Reconsider Displaying
Billboards or Bulletins During Setup

I used to think that the technique of displaying useful information on a billboard or the use of a similar metaphor was a great idea. It gives the user useful information about the program and helps the user pass the time. Now I'm not so sure. Why? Again, because the user doesn't want to be shackled to the computer during a long setup process. By displaying useful information in a way that appears only during setup, you make the user feel as if he might be missing out on something important. Furthermore, those using an automated installation won't see this information at all. A better technique is to provide access to such information the first time the program is run and to provide permanent access to it from the Help menu.

Bonus Setup Tips

A few final setup details to consider:

- Name your setup program Setup.exe. Place the setup program in the root directory of the distribution media. This is the name (as well as Install.exe) and location that is expected by the Add/Remove Programs Control Panel applet.

- Be careful with Custom installations. Since you want all user choices to result in valid installations, don't give the user the option to not install required files. All the custom choices should be to install optional files.

- Be careful with the Add/Remove Programs Control Panel applet. Not all users know that the way to remove Windows programs is through the Add/Remove Programs applet. Even fewer know that the way to add components to a Windows program is also through the Add/Remove Programs applet. Many users try to perform these tasks by using the original setup program. To eliminate this confusion, include options in your setup program to add components and to uninstall. If the user clicks these options, give instructions and then launch the Add/Remove Programs utility. This technique will make the process much more visible.

- If installing from a CD-ROM, use the CD-ROM drive as the default drive letter for installation source paths. If installing from a floppy, use the floppy disk drive letter as the default. Do not assume that floppies are on drive A.

- If the setup program uses multiple disks, it should never ask the user to install a disk more than once. Lay out the files so that the user doesn't have to reinsert the same disk multiple times. Use volume labels to make sure the user has inserted the right disk, and put the volume labels on the disk labels for easy identification.

- The setup program should always include a progress indicator to show users how far along they are in the setup process. This progress indicator should show the total progress, not the progress for an individual step, since the progress of a single step is meaningless to most users and the sight of a progress indicator zipping back and forth can be distracting.

PART
V

- Don't require access to the distribution media just to exit the setup program. I have been bitten by this several times. I install a program and then, thinking that I am done, remove the installation disk and put it away. Sometime later I discover a silly dialog box saying something like *Installation Complete!* but when I click the OK button the setup program insists on having access to the distribution media. This is totally unnecessary and very annoying.

- If you do need to restart Windows during the installation process, be sure to ask for permission first.

- Your setup program should always give the user a chance to cancel the setup process before it's finished. It should keep track of files that have been copied and settings that have been made so that it can clean up a canceled installation and restore the user's system to its original state.

- If you localize your program to other languages, be sure to localize the setup program as well.

How to Find Problems

Simply put, the best way to find problems in your setup program is to make the setup program an early deliverable and apply for the Designed for Microsoft Windows logo. Getting the logo is the best way to make sure that your program integrates well with Windows. After all, that's what it's for. The more your program integrates with Windows, the more valuable the logo requirements become. If your setup program is complex, it might be worthwhile to apply for the logo just to get independent verification that your setup program does what it should. You should make sure the setup program satisfies the logo requirements even if you could care less about using the logo.

Part of the logo testing process is to pretest your setup program by using the VeriTest Install Analyzer, a freeware program that can be downloaded from the VeriTest Web site. Instructions on how to do this are included in the logo requirements. Install Analyzer first scans the registry and your hard disk, has you run your setup program, and then checks the system changes to make sure that they comply with the logo requirements. I recommend that you perform this process on a machine that has little software loaded, since the scanning process takes a while. (And, whatever you do, don't use this program as a model user interface.)

CHAPTER
33

TIP   Test your setup program by using the VeriTest Install Analyzer.

Aside from the logo tests, I recommend that you do the following:

● Specifically instruct your testers to test both the setup program and the uninstall.

● Test the setup program on all supported platforms, such as Windows 95, Windows 98, Windows NT 4.0, and Windows 2000.

● Test the setup program on a variety of computers.

● Test the setup program on computers that have never been installed to before and on computers that have been installed to before.

Related Chapters

● Chapter 1—Know the Standards.
Discusses the importance of knowing the standards, including the Designed for Microsoft Windows logo requirements.

● Chapter 6—Beginning vs. Advanced Users.
Presents tips on how to choose a default program configuration that is suitable for beginners without modification.

● Chapter 15—Keep It Simple.
Presents tips on reducing the complexity of software in general.

● Chapter 23—Unnecessary Message Boxes Are Pure Evil.
Discusses the different types of message boxes and tips on how to identify and eliminate unnecessary ones.

● Chapter 30—Check Your Error Messages.
Gives a list of useful items to check to make sure that your error messages are necessary, helpful, informative, and easy to understand.

● Chapter 32—Check Your Help System and Documentation.
Presents tips on creating the readme file contents.

PART
V

Recommended Reading

- Cooper, Alan. *About Face: The Essentials of User Interface Design*. Foster City, CA: IDG Books Worldwide, Inc., 1995.

  Chapter 32, "Installation, Configuration, and Personalization," does a good job at identifying setup problems. While much of the material is useful, I find that some of the suggested solutions are impractical, cumbersome, and overly verbose. Also, many of the details mentioned relate to problems with installing programs in Windows 3.1, which have been fixed in Windows 98 and Windows NT.

- Easter, Leslie E. *Bulletproof Installs: A Developer's Guide to Install Programs for Windows*. Upper Saddle River, NJ: Prentice Hall PTR, 1999.

  This book presents everything you need to know to make logo-compliant setup programs by using InstallShield5, going well beyond the documentation included with the product. I highly recommend it for anyone using InstallShield5 for advanced setup programs.

- Microsoft Corporation. The Designed for Microsoft Windows logo requirements.

  A significant portion of the logo requirements cover setup-related issues, including sections on installing and removing programs, installing and removing components, using the registry correctly, saving data to the best locations, and cooperating with administrators.

- Microsoft Corporation. *Designing for the User Experience*. Redmond, WA: Microsoft Press, 1999.

  See the chapter on integrating with the system for useful information about integrating with Windows, setup programs, and using the registry.

- Microsoft Corporation. *Programmer's Guide to Microsoft Windows 95*. Redmond, WA: Microsoft Press, 1995.

  Chapter 10, "Installing Applications," presents useful information about installing Windows programs.

- Microsoft Corporation. "Installing Applications." MSDN, Platform SDK, Windows Programming Guidelines, Programming Tips and Techniques.

Presents useful information about installing Windows programs. This is roughly the same information that is in *Programmer's Guide to Microsoft Windows 95.*

- Norman, Donald A. *The Design of Everyday Things.* New York, NY: Currency/Doubleday, 1990.

  Chapter 4, "Knowing What to Do," states that if something needs a label, the design has failed. Similarly, I believe a setup program that requires step-by-step instructions means that the setup user interface has failed. Your setup program shouldn't need step-by-step instructions.

- Richter, Jeffrey M. *Windows 3.1: A Developer's Guide.* New York, NY: M&T Books, 1992.

  This book explains everything you need to create a setup program for Windows 3.1—a product of a time when installing Windows programs was relatively easy. Writing your own setup program is no longer recommended.

CD-ROM Resources

The CD-ROM included with this book contains the following resources related to this chapter:

- The Designed for Microsoft Windows logo requirements.
- Dependency Assistant, a program that detects dependent files for both compiled Windows programs and Microsoft Visual Basic programs. This program helps you make sure that you are shipping all the files required by your program.

PART
V

34

Use System Colors

Microsoft Windows maintains 28 system colors for painting various parts of the display. These system colors include colors settings for window text, backgrounds, and borders; dialog box text and backgrounds; shading of 3-D objects; and even tooltip text and backgrounds. By allowing the user to change the system colors, Windows provides a significant amount of flexibility in determining the appearance of the display.

You need to make sure your program correctly uses the system colors. Using the system colors correctly helps you display your program the way the user wants it displayed. It is also necessary to satisfy the Designed for Microsoft Windows logo requirements. In this chapter, I'll explore the implications of using the system colors in your code and give some suggestions for ways to make sure that you have done it correctly.

Let's start by looking at a typical dialog box screen. The window on the following page is the Background tab of the Display Control Panel applet.

In the center of this tab is a computer monitor graphic that gives you a preview of your selections. Since this is a graphic of something other than a standard screen element, it's acceptable that the graphic is drawn using various shades of gray that are independent of the system colors. On the other hand, everything else in this tab should be drawn using system colors. To see if this tab is drawn correctly, try changing the system colors. If done right, the monitor graphic should always look the same but all other elements should change to reflect the new settings. Furthermore, the changes should happen immediately and completely. You shouldn't have to close and redisplay the dialog box to see the change.

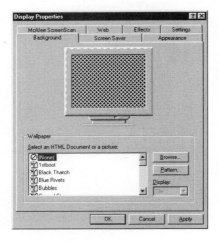

Using the system colors correctly has the following implications: You cannot assume that window backgrounds are always white, that dialog boxes are always light gray, or that text is always black. You cannot assume that 3-D shading is always done with white and dark gray. In short, you really can't assume anything about colors—you must always use the GetSysColor and GetSysColorBrush functions to create GDI objects for painting screen elements. On the other hand, graphics that are independent of the system objects, such as the monitor graphic example above, should not change with the system colors.

TIP

Do not assume that standard screen elements are drawn using shades of gray. Always use the GetSysColor and GetSysColorBrush functions to draw such screen elements.

Be careful when deciding which system colors to use. Select the system color that most closely matches the description of what you are using the color for. Do not make the selection based on the actual color itself on your system, since the actual colors have no significance. Note that many of the system colors come in sets, such as window text (COLOR_WINDOWTEXT) and window background color (COLOR_WINDOW). You should always use these sets of colors as a group and never mix and match them. For example, suppose you are creating a custom slider control that has text on the slider. Going through the descriptions of the system colors, it's clear that you should use the button color (COLOR_BTNFACE) for the slider itself. What color should you use for the text? Applying the above rule, the only choice is button text color (COLOR_BTNTEXT), since no other selection is guaranteed to be legible against the button color.

TIP Select the system colors based on their description, not their appearance. Do not mix and match system colors that are part of a set.

Windows sends the WM_SYSCOLORCHANGE message to all top-level windows when a change is made to a system color setting. These windows must forward the WM_SYSCOLORCHANGE message to the common controls (such as toolbars, list views, tree views, and tab controls), but forwarding to the basic controls (such as buttons and static text controls) is unnecessary. You also have to be careful how you manage GDI resources. Any bitmaps, brushes, and pens that use system colors that are kept in memory must be destroyed and re-created when your program receives the WM_SYSCOLORCHANGE message.

TIP Handle the WM_SYSCOLORCHANGE message so that color changes happen immediately and completely.

You cannot go wrong by using the system colors. You don't have to worry about preventing users from selecting ugly appearance schemes. Choosing an attractive appearance scheme is the user's problem, not yours. Using system colors correctly for standard screen elements is never a problem—using fixed colors that the user cannot change is.

When you cannot use the system colors for a screen element (which should be rare), do not use the system colors at all. For example, suppose you have a window that simply isn't legible if the background color isn't white. In this case, you can choose not to use the window background system color, but also make sure that you don't use the system colors for anything else in that window. Use black for text, and do not use the system color for

CHAPTER
34

window text. Why? Because the user can set the window text color to be white or a light color, making the text illegible on the white background.

Windows API Support

To help you draw rectangles and lines using the system colors, Windows provides the DrawEdge function. With this function you can select to draw any combination of raised or sunken inner or outer edges. You can also select which edges you want to draw, allowing you to draw individual lines. While it may take you awhile to figure out exactly which options to use, using this function eliminates having to create any GDI objects and guarantees that you are using the correct system colors.

Another useful API is the LoadImage function. If you call this function with the LR_LOADMAP3DCOLORS option, it transforms light gray to COLOR_3DLIGHT, gray to COLOR_3DFACE, and dark gray to COLOR_3DSHADOW. You can also use the LR_LOADTRANSPARENT option to let the parent window handle the system colors. You still have to handle the WM_SYSCOLORCHANGE to use these options, but this function helps make up for the fact that Windows currently doesn't have a transparent BitBlt function (although this function is coming with Microsoft Windows 2000).

How to Find Problems

To make sure your code is using the system colors correctly, the first step is to scan through your source files and look for suspicious code. Any color that is white, light gray, gray, dark gray, or black should be considered suspicious. While there are many functions that can result in color problems (such as the CreatePen, CreateSolidBrush, SelectObject, SetTextColor, and SetBkColor functions), I find it easier just to search for the RGB macro and the SelectStockObject function, since these are the primary ways of setting a nonsystem color. Searching for the SelectStockObject function is especially important, since this function is often used to incorrectly set pens and brushes, especially windows background brushes. When you find suspicious-looking code that is actually correct, I recommend labeling it with a comment for future reference, for example:

```
// Note: Nonsystem color
CPen grayPen(PS_SOLID,1,RGB(192,192,192));
```

The comment helps ensure that the code won't be accidentally "corrected" in the future.

However, the best way to find system color problems is to set your development computer's appearance scheme to one that doesn't use any of the default GDI colors, with the possible exception of black text. This includes just about all of the predefined Windows appearance schemes except for the Windows Standard scheme or any of the VGA schemes. My personal favorite is the Plum appearance scheme. Using such an appearance scheme immediately reveals any misuse of color.

TIP To help you find system color problems easily, always set your computer's Windows appearance scheme to one that doesn't use any of the default GDI colors.

The last test you should employ is changing the system colors while your program is running. On the Appearance tab of the Display Control Panel applet, change the colors while displaying various windows and dialog boxes. Again, the color changes should happen immediately and completely. If the changes aren't immediate, you need to handle the WM_SYSCOLORCHANGE message. If the changes aren't complete, most likely you need to re-create GDI resources using the new colors or forward the WM_SYSCOLORCHANGE message to child controls.

Recommended Reading

- Microsoft Corporation. The Designed for Microsoft Windows logo requirements, "Accessibility and User Interface."

  Provides the requirements for using system colors, for using the proper foreground/background system color combinations, and for ensuring compatibility with the High Contrast option.

- Petzold, Charles. *Programming Windows, Fifth Edition.* Redmond, WA: Microsoft Press, 1998.

  Chapter 9, "Child Window Controls," describes system colors, windows background brushes, and the WM_CTLCOLORBTN message.

CD-ROM Resources

The CD-ROM included with this book contains the following resource related to this chapter:

- The Designed for Microsoft Windows logo requirements.

CHAPTER 34

3 CHAPTER 5

Handle All
Video Modes

Microsoft Windows provides the user many display options through the Display Control Panel applet. The property sheet's Settings tab includes options for the number of colors, for video resolution, and for the size of the font used. Combined, these options give the user a wide variety of choices in how a program appears on the screen.

You need to make sure your program handles all video modes. After all, your users are going to be using various combinations of these settings, and they are not going to appreciate having to change video modes just to use your program. Given the number of display options available, however,

CHAPTER

35

this task is certainly easier said than done. For example, on my computer I have the following options:

- **Colors**   16 Color, 256 Color, High Color (16 bit), and True Color (32 bit)

- **Screen area**   640 × 480, 800 × 600, 1024 × 768, 1152 × 864, 1280 × 1024, and 1600 × 1200

- **Font size**   Small Fonts, Large Fonts, and Other (which allows a custom font size)

Not counting the Other font size category, these options provide for a total of 48 different video modes. Of course, it is simply not practical to develop and test all video combinations unless you plan on selling a whole lot of software. Instead, I recommend the following more realistic goals:

- Choose a minimum recommended video mode for your program.

- Make sure that your program fully supports that video mode or better.

- Provide "graceful degradation" so that your program is at least functional in modes less than the minimum recommended mode.

In the remainder of this chapter, I'll explore these goals and the steps necessary to achieve them.

Choosing a Minimum Recommended Video Mode

You should choose a minimum recommended video mode for your program. The standard minimum supported video mode for Windows 98 is 640 × 480 with 256 colors. If your interface is simple, you should support this mode. However, the more complex a user interface is, especially a complex MDI application, the less likely it is to work well in lower resolution modes. For example, try using Microsoft Visual C++ in 640 × 480 mode. It isn't pretty and it's fairly awkward, but it is functional. Had Visual C++ been designed to work well in 640 × 480 mode, its usability in higher resolution modes would have suffered greatly. Visual C++ simply has too much functionality to work well in this video mode, and forcing the interface design to accommodate the mode would have resulted in many unnecessary restrictions. As a result, the designers of Visual C++ chose 800 × 600 as its recommended minimum video mode.

PART

TIP   Choose a minimum recommended video mode for your program.

Your program should always support at least 256 colors. This is the hardest number of colors to support, since high color and true color modes don't use a palette. Users will probably use 16-color mode only if there isn't a suitable driver for their video hardware—a problem that is much more likely with Microsoft Windows NT than with Windows 98. Even if your program uses colors other than the 20 reserved system colors, it will most likely be functional in 16-color mode without any special programming effort.

Lastly, you should certainly support both large and small fonts in all video modes. While this sounds easy enough, there are some details you need to be aware of, as I'll describe shortly.

Typical Video Mode Problems

Generally, any element in your interface that is resolution-dependent is a source of video mode problems. Your goal is to make these interface elements resolution-independent, which in this context I define as looking and working well in all supported resolutions. The following sections present typical problems.

Graphics Problems

Bitmaps and icons are of fixed size, so they look different in different resolutions. For example, the following dialog box looks good in 800 × 600, Large Fonts:

35 CHAPTER

But it doesn't look so good in 800 × 600, Small Fonts:

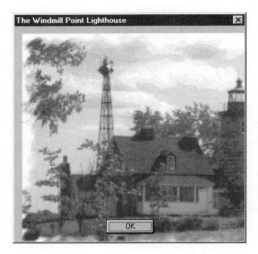

Here are a few suggestions for handling graphics in a resolution-independent manner.

Avoid using bitmaps and icons

Well, this is one way to avoid the problem. However, note that while bitmaps and icons are resolution-dependent, text (including symbols like Wingdings) and metafiles are not. A bitmap containing text is always going to give you more problems than straight text itself.

Leave plenty of space

Realizing that the origin of bitmaps and icons is stationary but that they grow or shrink on the right and bottom, you can make your graphics' resolution dependence less noticeable if you place them to the top and left of your windows and dialog boxes and leave plenty of space around them. This is at least one reason why icons in an About box are usually in the upper left corner. Placing a bitmap or icon in the lower right corner of a dialog box is asking for trouble.

Scale your graphics

Of course, if the above two approaches don't work, you should scale your graphics (by using the StretchBlt function instead of the BitBlt function) so that they size proportionally to your windows or dialog boxes. If scaling doesn't look good, you could create the graphics at run time by dynamically rendering them into bitmaps of the correct size. Alternatively, you could create different-sized graphics for different resolutions and select the best graphic at run time.

PART

V

Window Layout Problems

Since the number of windows you can display on the screen and the amount of information displayed in a window are resolution-dependent, handling the window layout of your program in a way that is reasonably resolution-independent is particularly challenging. The next two sections describe some typical problems.

MDI programs

The good news is that MDI programs allow users to lay out document windows as they choose. As long as your program gives the user plenty of flexibility in the screen layout and it has features to save and restore these settings, your users should be happy. The bad news is that MDI programs often have docking windows and complex toolbars and status bars that complicate matters.

MDI windows, especially docking windows, should be created with an initial size that scales proportionally with its contents. Typically, this means adjusting the window's size to the size of its text. For example, a window that docks on the left-hand side of an MDI program should set its width with code similar to the following:

```
windowSize.cx = max( 20 * fontSize.cx, appSize.cx / 4 );
```

This code makes the docking window wide enough to display 20 average characters (which, for the sake of argument, is the normal size of its contents) or at most a quarter of the width of the program window in lower resolution modes to prevent the docking window from taking up too much of the MDI client area.

The complexity of many MDI program toolbars means that the user should be able to create several independent toolbars and the toolbars should be movable and configurable. An application like Visual C++ would not be effective with a single static toolbar. On the other hand, Microsoft Outlook Express has a fairly simple toolbar, so a single static toolbar works fine.

The status bar should have at least one pane that stretches to fill any unused space (that is, have the SBPS_STRETCH attribute in MFC's CStatusBar class). Furthermore, you need to be careful with the text you place in the status bar. If you have lengthy text, you might need to have a short and long version of the text and display the long version only when you have the room. This is worth the extra effort, since the whole point of the status bar is to help the user and chopped-off text isn't especially helpful.

SDI programs

SDI programs suffer from basically the same problems as MDI programs but to a much smaller degree. Generally, SDI programs are much more resolution-independent than MDI programs. While you don't have to worry

CHAPTER 35

about laying out windows, you do have to worry about sizing splitter windows, as well as toolbars and status bars. You can use the suggested MDI solutions when needed.

Dialog Box Problems

Regardless of the minimum video mode you choose to recommend, you need to make sure that all your dialog boxes fit within at least 640 × 480 for your program to be minimally functional in this mode. A classic example of a dialog box that doesn't fit within 640 × 480 is the original Windows NT 4.0 Display Control Panel applet. (Note that this problem was fixed by a service pack.) It is so large that neither the title bar nor the OK, Cancel, and Apply buttons appear on the screen. This means that you can change your settings, but good luck actually making the change since you have to somehow click the OK button or the Apply button without seeing it or moving the cursor to it. (You can do it by using the keyboard but not the mouse.) Note that since the title bar is not visible, you cannot use the mouse to move the window to see the buttons. Also, it's unfortunate that the dialog box used to change video modes doesn't display in all video modes, as anyone who has ever tried to change the video mode in 640 × 480 in the original Windows NT 4.0 can attest.

TIP

Regardless of your minimum recommended video mode, make sure all dialog boxes fit within a 640 × 480 screen resolution.

However, there is a far more subtle problem with dialog boxes that happens a lot. Have you ever seen a dialog box that looked like this

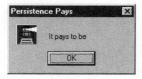

when it was supposed to look like this?

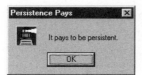

Why does this happen? The problem is the result of a conspiracy between fixed control sizes (in dialog box units in Visual C++ or twips in Microsoft Visual Basic) and static text controls. For Visual C++, dialog box units are the unit of measurement used in dialog box templates to determine the size of dialog boxes and their contents. The dialog box unit is based on the size of the text used in that dialog box, specifically one-fourth the width of the average character and one-eighth the height. While dialog box units are generally a good thing and make dialog boxes resolution-independent, they interact with static text controls in an interesting way. Note that Visual Basic has the same problem but with different units.

Static text controls are used to display text in a dialog box. They are multiline controls, so they display as much text as they can, perform a line break, and continue the text on the next line. But what if the control is only one line high? The line break still occurs, so the remainder of the text is displayed on the next, albeit invisible, line. This is why the whole last word dropped in the first of the two dialog boxes above.

But static text controls are sized using dialog box units, so how can this happen? The problem is that while the dialog box and its controls are scaled exactly according to the dialog box units, the specific text in a static control is not. Why? Because the specific text in a control does not necessarily scale exactly the same as average text. Some text might scale to the average, some text might be larger (for example, *WWW*), and some text might be smaller (for example, an ellipsis). So, although dialog box text can look good when you initially create the dialog box template, it might get chopped off in other video modes.

One final detail to remember is that dialog box units are not pixels—in fact, a dialog box unit is often about 1.5 pixels—so you should not try to achieve precise alignment in dialog box templates. For example, any effort to align two controls exactly one pixel apart is doomed to failure. It might look good in one video mode, but chances are it won't in other video modes.

Dialog Box Solutions

Given the fact that you cannot be sure that the static text in a dialog box will display properly in all video modes, and given the 48 possible video modes, what can you do to make sure your static text displays properly?

First, make sure your static text controls have plenty of room to grow. While you can try to make your static text controls exactly the right size, there is no downside to giving them plenty of room to expand. This practice helps you maintain the resources (especially if you often edit resources directly

CHAPTER 35

with a text editor, which I sometimes do), and it also helps if you localize your product.

Another solution is to develop your dialog boxes in the worst-case video mode. That way you can be confident that the static text will display correctly in all other video modes. Is there such a mode? I've found that using small fonts in any resolution seems to be the worst case. In fact, I've found that the font used in small-font mode is exactly the same in all resolutions, so the resulting dialog boxes display exactly the same as well. If you carefully lay out your dialog boxes while using small fonts and leave some extra space for good measure, you shouldn't encounter any chopped-off text in the large-font modes.

How to Find Problems

I've outlined the problems with handling video modes and have given suggestions on how to eliminate problems during development. However, there are no guarantees. To make sure that your program works in all modes, you need to do some testing.

Clearly, you cannot test your entire program in all 48 video mode combinations. Rather, a better approach is to test with a few strategic video modes, such as:

- **640 × 480, 256 Color**   The standard Windows driver, common mode for old hardware

- **800 × 600, 256 Color**   The target video mode for Windows 98, common mode for old hardware

- **Your program's minimum recommended video mode, Small fonts**   The target video mode for your program

- **Your program's minimum recommended video mode, Large fonts**   The target video mode for your program

PART

V

- **1024 × 768, 16-bit Color, Small fonts** Common mode for new hardware

- **1024 × 768, 32-bit Color, Large fonts** Common mode for new hardware

These six video modes should cover most of the bases. If your program has a simple interface (with no windows that need placement and sizing), if you developed using small fonts, and if you've made an effort to give all static text controls plenty of room to grow, you can probably get by with just doing the two minimum recommended video tests and 640 × 480 to make sure all the dialog boxes can be displayed in this mode. Note that the easiest way to make sure all dialog boxes fit in 640 × 480 is to view them as resources in Visual C++. You don't have to view them from the running program unless you change dialog box sizes during run time.

Lastly, you need to make sure that your program handles video mode changes while it is running. Typically, this means handling the WM_DISPLAYCHANGE message by recalculating object sizes, especially the average text size, and destroying any in-memory GDI resources that are resolution dependent, such as fonts and bitmaps, so that your program will re-create them using the correct metrics. Your program should be able to appear and function correctly after a display resolution change. Ideally, after a video mode change your program should look as if it was started in that video mode.

TIP Handle the WM_DISPLAYCHANGE message.

Recommended Reading

- Thompson, Nigel. *Animation Techniques in Win32*. Redmond, WA: Microsoft Press, 1995.

  Despite its title, this book is an excellent resource for basic Windows graphics information, even if you never plan on doing any animation. The first three chapters include an excellent presentation on device-dependent bitmaps (DDBs), device-independent bitmaps (DIBs), video modes, colors, and palettes.

35
CHAPTER

CD-ROM Resources

The CD-ROM included with this book contains the following resources related to this chapter:

- Resource Assistant, a utility that checks the resources in an executable, and Resource Assistant for VB, a utility that checks the resources in a Visual Basic program. Both programs verify that dialog boxes will fit on the screen in all video modes, static text controls and buttons (command buttons, radio buttons, and check boxes) are large enough to display their text in all video modes, the tab order of the controls has been set, the tab stop and group properties of the controls have been set, and control access keys are unique. Resource Assistant also extracts all resource strings so that you can check for spelling errors, and Resource Assistant for VB does the same for string resources, forms, and menus.

CHAPTER

36

Learn How to Play
QA Gefahren

Perhaps the most important
and challenging part of the QA process is dealing with the
feedback you receive. That feedback will come from all sorts
of people with all sorts of backgrounds, and some of it will be helpful and
some of it won't. In this chapter, I'll focus on dealing with feedback that
appears not to be good. Of course, handling good feedback is easy. The
suggestion makes sense and will improve the program; you say, "What a
great idea," and then act on that feedback. But a lot of feedback isn't so
good. In fact, some of it borders on the bizarre, and sometimes the person making the suggestion is very insistent. Worse yet, the person might
be your customer or manager, so they aren't going to go away.

I've noticed that most bad feedback has something in common. The
tester, QA person, customer, user, or manager—for simplicity, from now
on I'll generally refer only to testers—is not reporting a problem, per se,
but a change that the person would like to see made to the program. For
example, instead of reporting that it's difficult to accomplish a particular

task, the tester might suggest adding various menu items and dialog boxes without clearly stating what he wants to accomplish. I like to call this phenomenon QA Gefahren. (*Gefahren* is German for dangers, perils, hazards, risks, or jeopardy.) When you're playing QA Gefahren, instead of being given an answer and trying to figure out the question, you're given a solution to a problem (and often a bad solution) and you need to figure out what the problem is.

Once I discovered this phenomenon, my next major discovery was how often it happens, which is fairly frequently. In fact, with some testers, it happens the majority of the time. The first reason for this is that testers know what they like and don't like, but they are not software engineers or designers. They come up with a solution to a problem (perhaps without even realizing exactly what the problem is), but they aren't fully aware of the solution's drawbacks or implications for the system as a whole. The second reason is that testers want to be helpful, and they feel that providing feedback in the form of a solution is more helpful. Although this might be true in other fields, in software it is not. The saying "bring me solutions, not problems" is counter-productive in software testing.

How to Play the Game

The first step in playing QA Gefahren is realizing that you are playing it in the first place. A tester presents a bad solution to an unstated problem, and the next thing you know you're in a heated discussion on the pros and cons of a clearly bad idea. Everything you do to talk the tester out of this bad idea seems fruitless. You're even tempted to capitulate just so that you can talk about something else. Sound familiar?

Understanding QA Gefahren is especially important when dealing with customers. The motto "the customer is always right" can be bad advice in software development. A better motto for software development might be "the customer always knows what he wants but doesn't necessarily have a clue how to implement it." After all, if they knew how to do it themselves, they probably wouldn't have hired you. I've seen engineers spend a great deal of time implementing solutions that they knew were bad after doing little to try to talk the customer out of it. "Well, they're the customer, and they're paying for it" is usually the response.

However, once you understand that you're playing QA Gefahren, you will never let yourself get put in this position. How? By always asking the Magic Question.

PART
V

Asking the Magic Question

To prevent the anguish of wasting time debating the merits of an obviously bad solution, you should try to immediately shift the focus of the discussion away from the solution and to the problem. Once you've done that, a good solution is usually not far away. You make this shift by asking the Magic Question: "What problem in the program would this solution solve?"

> **TIP**
>
> When you receive feedback in the form of a solution that doesn't seem to make sense, always ask: "What problem in the program would this solution solve?"

The phrasing of the Magic Question is important because it allows you to shift the focus in a diplomatic way. Once you've asked the Magic Question, you and the tester should now be focused on the problem in a way that allows the tester to fully express his ideas. You are listening to the tester, and you are not being insulting or patronizing. Note that a response such as "what a stupid idea" doesn't have quite the same effect.

During the QA process, another important step is to make sure that any written feedback is clearly focused on reporting problems. Your problem report form should include specific sections, such as "Describe the Problem." Give instructions on how to report feedback, and clearly indicate that you are more interested in problems than solutions.

Let's Play a Round

For a bit of practice, let's play a round:

Tester: I really think the Output Window should use a 6-point font by default.

You: Why? A 6-point font is completely illegible.

Tester: Trust me, it would make the product much better.

Right now, an alarm should sound off in your head. You now know that you are playing QA Gefahren. You realize that the tester has a problem with the program and has presented you with a poor solution to the problem. Rather than wasting time debating the merits of 6-point fonts, you should immediately shift the focus away from the proposed solution to the actual problem. Ask the Magic Question!

You: What problem in the program would this solution solve?

Tester: Well, if I select the verbose option and display a summary in the Output Window, much of the information gets chopped off on the bottom. I then have to resize the window to see what I want. With a smaller font, I can see everything without resizing.

You: What if the Output Window had a vertical scroll bar so that information wouldn't get chopped off?

Tester: I thought of that, but another problem is that if I resize the window to be narrower than the default size, text would still get chopped off on the right unless we also had a horizontal scroll bar, which I definitely don't want.

You: What if the contents of the Output Window were to use a dynamic layout so that it would take advantage of whatever space is available when the window is resized? This approach only requires a vertical scroll bar.

Tester: Well, I guess that would work...

This example round also reveals another trick: you have to be persistent. When a tester decides to play QA Gefahren, he has already decided what the solution is. Your initial counter-solutions usually will not get a warm reception. And the tester might have several problems that he's trying to solve at once with the proposed solution, so you might have to make several attempts before you come up with something acceptable.

Believe it or not, this example is loosely based on an actual incident. Early testers of the original Macintosh wanted to have really small fonts so that they could get more information on the screen.

And Now for the Prizes

Once you become an advanced player of QA Gefahren, you will soon have a revelation. You will realize that almost all user feedback is useful in some way. You will realize that much of the bizarre feedback you readily dismissed in the past actually had some hidden insight waiting to be revealed. You realize that testers often have trouble presenting their ideas and that you need to work with them to help them express what they want to say. The final result of all this is better software, which is the grand prize when playing QA Gefahren.

PART

Related Chapters

- Chapter 8—Users Aren't Designers.

  Presents the concept that users aren't designers and that their feedback needs to be carefully interpreted. Unlike this chapter, Chapter 8 is more focused on understanding how to work with users during the design process.

Recommended Reading

- Borenstein, Nathaniel S. *Programming As If People Mattered*. Princeton, NJ: Princeton University Press, 1991.

  Chapter 13, "Listen to Your Users, but Ignore What They Say," states "There is never a shortage of suggestions and complaints from the people who use software. These complaints often come from people who are quite sure they know not only what the problem is, but how it should be fixed as well…. The world is full, accordingly, of bad user interfaces that were essentially designed (or redesigned) by nontechnical people with no real idea of what they were doing…."

- Capucciati, Maria R. "Putting Your Best Face Forward: Designing an Effective User Interface." *Microsoft Systems Journal*, February 1993.

  "User feedback should be analyzed for trends and common threads rather than taken at face value. Sometimes the best feedback comes not from users, but from looking at other products and talking with people who have a similar vision for the application."

36 CHAPTER

Keep Looking
for Improvements

User interface work is never done. After all, a program is never finished—it's just due. No matter how good your user interface is, you can always make it better. Even if your program is a huge success, there is always room for improvement. Creating great user interfaces is hard work and that means constant improvement.

Plan for the Next Release Now

If you want to release software in a reasonable time frame, you can't do everything in the first release. You will be exposed to all kinds of ideas and suggestions in the later stages of the development process and once the program is released. The sources of this information include the features and improvements you were not able to do before release, feedback from actual users, feedback from technical support, and feedback from product reviews. Start to gather this valuable information as early as you can, and plan for the next release now.

Get Feedback and Take It Seriously

You should actively try to get the best feedback you can. Try to talk to real users. Talk to your technical support team, and ask them to create a list of the most common problems and complaints. You can get feedback from other sources, such as user requests, newsgroups, and user surveys. If the feedback doesn't make sense, assume that either you don't fully understand it or that the person has trouble expressing his ideas. Don't be afraid to ask questions or discuss alternative approaches.

Take the feedback seriously and look for patterns. One user complaining about a feature doesn't necessarily imply that the feature is flawed. Research has shown that there is a 97 percent chance that at least one user will complain about every feature in a program, no matter how good it is. (Just kidding—there is no such research, but it is probably true.) But receiving several complaints about a feature is a clear sign of a problem. If you think a task is easy to do, yet users find it difficult, they are right and you are wrong. Always. Don't dismiss this feedback or try to defend the feature—just fix it.

Avoid the Second-System Effect

The problem of the *second-system effect* is best described by Frederick Brooks, who coined the term. He said, "An architect's first work is apt to be spare and clean. He knows he doesn't know what he's doing, so he does it carefully and with great restraint. As he designs the first work, frill after frill, embellishment after embellishment occur to him. These get stored away to be used 'next time.' Sooner or later the first system is finished, and the architect, with firm confidence and a demonstrated mastery of that class of systems, is ready to build a second system. This second is the most dangerous system a man ever designs. The general tendency is to over-design the second system, using all the ideas and frills that were cautiously sidetracked on the first one. The result, as Ovid says, is a 'big pile.'"

Use Restraint

Can the second-system effect be avoided? Ideally, you want to add power and functionality to your next release, but you also want to make the features easier to use. You can accomplish this goal by using more elegant user interface solutions, such as:

● Making apparently dissimilar features similar, as was done with the Microsoft Windows Shell Namespace used by Windows Explorer.

The Shell Namespace makes Control Panel, the Recycle Bin, Briefcase, and even Microsoft Internet Explorer look like files and folders.

- Making features more visible and easier to find.
- Using drag-and-drop functionality and other forms of direct manipulation.
- Fixing or removing problematic features.
- Simplifying interaction by using appropriate defaults.
- Eliminating unnecessary dialog boxes and message boxes.
- Making the program faster.
- Providing better system integration.
- Simplifying everything you can.

Another common problem with lack of restraint is to misuse new technology. Never add new user interface technology just because you can. Always have a reason.

I find it interesting to compare current versions of programs to previous versions. For example, in comparing Microsoft Word 97 to Word Version 6.0 (from 1993), I find the current version much more attractive and easier to use. The appearance is visually much cleaner. Although the current version is much more powerful, the screen layout and menu structure isn't more complicated. Unfortunately, this isn't always the case. You should try to make your user interfaces simpler over time, not more complex.

While it is possible to improve your program and avoid the second-system effect, don't expect it to be easy. You'll have to make many difficult trade-offs.

Don't Develop an Attitude

I've had many encounters with attitude, but I'll recount just one. I was porting a Windows utility I wrote to Apple Macintosh. I complained to the Macintosh expert I was working with (who at the time was wearing the traditional Mac programmer "I don't do Windoze" garb) that TeachText (the Macintosh equivalent to NotePad) didn't support the Delete key to delete text. He explained to me (apparently seriously) that using the Delete key was a Windows thing, not a Mac thing, and that the way to delete text on the Mac was to select the text with the mouse and use the Cut command or use the Backspace key. He went on to say that it was my mistake for being a Windows user and having incorrect expectations about what the Mac should do. Even though the Delete key is found on every modern

577

Macintosh keyboard (although Backspace is labeled "Delete" and Delete is labeled "Del"), it was apparently incorrect for me to expect that it would actually work. Now that's attitude!

The following are telltale signs of having an attitude:

- You think your competitors are idiots.

- You think your customers are idiots.

- You think your managers and your sales and marketing staff are idiots.

- You think your product is much better than the competition's.

- You think your product is good enough because it does the job.

The problem with such attitudes isn't that they are annoying but that they are destructive. They impair your judgment and prevent you from seeing the obvious. They prevent you from learning from others. They make you believe you are ahead of the competition when you may be behind. Worst of all, they prevent you from improving your software.

No matter how good your program is, always keep looking for improvements. Never be satisfied.

Recommended Reading

- Brooks, Frederick P., Jr. *The Mythical Man-Month*. Reading, MA: Addison-Wesley Publishing Company, 1975.

  Chapter 5, "The Second-System Effect," describes the importance of self-discipline in design and why the second system is especially dangerous. The specific examples given are terribly dated (from the IBM 360 era), but the principle is timeless.

- Tognazzini, Bruce. *Tog on Interface*. Reading, MA: Addison-Wesley Publishing Company, Inc., 1992.

  Chapter 28, "More Short Subjects," presents a letter from a reader of *Apple Directions* discussing some attitude problems common to programmers and how having an attitude can adversely affect usability.

Appendix

List of Tips

1. You should review the Designed for Microsoft Windows logo requirements, even if you could care less about obtaining the logo.

2. Conforming to the standards makes your job easier, not harder.

3. Violate the standards to go forward, not backward.

4. Use the same term to describe the same thing. Using different terms for items that have only subtle differences will confuse users.

5. A good name now is usually better than a perfect name later.

6. The responsibility for choosing names includes the responsibility for choosing the names in a timely manner.

7. Avoid choosing joke names.

8. Effective user interface style guidelines make your job easier, not harder.

9. Having user interface style guidelines doesn't mean that you can stop thinking.

10. User interface style guidelines supplement, not replace, the standards.

11. When appropriate, include the rationale in a guideline.

12. Use resource templates to create consistent-looking resources.

13. Think like a user instead of a programmer. Trying to understand why you feel the way you do about a program will help you improve your own programs.

14. Details matter! The fact that a program's problems are minor makes them no less irritating.

15. Good programs go out of their way to help users get their work done.

16. Menu bars are an excellent teaching tool.

17. Keep menus stable. Disable, don't remove, invalid menu choices.

18. Don't use fixed user modes. Provide enough flexibility and configurability so that users can create their own modes.

19. Make your program's default configuration very simple. Let users grow into the program at their own pace.

20. Applications are usually run maximized. Design applications primarily for advanced users.

21. Utilities need to work in a small screen space. Utilities are almost never run maximized. Design utilities primarily for beginning users.

22. SDI programs that manipulate actual documents must support running multiple instances.

23. Users are not you. You need to be an advocate for the user by putting the user's goals ahead of your goals.

24. Establish the target user to help you make design decisions.

25. Always identify a target user, even if your program will be used by a wide range of users.

26. Avoid designing user interfaces based on speculation of the user's needs and goals. Work from direct knowledge whenever possible.

27. Use specific target user information to make decisions about design details.

28. Having users evaluate a design through a prototype is much harder than it appears.

29. It is hard for a user to be as critical of a prototype user interface as of a real user interface.

30. Marketers aren't users.

31. While you should always listen to your users, you should not incorporate their suggestions without question. There is a difference between what users say they want and what users actually want.

32. Establish a shared product vision to make product direction and design decisions.

33. Rapid prototyping and careful design are mutually exclusive design techniques.

34. User-centered design shouldn't result in user-designed software.

35. Be an advocate for the user. Put the user's goals ahead of your goals.

36. Looking at the user interface from the user's point of view is the first step in creating great user interfaces.

37. There is more to making a feature visible than displaying it visually on the screen. The user has to be able to understand it.

38. Intuitive = Visible + Consistent − Standards

39. Make an extra effort to ensure that essential features are visible.

40. Visibility is the ultimate goal of a graphical user interface.

41. A user interface that is too visible draws attention to itself and breaks the user's focus.

42. Use a metaphor only if it is simple and helps the user accomplish the task without constraining the user to the real-world limitations of the metaphor.

43. Unnecessary dialog boxes and message boxes break the user's flow because the user is no longer in control of the program. Rather, the program is controlling the user.

44. Your job as a user interface designer is to make the translation from tasks to program features easy.

45. The ultimate user interface design goal is to create visible tasks.

46. The most invisible form of navigation is when the user has to access several unrelated windows to perform a task. Try to make the connection between such windows visible.

47. Users understand affordance through real-world knowledge, including knowledge of human anatomy, metaphors, and experience with everyday objects.

48. The need for a label indicates that a mapping isn't natural.

49. Good constraints eliminate invalid choices while making the remaining valid choices easier to use.

50. Conceptual models happen whether or not you intentionally design them.

51. Choose the least obtrusive feedback interface that does the job.

52. The goal behind learning from the Web isn't to be trendy but to make software easier to use.

53. Consider using HTML documents even if the document looks nothing like a Web page. They are flexible, powerful, and easy to program.

54. Users need to be able to predict where links will lead and differentiate one link from another.

55. Pretend that your command buttons are hyperlinks, and try to predict where they will take you.

56. Beginning users don't understand modal windows.

57. Consider single-clicking when selection isn't necessary, but make sure that there is a clear visual distinction between single-clickable objects and double-clickable objects.

58. Consider embedding commands directly in the context where they are needed. If you do, use the menu bar for universal commands that apply in most contexts.

59. Don't use multiple windows when a single window will do. Try to have users perform a single task in a single window.

60. Try to use more white backgrounds and fewer 3-D effects to give your windows a cleaner appearance.

61. The more time and effort you spend creating a prototype, the harder it is to change—defeating the very purpose of the prototype.

62. If you don't throw it away, it isn't a prototype.

63. Programming is programming, not matter what you call it.

64. Users know that a prototype user interface isn't a real user interface, so they use it and evaluate it differently. It is harder for a user to be critical of a prototype user interface than of a real user interface.

65. You need to interpret a prototype by creating a design document.

66. Avoid dangerous vaporware. Never prototype to give someone the impression that a program is further along than it actually is. Never prototype to make marketing demos. Prototypes are for design, not for marketing.

67. Use prototyping by example to design new user interfaces by modeling them after appropriate user interface elements of existing programs.

68. Paper and pencil are the most powerful, efficient design tools available. Use paper prototypes to create new designs.

69. Use scenarios to prototype specific tasks.

70. Use resource prototypes to create nonfunctional prototype programs without writing any code.

71. Prefer nonfunctional prototypes. Avoid writing prototype code.

72. If you must create a functional prototype, try to implement as little functionality as you can. Create either a horizontal or vertical prototype and establish a strict time limit.

73. Simplicity is the most important quality of good user interface design. Much of the user interface development process involves simplifying the interface in some way.

74. Windows typically allows you to implement a user interface feature in several different ways. Often the difference between a simple user interface and a complex one lies in making the right choices among these options.

75. A convertible dialog box is a good choice when either the modal or modeless state makes sense. It lets the user decide.

76. Context menus aren't visible, making them a poor choice for programs that are targeted at beginning users.

77. Static lines and text are a good alternative to group boxes because they don't take up as much space and don't add to the clutter.

78. Test the program using a trackball. All interactions seem more complex when using a trackball.

79. Make simple things easy, complex things possible.

80. Standard controls have a significant advantage over custom controls simply because they are standard. Users already know how they work.

81. Don't use custom controls just because you can. Always have a reason.

82. Choose custom controls that look and behave like standard controls. Ideally, users should have no clue that they are using a custom control.

83. Direct manipulation makes using software fun. It is the ultimate form of interactivity.

84. Direct manipulation usually involves using a mouse, but sometimes using a mouse feels indirect. The user's subjective feel of the manipulation is more important than the specific input device used.

85. Before you create a new dialog box, ask yourself whether you can create a way to perform the action directly.

86. A dialog box whose appearance mimics the window it supports can often be eliminated by direct manipulation.

87. You should indicate that an object can be manipulated by changing the cursor.

88. Prevent accidental manipulation. Avoid ambiguous manipulations, and limit the number of objects that can be manipulated.

89. A good default doesn't have to be right all the time.

90. Give the default value that is most likely to be right, given how the setting is used.

91. Defaults should change only as a result of user input.

92. Use placeholders to make it clear that a value hasn't been set.

93. Provide defaults based on the user's actual behavior.

94. Make carefully selected features visible by turning them on by default when the program is first installed.

95. Consider automatically saving file changes by default. Provide an Abandon All Changes command to allow users to revert to the original document.

96. Consider safety when selecting default values. Never use a default value that would surprise the user.

97. Dismissing an unchanged dialog box with the OK button should have the same effect as dismissing it with the Cancel button.

98. Make sure that an activity that has significant consequences requires explicit selection from the user. Disastrous actions should never result from the default.

99. Property sheets should always reflect the actual state of an object.

100. While having more options makes a program more configurable, it also makes it harder to configure. Avoid providing options that aren't useful.

101. Provide configurability to make your program accessible to all users.

102. Prefer implicit settings (that is, direct manipulation with persistence) to explicit settings (that is, property sheets or dialog boxes) whenever possible.

103. Simple configurations are better than powerful ones.

104. Always implement the Apply button in property sheets.

105. Consider providing a Restore Original Settings command to return the program to a configuration that is known to work.

106. Make multilevel configurations visible. Put related configurations in a single property sheet.

107. If you set rules for using an interface, you need to explain them.

108. Previews help users make choices and verify results by giving immediate visual feedback before the user makes a selection.

109. The type of preview to use depends upon how much accuracy you need to effectively indicate the results of a selection. Use the simplest preview type that does the job.

110. Preview animations with animation.

111. Don't explain a feature—show it with a preview.

112. Tooltips lose their value if there are too many of them.

113. Make your tooltip text informative yet brief. Avoid stating the obvious.

114. Aim tooltip text at intermediate to advanced users.

115. Dialog boxes break the user's flow.

116. The psychological effort to use a dialog box is probably more significant than the physical effort.

117. Having to constantly access a dialog box to perform a routine command is a sign of an unnecessary dialog box.

118. Consider combining several related dialog boxes into a single dialog box.

119. Create objects using appropriate defaults to free the user from having to set properties.

120. Use the toolbar to cancel toolbar commands.

121. Consider using the status bar to eliminate notification message boxes.

122. Consider using control enabling and animation to eliminate notification message boxes.

123. Consider using flash boxes to provide feedback that isn't essential for the user to know.

124. Consider providing an undo command to eliminate confirmations.

125. Don't confirm saving changes unless the user actually made changes.

126. Prevent invalid input to eliminate error messages.

127. If you fix problems automatically, make it obvious.

128. Use automatic features to help the user, but leave the user in control.

129. A program should restore itself to the state it was in when last quit.

130. Allow the user to fully customize automatic features and include the ability to turn them off.

131. Use automatic features to help the user, but leave the user in control.

132. The best programs go out of their way to help users get their work done.

133. Assign the initial input focus to the control that the user is most likely to interact with first.

134. Use the Rebase and Bind utilities to reduce your program's load time.

135. Let Windows automatically optimize drawing by not calling the UpdateWindow function unless really necessary.

136. Optimize drawing by passing the InvalidateRect function an invalid rectangle whenever possible. Try to invalidate the smallest area possible.

137. Avoid erasing the background unless really necessary.

138. Use the CS_HREDRAW and CS_VREDRAW styles only when necessary.

139. Consider rendering to a bitmap instead of rendering directly to the screen.

140. Improve drawing and scrolling performance by redrawing only the invalid area.

141. The programmer is primarily responsible for software quality.

142. The key to successful programmer testing is to change your perspective and use your program like a user.

143. As a programmer, you can find user interface problems that are impossible for other testers to find.

144. Evaluate the usability of your program with your team members by using a short list of high-level design principles.

145. Give a lot of demos to obtain valuable feedback, especially early in the development process.

146. Users aren't designers, but they can tell you if a design has usability problems.

147. User testing is the most realistic indicator of how users will react to your program. You have to watch real users struggle to use your program.

148. Some user testing is better than none. Don't feel guilty for using user techniques that are less than ideal.

149. Focus user testing on learnability. If users find the program easy to learn, chances are they will find it efficient, not error-prone, and enjoyable as well.

150. Testing with beginning users is more likely to reveal problems.

151. Ask the test user to think out loud, that is, to verbalize all thoughts while performing a task.

152. Avoid giving the test user assistance during the test. Encourage the test user to ask any questions—you just won't be able to answer them.

153. During the test, keep your eyes and ears open and your mouth shut.

154. Users want to be nice, so you can't always take what they say literally.

155. It can be a humiliating experience to watch someone trash your work. Consider having someone else conduct the user testing for your user interfaces.

156. Lighten up! Test users are doing you a big favor when they find problems in your user interfaces.

157. Your other team members want to be involved early in the development process.

158. Make sure that the other team members understand that their input is wanted.

159. Use graphic designers to improve your program's functional visibility and its visual appeal.

160. Technical writers are in a unique position to find user interface problems.

161. Don't document problems; fix them.

162. For dialog boxes with nondestructive actions, assign the default button to the command the user is most likely to choose.

163. For dialog boxes with destructive actions, assign the default button so that the user can make any single mistake without serious consequences.

164. For dialog boxes with catastrophic actions, assign the default button so that the user has to make two explicit mistakes in a row before there are serious consequences.

165. Assign the initial input focus to the control that the user is most likely to interact with first.

166. Never use assertions or TRACE statements as a substitute for error messages.

167. Don't use error messages as a substitute for assertions or TRACE statements.

168. Make the error message as specific as possible. There is no harm in eliminating unimportant options, but never eliminate important ones.

169. If an error can occur as the result of several conditions, provide a specific error message for each condition.

170.   Use the Windows Troubleshooters for solutions to system problems.

171.   Use progressive disclosure for complex error messages.

172.   Make sure that the string parameters to error message text constructed at run time aren't empty.

173.   For internationalization, always put the error message strings in string resources, and construct strings at run time using FormatMessage.

174.   Keep the recommended solutions practical. Never propose a solution that isn't likely to be right.

175.   If your program has a toolbar, provide direct printing.

176.   Make your print previews interactive when possible.

177.   You can find many types of printing problems by checking for incorrect assumptions in your printing source code.

178.   Use print previews to find many types of printing errors.

179.   Help should be helpful.

180.   Prefer task-oriented Help.

181.   Having exactly the same help online and in the printed documentation isn't helpful.

182.   The readme file is your last defense against technical support calls.

183.   Avoid restarting Windows during an installation.

184.   Reduce Start menu clutter by not adding installation, documentation, and technical support–related files to the Start menu.

185.   Reduce desktop clutter by not adding icons to the desktop, Quick Launch bar, or taskbar System Tray without asking permission.

186.   The best setup programs go out of their way to help the user control his system.

187.   Don't overexpose the readme file during the setup process.

188.   Avoid presenting unnecessary setup options.

189.   Never ask the user a question unless you really want to know the answer.

190.   All user choices should result in valid installations. Never offer the user a choice that could lead to a bad installation.

191.   Consider eliminating the need for installation of CD-ROM-based programs.

192.   If a setting requires the distribution media or is required for the program to run, make it part of the setup. Otherwise, make it part of the program itself.

193.   Test your setup program by using the VeriTest Install Analyzer.

194. Do not assume that standard screen elements are drawn using shades of gray. Always use the GetSysColor and GetSysColorBrush functions to draw such screen elements.

195. Select the system colors based on their description, not their appearance. Do not mix and match system colors that are part of a set.

196. Handle the WM_SYSCOLORCHANGE message so that color changes happen immediately and completely.

197. To help you find system color problems easily, always set your computer's Windows appearance scheme to one that doesn't use any of the default GDI colors.

198. Choose a minimum recommended video mode for your program.

199. Regardless of your minimum recommended video mode, make sure all dialog boxes fit within a 640 × 480 screen resolution.

200. Always give your static text controls room to grow to avoid resolution-dependent problems.

201. Always develop dialog boxes while using small fonts to eliminate static text control size problems.

202. Handle the WM_DISPLAYCHANGE message.

203. When you receive feedback in the form of a solution that doesn't seem to make sense, always ask: "What problem in the program would this solution solve?"

Summary of CD-ROM Resources

The CD-ROM that accompanies this book contains several resources to help you create excellent user interfaces. Chapter 1, "Know the Standards," encourages you to know, understand, and apply the standards for Microsoft Windows user interface design, so included on the CD-ROM is an electronic version of the *Microsoft Manual of Style for Technical Publications, Second Edition* (Microsoft Press, 1998), as well as the Designed for Microsoft Windows logo requirements. The online versions make this valuable information available with a few mouse clicks. While knowing the standards is crucial, there is enough flexibility within the standards to create an endless variety of user interface designs. Chapter 4, "Establish a Consistent User Interface Style," encourages you to create and apply companywide or projectwide user interface style guidelines to give your software a consistent appearance and behavior. The CD-ROM includes a copy of the sample user interface guidelines presented in that chapter (in Microsoft Word format) as well as sample resource templates.

In Part III, "Design Concepts," and Part IV, "Design Details," I make many suggestions on how to improve the usability of your programs. Most of these suggestions can be implemented directly using the Windows API or MFC, but a few of them can't. Since I know you're in a hurry and don't want to write any more code than you have to, I've created the DevUI MFC Extension library to help you get going. The full source code is included on the CD-ROM so that you can adapt this code to suit your user interface needs.

Part V, "Testing and QA," presents many user interface details to check during testing. Good user interfaces require a significant amount of testing and, although many aspects of testing user interfaces require hard manual labor, many common user interface mistakes can be detected automatically by processing a program's resource information. I have included three shareware programs that check for common user interface mistakes and setup problems. They should help make your interface testing much more efficient.

The DevUI MFC Extension Classes

- The McMessageBox function that provides a message box with options for customizable button text, customizable icons, HTML tagging in the text, an option to not display the message box in the future, and an automatic time-out.

- The McDetailsBox function that provides a message box with options for a Details button to show additional information, customizable button text, customizable icons, HTML tagging in the text, an option to not display the message box in the future, and an automatic time-out.

- The McFlashBox function that provides a flash box (which is a message box without buttons that goes away automatically) with options for customizable icons and HTML tagging in the text. The McFlashBoxModeless function does the same using a modeless dialog box so that it can be displayed while other processing continues.

- The CMcPropertySheet class to provide the ability to customize property sheet buttons.

- The CMcMRUList class to help manage MRU lists.

- The McShowZoomRect function to help show the relationship between a user action and its effect.

- The CMcColor class for colors, including functions to convert from RGB values to HSL values (hue, saturation, and luminosity) and back. Converting to HSL values is essential for color manipulation.

- The CMcWindowPlacement class to help save and restore window sizes and locations.

- The CMcTooltip class to help you create any kind of tooltip with any contents or format.

- The CMcProgressDialog class to display a progress dialog box.

- The CMcStatusBarProgress class to display progress on the status bar.

- The McGetProfileStringList and McSetProfileStringList functions to get and set string lists to help manage MRU lists.

Shareware Programs

- **Resource Assistant** A utility that checks the resources in an executable. It verifies that dialog boxes will fit on the screen in all video modes, static text controls and buttons (command buttons, radio buttons, and check boxes) are large enough to display their text in all video modes, the tab order of the controls has been set, the tab stop and group properties of the controls have been set, and control access keys are unique. It also extracts all resource strings so that you can check for spelling errors.

- **Resource Assistant for VB** A utility that checks the resources in a Microsoft Visual Basic program. It verifies that dialog boxes will fit on the screen in all video modes, static text controls and buttons (command buttons, radio buttons, and check boxes) are large enough to display their text in all video modes, the tab order of the controls has been set, the tab stop and group properties of the controls have been set, and control access keys are unique. It also extracts resource, form, and menu strings so that you can check for spelling errors.

- **Dependency Assistant** A utility that detects dependent files for both compiled Windows programs and Microsoft Visual Basic programs. This utility helps you make sure that you are shipping all the files required by your program.

Index

Numbers and Symbols

B

C

Index

F

F1 key, getting help with, 145
feedback
  with flash boxes, 370
  testing user interfaces for use of, 418
  using in programs, 186–89
  visual in good user interfaces, 139–42
feedback interfaces, types of, 187–89
feedback techniques, 187–89
filenames, editing in Windows Explorer, 92
files, saving by default, 304–5
Find command, notification message boxes
  with, 369
Find dialog box, animation in, 140–41
Find in Files toolbar button in Visual C++,
  technique that eliminates need for
  dialog box, 363
Find utility, techniques for eliminating
  repetitive tasks in, 387
fixed control sizes vs. static text controls,
  563
flashing, eliminating to improve drawing
  performance, 402–3
flash message boxes, 370
  vs. notification boxes, 368
fonts
  avoiding distracting, 153–54
  guidelines for, 68
  limiting use in user interfaces, 254
  recommended minimum support in video
  mode, 559
forgiveness
  building into good user interfaces, 420
  importance in programs for beginning
  users, 155
frames vs. splitter windows, 212
full screen setup, avoiding use of, 543
functional prototyping, 217–18, 232
  problems with, 115

G

GDI (Graphic Device Interface) objects,
  keeping in memory to improve drawing
  performance, 405

GetDiskFreeSpaceEx, determining amount of
  free disk space with, 9–10
GetFreeSpace API function, determining
  amount of free disk space with, 8–10
GetSysColorBrush function, to create GDI
  objects for painting screen elements, 552
GetSysColor function, to create GDI objects
  for painting screen elements, 552
goals, programmers vs. users, 125–29
grabbers, resizing windows with, 141
graphic designers, role in user interface
  design team, 449–50
graphics
  distracting, how to avoid, 154
  handling in a resolution-independent
  manner, 560
  using color in, 68
graphics problems, in video mode, 559–60
gray backgrounds, in Windows
  programming, 8–9
grids, using to organize items in windows,
  250
group boxes
  grouping related controls with, 244
  guidelines for, 59, 62
  vs. static lines and text, 245
grouping
  of related items in windows, 250
  of related user interface elements in
  dialog boxes, 462–63
group settings, managing configurability
  with, 320
guidelines. *See also* user interface guidelines
  for asking setup questions, 534
  for designing for the Windows
  environment, 6
  for eliminating unnecessary repetitive
  tasks, 392–93
  for establishing user interface style, 40–41
  for user interface style guidelines, 41–43
GUI Design for Dummies (Laura Arlov), 23–24

H

halftone palette, using for graphics, 68
handles, typical examples of, 288–89

N

Q

U

Z

About the Author

A programmer since 1975, Everett N. McKay is owner of Windmill Point Software, a firm specializing in providing consulting services and software tools for user interface design and development. Previously, he has worked for ADE Corporation, Sony Corporation, and Hughes Electronics. He has been developing Microsoft Windows programs since 1990, specializing in user interface design.

Everett graduated from MIT in 1985 with a B.S. and M.S. in electrical engineering and computer science. In his spare time, he enjoys photography, skiing, biking, and sailboarding on Lake Champlain. Everett and his wife Marie have two children: Philippe Mathieu, born in 1996, and Michèle Audrey, born in 1998. They live in Vermont, near the Canadian border.

You can reach Everett at *everett@uideveloper.com*.

The manuscript for this book was prepared and submitted to Microsoft Press in electronic form. Text files were prepared using Microsoft Word 97. Pages were composed by Microsoft Press using Adobe PageMaker 6.52 for Windows, with text in Garamond and display type in Frutiger. Composed pages were delivered to the printer as electronic prepress files.

Cover Graphic Designer
Tim Girvin Design, Inc.

Cover Illustrator
Glenn Mitsui

Interior Graphic Artist
Alton Lawson

Principal Compositor
Paula Gorelick

Principal Proofreaders/Copy Editors
Karen Lenburg/Patricia Masserman

Indexer
Carol Burbo

Editorial Assistant
Denise Bankaitis

MICROSOFT LICENSE AGREEMENT

Book Companion CD

IMPORTANT—READ CAREFULLY: This Microsoft End user License Agreement ("EULA") is a legal agreement between you (either an individual or an entity) and Microsoft Corporation for the Microsoft product identified above, which includes computer software and may include associated media, printed materials, and "online" or electronic documentation ("SOFTWARE PRODUCT"). Any component included within the SOFTWARE PRODUCT that is accompanied by a separate End user License Agreement shall be governed by such agreement and not the terms set forth below. By installing, copying, or otherwise using the SOFTWARE PRODUCT, you agree to be bound by the terms of this EULA. If you do not agree to the terms of this EULA, you are not authorized to install, copy, or otherwise use the SOFTWARE PRODUCT; you may, however, return the SOFTWARE PRODUCT, along with all printed materials and other items that form a part of the Microsoft product that includes the SOFTWARE PRODUCT, to the place you obtained them for a full refund.

SOFTWARE PRODUCT LICENSE

The SOFTWARE PRODUCT is protected by United States copyright laws and international copyright treaties, as well as other intellectual property laws and treaties. The SOFTWARE PRODUCT is licensed, not sold.

1. **GRANT OF LICENSE.** This EULA grants you the following rights:

    a. **Software Product.** You may install and use one copy of the SOFTWARE PRODUCT on a single computer. The primary user of the computer on which the SOFTWARE PRODUCT is installed may make a second copy for his or her exclusive use on a portable computer.

    b. **Storage/Network Use.** You may also store or install a copy of the SOFTWARE PRODUCT on a storage device, such as a network server, used only to install or run the SOFTWARE PRODUCT on your other computers over an internal network; however, you must acquire and dedicate a license for each separate computer on which the SOFTWARE PRODUCT is installed or run from the storage device. A license for the SOFTWARE PRODUCT may not be shared or used concurrently on different computers.

    c. **License Pak.** If you have acquired this EULA in a Microsoft License Pak, you may make the number of additional copies of the computer software portion of the SOFTWARE PRODUCT authorized on the printed copy of this EULA, and you may use each copy in the manner specified above. You are also entitled to make a corresponding number of secondary copies for portable computer use as specified above.

    d. **Sample Code.** Solely with respect to portions, if any, of the SOFTWARE PRODUCT that are identified within the SOFTWARE PRODUCT as sample code (the "SAMPLE CODE"):

        i. **Use and Modification.** Microsoft grants you the right to use and modify the source code version of the SAMPLE CODE, *provided* you comply with subsection (d)(iii) below. You may not distribute the SAMPLE CODE, or any modified version of the SAMPLE CODE, in source code form.

        ii. **Redistributable Files.** Provided you comply with subsection (d)(iii) below, Microsoft grants you a nonexclusive, royalty-free right to reproduce and distribute the object code version of the SAMPLE CODE and of any modified SAMPLE CODE, other than SAMPLE CODE, or any modified version thereof, designated as not redistributable in the Readme file that forms a part of the SOFTWARE PRODUCT (the "Non-Redistributable Sample Code"). All SAMPLE CODE other than the Non-Redistributable Sample Code is collectively referred to as the "REDISTRIBUTABLES."

        iii. **Redistribution Requirements.** If you redistribute the REDISTRIBUTABLES, you agree to: (i) distribute the REDISTRIBUTABLES in object code form only in conjunction with and as a part of your software application product; (ii) not use Microsoft's name, logo, or trademarks to market your software application product; (iii) include a valid copyright notice on your software application product; (iv) indemnify, hold harmless, and defend Microsoft from and against any claims or lawsuits, including attorney's fees, that arise or result from the use or distribution of your software application product; and (v) not permit further distribution of the REDISTRIBUTABLES by your end user. Contact Microsoft for the applicable royalties due and other licensing terms for all other uses and/or distribution of the REDISTRIBUTABLES.

2. **DESCRIPTION OF OTHER RIGHTS AND LIMITATIONS.**

    - **Limitations on Reverse Engineering, Decompilation, and Disassembly.** You may not reverse engineer, decompile, or disassemble the SOFTWARE PRODUCT, except and only to the extent that such activity is expressly permitted by applicable law notwithstanding this limitation.

    - **Separation of Components.** The SOFTWARE PRODUCT is licensed as a single product. Its component parts may not be separated for use on more than one computer.

    - **Rental.** You may not rent, lease, or lend the SOFTWARE PRODUCT.

    - **Support Services.** Microsoft may, but is not obligated to, provide you with support services related to the SOFTWARE PRODUCT ("Support Services"). Use of Support Services is governed by the Microsoft policies and programs described in the user manual, in "online" documentation, and/or other Microsoft-provided materials. Any supplemental software code provided to you as part of the Support Services shall be considered part of the SOFTWARE PRODUCT and subject to the terms and conditions of this EULA. With respect to technical information you provide to Microsoft as part of the Support Services, Microsoft may use such information for its business purposes, including for product support and development. Microsoft will not utilize such technical information in a form that personally identifies you.

- **Software Transfer.** You may permanently transfer all of your rights under this EULA, provided you retain no copies, you transfer all of the SOFTWARE PRODUCT (including all component parts, the media and printed materials, any upgrades, this EULA, and, if applicable, the Certificate of Authenticity), **and** the recipient agrees to the terms of this EULA.

- **Termination.** Without prejudice to any other rights, Microsoft may terminate this EULA if you fail to comply with the terms and conditions of this EULA. In such event, you must destroy all copies of the SOFTWARE PRODUCT and all of its component parts.

3. **COPYRIGHT.** All title and copyrights in and to the SOFTWARE PRODUCT (including but not limited to any images, photographs, animations, video, audio, music, text, SAMPLE CODE, REDISTRIBUTABLES, and "applets" incorporated into the SOFTWARE PRODUCT) and any copies of the SOFTWARE PRODUCT are owned by Microsoft or its suppliers. The SOFTWARE PRODUCT is protected by copyright laws and international treaty provisions. Therefore, you must treat the SOFTWARE PRODUCT like any other copyrighted material **except** that you may install the SOFTWARE PRODUCT on a single computer provided you keep the original solely for backup or archival purposes. You may not copy the printed materials accompanying the SOFTWARE PRODUCT.

4. **U.S. GOVERNMENT RESTRICTED RIGHTS.** The SOFTWARE PRODUCT and documentation are provided with RESTRICTED RIGHTS. Use, duplication, or disclosure by the Government is subject to restrictions as set forth in subparagraph (c)(1)(ii) of the Rights in Technical Data and Computer Software clause at DFARS 252.227-7013 or subparagraphs (c)(1) and (2) of the Commercial Computer Software—Restricted Rights at 48 CFR 52.227-19, as applicable. Manufacturer is Microsoft Corporation/One Microsoft Way/Redmond, WA 98052-6399.

5. **EXPORT RESTRICTIONS.** You agree that you will not export or re-export the SOFTWARE PRODUCT, any part thereof, or any process or service that is the direct product of the SOFTWARE PRODUCT (the foregoing collectively referred to as the "Restricted Components"), to any country, person, entity, or end user subject to U.S. export restrictions. You specifically agree not to export or re-export any of the Restricted Components (i) to any country to which the U.S. has embargoed or restricted the export of goods or services, which currently include, but are not necessarily limited to, Cuba, Iran, Iraq, Libya, North Korea, Sudan, and Syria, or to any national of any such country, wherever located, who intends to transmit or transport the Restricted Components back to such country; (ii) to any end user who you know or have reason to know will utilize the Restricted Components in the design, development, or production of nuclear, chemical, or biological weapons; or (iii) to any end user who has been prohibited from participating in U.S. export transactions by any federal agency of the U.S. government. You warrant and represent that neither the BXA nor any other U.S. federal agency has suspended, revoked, or denied your export privileges.

DISCLAIMER OF WARRANTY

NO WARRANTIES OR CONDITIONS. MICROSOFT EXPRESSLY DISCLAIMS ANY WARRANTY OR CONDITION FOR THE SOFTWARE PRODUCT. THE SOFTWARE PRODUCT AND ANY RELATED DOCUMENTATION ARE PROVIDED "AS IS" WITHOUT WARRANTY OR CONDITION OF ANY KIND, EITHER EXPRESS OR IMPLIED, INCLUDING, WITHOUT LIMITATION, THE IMPLIED WARRANTIES OF MERCHANTABILITY, FITNESS FOR A PARTICULAR PURPOSE, OR NONINFRINGEMENT. THE ENTIRE RISK ARISING OUT OF USE OR PERFORMANCE OF THE SOFTWARE PRODUCT REMAINS WITH YOU.

LIMITATION OF LIABILITY. TO THE MAXIMUM EXTENT PERMITTED BY APPLICABLE LAW, IN NO EVENT SHALL MICROSOFT OR ITS SUPPLIERS BE LIABLE FOR ANY SPECIAL, INCIDENTAL, INDIRECT, OR CONSEQUENTIAL DAMAGES WHATSOEVER (INCLUDING, WITHOUT LIMITATION, DAMAGES FOR LOSS OF BUSINESS PROFITS, BUSINESS INTERRUPTION, LOSS OF BUSINESS INFORMATION, OR ANY OTHER PECUNIARY LOSS) ARISING OUT OF THE USE OF OR INABILITY TO USE THE SOFTWARE PRODUCT OR THE PROVISION OF OR FAILURE TO PROVIDE SUPPORT SERVICES, EVEN IF MICROSOFT HAS BEEN ADVISED OF THE POSSIBILITY OF SUCH DAMAGES. IN ANY CASE, MICROSOFT'S ENTIRE LIABILITY UNDER ANY PROVISION OF THIS EULA SHALL BE LIMITED TO THE GREATER OF THE AMOUNT ACTUALLY PAID BY YOU FOR THE SOFTWARE PRODUCT OR US$5.00; PROVIDED, HOWEVER, IF YOU HAVE ENTERED INTO A MICROSOFT SUPPORT SERVICES AGREEMENT, MICROSOFT'S ENTIRE LIABILITY REGARDING SUPPORT SERVICES SHALL BE GOVERNED BY THE TERMS OF THAT AGREEMENT. BECAUSE SOME STATES AND JURISDICTIONS DO NOT ALLOW THE EXCLUSION OR LIMITATION OF LIABILITY, THE ABOVE LIMITATION MAY NOT APPLY TO YOU.

MISCELLANEOUS

This EULA is governed by the laws of the State of Washington USA, except and only to the extent that applicable law mandates governing law of a different jurisdiction.

Should you have any questions concerning this EULA, or if you desire to contact Microsoft for any reason, please contact the Microsoft subsidiary serving your country, or write: Microsoft Sales Information Center/One Microsoft Way/Redmond, WA 98052-6399.

Register Today!

Return this
Developing User Interfaces for Microsoft® Windows®
registration card today

Microsoft®*Press*
mspress.microsoft.com

OWNER REGISTRATION CARD   **0-7356-0586-6**

Developing User Interfaces for Microsoft® Windows®

FIRST NAME	MIDDLE INITIAL	LAST NAME

INSTITUTION OR COMPANY NAME

ADDRESS

CITY	STATE	ZIP

( )

E-MAIL ADDRESS	PHONE NUMBER

U.S. and Canada addresses only. Fill in information above and mail postage-free.
Please mail only the bottom half of this page.

For information about Microsoft Press®
products, visit our Web site at
mspress.microsoft.com

Microsoft Press

NO POSTAGE
NECESSARY
IF MAILED
IN THE
UNITED STATES

BUSINESS REPLY MAIL
FIRST-CLASS MAIL   PERMIT NO. 108   REDMOND WA

POSTAGE WILL BE PAID BY ADDRESSEE

MICROSOFT PRESS
PO BOX 97017
REDMOND, WA 98073-9830